Communic
with Data
Visualisation

Sara Miller McCune founded SAGE Publishing in 1965 to support the dissemination of usable knowledge and educate a global community. SAGE publishes more than 1000 journals and over 800 new books each year, spanning a wide range of subject areas. Our growing selection of library products includes archives, data, case studies and video. SAGE remains majority owned by our founder and after her lifetime will become owned by a charitable trust that secures the company's continued independence.

Los Angeles | London | New Delhi | Singapore | Washington DC | Melbourne

Communicating with Data Visualisation

A Practical Guide

Adam Frost   Jim Kynvin
Tobias Sturt   Sergio Fernández Gallardo

Los Angeles | London | New Delhi
Singapore | Washington DC | Melbourne

Los Angeles | London | New Delhi
Singapore | Washington DC | Melbourne

SAGE Publications Ltd
1 Oliver's Yard
55 City Road
London EC1Y 1SP

SAGE Publications Inc.
2455 Teller Road
Thousand Oaks, California 91320

SAGE Publications India Pvt Ltd
B 1/I 1 Mohan Cooperative Industrial Area
Mathura Road
New Delhi 110 044

SAGE Publications Asia-Pacific Pte Ltd
3 Church Street
#10-04 Samsung Hub
Singapore 049483

Editor: Aly Owen
Assistant editor: Hannah Cavender-Deere
Production editor: Ian Antcliff
Copyeditor: Richard Leigh
Indexer: Martin Hargreaves
Marketing manager: Ben Griffin-Sherwood
Cover design: Shaun Mercier
Typeset by: C&M Digitals (P) Ltd, Chennai, India
Printed in the UK

Library of Congress Control Number: 2021936953

British Library Cataloguing in Publication data

A catalogue record for this book is available from the
British Library

ISBN 978-1-5297-4376-0
ISBN 978-1-5297-4377-7 (pbk)

At SAGE we take sustainability seriously. Most of our products are printed in the UK using responsibly sourced papers and
boards. When we print overseas we ensure sustainable papers are used as measured by the PREPS grading system. We
undertake an annual audit to monitor our sustainability.

Contents

Discover your online resources

Whether you're working on your own data visualisations or looking to improve your ability to understand and interpret the work of others, this book is supported by online resources that will help you get to grips with the basics and refine your practice.

Visit https://www.addtwodigital.com/book for:

- **Tutorials and walkthroughs of the in-text exercises** so you can make sure you're on the right track.
- **Bonus content on statistics and visual storytelling** to give you more in-depth understanding of how to find, prepare, and design your data story.
- **A catalogue of key data viz rules** that you can use as tips on best practice—and justification for why it's okay to break all of them.
- **Downloadable hi-resolution versions of the main graphics** used in the book to use in teaching or quick-referencing.

Acknowledgements

Adam and Tobias would like to thank all the attendees of their *Guardian* masterclasses over the years (and the eternally splendid masterclasses team), who have remained enthusiastic, inspirational and, more importantly, patient, as we slowly discovered – out loud and in front of an audience – what it was that we actually thought about data visualisation.

All four of us would like to thank everyone at Sage and in particular our brilliant editor, Aly Owen. Finally, we will always be grateful to Tom Jackson for bringing the four of us together, and to Emma Whitehead for suggesting that we should teach other people what we do.

Credits

Photos via Unsplash from Dakota Corbin, Kevin Gent.

Images from Adobe Stock.

About the authors

Adam Frost has taught the *Guardian*'s data visualisation masterclass for the last 10 years. He has created infographics for the *Guardian*, the *New Statesman*, the British Film Institute and a range of corporate clients. He has also written a series of award-winning infographic factbooks for children. He is currently Content Director at Add Two Digital.

Tobias Sturt has taught the *Guardian*'s data visualisation masterclass for the last 10 years. He has been working in digital storytelling for almost three decades in all kinds of media, from web to TV to games to infographics. He is currently Creative Director at Add Two Digital.

Jim Kynvin is an award-winning infographic designer. He spent over a decade designing at the *Guardian*. He now designs for some of the UK's best-known brands, including John Lewis, IKEA and Google.

Sergio Fernández Gallardo has been a graphic designer for almost two decades. His work on Nestlé's Creating Shared Value project won a Digital Communication Award in 2015. His 'WPP BrandZ top 100 most valuable global brands' graphic was shortlisted for an Information is Beautiful Award in 2013. His own work has appeared on the *Guardian* website and in a range of other publications.

Introduction: Notes from the Underground

Adam Frost and Tobias Sturt

It may now be asked, to what purpose tends all this laborious bustling and groping to know...

John Graunt, demographer (1620–1674)

We both grew up just outside London in the 1980s, Adam in a suburb in the east of the city, Tobias in a suburb in the west. Although we wouldn't meet until 2010, when we were placed in the same team at the *Guardian*, it turns out that we both spent much of our childhoods doing the same thing: staring at the London Tube map and dreaming of escape.

London in the 1980s wasn't much to write home about: like most of the United Kingdom, it had been hit hard by Margaret Thatcher's cuts, which meant a rise in crime, an increase in social unrest and record levels of unemployment. Fifteen per cent of the population – over a million people – left the city between 1971 and 1991, meaning that fewer people lived there than at any point since 1901.[1] Getting into London was harder too: the Tube map looked as perfect as ever, but the experience of travelling by Tube had never been more arduous, with years of underinvestment leading to ageing trains, poorly maintained tracks and a demotivated workforce. The government's focus was on building more roads: the car was a symbol of individual freedom, whereas public transport was for 'failures'.[2]

But even though London was in bad shape, it didn't feel that way to us. It, still felt, well, cool: exciting, cosmopolitan and dynamic. Of course, part of this was down to our adolescent tendency to glamorise city life, but part of it really was down to Harry Beck's Tube map. In fact, not just the Tube map, but how the Tube looked more generally: the beautiful signs with their elegant Johnston Sans typeface, Leslie Green's stunning Arts and Crafts tiling in many of the central stations, and Charles Holden's modernist station entrances in the suburbs with their huge vertical windows letting in astonishing quantities of natural light.

The Tube train itself may have been dirty, overheated, overcrowded, late, slow and deafeningly loud, and the shops, cinemas and museums we were visiting might have been shabby or half-empty, but none of this prevented us from enjoying the Tube journey, because everywhere we turned, so much thought had been put into how everything looked and worked. Although we weren't aware of it, those brilliant designers were giving us an important lesson in why design matters: how it can turn a mundane experience into a great one, how this makes you want to repeat the experience, and how the best design continues to work long after trends and fashion shift.

We couldn't have been luckier. It's hard to imagine a better preparation for life as an information designer than being exposed to the London Tube map on a daily basis during your formative years. In 2006, the 200,000 people who participated in the BBC's Great British Design Quest put the Tube map in second place, beaten only by Concorde (which is, frankly, a travesty – up there with Banksy beating Michelangelo and Picasso in a 2019 YouGov poll to find the greatest artist of all time).

Before the innovations of Harry Beck, the Tube map was geographically accurate – which means the stations were positioned correctly, stations where you could change lines were not given any visual prominence, lines meandered between stations and the whole network was frequently placed on top of a London road map to further emphasise each station's physical location above ground.

---

[1]After the Conservative government fell in 1997, the city began to recover, and now has a population of over 8 million people.

[2]Margaret Thatcher allegedly accused anyone still travelling by bus over the age of 25 of being a 'failure'. Even if she was misquoted, her policies certainly suggested that she agreed with the sentiment.

Harry Beck changed every single one of these elements.[3] Rather than making a map for the people who built the Tube, he made a map for the people who used it. He worked out what passengers needed and reconfigured the design with these requirements in mind. In particular, he came to the following conclusions:

- Passengers needed to be able to find their own station and their destination. The overlaid road map was replaced with white space and the wiggly track lines were replaced with lines that were vertical, horizontal or at a 45-degree angle. The River Thames was added as the sole geographical marker, dividing north and south, but even this was stylised so that its meanderings were also horizontal, vertical or at a 45-degree angle. Beck was an engineer by training and his influence for this approach was almost certainly electrical circuit diagrams, which not only helped him to reduce clutter, but also acted as a subtle visual metaphor for how the Tube functioned: since the 1890s, when steam trains were phased out, it had been electricity ferrying all those passengers around the network.
- Passengers needed to be able to monitor their journey. Beck understood that people think of train journeys not in terms of distance covered, but of number of stops. So rather than spacing stations to mimic their position above ground, he placed a roughly equal amount of space between them.
- The majority of passengers needed to change lines and it was important that they didn't miss these stops. A clear diamond icon was placed at interchange stations, which made them feel very different from regular stations, marked with a simple tick mark on the side of the line.
- Most passengers were using the Tube in the centre of town, or to reach the centre of town. In the original (accurate) map, central stations were squashed together while suburban stations were spaced out. By using what he called

a 'convex lens' design, Beck reversed this, artificially amplifying the size of central London and bringing the size of the suburbs down. This not only meant the busiest stations were given more prominence, it also accurately reflected how the Tube had transformed the city – it had made the suburbs feel much closer to the centre and shrunk the distance between them.
- In earlier maps, font had been an inconsistent size or orientation. Beck used font clearly and consistently, always positioning it horizontally and at a size that was clearly legible. He also ensured that there were distinct amounts of white space between each label.

It's also worth remembering that Beck preserved what worked well in previous designs – in particular, the Lego-bright colours for the different Tube lines that may not work aesthetically (they clash violently, in fact) but are perfect for wayfinding, particularly if you are a commuter in a rush, or a tourist with a limited grasp of English.

Beck's Tube map survives, expanded and updated, to this day. Even though we have both lived in the city for half a century and know the Tube network off by heart, we still regularly gaze at it before any trip across town, partly to double-check our route, but mostly because, well, any excuse.

We're clearly not the only ones. The Tube map can be seen on mugs, coasters, T-shirts and posters; there are numerous parody versions ('Music on the Tube' is a particular favourite); and it has influenced transit maps in every city on Earth. The geographer Mark Ovenden has called it 'arguably the most recognised cartographic item in the western world' (Ovenden, 2013, pp. 152–3). In many ways, it has replaced the actual map of London, giving both residents and tourists alike an entirely illusory sense of which towns are in London (many of the city's districts don't have a Tube stop), where these places are and how well they know the city.

---

[3] It's worth saying that his innovative approach was influenced by earlier pioneers such as George Dow and F.H. Stingemore.

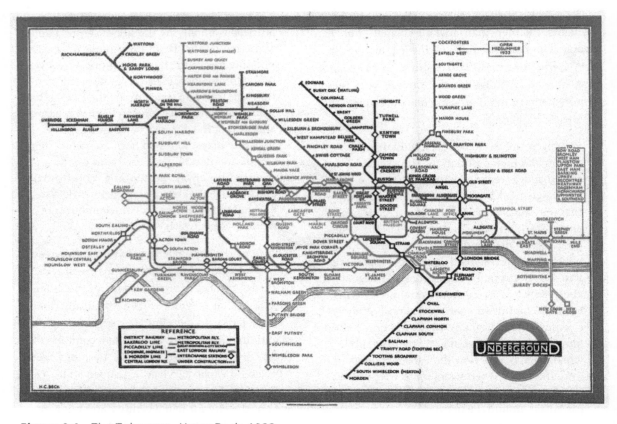

Figure 0.1   The Tube map, Harry Beck, 1933

We mentioned that we were lucky to have grown up with Beck's map as a daily inspiration. But perhaps everyone today is lucky. Even if you didn't grow up in London, you are likely to have had a similar example of great information design or data visualisation as a constant companion. Harry Beck is just one of the hundreds of design pioneers who have made it easier than ever for twenty-first-century humans to record, track and picture their lives.

Let's imagine a typical working day in the life of an average citizen in a modern city. You wake up and a clock or watch tells you the precise time. Perhaps you will pad to the bathroom and weigh yourself, a particularly thankless data collection ritual that rarely leads to any 'actionable insights'. On the way to the kitchen, you might check or adjust the thermostat in the hall or glance at the calendar on the kitchen door that maps out your itinerary for the week. As you eat your cereal, you might read the data table on the side of the box that breaks down its nutritional content. If you have children, there might be other charts on display. Perhaps crude pencil lines on the kitchen door frame, showing how quickly (and expensively) your children are growing. For young children, maybe a star chart on the wall rewarding good behaviour; for older children, perhaps a modified Gantt chart showing when they should be revising for exams. Indeed, the fact that children need monitoring will affect most rooms in the house. For example, the bathroom cabinet will almost certainly have a thermometer in it, to measure their temperature when they get sick. (If you don't have children, but want them, the same cabinet might have a pregnancy testing kit inside, to measure the level of hCG in urine and

4

then to display one or two vertical lines depending on the results.)

When it's time for work, you might glance at a weather map, and completely change your wardrobe based on the icon you see. When you set off, you might have a choice of transport methods. If you go by train, you might consult a map (Harry Beck's Tube map, if you're lucky). You might also check a timetable or departures board, to verify which lines are running and which are delayed. On the train, maybe you'll read a newspaper or news website and look at more data tables – the football league, the pop charts or the FTSE share index.

If you decide to drive, you'll be constantly consulting your car dashboard, which dynamically visualises your car's speed, fuel levels, oil levels, temperature, whether everyone is wearing a seatbelt and more. You might use a combination of physical maps, satnav technology, road signage and memory to get where you need to. Sometimes you'll have to stop at traffic lights, which encode stop and go by both the position and colour of halogen bulbs. If you need to refuel at a petrol station, more counters and dials will record how much fuel you've taken and how much money you've given to a large oil company.

Or perhaps you'll decide to jog to work. If you do, you may well have a fitness app which will monitor your location, speed, heart rate and calories burned. If you collapse halfway through your run, you'll wake up attached to various machines in a hospital, which will track and chart all of your body's vital signs. To give you a prognosis, the doctor will have to run tests and compare your results to an average or to other people with similar symptoms. (Medicine is, in essence, a science of data collection and comparison.)

If you wake up from your coma and the Earth is an apocalyptic wasteland, then a Geiger counter will help you to measure radiation levels by means of data sonification: a series of clicks per minute.

But if you don't collapse and fall into a coma, you will no doubt arrive at work, keen as mustard, and probably start up your computer. There's a high chance that at least some of your working life will involve data visualisation too.

This represents the first couple of hours in a typical day, but you get the idea. Even 100 years ago, few of these ways of collecting or displaying information existed. Now we seem to live in a late- or even post-data visualisation age. Centuries of innovation and refinement in disciplines as diverse as horology, cartography, medicine, engineering, economics, sports science and countless others have successfully created uniform units of measurement (from seconds to Celsius), built devices that can help people monitor themselves and their environment (rooted in these systems of measurement), and devised methods of displaying any stored data that can be readily understood with little or no specialist training.

Moreover, this unprecedented variety of data display does not faze us. We happily jump from beats per minute to miles per hour to three points for a win and glance from clockface to map to timetable to weather map. The only thing that might occasionally slow us down is if we are required to stop and read a page of actual words.

We are highly skilled interpreters of tables, charts and maps. The majority of us understand what the x-axis and y-axis mean on a line chart, what a line chart is good and bad at measuring, what contours mean on a map, what an average is (although more of this later), the difference between serif and sans-serif fonts and what clicking right-align might do to this paragraph.[4]

---

[4]We tested some of these assumptions about how quickly people read different charts in a collaboration with Jon Puleston of Lightspeed Research. Although we need to carry out further research to confirm some of our conclusions, our initial results can be found here: https://ana. esomar.org/documents/exploring-the-use-of-visuals-in-the-delivery-of-research-data

We can make our own charts too. It is easier than ever to access, store and explore large amounts of data, and to visualise what we have found. The software that is installed on a typical computer – regardless of whether it is a word processor, spreadsheet, presentation program or graphics editor – will usually have the ability to generate charts and maps. What is more, this software is usually low-cost, or free.

What this book will – and won't – do

All of this means that this book won't spend too long on the basic terminology and structure of key chart types. Just being alive today means that you use these charts and maps daily. Instead we will explore some of the difficulties that many people encounter when they make the leap from consumer to creator, and try to make a chart that is as intuitive and engaging as the one they just saw on the way to work – on a news website, on their fitness app, or on the wall of a Tube station.

Because this is the most frustrating paradox in our data-rich world. The fact that we are surrounded by excellent charts and by software that can make excellent charts deludes us into thinking that the process of making an excellent chart must be simple. However, although the tools have improved, the human ability to select and present data has not. The underlying task that faces any information designer is just as difficult as the task that faced Harry Beck in the 1930s when he was trying to fix the Tube map. In some ways it is harder, because the assumption that data can now be visualised quickly and easily is baked into the timeline of every project – whether you work in a newsroom, an investment bank or a laboratory. Even if you are given more time, it can still be a frustrating task, because tools marketed as 'user-friendly' are frequently not, and they often limit creativity by automatically dropping content into rigid labour-saving templates.

Our book will outline a series of strategies that should help you to overcome some of those obstacles. It will also recommend a process of working that has not materially changed since information design became a recognisable practice in the mid-nineteenth century. In particular, we will stress the importance of the following:

- **Take your time.** A chart shouldn't be something you quickly rustle up five minutes before a meeting. We will position data visualisation as a series of four equally important stages: **Find**, **Design**, **Make** and **Refine**. Rushing through any of them can damage the quality of your work.
- **Put your audience first.** If you are in a rush, you are more likely to copy and paste a chart from your analytics dashboard into your presentation or report. But what makes sense to you is unlikely to make sense to your audience. We will look at how visualising data for an audience is an act of translation.
- **Use the right tools.** At different stages of your project, you will require different tools. Sometimes this might be pen and paper, sometimes it might be a code editor. We will be looking at how to make sure the tools you are using are suitable for the task you are undertaking.
- **Work with the right people.** Because different tools and techniques are required, it is unlikely that you will be able to master them all. You need to work out what your core strengths are, and where you will need help from others. We will discuss the value and importance of collaboration.

This approach worked for Harry Beck, after all. He didn't rush his work. He spent months creating his Tube map – mostly in his spare time. He sketched his ideas first, with a pencil and paper, understanding that you shouldn't think about colour, font and alignment until you have worked out your underlying story or structure.

He had people around him who could influence and critique his ideas. When Beck made his map, the Underground was going through what we would now call a 'rebranding exercise', a hugely ambitious undertaking masterminded by Frank Pick that involved the creation of a new typeface, new stations and some of the most beautiful posters in British advertising history. Beck was not designing in a vacuum, but surrounded by talented colleagues.

These colleagues helped to improve his map. When Beck first submitted his map to the Underground publicity department in 1931, they rejected it for being too outré, so he made further improvements (most notably, creating tick marks rather than blobs for stations). Although his managers never fully 'got' Beck's work, they did agree to a trial run of this new version in 1932. At this point, the public took over, demanding more copies, and the trial run of 500 became a print run of 700,000. A month later, all 700,000 maps had been snapped up and an even bigger reprint was required. Beck's approach – working slowly and carefully, putting himself in his audience's shoes, refining his work after feedback – had been validated.

But Beck never became complacent. Even after the success of the 1933 version, he kept returning to his map, partly because his bosses requested modifications, but partly just to experiment with new visual approaches. He understood that audiences change, or change their minds, which means that a designer's work is never done. This is ultimately why we were lucky to grow up with Beck's Tube map alongside us. He taught us that good information design, like any work of art, only survives if it continues to mean something to an audience. You design it for them, and with them, and hopefully some of them will grow up and pick things up where you left off.

Part I
The Data Visualisation Process

Part I

One
Find, design, make, refine

Adam Frost

Our approach to data visualisation

Tobias and I have been running design agencies for the last two decades, most notably between 2011 and 2014, when we were part of a digital agency set up by the *Guardian* newspaper in the UK. Today we head up our own agency, Add Two Digital. For those of you who are unaware of the agency model, it's slightly different from a conventional design team set-up, in that you are not just working for one company or focusing on one subject. Even when we were part of the *Guardian*, our role wasn't usually to make graphics for the newspaper. We were set up to generate revenue for the organisation by offering *Guardian* skills to anyone outside of the business who might need them. These clients could be big corporates, charities, academic institutions or organisations such as the World Trade Organization or the European Union.

Most of the advice in this book will be drawn from this aspect of our careers. Although we both produce our own work, these personal projects tend to be less useful for teaching purposes, just because they are fuelled by our own obsessions and opinions, and we can freely choose what to make, how to make it and how much time to spend on it. Our client work is the opposite: the data differs with every project (simple or complex, qualitative or quantitative), the subject-matter varies (from trade treaties to toilet paper), the output can be static or interactive, it can be a PowerPoint presentation or a social media gif, it can be for experts or for everyone, the deadline can be tomorrow or next year, it can cost a little or a lot. No two projects ever look the same (see Figure 1.1).

However, the way we approach each of these projects *does* look the same. Explaining our working processes for client projects will form the basis of

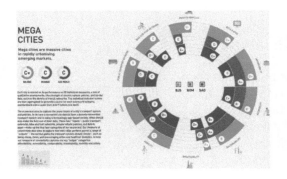

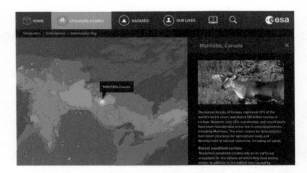

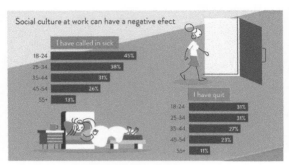

Figure 1.1 A range of client projects

this book because, in our experience, it is this framework that has proved most useful to our students, regardless of job role or previous experience.

Defining data visualisation

It will also serve as our definition of data visualisation (Figure 1.2). There appears to be widespread disagreement about what data visualisation is, whether it overlaps (or not) with infographics, whether it must (or need not) contain interactive elements, whether figurative graphics (illustrations and maps) count, or whether it is something else entirely.[1] For us, any work that adheres to the process we describe – selecting relevant data for an audience and turning it into its most compelling verbal and visual form – can happily be described as data visualisation. If any element is missing – for example, the data is flawed or the charts are unintelligible – then it isn't data visualisation. Because what you're visualising isn't data, or what you're doing to the data isn't visualising it.

One other side point: there is often disagreement about whether data visualisation is 'new' or 'old'. In other words, is it a response to the modern 'big data' and 'open data' revolutions in which unprecedented amounts of information are being collected and therefore new visual methods are required to interrogate and represent this data? Or is it simply a continuation of a discipline that has existed for at least two centuries, since the engineer, spy and blackmailer William Playfair invented the bar chart in 1786? (Or maybe since the Imago Mundi was created in the fifth century BC?) Both points of view have merit. You could compare it to the distinction between cinema and stage plays prior to 1900, or computer games, and puzzles and games invented before the 1970s. A lot of the conventions are the same, and the old and new media both satisfy a similar emotional need in their audience.

Likewise, anyone who makes charts today is performing a similar function to those early data visualisation pioneers. They are clarifying complex information using memorable text and visuals. This is no different to John Snow in the 1850s creating his seminal cholera map, or Otto and Marie Neurath in the 1930s designing the first isotype charts. However, at the same time, there is no question that technology has changed both the chart-making process and the end product in several important ways, enabling anyone with even basic software to make perfectly functional charts and anyone with more technical ability to add interactive elements that can dramatically expand the possibilities of what charts mean, in some cases delivering experiences that resemble the feature films and computer games mentioned above. So yes, data visualisation owes a lot to the past, and this continuity of purpose is important, but at the same time, it is easy to see why a new term has materialised to describe what feels like a rapid evolution in the form's potential.

But let's get back to our process – which, I should add, requires no prior knowledge of (or even interest in) the history of data visualisation. It only requires a willingness to study each part of the process, to understand that they are all of equal importance and to realise that each element adds an additional positive attribute to the final product.

---

[1]Valinda Chan's view is fairly representative: 'Infographics tell a premeditated story to guide the audience to conclusions (subjective). Data visualizations let the audience draw their own conclusions (objective)' (Prototypr.io, 6 June 2017). Kim Rees of the design agency Periscopic believes that an infographic is always static and data visualisation is 'most often' interactive (https://readwrite.com/2011/01/07/difference-between-datavisualization-infographics/).

	THE BIG QUESTION	WHO'S DOING IT?
FIND	What is the story?	Researcher, Analyst, Editor
DESIGN	Who is the story for?	Editor, Copywriter, Producer, Designer
MAKE	How do I put this story together?	Designer, Illustrator, Animator, Developer
REFINE	How do I make the best possible version of this story?	Editor, Designer, QA, Illustrator, Animator, Developer

REMEMBER   **1** Move through each stage one by one.   **2** You can move quickly through stages, but never skip them.

Figure 1.2 Our process

WHAT'S HAPPENING?	WITH WHICH TOOLS?	TO CREATE SOMETHING...?	
Find all relevant datasets. Check the provenance of your data. Find all potential stories in your data.	• Excel • R • Tableau • Google Sheets	Trustworthy	
Find the right story for your audience. Use comparison and context to augment your story. Wireframe your information hierarchy.	• Pen and paper • Google Docs • Photoshop • Pencil Project	Relevant	BEAUTIFUL
Choose visuals that help people see the story in the data. Use a consistent visual language. Use design elements to guide people through the story.	• Illustrator • Powerpoint • After Effects • D3	Clear	
Hone your story based on testing and/or feedback. Ensure the copy is as clear and the visuals are as engaging as possible. If necessary, adapt for different channels and use cases.	• Illustrator • Powerpoint • After Effects • D3	Useful	

3 Go back a stage if something isn't working.

4 If you need to go back two or three stages, work through the intervening stages again.

Find

This is where we look for stories in the datasets that we have found.

The first task is always to verify the provenance of the data. Few datasets are perfect of course – most have gaps or inconsistencies – so we often have to use our professional judgement to decide whether these flaws will undermine the validity of our work or sabotage any chance of creating readable charts. If our data passes this test (viability, and visualisation is possible), then we begin to analyse the data we have.

As we work, we try to keep as open a mind as possible. Sometimes we will have a hypothesis that we want to test or a client question which determines the order in which we examine the data, but, even in these cases, we try not to be restricted by these parameters, and to document anything interesting or unusual that we find. A journalist researching a story may have an angle in mind, but it doesn't stop them reading widely on the subject, and taking copious notes that may be of tangential relevance to the final piece. This kind of curiosity is a critical tool when you're analysing a dataset too.

Sometimes we visualise what we find in order to examine its significance. However, it is worth stressing that the visualisation tools we use when we analyse data (e.g. R, Excel, Power BI) and the charts we use (e.g. scatter charts, box plots, histograms) are rarely helpful when it comes to communicating what we have discovered to an audience. When we make charts for analytical purposes, there is usually greater information density, our language (textual and visual) is more technical and we're often using software that won't let us change design and interface elements even if we wanted to. Most importantly, these charts have an audience of one – the person making them. For this reason, they will play a very limited role in this book. For us, data visualisation is always motivated by the desire to make something clear and interesting for someone else. Without this element, it is like a journalist publishing the jottings in their notebook and calling it journalism. It is a fundamental part of the job but it doesn't have much in common with the finished product.

It tends to be analysts who carry out this work. If it is a simple dataset, then editors and journalists can usually manage it too (there are some examples of simple datasets in Figure 1.3). We use Google Sheets most of the time, although Excel is still useful, and Tableau is indispensable for large or dynamic datasets. Finding a solid dataset with a range of potential stories is the rock on which you build everything else, giving your work depth and integrity.

Design

Although the four stages of this process are all equal, this stage is more equal than the others. Perhaps because of our background at the *Guardian*, we believe that it is this part – designing a story that will resonate with your audience – that is at the heart of any successful data visualisation project. When a chart or graphic misfires, it is usually because the data has been visualised but little else. No thought has been given to removing superfluous data or arranging the data into a hierarchy of importance. There is often a sensible reason for this: designing a visual story is difficult and takes ages. It requires empathy (putting your audience's needs first), ruthlessness (deleting datapoints that you might find interesting but your audience won't) and creative ability (arranging information so that audience interest is sustained). When you finally get to the end, you often find that you need to start again. A quote attributed to Terry Pratchett feels relevant here: 'The first draft is just you telling yourself the story.' In other words, you need patience and persistence too, as you rework the same material over and over again until only the indispensable elements remain.

Number of stolen objects used to make the tunnels in Stalag Luft III in 1944 ("The Great Escape")

Knives	1219
Spoons	478
Forks	582
Pillow cases	161
Mess hall tables	52
Single tables	10
Chairs	34
Benches	76
Bed bolsters	1212
Bed boards	4000
Wall/ floor boards	1370
Double bunk beds	90
Mattresses	635
Bed covers	192
Lamps	69
Water cans	246
Shovels	30
Towels	3424
Blankets	1700
Tin cans	1400

Number of insect fragments permitted in foods (per 100g, US FDA, 2019)

Oregano (ground)	12499
Marjoram (ground)	11749
Marjoram (unground)	2499
Sage (ground)	1999
Nutmeg (ground)	999
Pepper (ground)	949
Cinnamon (ground)	799
Curry powder	399
Paprika (ground)	299
Wheat flour	149
Cocoa powder	149
Corn flour	99
Noodles/ Macaroni	99
Chocolate	59
Broccoli	59
Spinach (canned)	49
Asparagus (canned)	39
Brussels sprouts (frozen)	29
Peanut butter	29

Most common first names of female babies in England and Wales (1924–2014)

	2014	1984	1954	1924
1	Amelia	Sarah	Susan	Margaret
2	Olivia	Laura	Linda	Mary
3	Isla	Gemma	Christine	Joan
4	Emily	Emma	Margaret	Joyce
5	Poppy	Rebecca	Janet	Dorothy
6	Ava	Claire	Patricia	Kathleen
7	Isabella	Victoria	Carol	Doris
8	Jessica	Samantha	Elizabeth	Irene
9	Lily	Rachel	Mary	Elizabeth
10	Sophie	Amy	Anne	Eileen

Sources: *Daily Telegraph*, FDA *Food Defect Levels Handbook*, Office for National Statistics

Figure 1.3 It always starts with a dataset

Of course, some of you might be resistant to the word 'story'. In an exchange on Twitter, Moritz Stefaner warned of the 'power and danger of story-telling', and Scott Murray responded by referring to the 'toxic nature of the "storytelling" fad'.[2] These are two of the most celebrated information designers in the world, so if you'd prefer to think of data visualisation as something other than storytelling, then you are in good company.

However, all we can say is that our work became more focused and more effective when we began to think of ourselves as visual storytellers. Even when we are creating interactive explorers – which is what both Moritz Stefaner and Scott Murray primarily do – we ensure that we are aware of the key stories in our dataset, so we can make intelligent choices about the best charts to use, the default state of each chart, which datasets to exclude, and the interface elements that will guide our audience to the most interesting stories. We cede more control to our users than in a static chart, but this is still tightly circumscribed to ensure that they don't get confused or bored.

Before we thought of ourselves as storytellers, we would often create interactive charts that weren't too different from the charts we made during the **Find** (data analysis) stage of the process. We would argue that 'the user was the storyteller' and the audience could 'discover their own stories'. Which was convenient for us, as it involved a lot less work. And guess what – we discovered that, unless they *really* need the data, users tend to abandon dashboards that don't meet them halfway.

We found that we achieved better results when we thought of interactive data visualisation as allowing an audience to explore the stories that *we* had found, in an order that made sense to them. Of course it is a mathematical certainty that your audience will find stories that you weren't aware of (quality assurance can only test so many outcomes), but that's true of any storytelling medium. Authors are always pleasantly surprised at the meanings that readers find in their stories.[3] We will have more to say about the relationship between static and interactive storytelling in later chapters.

Although we call this stage 'design', it is not usually led by designers. It tends to be coordinated by journalists, producers or project managers, although sometimes graphic designers and user experience (UX) designers are involved. What is happening here is usually sketching and wireframing, defining the building blocks of our story, and arranging them so that information is released in a logical order. We stay focused on what is most relevant for our audience and the intellectual and emotional impact that we want our story to have on them. In terms of tools, for static graphics, we use pen and paper (as in Figure 1.4); for interactives, we start with pen and paper before moving on to wireframing software. For motion graphics, we start with sketched storyboards, before creating more worked-up versions in Illustrator.

The **Design** stage makes your work relevant and meaningful, creating an emotional bond with your audience.

---

[2]To see the full thread, go to: https://twitter.com/moritz_stefaner/status/550607190378414080

[3]Video game design is another example of this. If you play a sandbox video game such as The Legend of Zelda: Breath of the Wild, you are encouraged to explore and experiment. As any search of gaming videos on YouTube will demonstrate, gamers pride themselves in finding combinations of tools and tricks that the game designers couldn't possibly have imagined. However, there is always a narrative to follow (if you choose). And it is clear that most of the key player choices and pathways have been tested. It's the same when you design interactive data visualisation: users will have less fun if you haven't set up, signposted and tested the main pathways into the content.

20% of the country received food assistance.

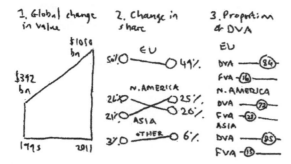

Value Added Origin of World Exports

Figure 1.4 Example chart designs

Make

Here we make what we've designed in the previous stage. We don't open any design or animation software or code anything until we've got a clear sense of what we are making. Like most digital agencies, we use agile methodology – which means that we accept change as an inevitable part of any project – so it's not as if our designs are set in stone. We share our work regularly with our client, and we accept that seeing a concept worked up into something more concrete can lead to us going back a stage and reworking aspects of the design.

However, it is best to see the **Make** stage as a separate part of the project as you are almost always

using different software and different team members. Your key focus is now 'Am I telling this story effectively?' rather than 'Is this story worth telling?' (You will have answered the second question already.)

It is in this phase that we agonise over the specifics. For example, let us say that we are creating a presentation and in the **Design** phase we have sketched something like Figure 1.5.

It is here that we will be thinking hard about what that icon at the top should be (see Figure 1.6). An ear of wheat? A farmer with a pitchfork? A tractor? A spade? Or should we just lose the icon? (Probably, yes.)

Should this stay as a column chart? Or should we make it a horizontal bar chart so we can read the labels? And rank it largest to smallest? Add labels to the bars? Leave off the *y*-axis and the gridlines, since we have labels? (See Figure 1.7.)

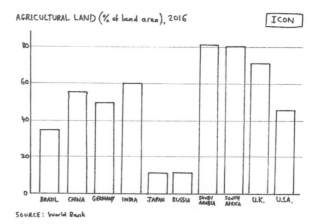

Figure 1.5 Percentage of land in each country used for agriculture, 2016

Figure 1.6 Potential agricultural icons

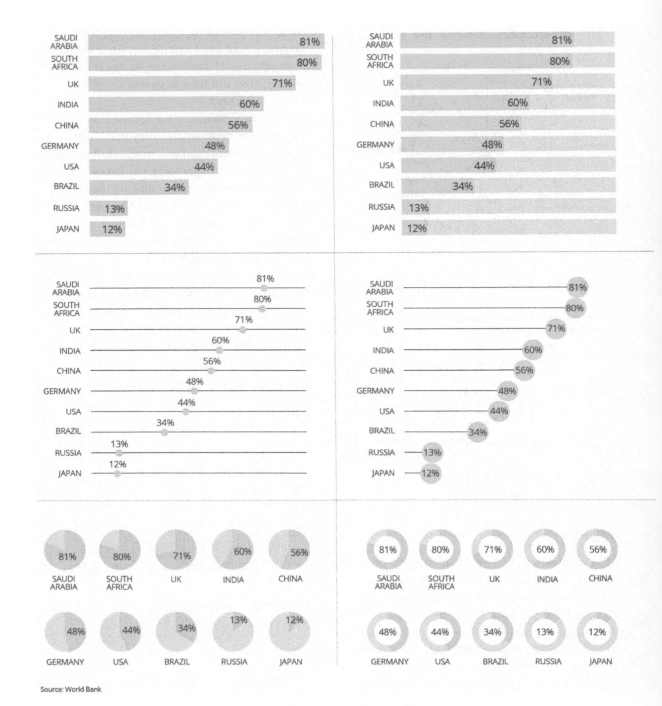

Source: World Bank

Figure 1.7 Agricultural land (% of land area), 2016, in 12 different charts

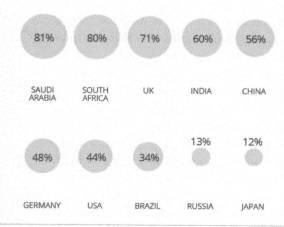

SAUDI ARABIA	SOUTH AFRICA	UK	INDIA	CHINA
81%	80%	71%	60%	56%

GERMANY	USA	BRAZIL	RUSSIA	JAPAN
48%	44%	34%	13%	12%

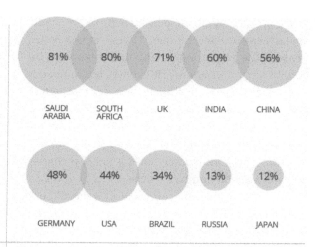

SAUDI ARABIA	SOUTH AFRICA	UK	INDIA	CHINA
81%	80%	71%	60%	56%

GERMANY	USA	BRAZIL	RUSSIA	JAPAN
48%	44%	34%	13%	12%

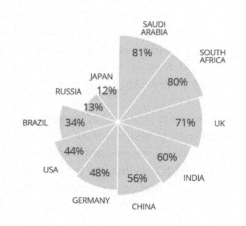

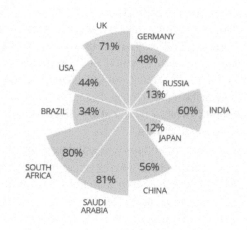

SAUDI ARABIA	SOUTH AFRICA	UK	INDIA	CHINA
81%	80%	71%	60%	56%

GERMANY	USA	BRAZIL	RUSSIA	JAPAN
48%	44%	34%	13%	12%

We are talking about percentages, so we could make them 100%-width bars. That gives us a better sense of the proportion of land that is taken up by farming, but it makes the differences less dramatic.

An alternative to this might be a dot plot (effectively, an abacus) which makes the end points stand out, although there is usually no room for the labels. If you want the labels to stay, a variant of a dot plot – sometimes called a lollipop chart – keeps the actual numbers visible.

Since we are charting composition, we could use pie charts. (We'll talk more about pie charts in the next chapter.) They are harder to read than bars, but they catch the eye, like those rows of clocks that show the different times in different cities. If we change the pies into doughnuts, this makes them less legible as charts, but we can add the number in the centre, which aids comprehension.

We could hark back to our *Guardian* days and go for rows of bubbles. (Some designers like making the bubbles overlap to signal the largeness of the largest value – I don't.)

If we wanted to add more visual drama, we could try a polar area chart. Maybe arranged largest to smallest? Or oriented so it matches each country's approximate geographical location?

But this is about agricultural land, so how about using squares to resemble fields seen from above? That might work better as a visual metaphor.

This is global data and people love maps, so we could also experiment with a cartogram.

Throughout this process, we will be thinking about who our audience is (will they tolerate a more 'creative' chart?), what our story is (is ranking the countries helpful or distracting?) and where in our story this chart occurs (is it at the beginning or the end? Have we just had ten bar charts in a row?).

The story also affects any colour choices we make and annotations we add. Here we have assumed our presentation is a general introduction to the subject for a global institution (say, the World Trade Organization), so we haven't highlighted any specific country. But if it were for OPEC and it was about Saudi Arabia's successful programme to 'make the desert bloom', we would be highlighting Saudi Arabia both here and in every chart in our deck.

There are limits to our experimentation, however. You will notice that none of the charts in Figure 1.7 has any 3D elements. In nearly every case, adding 3D to a chart renders it unattractive and confusing. The same applies to drop shadows and gradients: they don't help (see Figure 1.8). Although we are charting different countries, we have resisted the urge to add flags, because the flag colours clash with each other, they distract from the data, and few people know more than a handful of flags so we would have to add labels anyway. Of course, if a client absolutely insists that we include these elements, then in they go, but we would never include any of these design elements without being told to.

It is also worth saying that all of these charting options suit a static presentation, but not an interactive one. If this were a dashboard about land use, particularly one that had to be usable on mobile devices, the number of potential charts would be more limited (probably to horizontal bars, line charts, maps and tables) and we would be worrying less about making the charts immersive and more about making the user journeys *between* charts immersive.

The **Make** stage typically involves teams of designers, illustrators, animators, front-end developers, software developers and quality assurance managers. There is usually an internal project manager, and an account manager who interacts with the client – but for small projects, you can usually merge these roles. The tools used vary hugely: for static graphics, it is usually Inkscape, Illustrator, InDesign or PowerPoint. For interactive charts we use JavaScript libraries such as Highcharts and D3, and for animations we use After Effects. But new tools and charting libraries appear all the time, so it is worth keeping your

Percentage of land in each country used for agriculture

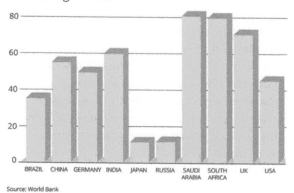

Source: World Bank

Percentage of land in each country used for agriculture

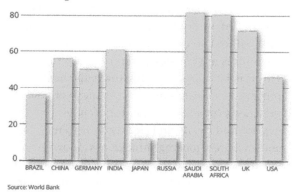

Source: World Bank

Percentage of land in each country used for agriculture

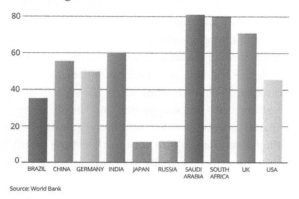

Source: World Bank

Figure 1.8 Experiments to avoid

eye on data viz blogs to see what practitioners are currently recommending.

This part of the process brings clarity and comprehensibility to your work. The objective is to enlighten your audience.

Refine

Last, but not least, you refine your work. This means correcting any spelling mistakes and double-checking the data, testing it for bugs (if it is interactive), sharpening up the visuals, and running it past key readers or users.

Every member of the team is involved in this part of the process. Quality assurance teams test for bugs; developers fix errors; editors and producers correct and rework copy; designers and front-end developers make sure any graphical elements are as engaging as possible, finalising font choices, colour palettes and layout. This last aspect is more important than it has ever been, just because the amount of competition is growing all the time. Thousands of charts and graphics get published every day, and if your work looks distinctive, then people are more likely to stop and listen to what you're telling them. Certainly we have seen many important stories sink without trace because of flat copy or unappealing visuals.

It is also during this stage that we process most of the client feedback. Let joy be unconfined.

Of course clients will have fed back at earlier stages too, but this is where the senior people get involved, with reliably hilarious consequences. 'The Eiffel Tower just doesn't say "Paris" to me', 'Surely you can rework that web page over the weekend?', 'Could you make us an icon for creative synergies?' and the timeless classic 'Make the logo bigger'.

The thing is, even if it's awful, most client feedback is a *good thing*. Your client is usually much closer to the intended audience of your chart or interactive than you are. Their solutions might be wrong, but they are sometimes putting their finger on a weakness in your work. Even when we are making our own graphics, uncommissioned by anyone, we draft in friends or colleagues to act as proxy clients, because that cycle of feedback and refinement is so useful in creating a piece of work that connects with others, that pre-empts where an audience might need more or less information, and that anticipates where design elements can speed up understanding.

I'm not saying that doing this is easy; it's not. It's painful to throw work away. But unfortunately an audience doesn't care how long it took you, or how hard you worked. Do *you* care how long it took your favourite artist to make that incredible painting or song or novel? They either got it right, or they didn't. Having access to a critical friend – which is what the best clients are – can give you a valuable competitive edge, and is usually a cause for celebration rather than dread.

And I should stress, although I'm using the word 'client' here, I mean anyone who has oversight of your work: it could be someone editing your news story, or an academic peer-reviewing your journal article. They are performing the same role: acting as a test audience. The refinement stage makes your work truly useful. If you don't go through this part of the process, you might have a solid story, but few people will notice it and fewer still will share it. We often compare it to the difference between *The Spanish Tragedy* by Thomas Kyd and Shakespeare's *Hamlet*.

So – have you read Kyd's *Spanish Tragedy*? Do you know any of the characters' names? Are you aware of the basic story? Could you quote any of the lines?

What about *Hamlet*? Do you know the plot of Shakespeare's play? It's likely that you do. Maybe you know a few of the lines too: 'To be or not to be', 'Alas, poor Yorick', 'Get thee to a nunnery', 'To thine own self be true'.

Well, *The Spanish Tragedy* and *Hamlet* are essentially the same play. Similar plot, similar characters.

Shakespeare stole the whole thing, just like he stole the plots of all of his other plays except (possibly) *The Tempest*. But we remember *Hamlet* and we have forgotten Kyd's earlier tragedy because of the way in which Shakespeare refined the story. He changed and rearranged scenes to make the plot more exciting, and gave the characters psychological depth to make their actions more credible. Above all, he added *style*, the poetry that makes his characters' words so memorable.

Refining has another meaning too. As a culinary term, it means breaking things down, getting rid of the lumps. When you're making a graphic, those lumps are *you* – your taste, your interests, your *stuff* getting in between the story and the audience. Of course you have interpreted a dataset and crafted a story for your audience; it wouldn't exist without you. But for an audience to lose themselves in your story, you have to get lost too. This is what happens during the refinement process: you are erasing as many traces of your presence as possible, so the story can be experienced clearly and cleanly, as if your audience were looking through a window.

This is ultimately the purpose of refinement. It is getting to the best possible expression of your story. That's why people will share it, quote it and use it in their own work, because they are unlikely to find a better version.

There is one final reason why refinement is so important. Although you build your story from the ground up – working with the data, building a story, making it look and sound distinctive – your audience will be experiencing it in the other direction. They will often notice the superficial features first – the snappy title and the attractive charts – and only if they find these appealing will they spend longer with your work, getting drawn into the story and finally acquiring a deeper understanding of the data. If you haven't spent time perfecting your work, then your audience may never get past these superficial elements, and all that work you put into finding, designing and making your story will be wasted.

To put it in architectural terms, your house might be built on solid foundations but if it's a dump, no one is going to come and visit.

That first impression of your work is also linked to one of our most fundamental emotions: approach–avoidance conflict. Should I get closer to this? Or should I move further away? Any information source is going to require effort to understand, and it is impossible to predict in advance whether it will be worth the time you invest in it. But an intriguing appearance can overcome some of this ambivalence, because it gives pleasure in itself, and so offers emotional rewards before any of the information has even been assimilated.

Of course, refining a bad story is unwise. In fact, a story that looks and sounds beautiful will get noticed, which means that experts will start to pay attention, because they are usually very wary of newcomers (especially *designers*) trespassing on their particular area of expertise. It is at this point that any shortcuts or errors you made during the **Find**, **Design** and **Make** stages will be uncovered. Therefore it is a mistake to think that beautification can save a bad story. On the contrary, it will only make any shortcomings in your story more visible.

One example: in 2017, I made a graphic on Jane Austen for the *Guardian*, along with designer Jim Kynvin and illustrator Amy Watt. I read all the books twice and checked the data dozens of times. But I got the first name of one of the minor characters wrong, the sub-editors didn't pick it up, and that is now reflected in the (furious) comments for ever, even though we corrected the mistake within half an hour of the graphic being published. Without the beauty of Jim Kynvin's designs, the *Guardian* probably wouldn't have published it, and if they had, few people would have noticed the mistake. I'm glad these people did notice, but the point is, augmenting and amplifying your story also amplifies its errors.

Why teamwork matters

So that is our process. We do not pretend that it is unique; most agencies will have created a similar diagram of their working practices, if only so that clients don't think they are making it up as they go along (even though everyone is, a bit). However, we do find that it helps us to keep projects on track, provided we have the right team in place.

Which leads us to the next point. You might have noticed that there are a range of different job roles, skillsets and software options included in the table of our process (Figure 1.2). We are often asked by clients to recommend a 'data visualiser' to them, because they want to build up their skills in this area. We tend to reply by saying we don't really know any. There may well be a modern da Vinci who can handle all the different aspects of the data visualisation process: a statistician, data analyst, editor, copywriter, project manager and graphic designer (as a minimum), but also an illustrator, animator, front-end developer, back-end developer, UX designer and quality assurance manager. To be honest, we're happy if we can find people who can combine two of these skillsets: a designer who can work with Excel, or a coder who can also make charts look attractive. But these people don't come along very often. So that is our other key piece of advice: work with other people. It is unusual for good data viz to be produced by individuals working alone. Writing, data analysis, designing, coding – it can take a lifetime to master just one of these disciplines. So finding people to work with – people who complement your own abilities – is important.

I was trying to think of a school subject that data visualisation doesn't draw on, but I think they are all relevant. In a typical week, I will be using skills I learnt in English, maths, history, geography, computer science, art and design, modern foreign languages and more. It is why there is no single route into data visualisation, no area of expertise shared by all practitioners.

Having said all this, it is still worth learning about each part of the process above. After all, you might turn out to be a modern da Vinci who does excel in multiple fields. (They do seem to be out there: Nathan Yau, Maarten Lambrechts, Nadieh Bremer and others.) However, even if this isn't the case, learning about the key tools and techniques used by other members of the team makes the process of collaboration so much easier. If you are an analyst and you know a little about Adobe Illustrator, it means that when you're putting together a brief for a designer, you'll be speaking a similar language. Likewise, if you're an editor talking to developers, understanding the basics of a JavaScript library like D3 means you'll know more about what it can and can't do. A little learning *isn't* a dangerous thing in data visualisation, it's a necessary precondition for effective working relationships. In fact, the technology develops so quickly that a continual willingness to try out new tools, approaches and visual effects ought to come as naturally as breathing.

The process in action

Here is one example of what the whole process looks like in action (Figure 1.9). 'What's in a Name?' is a piece that I created with the designer Zhenia Vasiliev and published on the *Guardian*'s Datablog in 2013. It's about people's names in the UK and how they tend to be a marker of age, ethnicity and social class.

Find

To find this story, I started by asking a range of professional bodies to supply me with the most

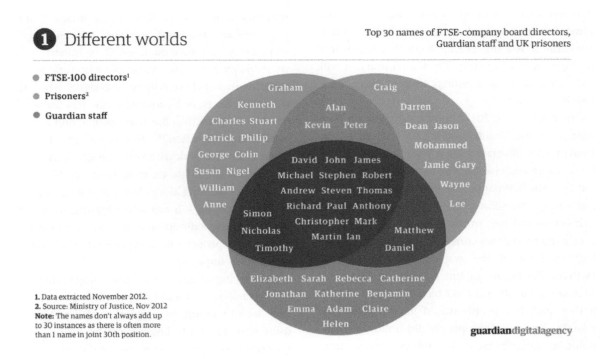

1 Different worlds

Top 30 names of FTSE-company board directors, Guardian staff and UK prisoners

● FTSE-100 directors[1]
● Prisoners[2]
● Guardian staff

Graham
Craig
Kenneth   Alan   Darren
Charles Stuart   Kevin   Peter   Dean Jason
Patrick Philip   Mohammed
George Colin   David John James   Jamie Gary
Susan Nigel   Michael Stephen Robert
William   Andrew Steven Thomas   Wayne
Anne   Richard Paul Anthony   Lee
       Simon   Christopher Mark
     Nicholas   Martin Ian   Matthew
      Timothy   Daniel

Elizabeth Sarah Rebecca Catherine
Jonathan Katherine Benjamin
Emma Adam Claire
Helen

1. Data extracted November 2012.
2. Source: Ministry of Justice, Nov 2012
Note: The names don't always add up to 30 instances as there is often more than 1 name in joint 30th position.

guardiandigitalagency

Figure 1.9 An example of **Find, Design, Make, Refine**

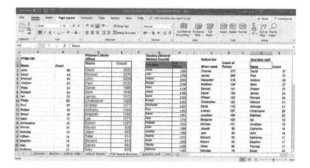

Figure 1.10 The original spreadsheet for 'What's in a name?'

Home Office. After analysing dozens of datasets, we decided to focus on the six groups that contained the most interesting stories – doctors, company directors, footballers, prisoners, Oxford University students and *Guardian* employees (Figure 1.10).

I looked for any interesting patterns and relationships in these datasets (Figure 1.11). I isolated the female names (there were only two female names in the top 30 company directors), and those commonly associated with an ethnic minority group (there was one – Mohammed – in the list of most common prisoners' names) and explored how names fall in and out of fashion (lots of doctors and FTSE company directors called John, but no Johns in the top 30 Oxford undergraduate names).

common first names of practitioners in their field. I supplemented this with publicly available datasets (e.g. the names of company directors). I also contacted government bodies such as the UK

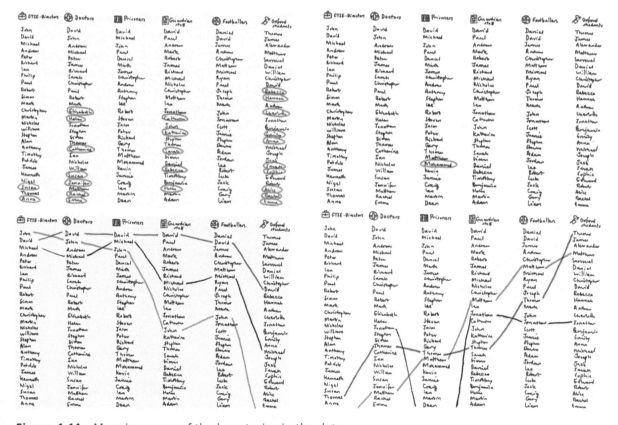

Figure 1.11 Mapping some of the key stories in the data

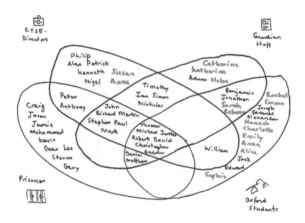

Figure 1.12 Names that only appeared in one of the datasets

However, what soon became apparent was that the real story lay in what these lists *didn't* have in common. There were names that only appeared in one of the top 30s but not in any of the others (Figure 1.12). This would become our story.

Design

Next, we needed to come up with a visualisation that showed our audience which names appeared to *impede* you from passing freely from one profession

to another. We needed a visual language of inclusion and exclusion, which led us towards the overlapping circles of a Venn diagram. The **Design** stage involved dozens and dozens of sketches. At first, we wondered if we could have more than three circles (Figure 1.13) and include four different professions, but this didn't tell a clear story at all. This is why sketching is a good idea – because your first ideas are usually wildly overambitious.

After we accepted that three overlapping circles would be easiest for our audience to process, we selected the three professions that told the most dramatic story – FTSE directors, prisoners and *Guardian* staff. Then we moved on to the question of how many names to show. We sketched Venns with the top 50 names in each group (adding more evidence for our case, but harder to read), top 10 (too few names undermined our point because the interesting variations started lower down the list) or top 30 (which is where we ended up, Figure 1.14). We couldn't have a hard cut-off at 30 though. There were five FTSE director names in joint 30th place, so we had to have 34 names in that circle.

After we had finished the sketch of the first Venn diagram, and established our design language, we decided to create three more Venns

Figure 1.13 No. Just no.

Figure 1.14 The final sketch of 'What's in a name?'

to show interesting relationships between other groups in our dataset – just two circles this time. We sketched FTSE directors v. doctors (to tell the gender story), male Oxford undergraduates v. footballers (focusing on class), and female Oxford undergraduates v. most common female names for that birth cohort (again, a class focus). At the end, to provide wider context about how the meaning of names changes over time, we looked at historical baby names data from the Office for National Statistics. For this, we devised two Venn diagrams, both with three circles, to show how there was some overlap for boys' names between generations (for example, James has been a permanent feature in the top 15), but none at all for female names (Figure 1.15).

Note that we continued to look for contextual and supplementary data even when we had started to design our story. Although it's ideal if you find and analyse all relevant data in the first part of your project, it is frequently the case that you won't understand which dataset will provide the best context until you know for sure the final focus of your story. Each of our four stages – **Find**, **Design**, **Make**, **Refine** – overlap to some degree.

At the end of the **Design** stage, we had a series of five charts: a story with a beginning, middle and end, covering the key stories in our dataset (gender, class, ethnicity and change over time) in a format that the *Guardian*'s Datablog would like (the editor preferred individual charts to single long, scrolling jpegs), legible for readers on both mobile and desktop, and on a subject that we thought *Guardian* readers would find interesting.

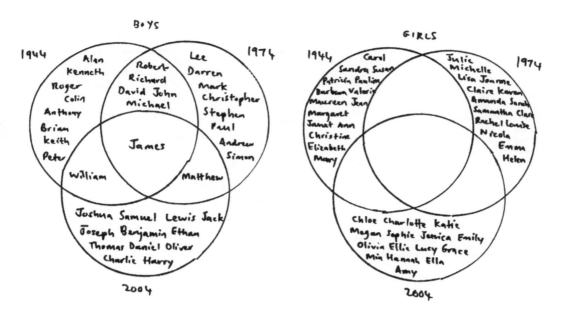

Figure 1.15 Boys' and girls' names – change over time

Make

After I had designed the charts, it was time for Zhenia to make them. I did the first part, transferring my sketches into PowerPoint slides, so Zhenia would have a digital version with all the names correctly spelt and located in the relevant section of the Venn. This is where errors creep in, so the more you can do to ensure consistency across iterations, the better. Suggesting that a designer retypes text from a hand-drawn sketch directly into Illustrator is asking for trouble.

Zhenia started with the first Venn, the hardest one, where we had over 50 names to fit into three circles. His first version (Figure 1.16) looked nothing like the finished version.

He used Arial as a typeface; he chose light shades of primary colours; he also pulled the names in the central overlapping section out of the chart because he was convinced he couldn't fit them in. But doing this meant we lost the central plank of our story: it was no longer possible to clearly see the difference between names that sat in *all* the circles and names that only sat in *one* of them. Believe it or not, this is quite a common issue. When you make a chart, your first attempt can make the wireframe *worse*, because you've started to tease out some of its structural problems without yet alighting on solutions. It's why a lot of PowerPoint presentations are hard going, because the presenter has never moved beyond a first iteration of their chart, and so hasn't ironed out any kinks in the translation from page (or brain) to screen.

The next iteration was much sharper (Figure 1.17). We lost Arial and used Guardian Egyptian – a less functional font.[4] Zhenia also began to bend the rules

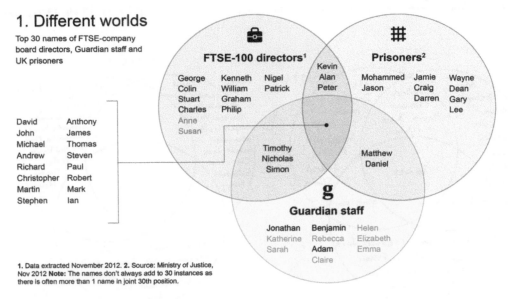

Figure 1.16   The first version of 'What's in a name?'

---

[4]Note that for licensing reasons, we've used Merriweather here. This is a clear and elegant free font that looks a lot like Guardian Egyptian, but you can download it and try it in your own designs for no cost.

❶ Different worlds

Top 30 names of
FTSE-company board
directors, Guardian staff
and UK prisoners

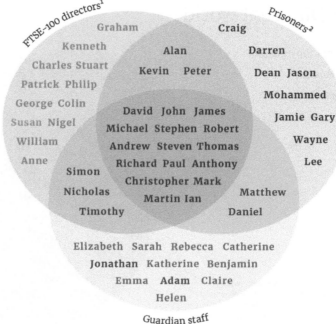

1. Data extracted November 2012.
2. Source: Ministry of Justice, Nov 2012
Note: The names don't always add up
to 30 instances as there is often more
than 1 name in joint 30th position.

Figure 1.17   The second version of 'What's in a name?'

a little. This is a vital part of any second iteration, even if you end up bending the rules back again. As any information designer will tell you, rules on charting are only guidelines: what accelerates information transfer for one audience can impede it for another.

Here Zhenia tried *squashing* the circles. After all, this wasn't a *scaled* Venn, where the size of the circles had a mathematical link to the number of elements contained within; we were under no obligation to use perfect circles. By distorting the circles slightly, Zhenia could put all the names back in the central section. As a side benefit, there was more horizontal space for the other names, so they became more legible too.

Zhenia also thought hard about the use of iconography. In my sketches, I'd placed small icons with each of my diagram labels, probably out of fear that there wasn't much visual interest otherwise. In the first iteration Zhenia dutifully kept these, but in the second the icons are gone. We

both sensed they were now surplus to requirements. Icons only work if they serve the story, and by 'serve' I mean that they save time, save space, increase visual interest or speed up understanding. Think of how icons are used on, say, an online video player – Play, Pause, Rewind, Full Screen, Minimise and so on. They are sensible choices, simplifying the interface. In the first iteration of our Venn diagrams, the icons do not save us time (we have to read the labels to understand them), they don't save any space (they cannot replace the labels), they don't increase interest (they distract from the circles) and they don't enhance understanding (the meaning of the labels isn't difficult). So Zhenia put the icons out of their (and everyone else's) misery. It's not a bad habit to get into – deleting icons. If only to see if your chart actually works better without them.

In the final iteration (Figure 1.18), everything came together.

① Different worlds

Top 30 names of FTSE–company board directors, Guardian staff and UK prisoners

- FTSE-100 directors[1]
- Prisoners[2]
- Guardian staff

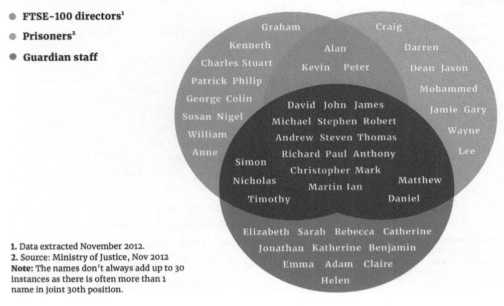

1. Data extracted November 2012.
2. Source: Ministry of Justice, Nov 2012
Note: The names don't always add up to 30 instances as there is often more than 1 name in joint 30th position.

Figure 1.18 The final version of 'What's in a name?'

The big breakthrough here was colour – those beautiful solid discs of red, orange and blue – creating four new colours at the points where the circles overlapped.

It was my fault that this took Zhenia a few iterations to get right. In my sketch and in my PowerPoint slide, I had put female names in a different font colour – as this felt like an important layer of the story. In the first two iterations, Zhenia preserved this – male names were in a different colour (iteration 1) or different shade (iteration 2) than female names. But this aspect of the wireframe was tying Zhenia's hands, preventing him from using bold colours elsewhere. More critically, it was preventing him from supporting our main story. Colour is one of the most powerful weapons we have for signalling groups or categories. Here our main categories are FTSE directors, prisoners and *Guardian* staff. Within these groups, some names are male and some names are female, but this is a secondary grouping. We need to understand those top-level groups first and so that is where our colours should be brightest and boldest. By trying to share colour meanings too widely (as we did in Figures 1.16 and 1.17), *all* the layers of our story end up weaker. By using colour to support our main story *only* (Figure 1.18), every component of our story benefits, because a stronger visual engages people for longer, and they see not just our main story, but secondary stories, and stories that are relevant only to them.

So the font colour in our circles became one colour – white – and our brightly coloured circles became the clear heroes of our graphic.

The other reason I found Zhenia's breakthrough so inspiring is that it brought home the degree of social breakdown so clearly. In a fair society, there should be almost complete overlap: the same names in the centre of those three circles, the same life chances regardless of gender, class, age and ethnicity. Because the contrast in that central section – white font on a dark crimson background – was stronger than anywhere else in the graphic, this increased the prominence of these names, and made them almost push in front of the others, just as they had pushed past them in life.

The new colours had another beneficial side-effect. Because they were so distinct, we could move the circle labels into a key. Before, these labels had been inside the circles (Figure 1.16), taking up valuable space, or they'd curled round the outside, almost apologetically (Figure 1.17). Now they were out of the way, but still close enough to the chart.

In fact, the information hierarchy improves overall: the title and subtitle are at the top, ruled off from the graphic, the key is top left, the footnotes are bottom left; the relative importance of each element is clearly signalled.

Once Zhenia had set up this design language, he was able to use it in the other four Venn diagrams in the series (Figure 1.19). Note that we 'solved' the first graphic before starting any of the others, as this meant that any edits only had to be done in one place, not five.

Refine

So we have worked through **Find**, **Design** and **Make**. Fortunately for these charts, the **Refine** stage was fairly speedy. The Datablog editor, Simon Rogers, accepted the graphics with minimal edits. The only real changes were reformatting the charts for different use cases: creating crops for social media and for specific image slots on the *Guardian* website. We also prepared a single long jpeg version so that we could publish it on specialist infographic sites and enter it for competitions that stipulated single-image submissions (Figure 1.20).

This is a dull but vital part of the job. When the graphic is finished, it isn't finished – as you are rarely just publishing that image in one place. If you don't create custom versions, then a bored sub-editor or an algorithm will, and people may never click through if what they see is confusing, blurry or doesn't match the supporting text.

4 Head Girls

Top 50 names of female Oxford undergraduates and women born in 1994.

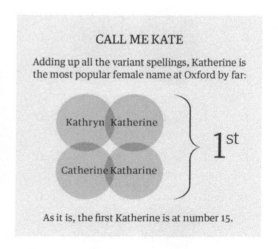

● Oxford undergraduates[1] (female)　● Most popular baby girls' names[2] (1994)

1. Source: Oxford University 2. Source: ONS, Most popular names in England and Wales.

guardiandigitalagency

Figure 1.19 Another chart in the 'What's in a name?' series

One increasingly important part of the **Refine** stage is creating animated versions of graphics, particularly for social media. We didn't create one in this instance (it was 2012, life was simpler then) and by the time you read this, perhaps animated gifs will have been replaced by something even more insufferable. But what is unlikely to have changed is the need to think about different audiences discovering your work in different places.

The importance of each stage

Each stage – **Find**, **Design**, **Make**, **Refine** – is essential (Figure 1.21). With our Venn diagrams, if we had rushed or skipped a stage, we would have compromised on accuracy, interest, clarity or usefulness, marring the beauty of the whole. For example, refining a design is often seen as 'adding the finishing touches'. But if you look at our Venn diagram, you'll see that *at no point* before the final iteration (Figure 1.18) was the graphic finished. Even going one step back (Figure 1.17), the colours are washed out and the meaning is less clear. If we had stopped at this point, it is unlikely that the chart would have had the same impact, and all the time and effort we had spent finding and designing the story would have been wasted. Colour, font and layout are not 'finishing touches'; they are your audience's starting point, and an integral part of how your story will be understood.

Although this was a series of static graphics, we go through the same process whatever we are

Figure 1.20 Cropping and customising your graphic

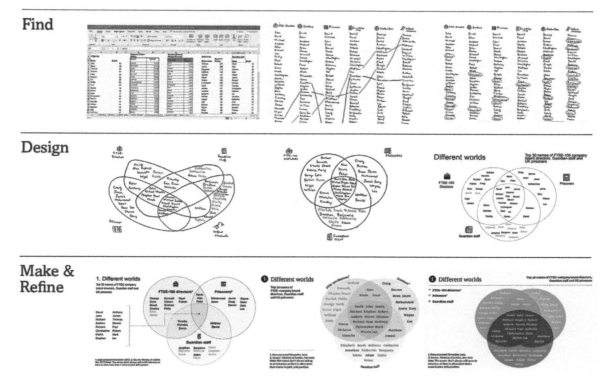

Figure 1.21   Find, Design, Make, Refine

making: an animation, a PowerPoint presentation, a dashboard or a physical installation. The media, audience and subject-matter changes, but there is always a story to be found, designed, built and refined.

The only further point to make is that sometimes the story and media type are fixed by our client and this limits the work we can do in the first three stages – **Find**, **Design** and **Make**. For one example of how we approach projects like these, see Appendix A, which you can find online here: www.addtwodigital.com/book

─── ∴ ─── **Try it yourself!** ───

Whatever your data viz dilemma, you can bet that someone else has already encountered it, and probably come up with a pretty good solution. The more you're aware of data visualisation's past, the easier you'll find it to come up with your own answers. Try the following:

- Monitor the best data viz sites and practitioners and create a (real or virtual) scrapbook of the

(Continued)

work that you find most inspirational. Some suggested starting points: *The Economist*, the *Financial Times*, the *New York Times*, the *Washington Post* and *National Geographic*.

- Have a look at the recent shortlisted entries for a data viz award, such as the Information is Beautiful Awards or Malofiej. Do you think the judges made the right decision? Would your winner have been different? Have a look at previous winners too.

- Is there a particular subject or theme that you care about, or that is important for your work? Identify the graphics or interactives on this topic that you think are particularly successful. What makes them work so well? Consider writing a blog post about what you've discovered: 'The five most inspirational graphics about crime/health/outer space' (or whatever it might be).

Two

A spectrum of right answers

Adam Frost

Chapter contents

We don't have any other hard-and-fast rules.

We recommend that you stick to our process – starting with finding the data, and working through each stage in order – and we advise you to collaborate with people whose skills complement your own. But that's about it.

Over the years, we've encountered plenty of diktats about the right and wrong way to put a chart together: 'Never use a RAG scale', 'Never put more than 10 lines on a line chart', 'A *y*-axis should always start at zero'. If you are designing a chart for the person who invented these specific rules, then you should probably stick to them. But in most cases, your audience is relying on you to make a judgement about which rules will serve the story best. After all, many rules contradict each other: an election map that uses the correct political party colours will often fail colour-blindness tests (lots of parties use red and green). Other rules have vital exceptions. For example, starting a *y*-axis at zero is essential for bar charts, but for line charts it entirely depends on whether starting at zero will make important changes invisible.

Brand guidelines often conflict with good design principles too. For example, we might advise one client: 'Use red sparingly. It should be used as an alert colour only.' But they might reply: 'I work for Coca-Cola. Everything has to be red.'

For more rules, and why following them can be problematic, check out the '99 Data Viz Rules' project on our website: www.addtwodigital.com/book. At the time of writing, we've only found three rules that you should always stick to all of the time (to find out which ones, you'll have to visit the site).

Rather than outlining a set of strictures, we prefer to say that there is a spectrum of right answers, and as long as you stay broadly within this spectrum, tailoring the story you've found to your audience's needs, then you should end up in a sensible place.

We've provided a simplified overview of our good practice spectrum in Figure 2.1, with some of the key practitioners who can help you communicate with each audience type. This is subjective of course, although we have been strongly influenced by recommendations from our students. There are many other authors and designers that we could have included, but we wanted to keep our recommendations to a manageable number.[1] We're also aware that this list is: skewed towards UK/US authors and publications, likely to become out of date very quickly, and likely to cause disagreements about whether specific individuals are positioned correctly on the spectrum. But, leaving all of this aside, we hope that it successfully conveys the fact that there are a range of useful approaches depending on what you are saying and to whom.[2]

We would advise against you straying outside of this spectrum. If you move too far to the left-hand side, you will find yourself in the world of business intelligence dashboards and statistical software, and it's harder to clearly communicate ideas with these visualisation approaches. If you

---

[1]If you're looking for more of an overview of everything, try Andy Kirk's *Data Visualisation* (2019), which is full of good sense, Isabel Meirelles' *Design for Information* (2013) or *The Wall Street Journal's Guide to Information Graphics* by Dona Wong (2010). Also bridging at least two of the schools of thought is Simon Rogers' superb *Facts Are Sacred* (2013).

[2]I'm also aware that focusing on individuals undermines what we said earlier about the need for a team. However, many of the people on this list have teams working with them. In Edward Tufte's books, he frequently credits designers for producing artwork; David McCandless collaborates with designers and researchers; and Valentina D'Efilippo worked with the investigative journalist James Ball on her book *The Infographic History of the World* (D'Efilippo and Ball, 2013).

The good practice spectrum

Who are you talking to?

Expert or analyst audience	**A mixed audience (experts and non-experts)**	**The wider public**
Try reading	**Try reading**	**Try reading**
Edward Tufte	Nathan Yau	David McCandless
William Cleveland	Nate Silver/FiveThirtyEight	Nigel Holmes
Naomi Robbins	Hans Rosling/Gapminder	Valentina D'Efilippo
Stephen Few	Alberto Cairo	The *New York Times*
Leland Wilkinson	The *Financial Times*	The *Washington Post*
Office for National Statistics style guide (UK)	*The Economist*	*The Guardian*
	Bloomberg Graphics	*National Geographic*
		South China Morning Post
For scientific context	**For business presentations**	**For infographics/data art**
Colin Ware	Jon Schwabish	Stefanie Posavec
Stephen Kosslyn	Nancy Duarte	Giorgia Lupi
Katy Borner	Cole Nussbaumer Knaflic	Nadieh Bremer

Other useful people

Interactives/coding :
Hadley Wickham, Kieran Healy (R), Scott Murray (D3), Lisa Rost (Datawrapper blog), Steve Wexler, Andy Cotgreave, Jeffrey Shaffer (Tableau), Moritz Stefaner, Maarten Lambrechts (best practice)

Miscellaneous (but all brilliant):
Randall Munroe, Mona Chalabi, Christian Rudder

Historical examples:
William Playfair, Charles Minard, John Snow, Otto and Marie Neurath and Gerd Arntz

Not about data viz directly, but will change your life:
Daniel Kahneman and Amos Tversky, Barbara Tversky, Don Norman, George Lakoff & Mark Johnson, Scott McCloud

Figure 2.1 Key figures in the data viz spectrum

move too far to the right, you are in tabloid territory – Fox News and the *Daily Mail* – and this should be avoided too, because the storytelling can be distorted by ideology (i.e. propaganda) or sensationalism. If you stay within the good practice spectrum, then your objective is always revealing the truth to an audience and it just becomes a question of the best way of achieving this.

Let's briefly examine the constituent parts of our spectrum. How do all of these designers differ?

Audience 1: The experts

Most of the people on the left-hand side of our spectrum started out as statisticians or scientists before becoming interested in information design, and this is perhaps one reason why their work appeals primarily to people whose lives have followed a similar trajectory. They often hold (or held) academic positions: William Cleveland taught at Purdue, Edward Tufte has taught at Yale and Princeton. Or they have worked in the research and development departments of large firms: both William Cleveland and Naomi Robbins worked at Bell Labs. It's also worth mentioning two 'forefather' figures: John Tukey, a statistician and polymath who divided his time between Bell Labs and Princeton University, and Jacques Bertin, a French cartographer who acted as Director of Studies at the École des Hautes Études en Sciences Sociales in Paris.

This group can loosely be described as embodying the 'analytical' or 'academic' approach to information design. Their statistical background means that they are more likely to see information design as a science rather than an art, with universal rules and principles just like 'mathematics and the laws of Nature', as Edward Tufte has put it (Tufte, 2006, p. 9). They often articulate a belief in an 'objective school of knowledge that says this is "right" and that is "wrong"', in Stephen Few's words (Rogers, 2013b). Designers in this 'school' are deeply uncomfortable with the idea of charting being subjective, with Cleveland writing: 'It is a continual challenge in developing principles for graphs not to degenerate into simply expressing personal preferences' (Cleveland, 1985, p. 18). You shouldn't just choose a chart because you like it, or because you think your audience will like it: you should use scientific research to help you find the most effective chart.[3]

The fact that most members of this group are rooted in academia and research also influences their approach. They are accustomed to addressing a student or expert audience who have existing knowledge of key statistical concepts and chart types, the willingness to expand their knowledge further, the time in which to do this and the patience to cope with more detailed examples.[4] Furthermore, these authors are used to formulating their arguments in a didactic fashion, so that their students can readily apply them, and prepare 'correct' answers in any presentations or assignments. Edward Tufte is perhaps the best-known embodiment of this tendency: his books provide both a range of clearly expressed precepts and a variety of superb

[3]This is often accompanied with a conflation of good design and moral goodness: 'Making an evidence presentation is a moral act', and presenters must be held 'ethically responsible' for their work, Tufte writes in *Beautiful Evidence* (Tufte, 2006, p. 9).

[4]Cleveland wrote: 'The important criterion for a graph is not simply how fast we can see a result …. If a graphical display requires hours of study to make a discovery that would have gone undetected without the graph, then the display is a success' (Cleveland, 1985, pp. 97–8). True, charts don't always need to be understood quickly, but not every reader will have the time or inclination to devote 'hours of study' to a chart.

historical examples which show how these precepts might be put into practice.

Audience 2: The general public

At the other end of the spectrum, we have what we might call the 'journalistic' approach. As well as individual designers such as David McCandless and Valentina D'Efilippo, there are the graphics departments of news organisations such as the *New York Times* and the *Washington Post*, and magazines such as *National Geographic*. Outstanding individual writers and designers associated with these organisations include Simon Rogers and Michael Robinson (formerly of the *Guardian*), Amanda Cox, Steve Duenes and Mike Bostock (*New York Times*), Adolfo Arranz and Alberto Lucas López (*South China Morning Post*), Jane Pong (*SCMP* and *Financial Times*), Francesco Franchi (*Repubblica*) and Juan Velasco and Fernando Baptista (*National Geographic*) and countless other designers and developers who will be creating world-class visual stories as we speak.

The most important precursors of this approach were arguably Otto and Marie Neurath and Gerd Arntz, founders of the isotype movement. Based in 1920s Austria, they skilfully used iconography to bring dry social, economic and historical data to life. Their goal was, in Marie Neurath's words, to create charts 'meaning something for everyone', charts 'that excluded nobody' (Marcus, 2018, p. 140). The Gerd Arntz web archive is a good place to start if you want to find out more.

Many of the people in this group have a background in the humanities (often literature, history, or art and design), rather than science. However, it's not correct to define their approach as 'unscientific': most data journalists use statistical methods to analyse and verify their source data. It's more that when it comes to *presenting* what they've found, journalists will tend to balance the need to be understandable (sticking to tried-and-tested rules)

with the desire to be novel (extending or subverting the rules). There is science behind this, but it's psychology rather than statistics.

The journalistic approach assumes a very different set of audience expectations. Books at the analytical end of the spectrum are often 'designed as a learning experience', and you are invited to approach it 'with the curiosity of a student' (Few, 2012, pp. 12–13). Journalists, on the other hand, tend to assume that their audience is not at work or college (though they might be on the way there); this is their free time, and therefore anything you produce is competing with other leisure activities. If a teacher's audience is leaning in, a journalist's audience is leaning out. The reader of a news story may have no prior knowledge of the subject (which means that journalists simplify) and no prior interest in the subject (which means that journalists dramatise). Most of the time, journalists also write with a clear perspective or point of view, which is sometimes shaped by the organisation's proprietor but is often just dictated by the nature of the form. The visual journalist David McCandless put it this way: 'statisticians need to present their work objectively ... But my goal is to communicate with a wide audience ... I have to use framing and storytelling to get people to pay attention' (Tarran, 2015).

All of this means that visual journalists have fewer top-down precepts about what a right answer looks like. If it serves the story in the data well and connects with an audience, then your chart works. They are practitioners, testing what cuts through and what doesn't on a daily basis, making and unmaking charts at high speed, working under intense commercial pressure.

Audience 3: A mixed audience

In the centre of our spectrum, we have people who synthesise elements of both the 'statistical' and 'journalistic' approach. They are useful guides when you are talking to a mixed audience, for example in a company meeting where members of both the data science team and the marketing team are present. Or perhaps you work for a market research organisation or are a researcher at a university. You have a reputation for providing reliable data – and you need to protect this – but perhaps you struggle to present your data in accessible ways.

This 'hybrid' group includes people who started out as statisticians (such as Nate Silver) before embarking on journalistic careers, or who started out as journalists (such as Alberto Cairo) before becoming academics. Sometimes they are trained journalists who are still journalists, but who write for an expert audience, such as the Bloomberg Graphics team or the data visualisation teams at *The Economist* and the *Financial Times*. They often use more 'analytical' charts – scatter plots, steam-charts and alluvial diagrams – and incorporate important statistical concepts such as uncertainty and margin of error. As *The Economist* puts it, their goal is not to follow the path of least resistance, but to produce 'mind-stretching' journalism (Leo, 2019). However, they also understand the importance of good design: for example, a typical chart in *The Economist* will have a clear title and annotations, it will use brand fonts and colours consistently, and it will strike a balance between being comprehensive and being succinct enough to make sense on a mobile phone or speeding past on a social media timeline.

Although this group offers advice – a good starting point is Alan Smith's Chart Doctor column for the *Financial Times* – they are more pragmatic than the 'statistical' group and rarely prohibit charts or visual approaches unless they are actively fallacious. A statistical writer such as Cleveland compares charting rules to grammatical rules: 'Our written language has grammatical and syntactical rules that govern the details of word and sentence construction; most of [my] graphical principles … are analogous to these rules' (Cleveland, 1985, p. 89). But writers in the centre of our spectrum understand that grammar evolves, and is routinely ignored by native speakers if it slows down communication. In his seminal book *Data Points*, Nathan Yau puts it this way: 'In writing, there is grammar and syntax that is good to know, but where you can bend the rules is also important' (Yau, 2013, p. 89).

The pie chart test

So how do these different approaches look in practice? There are many examples I could cite, but sometimes it feels like it all comes down to pie charts. If you want to understand where a designer sits on the good practice spectrum mentioned above, ask them what they think about this chart type.

Let's start with the analytical group. Edward Tufte is unequivocal: 'Pie charts should never be used' (Tufte, 2001, p. 178). Other designers from a statistics background agree, with Stephen Few labelling them 'by far the least effective' graph (Few, 2007). Jorge Camoes (who describes his reading of Tufte as 'love at first sight') calls pies 'a sign of low graphical literacy' and 'the Comic Sans of data visualisation' (ouch!) and Cole Nussbaumer Knaflic states simply: 'They are evil' (Camoes, 2016, p. 206; Knaflic, 2015a, p. 61).

And don't get these guys started on doughnut charts or bubble charts. Here is Knaflic again: 'My hatred of pie charts is well documented. Donuts are even worse.'[5] Jorge Camoes writes: 'Every bad thing you can say about pie charts can be applied to donut charts, and then some' (Camoes, 2016, p. 210).

---

[5]See https://www.storytellingwithdata.com/blog/2011/07/death-to-pie-charts for more on this.

In a conversation with Simon Rogers, the *Guardian*'s Datablog editor, Stephen Few called bubble charts 'an ineffective quantitative display' and slammed Rogers for publishing the work of David McCandless 'who is particularly fond of bubbles' (Rogers, 2013b).

Indeed he is. Not just McCandless, but many visual journalists use bubble charts, doughnut charts and pie charts. Are they out of their minds? Haven't they read the scientific literature on how bad humans are at comparing the sizes of areas and angles compared to rectilinear shapes?[6] Look at a pie chart and try to judge the sizes of those tapering wedges as they jut into the circle from different angles. Put the same data in a bar chart and it's simple: you can instantly make out the largest and smallest bar, and make a pretty accurate guess at how much bigger one bar is compared to its neighbours.

So why do journalists persist in using circles in their visualisations? Why use a 'bad' chart?

Because people *love* them.

Circles are, without doubt, the world's favourite shape: the shape of the Sun and the Moon and human faces and pizza and biscuits. The designer Manuel Lima argues that this is 'deeply rooted in our biology': from the age of five months, babies show a clear preference for curved over angular objects. Certainly when we glance at another person, we invariably look at their eyes first to interpret their mood and intentions. And what we see when we're looking – our visual field – is also roughly circular, blurring at the edges.

Given that our ability to glean information from circles may have conferred an evolutionary advantage, it is no surprise that the shape is the cornerstone of many cultures and religions. Classical authors made it the symbol of unity and divinity, and shortly afterwards the halo became a visual shorthand for perfection.

If you want to remember that paragraph, then you'll probably draw a circle round it, not a polygon.

Journalists like McCandless know that circular charts take slightly longer to decode. But they are willing to sacrifice a little perceptual accuracy for the visual appeal that circles provide. It's because they are trying to reach a wider audience; they are attempting to make people pay attention to information that they might not usually care about, and they are willing to use more direct methods to make people look and listen.

When in 2009 the *Guardian* decided to chart annual government spending, an open dataset that had previously attracted little public interest, they chose a modified spider diagram to do it, a double-page spread of multi-coloured circles. We have re-created a simplified version of it here, using similar data (Figure 2.2).

As an agency, we went on to work with several UK government departments, and the *Guardian*'s public spending chart was referenced time and time again ('we want one like that') and in some instances displayed as a poster on office walls. It appealed not only to *Guardian* readers, but also to the data owners. It might be hard to accurately compare the size of circles, but the fans of that chart didn't care. A previously neglected dataset had been transformed into something that was both understandable at a glance but also attractive enough to invite further study.

There is no use telling these people that, scientifically speaking, bubble charts are 'an ineffective quantitative display'. Sometimes your primary goal is not to facilitate highly accurate comparisons. For newspapers, the scientific studies

---

[6]William Cleveland's *Elements of Graphing Data* (Wadsworth, 1985) is the seminal work on the 'effectiveness' scale. For example, he writes that *any* chart that relies on the judgement of area (pies, doughnuts and especially bubbles) should be avoided or 'redesigned to replace the area judgements by position or length judgements' (p. 282). We will explore this further later.

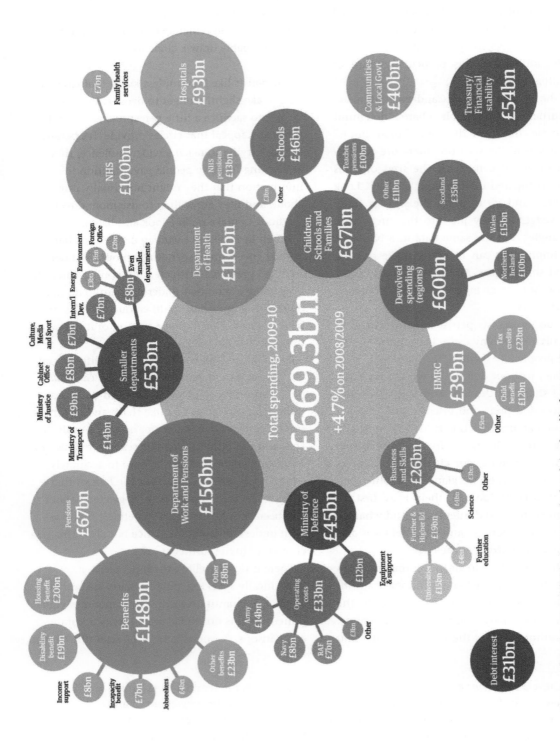

Total spend is greater than £669.3bn due to some budgets being shared by departments.

Figure 2.2 Government expenditure in the UK, 2009–10, based on a design by Jenny Ridley; original creative direction by Michael Robinson

that they are interested in do not take place in universities, with base sizes of a couple of hundred people; they are their daily analytic dashboards, which consist of millions of users, and which monitor every click that these users make, how long their users look at a story, whether they comment on it, and how often they share it. A bubble chart or a pie chart may be less accurate than a bar chart, but it is not a lie – it is a legitimate chart type – and if readers respond to it more readily than to the same information in a bar chart, then why on earth would a newspaper risk losing readers, depriving them of the chance of engaging with vitally important data, for the sake of a set of guidelines designed for a completely different use case?

But back to pie charts. Of course pie charts can be used badly. I suspect that this is a key reason for their unpopularity with the analyst community – that they are so easy to get wrong. But for a few types of story, pies are an acceptable choice. In the use cases displayed in Figure 2.3, I'd argue that they are at least as good as bar charts, and arguably better.

This is why journalists such as David McCandless use pie charts and other circular charts. It can be the right choice for your story, or it can offer visual variety, or it can emphasise important parts of your story. Note that in all the cases above, we are ensuring that we start our pie charts at 12 o'clock to exploit the human facility at reading clock faces, we are using colour with care, there are no exploding slices or any other visual trickery, and we are not trying to make pie charts do something they can't. Furthermore, we'd avoid using pie charts *at all* in charts designed for analysts or for business intelligence dashboards, where small differences in our data can have major repercussions. Likewise where the subject-matter is sober or serious and pie charts

might risk trivialising the content. But 'use pie charts carefully' is not the same as 'never use pie charts'.

Certainly if we move back to the group in the middle of our spectrum, we'll see a bit more tolerance towards pies. Nate Silver uses pie charts on two occasions in *The Signal and the Noise* (2015), and in one case, uses a *proportionately sized* pie chart, which would upset the analyst group on two counts because it's like a bubble chart and pie chart combined (we've created an example of our own in Figure 2.4).

Nathan Yau happily puts 'pie chart' first in his list of charts designed to show 'parts of a whole' and appears to prioritise them over stacked bars. Bubble charts are also defended by Yau – and he argues that they can be better than bars when you have a significant difference between your largest and smallest value.[7] I'd agree with this and add that it is particularly applicable where you have small datapoints that you nonetheless have to include because it would be confusing or deceptive to leave them out (see Figure 2.5).[8]

Hans Rosling, another practitioner whom we would place roughly in the middle of our spectrum, uses proportionally sized bubbles in his Gapminder tool, as we will see later. Alberto Cairo is more sympathetic to the Cleveland–McGill scale (we'll discuss this more later) which is often a key justification for dispensing with pie charts, but at the same time he can't quite bring himself to ban them: 'The reason why pie charts are still so widespread despite their obvious shortcomings escapes me. I think that people keep using them because they are fun and aesthetically pleasing' (Cairo, 2016, loc. 962). 'Fun and aesthetically pleasing': if I were described in this way (this has never happened), I'd definitely take it as a compliment.

---

[7]'Area is more useful when there are exponential differences between values … Bubbles let you put large and small counts in the same space' (Yau, 2013, p. 208).

[8]Other charting applications may be different, but in the bar chart tools in Microsoft Excel and Adobe Illustrator, Mercury, Venus, Earth and Mars are all encoded as one pixel high. In a bubble chart, the difference is more perceptible.

Over half of the UK's shoppers say that Supermarket A is their favourite

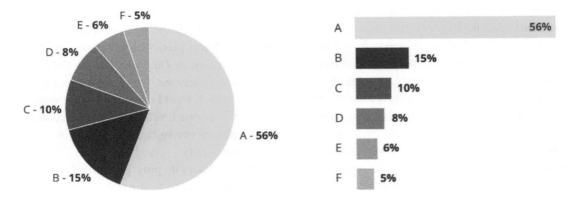

Parties A and B have more chance of forming a coalition than parties D and E

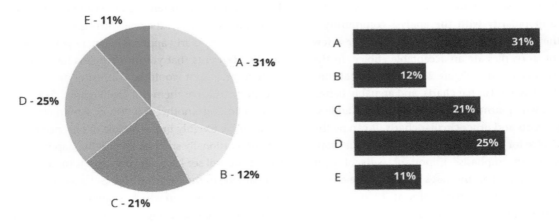

There is no single dominant brand in the UK supermarket sector

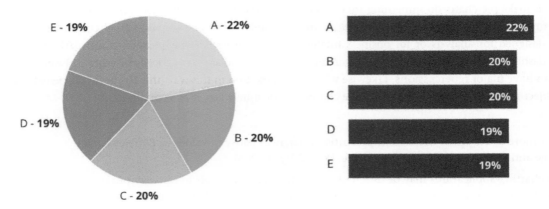

Figure 2.3   Five examples of pie charts working just fine

Over three quarters of senior positions in politics, law and medicine are occupied by men

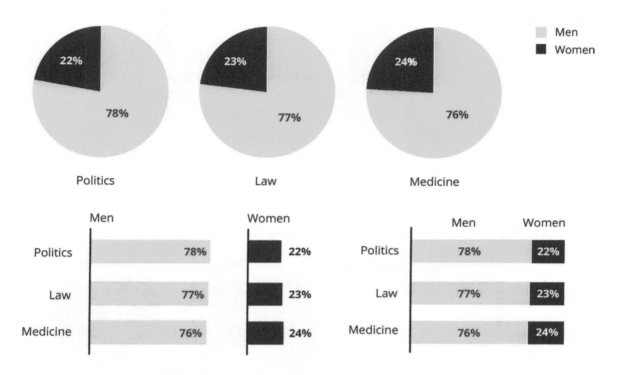

Supermarket A's market share has more than doubled in a year

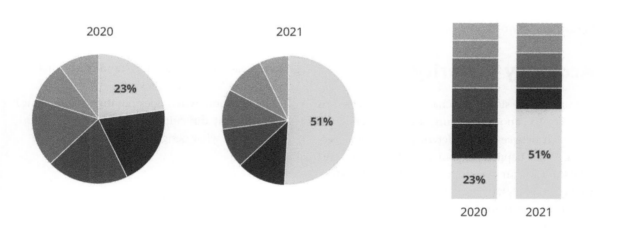

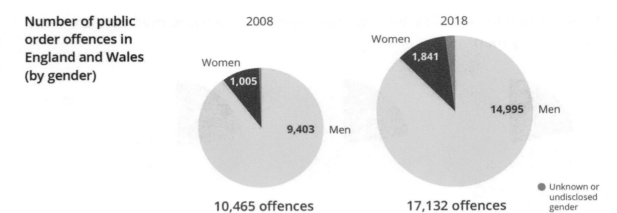

Number of public order offences in England and Wales (by gender)

Figure 2.4 Public order offences, 2008 and 2018

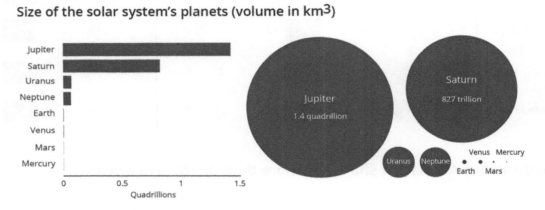

Size of the solar system's planets (volume in km³)

Figure 2.5 Two ways to chart the solar system's planets – biggest to smallest

Accuracy v. clarity

I'm sure you're sick of pie charts by now. Let's turn instead to another significant difference in approach between the different parts of our spectrum. What happens if your data doesn't behave? By which I mean you chart your data and the story isn't clear enough – maybe the labels are overlaying each other, or there are outliers spoiling an otherwise dramatic story, or an interesting secondary story is now invisible. Do you think your chart should always be a 100% accurate representation of the numbers in your spreadsheet? Or do you think visual 'cheats' are sometimes required to make your

chart clear and easy to understand? And what constitutes 'cheating' anyway?

The question 'when does tidying become lying?' is surprisingly difficult to answer and takes us to the heart of what designing for an audience is.

Accuracy v. clarity: The journalistic approach

Let's start with the journalistic approach – the right-hand side of our spectrum – and use a chart based on David McCandless's 'Billion Pound-o-Gram', which was first published in the 'Show and

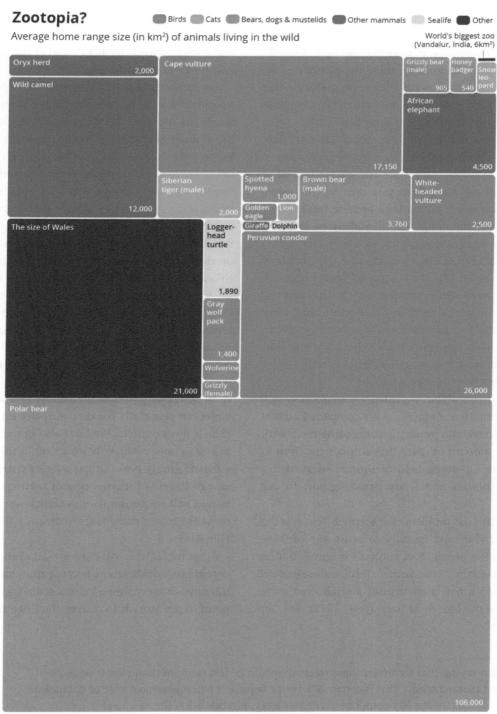

Figure 2.6 Animal home ranges

Tell' section of the *Guardian*'s Datablog in 2009. McCandless's original, which you can also find in his book *Information is Beautiful* (2012), is a modified treemap, designed to show the global cost of the financial crisis in 2008. Here we are using the same chart type to show a different dataset: average animal home range sizes (Figure 2.6).

We often use these kinds of charts. They are particularly effective when you are trying to make a general audience appreciate the magnitude of a large number. Of course you can do this using other chart types, but perhaps because this is still a reasonably unfamiliar chart, audiences seem to find this approach engaging in a way that a bar, stacked bar or pie chart wouldn't be. The fact that you can use big blocks of colour to signal categories helps to make it eye-catching, and the fact that the first part is nonlinear (you can explore the blocks in the first half in any order you want) seems to make it more intriguing than a chart that has been ranked in some way, whether alphabetically, largest to smallest or whatever it may be.[9]

It also helps if your chart has a metaphorical link to the data. Here, because we are comparing animal home ranges, and implicitly contrasting them with the tiny amount of space that animals are given in zoos, the top-down field of squares suggests distinct territories and lends visual support to our theme.

So what's the problem? For Stephen Few, it is the fact that you can't usefully compare any of these boxes. After seeing McCandless's original 'Billion Pound-o-Gram', Few wrote: '[McCandless] could have used a bar chart instead and allowed us to compare the length of bars' (Few, 2011). For our treemap, we did start by putting our data in a bar chart, but it looked dull, it didn't suit the story and it undermined the 'big reveal' of the polar bear home range at the end.

Another objection might be that we've hugely simplified the data. Some estimates of animal ranges are more reliable than others, just because the animals have been observed more often or for longer periods. Some animals have a fairly stable home range size; for others, range size varies hugely depending on whether it's mating season, whether it's summer or winter, whether there's plenty of food, as well as a multitude of other factors. We are showing none of this uncertainty on the chart – you would have to follow the link to our original data table for any of these caveats. We have left out a lot of the complexity too. There is no mention of the difference between territories (which are vigorously defended) and home ranges. A male Siberian tiger actively polices his 2,000 km^2 area and fights any other males that enter it, while a wild camel in the Gobi desert may wander around an area six times larger but peacefully coexists with any other camels it encounters. We have also not factored in size (a honey badger is a fraction of the size of a female grizzly bear but has a larger range) or ease of travel (a Peruvian condor soaring over its terrain will encounter considerably fewer obstacles than a snow leopard crossing the Himalayas).[10]

All of this is true. We did leave all of these details out – deliberately. Because this chart is intended as (very simple) visual journalism. The point of our story is to convey the huge amount

---

[9] It's worth saying that a conventional treemap would be less random than this; it would be organised hierarchically. This is certainly a better approach when you have a lot of datapoints or when hierarchy is a key component of your story. But neither is the case here.

[10] See Chapter 9 of Tim Harford's *How to Make the World Add Up* (2020) for a critique of mixing different data types in this way, with particular reference to McCandless's work. Even if you disagree with Harford (which I do), it's a bracing read.

of space that animals are accustomed to, and adding caveats or confidence intervals or overlaying additional datasets would obscure our main story. This chart isn't intended for experts; it's intended to introduce an unfamiliar subject to the widest possible audience.

We are biased too. We have called our chart 'Zootopia?'; we have included a tiny box representing the world's biggest zoo (the entire zoo is about the size of a gorilla's home range) and we have added a footnote explaining how a polar bear's zoo enclosure is a million times smaller than its typical home range. We have deliberately chosen animals that you might find in zoos, and prioritised those with the largest home ranges. There is nothing here about the fantastic conservation efforts that many zoos participate in, or the fact that zoos often introduce people (particularly children) to species that they might not otherwise have heard of, and can foster a lifelong love of the animal kingdom – because our story is about how awful zoos must be for the animals that live inside them. We found the data on home ranges shocking, we want our audience to feel shocked too, and we have removed anything from our chart that might interfere with this emotional response.

There is one more objection to consider. Stephen Few has dismissed McCandless's graphics as 'often inaccurate' and he could well have had the original Billion Pound-o-Gram in mind (Few, 2011). Certainly we have followed the approach of the original McCandless graphic here – he later created more accurate versions – and we have also replicated McCandless's footnote: 'Slight visual cheating to make things fit.'[11]

If you look back at our Zootopia? graphic, you will notice that the boxes are suspiciously legible and

well aligned. When you make a treemap in your software of choice, does it *ever* look like that? Figure 2.7 shows what happened when we asked the chart-making tool Raw (which is brilliant, by the way) to make us a treemap with the first part of our home range data.

At least it is accurate now. Or rather, *at most* it is accurate. It doesn't have any other redeeming features.

In our original Zootopia graphic, we tweaked and rotated some of the boxes to make sure the text could fit inside them and still be legible. We moved some boxes around so that there weren't too many similarly coloured boxes next to each other, and shifted some up so that the size of Wales was next to the polar bear's home range.

The resizing wasn't consistent (this box got very slightly bigger, that box got very slightly smaller); we were guided purely by whether it made the story *look* clearer. We also rounded the edges of the boxes, partly because this helped convey the idea of approximation (this box is *roughly* this size) but partly also for aesthetic reasons: rounded edges look friendlier than sharp edges (sometimes known as the contour bias).

When cheating is helpful

This is indefensible, right? You trusted us to give you an accurate picture.

Or did you? Look again at the accurate treemap (Figure 2.7). Doesn't this cause even bigger trust issues?

I'd argue that the small inaccuracies we introduced into our treemap are, for a general audience, not only justifiable, but commendable.

---

[11] The 'slight visual cheating' line is an example of another important aspect of McCandless's approach: wit. He wants to make his readers smile.

Figure 2.7 An accurate treemap

Labels within the treemap:

Brown bear (male), 3760

Black bear (

African elephant (female), 4500

Cheetah (Gray wolf pack, 3450 Gray bear (fema

Gray wolf pack, 3450

Grizzly bear (male), 905

Honey badger, Jaguar (male pride5

Oryx herd, 2000 Sand cat

Loggerhead turtle, 1890

Cape vulture, 17150

Andean condor, 26000

Siberian tiger (male), 3600 leopard hyena (India),

spotted hyena (India), Tiger

Wild camel, 12000

Wolverine (m

Off the scale: How far is too far?

In our 'Zootopia?' chart (Figure 2.6), we made cosmetic changes to our chart to help with readability. Compare this to a chart that blatantly distorts the truth – like Figure 2.8, which we have based on a Fox News original from March 2014.

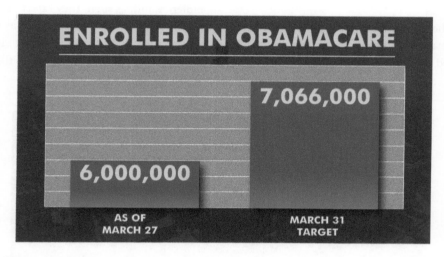

Figure 2.8 Wrongness as an art form

This chart deliberately sets out to prove something that isn't supported by the data – that Obama's Affordable Care Act is failing. The actual story (which most other news outlets reported) was that 1 million people had signed up to Obamacare in the 10 days before 27 March, taking the number of people enrolled from 5 million to over 6 million, exceeding the Congressional Budget Office's estimate. To ensure that Fox News viewers were not troubled by this inconvenient truth, the chart authors tracked down a much older, much higher estimate and then placed this out-of-date estimate (which they reported precisely as 7,066,000) next to the Obamacare numbers (which they rounded down to 6,000,000). Finally, because the difference between 6 and 7 million would have looked less dramatic on a bar chart that started at zero, they started their y-axis at 5,400,000, so that the Obamacare bar looked around a third the size of the (outdated, inflated) estimate. The fact that the chart starts at 5,400,000 can only be laboriously

deduced from the gridlines, as the y-axis and all of its labels have been removed. The only thing that stops this being the most perfect example of how to violate every data visualisation principle on Earth is that they started the y-axis at 5,400,000 and not 5,800,000 – and therefore missed the opportunity to lie on an even grander scale.

In our Zootopia? chart, as in McCandless's original Billion Pound-o-Gram, the intended goal is not to deceive. The motivation is to try to make our audience see something we have found in our data. Fox was motivated by the opposite – hiding the truth from their audience. They reversed our process: they did not start with the data, design a story based on what they found, and then make a chart to dramatise this story. Instead they started with the chart – which had to show that Obamacare was failing – and then concocted a story to make this chart work: let's compare it to an old estimate and slice off 5,400,000 from the y-axis.

For a start, the degree of distortion is not huge (2,000 km² is still about twice the size of 1,000 km²) and only affects the visuals. The numbers in the boxes have not been changed. We have been open about our 'visual cheating' and there is a link to our data should anyone wish to recreate a 100% accurate chart.

Secondly, the data we are using consists of estimates and approximations. Home ranges are always 'rough guesses' based on limited sample sizes. Creating a

chart that suggests pinpoint accuracy and precision might not be appropriate here.

Most importantly, this is not for an audience of experts. This is not something a zoologist or wildlife park architect would use to inform their professional decisions. This is for a general audience and, as such, they *expect* us to help them see the story in this chart. As long as that story is true, and we are not massaging the visuals to obscure what the data is telling us, then we are

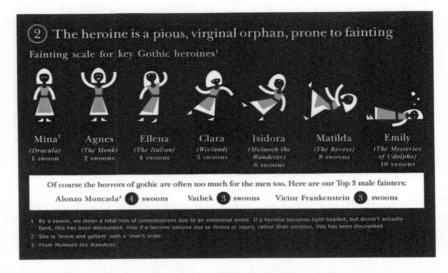

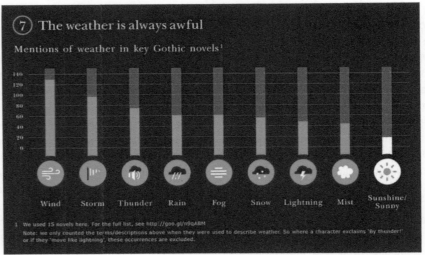

Figure 2.9 Examples of the journalistic approach

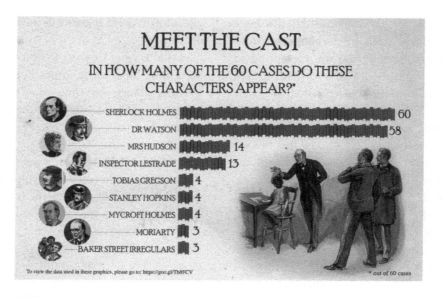

serving our audience well if we use aesthetic techniques to increase the level of readability and drama.

I realise that being deliberately 'inaccurate' might still sit uncomfortably with you – particularly if you are from a statistical background. But, as I will explore later, statisticians are also prone to their own type of creative rearrangement. It's also worth stressing that you should always be accurate first, by default, and only think about visual adjustments if the accurate chart fails to give a clear, truthful picture. Furthermore, this Zootopia? graphic should be seen as the outer limits of what an acceptable degree of 'cheating' might be. (Compare this to an unacceptable degree of cheating, outlined in 'Off the Scale' p. 53).

However, what I would say is: even if you are wedded to the idea of 100% accurate charts at all times, consider adding the McCandless style of bold, biased storytelling to your design toolkit.

I mentioned a general audience, but we have seen this approach work in corporate environments too, particularly if you are presenting to someone who is pushed for time or with only a fleeting knowledge of the subject-matter.

We have included some other charts that we have made that follow an even more stridently journalistic approach (Figure 2.9). The first two are from a series of graphics I worked on about the Gothic novel (design by Zhenia Vasiliev), the second two are from a series on Sherlock Holmes (design by Jim Kynvin), both for the *Guardian*.

Of course there is risk when you use 'data decoration' so blatantly. Subject specialists might not take what you're saying seriously. But, whichever approach you take, there is risk. There will always be a section of your audience that will be baffled by your choices.

Accuracy v. clarity: The analytical approach

For example, if we look at a graphic from the analytical end of our spectrum, you will see that there is also risk. I'm going to use a chart popularised by Edward Tufte: the slope chart. The original version is in Chapter 7 of Tufte's first book, *The Visual Display of Quantitative Information* (2001), where he plots tax receipts for different countries between 1970 and 1979. I've updated the data to reflect the OECD's most recent assessment of the tax take during this period, and switched a couple of the countries to keep the main story intact, but in all other respects, the chart is a faithful homage (Figure 2.10).

This is about as different from a standard newspaper infographic as it is possible to get. In a Tufte slopechart, there should be no waste and no clutter. Any designer should be mindful of the data-to-ink ratio, which should ideally be 1:1 – every drop of ink is linked to a datapoint. Otherwise you risk filling your work with 'chartjunk', Tufte's word for

visual elements that are unnecessary or distracting.

So that is what we have here: a chart with everything superfluous stripped out. A chart showing change over time would usually have a *y*-axis of some kind, often gridlines, possibly some annotations, but for Tufte these are unnecessary. All we have are the datapoints for 1970 and 1979, data labels and a line linking the two datapoints.

The chart is also black and white. You might have been tempted to make the UK line a different colour so that it stands out. After all, isn't this the story? The fact that all the lines are rising or staying the same except the UK? However, not only would this be biased (telling the audience where to look first) and risky (what if you choose a terrible colour?) but most of all, it would be superfluous – the line's sharp drop is dramatic enough by itself.

I think charts like this are beautiful: clear and minimalist, heavily influenced by the Japanese calligraphy and fine art which Tufte admires, making skilful use of white space to frame their simple stories. But they are certainly not for everyone. When we have tried to persuade our students of the benefits of slopecharts, it is fair to say they have met with a mixed reception. People who like them *really* like them, but for the majority the response has been that they are 'boring' or 'dry.' Jen Christiansen, the Graphics Editor of *Scientific American*, has commented: 'When I developed magazine graphics according to [Tufte's] philosophy, they were most often met with a yawn' (quoted in Kirk, 2019).

We have found that an Edward Tufte chart is as risky a choice as the journalistic approach, but for different reasons. You risk boring or alienating non-specialists. Among our clients, it has been the right approach for the *Lancet* (the UK medical journal) and Lloyd's of London (an insurance company). It has also been the right approach for clients who need to be seen as purveyors of objective data, such as the World Trade Organization. In these cases,

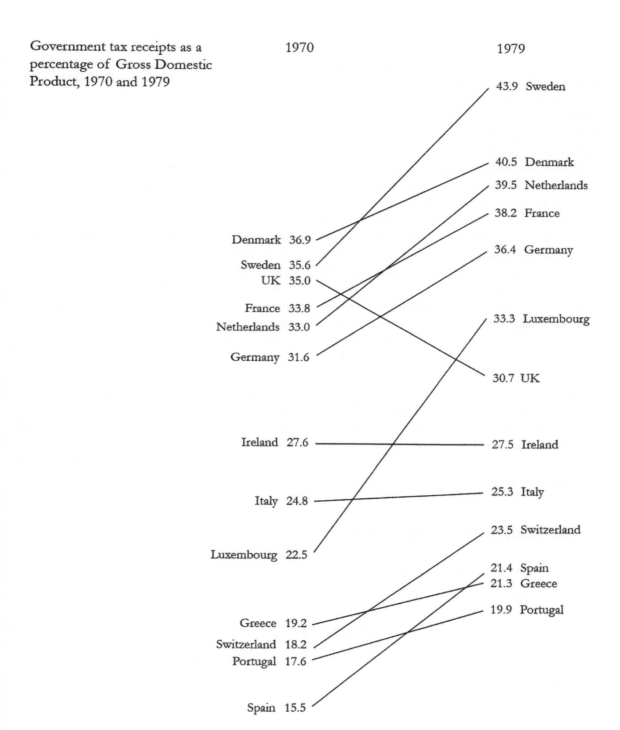

Figure 2.10 Example of a slopechart

clear, simple charts rendered in a plain style without excessive ornamentation have been the best way of signalling that they are presenting accurate data without undue bias.

However, there is a vital caveat to be made. This slopechart – like Tufte's original – only *appears* neutral. Making a chart look this plain and objective involves a multitude of small, subjective decisions.

The data has been selected to tell the most dramatic story. Not every country in the world has been shown, just 13 of them. The year 1970 is compared to 1979 because showing the years in between not only adds visual interference, but tells a different story (see Figure 2.11), as does starting earlier or finishing later.

We have also imitated the dimensions of Tufte's original – long and narrow. Not landscape, like a standard line chart, which would diminish the drama of those changes, and make some of those shallower angles (like Greece or Portugal) look almost flat.

Note too we have not started our slopechart at zero but at 15, which also gives the lines more zip. Furthermore, there is the fact that we have chosen this chart because it suits our story. As in Tufte's original, one line is behaving very differently compared

to the others. All our lines are rising or staying the same except one (UK). If our dataset were different, this chart might not be a sensible choice, as Figure 2.12 shows.

A slippery slope

Most vitally of all, there is the question of accuracy. In his original chart, when datapoints start or end at similar places, Tufte manually moves the lines and labels up or down so they don't overlap. We have done the same thing in Figure 2.10. Greece ends at 21.3, Spain ends at 21.4 so we have nudged Spain up and Greece down so the lines and labels remain clear and readable. UK at 35.0 was snug up against Sweden at 35.6 so we shifted Sweden up a bit too. There is slight visual cheating to make things fit!

Of course, the cheats we are using here aren't on the same scale as the box-stretching we indulged in for the Zootopia graphic. We are nudging the lines up and down *a little*. However, it remains the case that the purpose of an Edward Tufte slopechart is to communicate clearly and gracefully. If accuracy interferes with this, then it is the designer's job to fix it.

Tax receipts as % of GDP (1970-79)

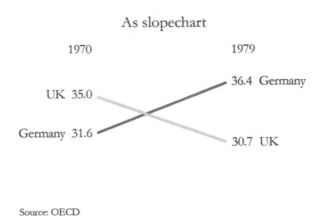

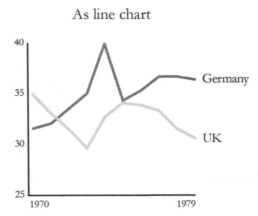

Source: OECD

Figure 2.11 Different frames, different stories

Too many lines, no real story

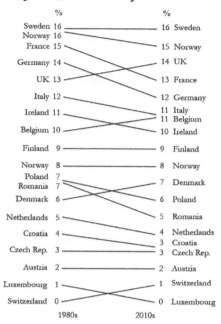

Lots of lines starting or ending at the same point

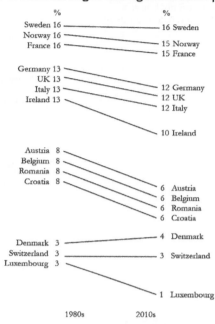

Lots of criss-crossing lines

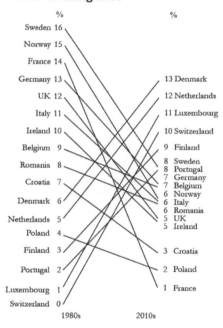

One huge outlier

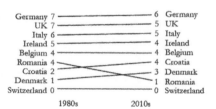

Figure 2.12 Four ways to break a slopechart

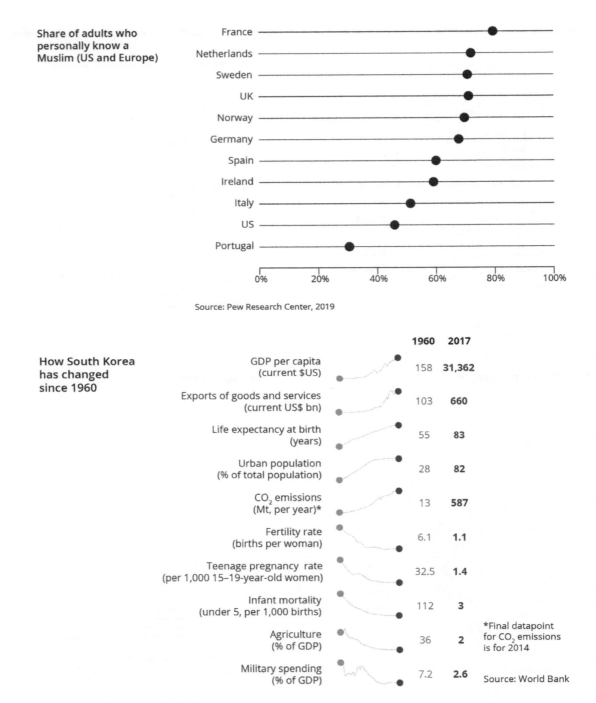

Share of adults who personally know a Muslim (US and Europe)

France
Netherlands
Sweden
UK
Norway
Germany
Spain
Ireland
Italy
US
Portugal

0%　20%　40%　60%　80%　100%

Source: Pew Research Center, 2019

How South Korea has changed since 1960

	1960	2017
GDP per capita (current $US)	158	31,362
Exports of goods and services (current US$ bn)	103	660
Life expectancy at birth (years)	55	83
Urban population (% of total population)	28	82
CO$_2$ emissions (Mt, per year)*	13	587
Fertility rate (births per woman)	6.1	1.1
Teenage pregnancy rate (per 1,000 15–19-year-old women)	32.5	1.4
Infant mortality (under 5, per 1,000 births)	112	3
Agriculture (% of GDP)	36	2
Military spending (% of GDP)	7.2	2.6

*Final datapoint for CO$_2$ emissions is for 2014

Source: World Bank

Figure 2.13　Other examples of charts with a high data-to-ink ratio

Lifetime earnings by bachelor's degree (US)

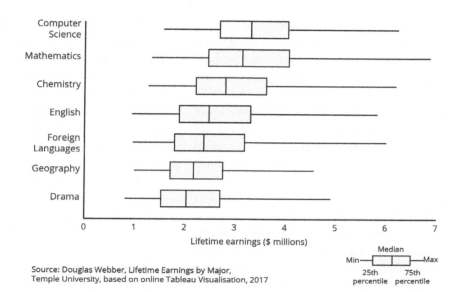

Lifetime earnings ($ millions)

Source: Douglas Webber, Lifetime Earnings by Major,
Temple University, based on online Tableau Visualisation, 2017

Median

Min ⊢ ⊣ Max

25th percentile   75th percentile

Number of lines spoken by each character in selected Shakespeare plays

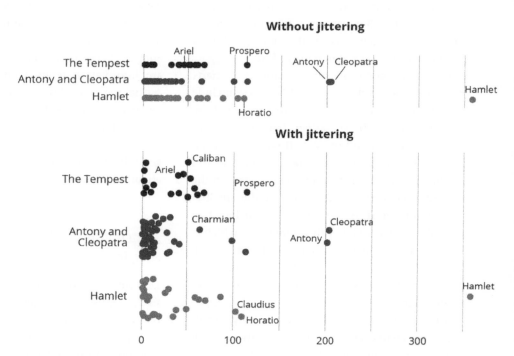

Without jittering

With jittering

Source: Open Source Shakespeare

This is why the accuracy question sits at the heart of communicating with data. Because when you analyse data, you should always use accurate charts. But when you communicate what you have found to others, there is invariably an element of cheating and it is impossible to quantify precisely how much cheating is acceptable. Our spectrum of good practice suggests some boundaries – Edward Tufte at one end (cheating a little) and David McCandless at the other (cheating a little more) – based on how important accuracy is for their respective purposes and audiences.

Bur just as we would say that going 'beyond McCandless' into tabloid territory is unwise, so we would say that going 'beyond Tufte' and being 100% accurate at all times is little short of cata-strophic. It is what computers do – they are accurate to a fault, even when the charts they out-put are illegible. But you are a human talking to other humans and your content and design choices should make this fact abundantly clear.

We have created some other examples of charts in the analytical style in Figure 2.13. These include our interpretations of dot charts (invented by William Cleveland), sparklines (another Edward Tufte invention) and box plots (invented by John Tukey). They all have a high data-to-ink ratio and aim to convey 'the greatest number of ideas in the shortest time with the least ink in the smallest space' (Tufte, 2001, p. 51). I have also included an example of a strip plot with jittered data which is another example of a more 'analytical' chart which deliberately introduces inaccuracy (the position of the dot on the y-axis is random) to make the chart easier to read.

Just to reiterate the point above, many people find these charts hard to warm to. Although this approach is frequently called 'scientific', there is very little evidence that charts in this style are more

effective or memorable than those laden with 'chartjunk'. As Leland Wilkinson puts it in *The Grammar of Graphics*: 'The crusade against chartjunk is not supported by scientific research and psychological theory' (Wilkinson, 1999, p. 281).

So do not imagine that when you use these charts you are abiding by what Tufte calls 'universal' principles of analytical design, 'not tied to any particular language, culture, style, century, gender or technology' (Tufte, 2006, p. 10). You are in fact using design principles that are tied to a very *specific* use case – talking to well-educated analysts and academics in the early twenty-first century.

But this is why it is important to study and value this approach. Not because it's scientifically robust, but because many scientists like it, and believe it's more scientific because they like it, and trust information more readily when it is delivered in this style.[12] This means that the analytical approach is an invaluable resource for any information designer. I'd go further: Tufte's central message – less is more – is useful advice in *all* circumstances, as it encourages you to stop and think before adding decorative elements to your charts and helps you to focus on the fact that good design is often less about addition and more about taking away.

Accuracy v. clarity: A mixed audience

Let's finish up in the middle. How do practitioners in the centre of our spectrum approach the question of bias and accuracy? I'll use as my main example one of the greatest scientific communicators (and amateur sword swallowers) of the last twenty years: Hans Rosling, a man

---

[12]What I mean here is that Tufte should not be seen as someone who formulates universal principles, but as someone who usefully embodies and systematises a particular strain of academic taste.

whose combination of statistical rigour and powerful storytelling has won over people at both ends of the data visualisation spectrum, from Stephen Few, who believes that Rosling's 2006 TED talk sparked 'a new era of quantitative storytelling' (Few, 2012, p. xvii), to David McCandless, who described Rosling as 'the world's greatest data storyteller' and wrote on the occasion of Rosling's death in 2017: 'His spectacular talks convinced me that data stories could be enlightening, illuminating, and entertaining – all at the same time' (McCandless, 2017). He was unanimously believed to have struck the perfect balance between authority and accessibility, becoming in the process 'a pop-star statistician' (as the *New York Times* put it).

So what does 'pop-star' statistics look like? At first glance, it looks a lot like regular statistics. Rosling is best known for cofounding the Gapminder Foundation, an organisation devoted to 'minding the gap' between the developed and developing worlds. Its most famous product is the Trendalyzer, an interactive scatter plot devised in partnership with Rosling's son Ola Rosling and his daughter-in-law Anna Rosling Rönnlund, which

allows users to play through 200 years of human history (Figure 2.14).

The *x*-axis is income, the *y*-axis is life expectancy. In 1800, all countries are poor and sick – down at the bottom left. The Industrial Revolution means that Western countries pull away and start heading for the top right – rich and healthy. The green circle is the United States, the yellow circles are European countries like Britain, France and Germany. There are a few blips – the First and Second World War, for example – but essentially the Western countries keep powering upwards while the developing world stays down at the bottom left. Then, after the Second World War, former colonies gain their independence and start catching up with the Western world. In 2018, most Asian countries – India and China are the big red circles – have moved into the top right quadrant. Most African countries – the blue circles on the left – are still poor, but even they have enjoyed dramatically improved life expectancy. You can play with the tool yourself at https://www.gapminder.org/tools/ and if you search for Hans Rosling on YouTube,

Figure 2.14 The Trendalyzer interface on the Gapminder site

(Continued)

Figure 2.14 (Continued)

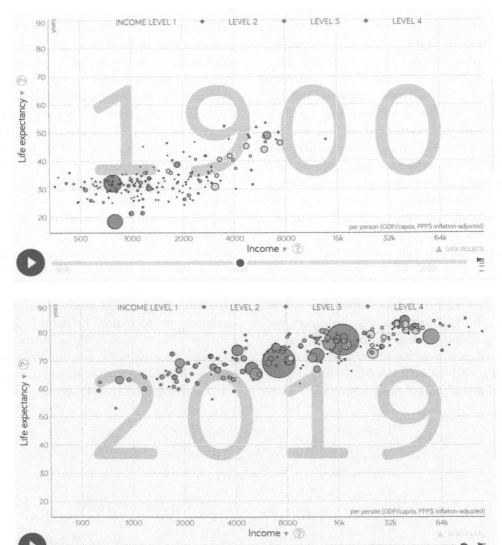

you can see him walking you through the story himself. Please do – it's as good as data visualisation gets.

To achieve his ends, Rosling brilliantly combines both the analytical and journalistic approach. The analytical aspect is clear enough. This is not the prettiest chart – you would never mistake it for a chart produced by the *New York Times* or the *Guardian*. It has lurid primary-coloured circles overlaid on top of each other.

Furthermore, it is a scatter plot, which is not a chart type that is commonly used outside of the statistical or market research community. This is perhaps because it can only really be used to tell one story – correlation (or a lack of it) – and this is a less common story than comparison, composition or change over time. When it is used by news organisations – for example, have a look at the *New York Times*'s 'Why is Her Paycheck

Smaller?' – it is usually heavily annotated to prevent confusion, or there is a walkthrough of some kind so that, as you scroll, more elements are added or explained. Don Kopf has put it this way: 'While line charts and bar charts are far more common in newspapers and business presentations, the scatter plot dominates science journals. Edward Tufte once estimated that more than 70% of all charts in scientific publications are scatter plots' (Kopf, 2018). By choosing a scatter plot as the Trendalyzer's landing page and default view, Rosling seems to be saying – loudly and clearly – 'Made by a scientist'.

But it goes deeper than this. Before you click Play, you might think that it's for scientists too. The default view here shows wealth and health, but if you click on either of the axes, there are a bewildering number of datasets you can load on to this chart. You can find out if 'bad teeth per child' correlates with 'number of murders' or if 'hydroelectricity production' correlates with 'broadband subscribers'. Then you can click Play and see if they correlate in 1800. It appears to be a sandbox for statisticians.

Logarithmic gymnastics

Moreover, the default dataset on the *x*-axis – wealth – is shown on a logarithmic (or log) scale. A log scale is a reasonably common charting tool – at least among statisticians. In *Elements of Graphing Data*, William Cleveland recommends the use of log scales frequently and often (Cleveland, 1985, p. 101). A normal (linear) scale goes 1, 2, 3, 4, 5 or 10, 20, 30, 40, 50. A log scale is based on an order of magnitude, so for example a base-2 log scale would go 2, 4, 8, 16, 32 (you are multiplying by 2). A base-10 log scale would go 10, 100, 1000, 10000 (you are multiplying by 10).

Why on earth would you do such a thing? The first reason is because you might have a huge outlier (three bars at 10, 20, 30 and a fourth bar at 5,000) and a linear scale would make your first three bars look the same size – or else they would

vanish entirely. The second reason is when you need to understand what Cleveland (1985, p. 101) called 'percent change or multiplicative factors'. For example, you might be charting a phenomenon such as hyperinflation where the value of a currency doubles or triples over short periods of time and your chart needs to keep up.

Log scales are more common than you might think. For example, take the phenomenon of measuring sound. Decibels are measured on a logarithmic scale (base 10). This is because, for humans at least, we detect large differences between quiet noises and hardly any difference between loud ones. We need a scale that reflects the fact that someone whispering, someone talking and someone shouting all sound extremely different to us, even though on a linear scale that difference would not be so dramatic. On the other hand, even though there is a huge difference between the noise a road drill, a rock concert and jet plane make, we hear them all as just *really loud*. For example, a rock band is about 110 decibels (dB) and a fighter jet taking off is 140 dB – so a fighter jet is 1,000 times louder than a rock band. But we detect little difference between them. If we use a base-10 log scale, we stretch out the lower part of our scale (where we need it) and shrink down the upper part (where rock bands and jet planes are all just 'loud'). It means we can keep all these phenomena on one scale – using readily understandable numbers (10 dB, 20 dB), rather than scientific variations (10^{-1}, 10^8 and so on). Incidentally, 150 dB will make your eardrums burst and 190 dB will kill you.

This is one reason why Rosling has used a log scale on his income axis. If you are on $1 a day, and your pay increases to $2 a day, this is not felt in the same way as someone on $1,000 a day getting a pay rise to $1,001. The second person would need their pay increased to $2,000 to experience the same sensation of a doubling of income. Therefore, each of Rosling's *x*-axis intervals will mirror this doubling.

However, Rosling's use of a log scale takes us to the heart of why Rosling is as much a showman as a scientist. Log scales are fine when you are talking to statisticians. They are not fine when you are talking to the general public. In our experience, when you are presenting to non-experts, charts with a logarithmic scale are either seen as regular charts, and misinterpreted, or if they are explained, the audience is baffled as to why you would use relatively sized shapes to tell a story that obliges you to ignore or reimagine their relative size and/or position. Bar 1 might look twice the size of bar 2, but it represents data that is ten times the size. How is that helpful?

I'll give you one example of this issue. In 2013, the British government used a logarithmic scale to represent how much it had spent on infrastructure projects (Figure 2.15).[13] They knew that the public would assume that more had been spent on flood defences and waste than was actually the case. It was only after a Labour Treasury minister spotted the 'mathematical cheating', and alerted the UK Statistics Authority that the public was given a more truthful picture. The Statistics Authority

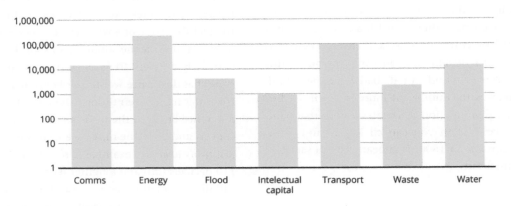

Figure 2.15 The original government chart

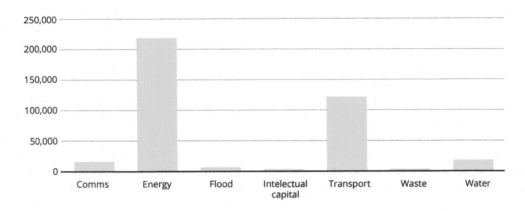

Figure 2.16 The chart reissued by the UK Statistics Authority

[13]See https://www.telegraph.co.uk/news/politics/10625168/Treasury-rebuked-over-misleading-flood-spending-graph.html

released a chart with a standard scale (Figure 2.16), and ruled that the original chart 'could leave readers with a false impression of the relative size of investment between sectors'. A 'false impression' is a polite way of putting it.

A more recent example is Covid-19 data, which was often charted using a log scale, in spite of research from the London School of Economics confirming that these charts were poorly understood by the general public, with around 60% of people misreading them, compared to just 16% of people misreading Covid data on a linear scale (Romano et al., 2020a, 2020b). The intentions of the people making these charts were often well meaning.[14] However, take a look at Figure 2.17, which shows a chart of Covid data from September

2020 that was plotted on a log scale by various publications, including *The Economist* (we have created our own version here). Try to answer the following questions: Roughly how many new confirmed cases of Covid were there on 30 September 2020? How about on 30 June 2020? What was the rate of increase? Do you think people's behaviour should have changed as a result of the data on this chart?

The correct answer is: the number of new confirmed cases had almost doubled in 3 months, rising from around 170,000 cases on 30 June to 300,000 on 30 September. Using a log scale makes this huge and important increase invisible.

So why has Rosling used a log scale when Gapminder is aimed at a general audience and he

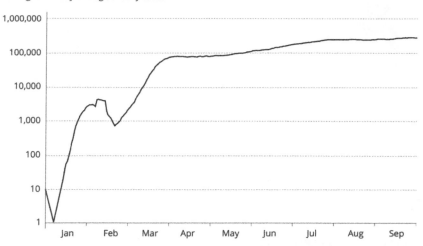

New confirmed COVID cases each day

Rolling seven-day average of daily cases

Health warning: The number of confirmed cases shown on this chart is considerably lower than the number of actual cases. This is mostly due to low levels of testing in many countries. The amount of testing has also increased over time which also means that this chart's level of accuracy has changed dramatically in recent months.

Source: European CDC, Our World in Data

Figure 2.17 Global Covid cases on a log scale

---

[14]For example, one of the reasons that the (excellent) *Financial Times* journalist John Burn-Murdoch gave for avoiding linear charts was his wish 'not to panic people' with hockey-stick charts: https://www.youtube.com/watch?v=4lm3MWTVAK0

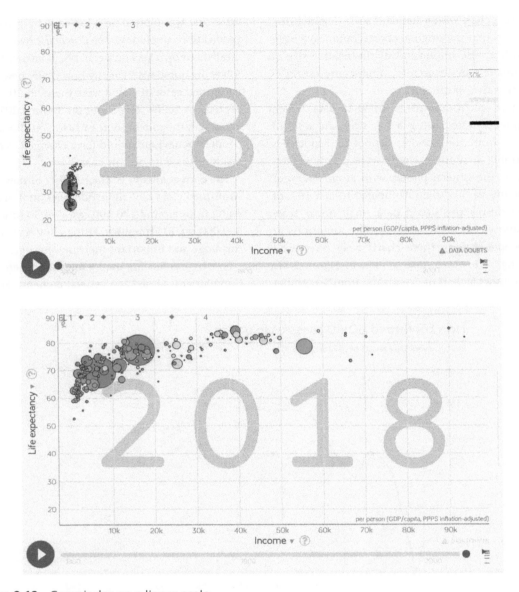

Figure 2.18 Gapminder on a linear scale

must know that a log scale risks creating a 'false impression'?

The answer is simple: his story breaks without it. And he has one hell of a story to tell. When Rosling first mapped his income v. life expectancy data, he would have almost certainly used a linear scale. And his data would have progressed as shown in Figure 2.18.

Oh dear. The 1800 data is now squished together, and by 2018, the poorer countries don't look like they've caught up with the rest of the world at all. People are living longer, but not getting much richer. Most of the circles are in the top left, not the top right.

Using a linear scale means that Rosling's story dies, so he has to use statistical trickery to rescue it.

He is counting on the fact that anyone watching his YouTube video or TED talk (where the use of a log scale is not even mentioned), or anyone going to the website and pressing Play, will be so swept away by the story that they won't care that the values on the x-axis keep doubling, which is not how most charts *work*.

The world as it really isn't

Likewise, they won't care about the data quality either. Gapminder happily shows data for average income per person for countries such as Croatia and Uzbekistan in 1800, even though those countries wouldn't exist for almost 200 years, and any income data collected in 1800 must surely be dubious. This might well lead us to click the 'data doubts' button which reveals this text: 'Comparing the size of economy across countries and time is not trivial. The methods vary and the prices change. Gapminder has adjusted the picture for many such differences, but still we recommend you take these numbers with a large grain of salt.'

A large grain of salt? But hang on – the scatter chart, the log scale, the gridlines, the accurate-sounding axis label ('Income per person, GDP/capita, PPP$ inflation-adjusted'). I thought this was science.

Well, not really. And it's all the better for it.

That's why Rosling sits in the centre of our spectrum. Yes, he is a statistician who uses solid data sources and gives his audience access to the data so they can question his conclusions. But he is also a brilliant storyteller who grabs his audience by the arm and drags them in a very particular direction. The clue is in the title – Gapminder. Everything is designed to show how the gap between the developed and developing world is narrowing, and anything that obscures this story (like a linear scale, or starting the timeline when the data becomes more reliable) is dropped.

Let's think again about the default view. Although there are hundreds of datasets in Gapminder, the first story we see – and the story that

Rosling dramatises in his video walkthrough – is income versus life expectancy. This immediately primes us for a particular kind of story. We will explore the correlation between wealth and health: they are the two heroes of our narrative. As the story unfolds, we are encouraged to cheer for countries as they become 'emerging economies' and catch up with their wealthy neighbours. The implication is that this rush towards greater wealth is an unqualified good.

This is a powerful story, but not an objective one. It won't surprise you to know that Rosling is widely viewed as a central figure in what gets called the 'New Optimism' movement. Along with thinkers such as Steven Pinker, Johan Norberg and others, he is seen (a little unfairly) as playing down the negative aspects of the modern world and emphasising the benefits of market economies. After all, Gapminder doesn't start with income per person on the x-axis and CO_2 emissions on the y-axis. Then the story would appear to be how capitalism has ravaged the planet. It doesn't start with income on the x-axis and the Gini inequality index on the y-axis, because then we'd see China and India become more unequal societies as they grew superficially 'richer'.

None of this is to downplay Rosling's achievement. On the contrary, it is Rosling's bias that makes Gapminder so engaging. This bias is not openly acknowledged – Rosling believes that he is showing us the world 'as it really is' – but that doesn't mean the bias isn't there. This is why it is possible to load entirely different datasets into the Gapminder interface and tell yourself a story that contradicts what Rosling says.

So this is what a good balance between statistics and storytelling looks like. When you are presenting to a mixed audience, trying to engage both experts and novices, scientists and non-scientists, then the Rosling approach is indispensable. It must look and feel like science and allow users access to all the data (Rosling's story is just one of the stories that Gapminder can tell). But it must also be motivated by a journalist's passion for novel and provocative information (Rosling's own interpretation is strongly fore-grounded by his content and design choices).

Other examples of the third way

For other examples of this hybrid approach, I'd recommend looking at how government bodies, museums and technology manufacturers interact with the public. These organisations often have to think hard about how to produce easy-to-understand information without compromising their reputa-tion for integrity or safety. Let's look at three quick examples.

First, transit maps. In the introduction, we men-tioned how we find daily inspiration in Harry Beck's London Tube map. The design is grounded in empirical facts – all the stations are included. Beck does not leave out boring or underused stations or grey out his least favourite lines: he is not selective like a journalist – all the data is there if we need it. But, at the same time, the data is arranged so unim-portant information is omitted (the exact shape of the lines, the distance between stations) and the most important information dominates (the inter-change stations, the stations in central London). It acknowledges that all stations are not equal but all passengers are – and most of them will be working or changing lines in the middle of the city.

Weather maps for the general public are another good example. They are almost always rooted in high-quality data, collected by experts at hundreds of weather stations and carefully analysed by mete-orologists. Their findings are plotted on recognisable maps, using universal icons for sun, rain, fog and so on, along with a temperature value (usually Celsius) to add further context. Again, there is no journalistic 'take' – if the person who assembles the data happens to love snowy days, you wouldn't know it from looking at the map. However, as with the Tube map, there is an unswerving commitment to audience needs – which means that if an audience wants inaccurate data, they get it. For example, Nate Silver discovered that weather reports have an inbuilt 'wet bias'; they overreport the chance of rain. This is because their audience would rather carry a raincoat that they don't need than get drenched by an unexpected downpour. Weather reports also make completely baseless predictions. Any weather report for more than a few days in advance is total fiction. In fact, Silver found that after 8 days, any forecast will be worse than just guessing based on the weather last week or the weather this time last year. But most weather channels and websites happily predict 'next week's weather' because their audience wants them to. People prefer something to nothing – even if the end result is more like astrology than meteorology.

One final example is a car dashboard. This ostensibly gives you accurate real-time information about your car's speed, fuel levels, temperature and so on. Intuitive charts and dials are used to show this information. But imagine for a moment if your dashboard did show you a completely accurate estimate of your speed. If you are trying to abide by the speed limit, you will probably drive with the needle sitting on or around the maximum speed limit mark. Every few minutes, your attention will drift, your speed will increase and you will break the law. Car manufacturers understand that the purpose of the speedometer isn't just to track your speed, it's to stop you getting fined for speeding. This is why all car speedometers tell you that you are going slightly faster than you are. Law-makers understand the importance of this too. The European standard for speedometers states that they must never indicate a speed that is lower than the vehicle's true speed, but they can legally show a speed that is greater than the vehicle's true speed by 10% plus 4 km/h. So if you are travelling at 30 km/h, your speedometer can show you 37 km/h. According to the AA, this also suits police officers, because it means that motorists are unable to use the excuse 'But my speedometer told me I was under the speed limit' because no speedometer is legally permitted to do this (AA Motoring, 2019). Across your dashboard, your manufacturer will be reinterpreting the data that the car is collecting to ensure that the information displayed is reassuring or useful for the driver.

Another example would be the fuel gauge. One Ford engineer explained in a recent interview that their car's fuel gauges are calibrated to 'stick' for a while on full – because customers 'want it to stay on full for an amount of time' so they don't feel like they're burning through gas seconds after they bought it (Shea, 2016). The gauges are also designed to hit empty well before the tank is empty (which means that the real 'empty' point of a tank is not visualised). Of course Ford can't have a gauge that cheats too much – or customers get angry or worry that it's broken. Like a lot of data visualisation, it's as much a psychological exercise as a mathematical one.

So this is the hybrid approach, where a mixed audience of experts and novices must be catered for. It is not journalism, it is not storytelling in an overt sense, but it still allows the organisation's goals or the audience's needs to distort the way in which content is selected and displayed.

A common enemy

I think this is ultimately why the world of data visualisation practitioners should be called a spectrum, because what unites these varying approaches is more important than what differentiates them. The purpose is the same: giving truthful, clear, useful information to an audience. And the enemy is the same. It is the dashboard in Figure 2.19.

Different schools of thought will dislike it for different reasons. The statistician because it is misleading, the journalist because it is dull, the designer because it is vulgar, the ordinary user because it is hard to understand. But everyone knows what bad looks like, probably even the person who made this, after they look at it again in a few days.

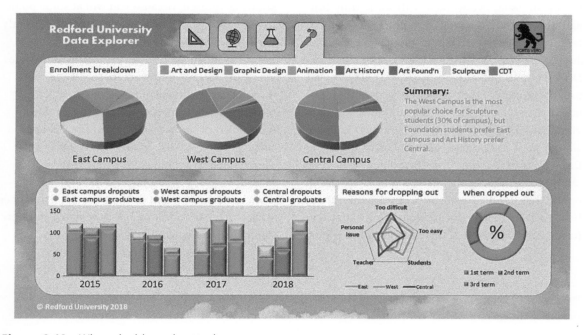

Figure 2.19 When dashboards attack

Everything else is just a question of priorities. Is detail more important than speed of understanding? Is accuracy more important than clarity? Are you providing evidence or information? Most successful data visualisation projects begin with a very clear statement of purpose: who is speaking, about what, to whom, and to what end. Getting that straight means that when the data isn't well behaved (which it rarely is), you will have a better understanding of where you can compromise and where you cannot.[15]

10,000 hours of practice

The approaches outlined above give you a very general sense of what can work with particular audiences (see Figure 2.20 for even more approaches). But it's worth stressing that each data visualisation project is unique and has its own specific character. You may find that past practitioners offer little help with your particular visualisation problem. Or perhaps you don't have enough time to read any or all of the books mentioned above. This need not be an issue. I've worked with some truly brilliant information designers and not many of them read books, let alone books about data visualisation. The title of Austin Howe's book *Designers Don't Read* is not entirely a joke. Designers will usually monitor other designers' work; they frequently love the more artistic kinds of data visualisation (Stefanie Posavec, Valentina D'Efilippo, Giorgia Lupi and others), and they will happily flip through anthologies of infographics, but they rarely read textbooks about bar charts. As for developers, they tend to read brick-sized books about how to learn particular programming languages (or digested versions of this information on help forums); they don't as a rule pore over Edward Tufte or Nate Silver. As for editors and copywriters, they read about the content. If the project is about 100 years of the Oscars, they read about the Oscars.

So you don't need to read about data visualisation to do it well. It is a multidisciplinary field and, as such, it can be approached from oblique angles. In fact, if you want to improve your work, I would always recommend sitting down and making something rather than reading a book – and that includes this book. The truth is, nobody else can help you in those initial stages of a project when it's just you, sitting in front of a blank sheet of paper, facing an entirely new problem, and the more practice you have in taking that initial leap into the unknown, the better.

As for connecting with your audience, yes, the practitioners above can help you to anticipate what different readers might find useful. But ultimately the more data visualisation you make, the better you will get at putting yourself in your audience's shoes. This is often a question of knowing yourself, because you will at some point have needed exactly what your audience currently needs. In a typical day interacting with information, everyone's taste is elastic: sometimes you want a simple transit map, sometimes you want a chart that explains a news story, sometimes you want a detailed demographic breakdown of the sales figures for the Greater Manchester area – depending on your role and identity at that moment. To paraphrase Walt Whitman, you contain multitudes, and your audience does too, and so the trick is to remember what it felt like to want what they want, and how happy you felt when you got it.

---

[15]We haven't spoken much about the importance of a good brief here, because this is not normally something we can control. However, we do try to question any brief from a client that doesn't make its scope, purpose and audience clear from the start.

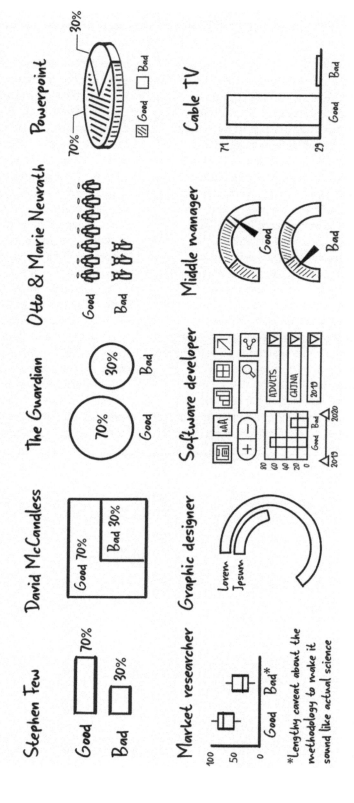

Figure 2.20 How bad was Chairman Mao? by Adam Frost

Try it yourself!

1. Imitation is a brilliant way of learning. Try to make a chart in the style of Edward Tufte, David McCandless, Hans Rosling, Giorgia Lupi or another practitioner whose work you admire.

2. For an Edward Tufte slopechart, start by finding change-over-time data that works well in a slopechart format. (Figure 2.12 shows the kind of data that *doesn't* work.) If you are a designer, you can use the line chart tool in Illustrator to create a slopechart. There is a great tutorial here: http://datavizcatalogue.com/blog/creating-slopegraph-adobe-illustrator/

3. Otherwise we'd recommend Datawrapper or Flourish which both contain easy slopechart templates. This blog from the Datawrapper academy walks you through the basics: https://academy.datawrapper.de/article/152-how-to-create-a-slope-chart. Note that if you are googling other tutorials, you should search for slopecharts and slopegraphs (both terms get used).

4. For a David McCandless 'Billion Dollar-o-Gram', try RAWGraphs (rawgraphs.io), a free charting tool which contains a treemap template. If you are more familiar with Microsoft products, then more recent versions of Excel and PowerPoint also contain treemaps.

5. You can make your own Gapminder chart using Flourish. Flourish have placed it in the 'scatter' category and called it a 'Hans Rosling chart' (quite right too). At the time of writing, it came with the population v. GDP data pre-loaded, just to make it even easier for you to get started.

6. If you are a user of R, you will know that you can also make all of the above with R packages such as ggplot (indeed, the Gapminder dataset makes frequent appearances in R and ggplot tutorials). Similarly, if you are a dashboard user, you will know that these charts are available in Tableau and Power BI. If you are unfamiliar with these tools, however, you might find the learning curve a little steep, whereas Raw, Datawrapper and Flourish are designed for novices and can all be picked up in less than an hour. Furthermore, new charting tools are invented constantly, so it is always worth checking data viz blogs for any recent arrivals. We also keep this Google doc updated with new tools: https://bit.ly/data-viz-best-practice

Three
Find

Adam Frost

Chapter contents

In the previous chapter, we talked about the inevitability of visual trickery when you are presenting data stories to an audience. In this chapter, we will be going back a step: finding the story in the first place. And here, when the audience is yourself, there should be no tricks.

Over the next few pages, we will look at how you lay the foundations for your story: building it on solid ground, so that when others seek to verify it or visualise it themselves, they find that what sounded unbelievable is actually the real thing.

The **Find** stage can be broken down into five overlapping activities:

1 Know your statistical terms
2 Find your data
3 Verify your data
4 Prepare and clean
5 Analyse and explore.

Sometimes this process can be swift. If you are familiar with the subject-matter, you know that your source is reliable, the data is clean and well structured, and the stories are interesting and easy to spot, then lucky you: you can take your sketchbook out and move on to the **Design** stage. But in the majority of cases, the **Find** stage is the most labour-intensive part of any project, just because most datasets take time to understand, and often contain nothing useful at all, so you have to keep starting again with new ideas and new data. Henry James said, 'It takes a great deal of history to produce a little literature', and it usually takes a great deal of data to produce one interesting chart.[1]

What you are doing in this first stage is discovering all the stories that your audience might potentially find interesting. You will rarely visualise them all, but understanding everything that you *could* show is a critical first step. It's also sensible to keep a relatively open mind, provided you

have time and budget to do so. Even if you have been given a specific brief or hypothesis, put this to one side for at least the first part of the analysis stage, so that the data determines the shape of your story, rather than the other way round.

Know your statistical terms

I'll start by letting you into a secret. It's perfectly possible to know nothing about statistics and still produce great visualisations. If you are dealing with simple datasets, or you are revisualising existing charts, then you may never need to go near Excel or even a calculator.

However it's also possible to go and live in France without ever learning any French. You will no doubt have plenty of great experiences, but you'll miss out on a lot, and probably make a lot of embarrassing mistakes too.

This is *data* visualisation, after all. Your dataset exists because a statistician collected, analysed and tabulated it. Every term you use to describe, benchmark, recalculate or represent your data will be derived from statistics. It is so central to any understanding of data that it has long ceased to be the exclusive preserve of mathematicians, and is now an essential component of dozens of academic disciplines: physics, political science, computer science, geography, sociology, economics, psychology, medicine, marketing and more. The relationship between statistics and chart-making is particularly close – in fact, the two disciplines have coevolved, advances in one stimulating advances in the other. Starting in earnest in the late eighteenth century, when William Playfair responded to the establishment of statistics as a distinct discipline by inventing the bar, line, pie and bubble charts, statisticians

[1] In fact, it is worth adding that exploratory data analysis (EDA) is a discipline in itself, established by John Tukey in the 1970s, with its own specialist methods and tools. EDA is outside of the scope of this book.

have continued to pose questions – How is this data distributed? How do these two datasets correlate? What is the information hierarchy in this dataset? – only for new visualisations (box plots, scatter charts, treemaps) to suggest answers. If you make your living by creating, analysing or presenting charts, then you owe it all to statistics.

If this isn't enough to convince you that having a good grasp of statistics is a sensible idea, then let me give you a few more practical reasons. If you visualise data without any statistical knowledge:

- you are more likely to make errors
- you are more likely to be misled by purveyors of dodgy data
- you will miss important stories in your data.

You will also miss out more generally: statistics is fascinating.

Having said all that, this is a book about data visualisation, not statistics. And I realise that many of you will be familiar with the key concepts already. So I'm not going to include a long list of detailed statistical explanations in this chapter. However, I have created a series of appendices, which you can find here: addtwodigital.com/book

- Appendix B: The statistical basics
- Appendix C: More advanced statistical terms
- Appendix D: Mistakes and misunderstandings

If you'd prefer to sit down with a more comprehensive statistics textbook, then Sally Caldwell's *Statistics Unplugged* (2004) is excellent. Alternatively, Charles Wheelan's *Naked Statistics* (2012) is an enjoyable and accessible primer.

Certainly I'd advise you *not* to read on if you have no idea what the following terms mean:

- mean, median and mode
- frequency distribution
- standard deviation
- random sample
- standard error
- confidence interval.

You don't need to be able to calculate them yourself, but you do need to understand why they're important and when they can be used to hide or skew stories. So if you're a statistical novice, do take the time to read the appendices or similar introductory material before moving on to the next section.

Find your data

I imagine that, for many of you, finding data isn't a problem – data finds you just fine. Every Monday morning, there it is: a new set of sales figures, or performance indicators, or website analytics. Alternatively, you may find data for a living; for example, if you work in a scientific or market research organisation, you will be used to designing experiments and surveys, and pulling the results into data tables.

However, even if you are accustomed to finding data with minimal effort, it is a good idea to be aware of the unprecedented variety of trustworthy, high-quality data that exists, partly because it might be more useful than the data you have, partly because it can provide valuable context for your data, and partly because you can learn a lot from how public-facing organisations structure and categorise their datasets.

For example, do you have global data? If so, what are you calling the (roughly) 200 countries in your dataset? Are you using country codes, and if so, do you favour the two- or three-letter system? Are you grouping these countries by continent? If so, which continent are Russia, Georgia and Turkey going to be placed in? Or are you grouping by business region? Or level of economic development? If so, which groupings are you using? At the time of writing, the World Bank uses Hans Rosling's four categories: high, upper-middle, lower-middle and low income economies. The IMF talks about countries with advanced, emerging and developing economies. The UN groups countries by very high, high, medium and low human development.

Countries are not treated consistently across these different systems: for example, Nigeria is ranked as low in the UN Human Development Index, but is classified as an emerging economy by the IMF. (And this, of course, will almost certainly change.) The point is: there are accepted structures for classifying (and spelling) countries, so rather than agonising about how to create a consistent system of your own, it is often easier to adopt, say, the World Bank or United Nations approach, depending on which taxonomy suits your own organisation's needs.

There are a few ways of finding good-quality data but the most common are: organic search (e.g. typing 'data about GDP' into Google), direct search (e.g. typing 'worldbank.org' into a browser), requesting it (e.g. contacting someone in a government department or using Freedom of Information requests), buying it (there are a ton of specialist databases), or creating your own data. Most projects combine several of these methods.

Organic search

If you are using Google or another search engine to find data, there are ways you can make your life easier. Google has a tool (currently called Google Dataset Search) that only looks for freely available online data. Alternatively, if you are running a standard search, there are a wide range of search operators available that can help you to target specific results. Here are a few examples:

(i) **Quotes for "a specific phrase"**. If you put double quotes around a phrase, then Google will look for these precise keywords in this exact order. You can combine this with a standard search too. For example: *"Central Statistics Office" India*.

(ii) **OR**. Using OR is a good way of combining two or more searches into one. For example: *GDP data World Bank OR IMF*. (If you want to search for the World Bank AND the IMF, you do not need to use AND, as any Google search uses AND by default.)

(iii) **A minus symbol to exclude words**. I'm a fan of the British comedian David Mitchell (check out *Peep Show* if you've never watched it). I also like the British novelist David Mitchell (author of *Cloud Atlas*). If I search *David Mitchell -comedian*, then I'm more likely to get search results for the latter.

(iv) **filetype**. If I just want to search for a particular filetype (for example, xlsx), then using 'filetype:' in tandem with a standard search will only return files of that type. For example, *World Bank filetype:xlsx* will only give me World Bank Excel files. No space after the colon (so not 'filetype: xlsx') or it won't work.

(v) **site**. If I only wanted GDP data that was on the World Bank site, rather than GDP data that mentioned the World Bank somewhere, then searching *GDP data site:World Bank* would do the trick. Again, no space after the colon.

(vi) **Bringing it all together**. Combing these terms will give you even more precise results. *"GDP data" filetype:xls x site:World Bank*. My personal favourite? *-filetype:pdf*. This excludes any pdfs from my search results. Given that pdfs are (at the time of writing) the worst possible way of sharing data, banishing them from your search results will save you hours of pain.[2]

---

[2]That said, there are an increasing number of tools out there that can help you extract data from a pdf – for example, Tabula, which is open source and easy to use. It's not foolproof, but it can usually get you most of the way there. WebPlotDigitizer is recommended for extracting data that sits behind charts. Both of these might have been superseded by better tools by the time you read this.

Direct search

Most international organisations have their own data repositories – some better than others – but it increasingly means that you can go to their sites directly. Examples would be the World Bank, NASA, UNESCO, the OECD and the FAO. Their data is often a year or two old, mostly because they need to ensure it is accurate and comprehensive, and that isn't a quick or easy task. But what they lack in timeliness, they make up for in credibility. Plus, the data is all free.

There will also be datasets that are relevant to your country, including data released by national statistics offices (e.g. censuses), government departments and charities. Furthermore, there will be repositories that relate to your sector; for example if you work for a health-care company in Britain, you will no doubt be aware of WHO, UNICEF, Global Health Data Exchange, National Health Service data and other sources.

I should also mention Our World in Data, which collates data from all of these sources and more. Not only does it allow you to download the raw numbers, but it also puts them in context with extremely useful articles and equally useful charts and maps. It is comprehensive, well organised and completely invaluable.

Different people have different ways of staying on top of this abundance of useful data, whether it is following these organisations on social media, bookmarking the most useful links, or creating folder structures on a shared drive with these datasets categorised. There are searchable community hubs (e.g. Kaggle), where users upload open datasets and share code and advice. Some organisations have APIs where the most useful public data is pulled into an in-house dashboard, meaning that any updates are available automatically.

The point is: whichever method you decide to use (or maybe you already use all of them), it is important to have some kind of system for navigating this ecosystem of free, high-quality data, because otherwise you can miss important stories, or lose track of which organisation owns which datasets, or redownload data you've already formatted and cleaned. It's likely you will do all of these things *anyway*, but the idea is to minimise their occurrence.

Other free databases

I'm sure many of you have lost hours of your life to free tools like Google Trends and Google Books Ngram Viewer.[3] There is also Wikipedia, of course, which everybody pretends they never use, even though everybody does. If you are regularly copying data from webpages, I'd consider using a scraper of some kind. There's a free extension on Chrome – Data Miner – that is currently the easiest way of getting data from a webpage into a spreadsheet in an accurate, readable format (copy and paste tends to give you a mess).

Other free ways of getting useful data include the following:

- Making a Freedom of Information request if your country has the relevant legislation in place. In the UK at least, if the data exists, and doesn't involve significant extra work to prepare, then they are meant to give it to you within a specific time period.[4]

---

[3] Google Trends analyses the popularity of search terms across a range of countries; Google Ngrams searches over 200 years of Google Books data. It is best to use these sources to add a 'fun' dimension to your data story, rather than suggesting they are scientifically solid, as there are obvious limits to the representativeness of the data.

[4] If you are a journalist or you work for a high-profile organisation, then you can always try crowd-sourcing data, although bear in mind the unrepresentativeness of your sample and think hard about how much freedom you give your contributors (drop-downs and checkboxes are good, free text boxes are usually bad).

- Making your own contacts, particularly with people who work in organisations that regularly release data to the public.
- Getting involved in Q&A communities like Stack Exchange, especially those that cater for specific disciplines. When I was writing an astronomy factbook for children, the Physics Stack Exchange community were endlessly patient when answering questions like 'If you built a slide from the Moon to Earth, how fast would you end up going?'
- Going to libraries and reading books. You would think it would go without saying but, increasingly, it doesn't. For contextual data and richer stories, you won't always find the information you need in a digital format.

The limits of free data

Just because the data is free, that doesn't mean you don't owe the author anything. At the very least, you will need to give the creator a credit. In most cases, how you credit the creator will be stipulated on a licensing page. Although most of the organisations I've mentioned above abide by Open Data standards and their licenses are Creative Commons, it's still important to under-stand what you're permitted to do (and not to do) with their data. There are currently, for example, six types of Creative Commons licence, ranging from the most permissive (you just have to credit the creator, and can use the data however you wish) through to the least permissive (these limit how much you can adapt the data, and/or whether commercial organisations can use it for free).[5] Get into the habit of reading data licensing pages before you click Download, and add any wording to your spreadsheet so you're aware of any terms or limitations as you analyse, adapt and visualise.

---

[5]https://creativecommons.org/about/cclicenses/

Buying data

There are an increasing number of companies that sell data. When we work with big companies, they usually subscribe to a bewildering number of databases such as TGI, Nielsen/IRI, Kantar Worldpanel and many others. On top of this, they might also commission bespoke surveys from market research companies, perhaps to test a new product, or a new advertisement, or to assess metrics such as brand loyalty, brand engagement or whatever it might be.

Rather than recommend data providers here, what we will say instead is that it is a good idea to understand who is selling data in your particular field, and which companies have the best reputations for quality, insight, value and customer service. And, of course, remember that they are businesses, so be on your guard for any areas where the pursuit of profit might be negatively affecting the data they are selling. In our experience, the data is usually pretty solid; it is the visualisation that can be problematic.

There are a number of commercial APIs where you can pull in maps, social media data, weather data, stock exchange information, news feeds and more into your own dashboards, web pages or wherever you might need the data to go. The Programmable Web has a full catalogue of all the APIs available.

I'd also like to mention the ProPublica datastore. As investigative journalists, they intuitively understand how data can generate powerful stories. Their datastore is a mixture of free and paid datasets that are always cleaned and organised to the highest possible standards. They also offer a number of APIs.

Mixing them all up

In most cases, you will use a variety of these different approaches. To take one example, in

2012, Jim Kynvin and I were asked by *Guardian Books* to look into the data behind the Booker Prize, a prestigious literary award that had been running for the previous 42 years (and is still going strong). This wasn't a dataset that existed so I had to create it myself. It involved visiting libraries and finding biographical information about the winning and shortlisted authors. I had to read the winning books in order to classify them by genre, setting and subject-matter. We used Nielsen sales data to look at the impact winning has on an author's sales (both their winning book and their backlist). We also ended up exploring the background of Booker Prize judges in an attempt to understand why a disproportionate number of winners were white, privately educated and British, in spite of it being open to writers from 56 countries. This ended up giving us our story: not only were the vast majority of the judges British and from privileged backgrounds, but 21 of them had been shortlisted or won the award themselves, or would go on to win it. In fact, three of the judges (Beryl Bainbridge, Paul Bailey and Nina Bawden) were nominated for the prize, then acted as judges, then were nominated again. Although the winning book was billed as the 'best original novel written in the English language' published that year across the 56 eligible countries, it was hard to see how that could be true. We could not have discovered any of these stories – or been able to visualise them – without drawing on a wide variety of data sources, print and digital, free and paid for, pre-existing and self-created.

Verify your data

Once you have found an interesting dataset, you need to check that it's not too good to be true. Even reputable data providers can make mistakes, and if you publish a story based on that data, then you are the one who can end up in trouble – sometimes serious legal trouble.

Let's imagine you were given a dataset by a company. We are imagining it is from a fictional photo-sharing website (Facesmash!) and it purports to show the world's favourite photo topics. The top five are: (1) cats; (2) selfies; (3) plates of food in a restaurant; (4) people at a hen/stag party; (5) blurry photos of speakers at a conference in front of awful slides.

What could possibly be wrong with this dataset? It sounds like it could make for a fun story. First of all, this is Facesmash! giving you Facesmash! data. It is not independent and any data damaging to the company's reputation is unlikely to have been included. The most common topics might in reality have been far-right propaganda or German erotica, but this is not something the company would want to disclose.

Who is in this dataset? Even if it is all of Facesmash!'s users, does this skew young, urban, wealthy, American? Can we talk about the 'world's' favourite photo topics if it is one tiny subset of one country's population?

How did Facesmash! collect the data? Did they just sweep every photo posted by every user? How were the photo categories decided? Did users tag them, or did a machine learning algorithm decide? (Both have flaws.) Did the company remove fake accounts? Duplicated accounts? Accounts that haven't been used for a year? If one user posts 100 photos a day, and all the photos are of their cat, are their photos weighted in the same way as a user who posts one photo a day?

How far back did they go? Is it just a single year of data? Or every single year of the company's existence, even though there were more photos posted in the past year than in the previous five years combined?

What about ethical considerations? Can Facesmash! prove that their users have given their informed consent for their personal data to be used in this way?

Finally, *why* did the company collect this data? And why are they telling you about it?

You ought to be as sceptical as any journalist being given data by a source. Are you using the data, or are you being used by it? The story might actually be why the data was collected, not what it contains.

In 2019, Jessica Glenza, a health reporter for *Guardian US*, found out that the Malaysian government was planning to increase taxes on cigarettes, in line with WHO recommendations.[6] However, a think-tank called the Institute for Democracy and Economic Affairs (IDEAS) quickly released a report showing that raising taxes would only increase the number of illegally traded cigarettes, without reducing the number of smokers. One in two cigarettes in Malaysia were smuggled, they showed. The statistic was repeated by cigarette manufacturers in the region. As a result, the proposal to increase taxes on cigarettes was dropped by the government 10 days later.

Rather than simply reporting these events, Glenza decided to look into who had released this report and why. IDEAS accepted donations from Philip Morris (a cigarette company) and Japan Tobacco International. As for the data on smuggling rates, Glenza looked into this too. Two reports backed up the 'one in two' figure. One from Nielsen showed that 57.1% of cigarettes were smuggled, and another from Oxford Economics claimed that 52% were illegally-traded. Both reports were funded by the tobacco industry. Glenza found that data not connected to the tobacco industry put the smuggling rate at 35%.

Glenza asked Nielsen for a copy of the report with their smuggling data in, but Nielsen said they weren't able to share it.

Because of Glenza's decision not to take the data at face value, her story became richer and more wide-ranging. This wasn't just about raising taxes in Malaysia anymore, it was about how tobacco companies and free-market think-tanks appear to be using data to influence government policy. She looked at how similar methods were being used to fight tobacco controls all over the world, including in Chile, Ghana, Australia, Nigeria and Hong Kong (Figure 3.1).

So that's the first – and most important – part of the verification process: checking your data is trustworthy. The next part is making sure that it is the right data for your project. In recruitment terms, the first part is checking your candidate's employment history and references. Now it is time for the interview. (I don't mean to overdo this 'your data is a person' metaphor, but I do think it's helpful. It gets you into the habit of thinking about the people that made the data before you think about the people *in* it.)

What I mean by an interview is a quick review of your data's structure and content. Is it too messily organised to provide any reliable stories? If there are stories, are they interesting enough to warrant further exploration? Before you go through the lengthy cleaning and analysis stages (see below), it's worth getting a broad sense of whether the data has potential, whether it will help you achieve your objectives and whether your audience will find it valuable. It's less about checking veracity, and more about checking suitability. It's especially important when you have multiple datasets and data sources competing for your attention.

Clean your data

In the previous section I emphasised the importance of being thorough in verifying your data: making sure you have a comprehensive dataset with no omissions or errors. The only downside of this approach is you can end up with a *lot* of data. This data might have come from

[6]https://www.theguardian.com/world/2019/jan/23/tobacco-industry-free-market-thinktanks-cigarette-controls

Tobacco: A deadly business

Free-market groups and the tobacco industry - full database

More than 100 free-market thinktanks have argued against tobacco control policies or accepted donations from the tobacco industry, research by the Guardian shows

● Revealed: the free-market thinktanks helping the tobacco industry

by Jessica Glenza, Sharon Kelly and Juweek Adolphe

North America

American Conservative Union Foundation

Country	Region	Years accepted donations
United States	North America	-

The American Conservative Union Foundation, best known for the highly influential conservative conference called the Conservative Political Action Conference, called "Woodstock for conservatives" by anti-tax Republican Grover Norquist. ACU has repeatedly opposed cigarette taxes and other tobacco regulations. In 2016 the group opposed a cigarette tax hike in Pennsylvania, which public health experts said is one of the most effective ways to discourage youth smoking. In 2018, the ACU opposed plain packaging, a tobacco control tactic which removes branding from cigarette packs. When the US Food and Drug Administration proposed banning menthol cigarettes, ACU argued it would hurt jobs, according to Slate.

American Enterprise Institute

Country	Region	Years accepted donations
United States	North America	2011, 2012, 2013, 2014, 2015, 2016, 2017

The American Enterprise Institute has aligned itself with the tobacco industry on many issues. AEI has said researchers should take money from big tobacco to conduct their research; that cigarette tax increases fund organized crime and terrorism; and argued, cigarette taxes cause smuggling, a claim health authorities say tobacco firms exaggerate. In 2017, the AEI wrote a letter to the US Food and Drug Administration (FDA), encouraging the agency to approve Philip Morris International's IQOS product for sale in the US. The product heats tobacco, but does not burn it. The letter said: "It is imperative that current US smokers have access to and be properly informed about safer options." An FDA advisory panel rejected Philip Morris's claims that the stick would be safer than smoking. AEI accepted donations from Altria, owner of Philip Morris USA, every year between 2011 and 2017. It is unclear what proportion of its budget is funded by tobacco companies. AEI was rated "highly opaque" by the watchdog group Transparify, which campaigns for thinktank transparency.

Figure 3.1 The *Guardian*'s story about the link between rightwing think-tanks and tobacco

different sources, and use different taxonomies. You will usually need to clean your data up before you analyse it.

Often this can all be done in Excel. The most common tasks are:

- deleting blank rows and columns and/or hiding irrelevant ones
- standardising names (e.g. USA, U.S.A., United States, United States of America) and classifications (M, Men, Males)
- standardising values (e.g. different types of measurement, different types of rounding)
- making everything readable (e.g. sorting out text wrapping, autofitting row height and column width)
- making everything easy to manipulate and filter (e.g. unmerging cells, splitting text fields – like the town, city and country in an address – into separate columns).

All of this is very straightforward to learn in Excel if you don't already know how. A simple Google search (see the organic search tips above) should lead you to useful resources, and books like *The Excel Bible* (2018), which is continually updated, are also useful.

If you have very messy data or a very large dataset, then there are a range of cleaning tools available. Open Refine from Google is a popular free option. This can quickly sweep through your data and make intelligent suggestions about anomalies and duplicates, and apply transformations in bulk across multiple cells. There are tutorials online to walk you through the basics. If you are a data analyst, you will be familiar with Stata, SPSS, SAS and other similar (paid-for) tools.

Data cleaning is important for selfish reasons – it makes your data easier to analyse. But it is not just for your benefit; it is also about establishing data integrity. Clean data means that it is easy for others to check the numbers and methodology behind your story. Most data journalists think this way – their data will be published and should be judged by the same criteria as anything else they publish –

and it is a good habit to get into. It also makes it simpler for other users to explore your data and find stories that you overlooked.

Analyse your data

Now you are ready to start analysing. Maybe.

Before we dive into a sample spreadsheet, it's worth emphasising that even a clean and credible dataset can contain errors. But these will be errors that you introduce, due to what Leland Wilkinson has called our 'systematically suboptimal' brains (Wilkinson, 1999, p. 466). We fabricate, overreact and jump to conclusions, getting further and further away from the data with each sweeping statement. Being on your guard against these cognitive biases can help you to see your data clearly and objectively. You can never overcome them all (believing that you can is a cognitive bias in itself), but you can at least be aware of the tricks that your mind likes to play. There is an entire literature on this subject (well over 100 cognitive biases have been identified at the time of writing) but in Table 3.1 I have focused on the handful of biases that are most likely to trip you up during the **Find** stage.

How software affects what you see

Other cognitive problems can be introduced by the circumstances in which you carry out your analysis. The most persistent offender is data exploration software. This unleashes the four main biases mentioned in Table 3.1 – and adds a few more as well. Although every tool is different, the main issues are:

- automatically dropping any data you upload into a chart
- suggesting a chart type, or offering you a limited range of common chart types

Table 3.1   A table of cognitive biases

	What happens	Why it happens	Example experiments	Strategies for minimising it
Confirmation bias	'The mother of all cognitive biases', according to Michael Shermer. We are drawn to information that confirms our existing beliefs. In data analysis, this is most likely to occur when you have found an exciting story and you are looking for data to corroborate it. Data that undermines your story is screened out, because you want the original story to be true.	In Michael Shermer's analysis, it is because humans possess a 'believing brain'. We believe something first, and find reasons for it afterwards. These beliefs shape our understanding of reality and give us mental shortcuts for dealing with daily situations. Changing these beliefs or admitting you are wrong involves effort, causes anxiety, and can lead to a loss of status.	In a 1951 study, academics showed footage of an American football game between Princeton and Dartmouth to 324 students from both universities. Students were twice as likely to see fouls committed by the opposing team. In a 1983 study by Darley and Gross, people graded an identical test paper differently, depending on the social class that they were told the pupil came from. The pupil from the higher class was 'upgraded'.	Try not to start with a fixed story in mind. Start with the idea: 'I'm looking for anything that might be interesting to my audience.' If you do find something interesting, check to see if another aspect of your data – or a different dataset – contradicts or undermines this story. Give yourself time to change your mind: it is not a fast process.
Overconfidence bias	When Daniel Kahneman was asked which bias he would like to eliminate if he had a magic wand, he chose this one: overconfidence (Shariatmadari, 2015). We imagine that we understand things when we don't. In data analysis, this can involve overconfidence in our abilities (imagining that we can analyse a dataset faster than is likely), our knowledge (believing that we have fully mastered a complex subject) or our conclusions (making an assertion with absolute certainty).	In Kahneman's words, the confidence we have in our beliefs is 'preposterous' but 'also essential' (Kahneman, 2011, p. 209). If we knew how little we know, we couldn't function. Believing that we know what we are doing, and others know what they are doing, is essential for personal happiness and social cohesion. It is so highly prized that the most overconfident among us are frequently given leadership roles, often with negative consequences.	In a series of studies, Rozenblit and Keil asked a group of people if they knew how everyday objects worked (e.g. sewing machines, zippers, flush toilets). Most said they did. But when asked to actually describe how these objects worked, the test subjects failed miserably (Rozenblit and Keil, 2002). The illusion of knowledge is also linked to the illusion of superiority. In a famous experiment from 1981, Ola Svenson found that 93% of US drivers rated their driving as better than average (Svenson, 1981).	One way of minimising overconfidence – invented by Gary Klein – is to imagine that you have published your story or visualisation, and that it was an unmitigated disaster. Everything you said in it was 100% wrong. Now list the reasons why you might have messed up so badly. Klein calls this a 'pre-mortem'. By thinking about how you might have misjudged or misrepresented the data, you correct for overconfidence (if you're lucky).

(Continued)

Table 3.1 (Continued)

	What happens	Why it happens	Example experiments	Strategies for minimising it
Availability bias	This is the belief that examples of things that come easily to mind are more common or meaningful than is actually the case. It can easily affect data analysts. Subjects with a frequent media presence can 'jump out' in your data, just because your brain is likely to spot them first. When you are looking for causes of particular trends, you may reach for easy explanations rather than analysing possible causes more methodically.	This mental shortcut could have been evolutionarily useful because it involves serving up 'good enough' information quickly, and doesn't involve effortful analysis or painstakingly searching our memories for more reliable information. It is also linked to our tendency to overreact to new information, which might have been important when any disruption in our environments could have had life-changing consequences.	Slovic, Lichtenstein and Fischhoff asked people to estimate the chances of dying from particular causes. Tornadoes were seen as more deadly than asthma (asthma is 20 times more deadly) and death from an accident was judged 300 times more likely than death from diabetes (diabetes is four times more deadly). Tornadoes and tragic accidents receive more media coverage and are more 'available' as causes of death (Kahneman, 2011, p. 138).	One good method is to try to come up with seven reasons why your story is valid. If you genuinely find a multitude of datapoints or explanations or perspectives that back up your findings, and you don't feel your confidence ebbing away when you get past reason 3 or 4, then you have probably interrogated your dataset thoroughly and not just relied on the easy-to-spot information.
IKEA bias	OK, this isn't as scientifically well established as the others, but it's a personal favourite. Based on the work of Norton, Mochon and Duke (2011), it describes people's propensity to overvalue objects that they have partly created, even if – as in IKEA furniture – the end product is poorly assembled and of low quality. There is an obvious parallel with data exploration. When you find and chart a story, particularly if it takes you some time, you will often think it is more coherent and interesting than it is.	There are various theories as to why humans do this. Successfully completing a task is pleasurable, and this warm feeling is transferred to the product itself – even if it's poorly made. Humans don't like admitting they've done a bad job – a bias linked to the sunk cost fallacy, where companies continue to invest money into failing projects because of the amount of money already spent.	In an experiment published in 2011, Norton, Mochon and Duke asked subjects to build IKEA furniture. The researchers then tested how much the subjects were willing to pay for the furniture they had assembled. The answer was 63% more, compared to furniture that someone else had assembled. A second experiment found that the more you built of an IKEA product, the more highly you valued it.	You overcome this bias just as you would when you actually build IKEA furniture. Ask someone you trust if you've done a good job. Are the shelves wonky? In data visualisation terms, it could be: Does this make sense? Do those numbers look right? Is that the best chart to tell this story? You are not going to be able to judge this accurately yourself. Another good habit is to put your story to one side for a few days and come back to it once 'effort justification' biases have worn off.

- assuming you are a novice and building the whole chart for you
- choosing how much of your data will appear in that chart (usually too much of it)
- turning on every possible annotative feature, including axis labels, data labels, gridlines, legends and titles
- automatically choosing fonts, colours and graphical effects which add nothing to the data or actively distort it
- constraining the extent to which you can change these defaults.

All of these elements change how you read your data. It is onerous to create chart templates that undo these defaults, or to patiently declutter your chart so that you can see the stories clearly. In the majority of analytical dashboards that we encounter, users have strayed little – or not at all – from the default settings. The biases this introduces include the following:

- *Overconfidence*. As soon as you put data in a chart, it can seem more authoritative, interesting and worthy of preservation.

- *Framing*. The number of datapoints shown, the chart type used and the colours chosen affect the story you see (more on this in Chapter 5).
- *Availability*. Data charted is more memorable, even if it looks awful. Data that happens to 'work' better when you chart it may also be remembered for longer, even if the story is weak.

How to minimise bias

To (partly) overcome these biases, we avoid charting our data unless it's absolutely necessary. We keep our data in tables and use spreadsheeting tools to look for initial patterns and trends. Each cell takes up the same visual space on the page; stories can be easily made and unmade by sorting or filtering, so this minimises the IKEA effect (see Table 3.1). In most cases, a well-organised spreadsheet is easier for a data-literate person to interpret than a pre-populated dashboard full of charts.

When we find a story we want to remember, we save that cut of the data as a table, write down a

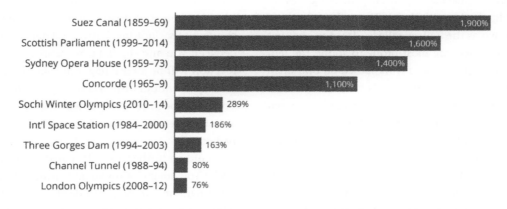

Overconfidence bias in action

Percentage by which each project exceeded its original budget

Project	Percentage
Suez Canal (1859–69)	1,900%
Scottish Parliament (1999–2014)	1,600%
Sydney Opera House (1959–73)	1,400%
Concorde (1965–9)	1,100%
Sochi Winter Olympics (2010–14)	289%
Int'l Space Station (1984–2000)	186%
Three Gorges Dam (1994–2003)	163%
Channel Tunnel (1988–94)	80%
London Olympics (2008–12)	76%

Economics professor Bent Flyvbjerg believes that on average only one in 1,000 large engineering projects delivers the promised benefits on time and on budget.

Source: *Forbes*, *New Statesman*

Figure 3.2   Overconfidence

simple text description of the story and/or sketch some initial thoughts about how it might be charted. Using pencil and paper. Again, the emphasis is on disposability and provisionality. This chart is one of many that might make the final cut, but we are not going to decide on the winners yet.

If your dataset is vast, multivariate and continually changing, it will be harder to do this, but even in these circumstances, looking at the data tables for as long as possible can save you pain further down the line. Your analysis software is a tool, not a coauthor, so it's sensible to minimise the number of times you ask it to 'help' find stories. If you do need to chart the data to make any sense of it, then tools that allow you to create basic charts quickly (R and ggplot are good at this) are preferable, because you are less likely to mistake their crude output for a clear and final story.

In the next chapter, we will talk more about how these biases can become your friends when it comes to telling a story to an audience. But during the analysis stage, you do need to be alert to the fact that our minds have evolved to help us survive, not to see the world truthfully. Analysis is not our natural, default state; we have to force ourselves to do it. But it is vital to try to see your data without bias, because otherwise you can end up visualising a mistake, and then your work – every part of it – will be dismissed. This is also a type of bias known as the 'fallacy fallacy'. It is the one that expert audiences are most prone to adopt: the tendency to reject a piece of work, based on one small error. The delivery is slightly flawed, so the whole argument must be flawed. It's not fair, but it's what happens, and if you don't want to be a victim of it, make sure you've checked, cleaned and analysed your data to a high standard.

I realise all of the above makes it sound as if data analysis is no fun. To be honest, a lot of the time it isn't. It should be tedious sometimes, because being thorough means checking everything, even the dull stuff. But, at the same time, getting overly bored introduces bias too, as you are likely to miss things or overreact to the faintest glimmer of a story. There is a balance to be struck.

So I do want to caution against being too obsessive about tracking and stamping out your biases. You need to be aware of them, but if that's all you are aware of, then you stop seeing the data, and all you see is yourself reacting to the data. You police every thought that crosses your mind. Your story becomes about the limits of what you can say, which is more of a philosophical rumination than a story.

Emotion plays an important role in data analysis. As you explore your dataset, you will be surprised, delighted, angered, afraid. You need to remember these emotions because when you come to tell your story, these are the emotions that you will want to reproduce in your audience. Yes, you will need to check that you have not been duped into feeling this way by cognitive bias. Some of these stories will be mirages and will need to be discarded. But many will not: they will be true stories, and the truth that they convey will be an emotional one. *There has been a dramatic rise. This datapoint is unlike the others. I've worked out what might have caused that.* Your pulse will quicken; you're a journalist with an exclusive; you have to tell other people what you've found.

Data analysis is often characterised as neutral and bloodless, but it isn't. You are looking for connections – not just between datapoints, but between you and the data. Sometimes your reaction will be a false flag, but that doesn't mean you should dispense with your emotions. They may be unreliable sometimes, but emotions are ultimately how you tell a good story from a bad one.

I could go further: isn't data analysis a story in itself? You are going on an adventure into the unknown, on a quest for understanding. The whole process implies the fiction of a settled, stable, rational self with a clear, knowable purpose. There will be challenges (cognitive biases to overcome, data discrepancies to untangle) but these can surely be overcome and the hero (you) can triumph over the forces of darkness and bring back the priceless treasure (truth). You can't do the job properly without creating a semi-fictional framework to support you. This is why you have to be careful when it comes to policing biases and errors, because you might end up shutting down the biases that allow you to function as an analyst in the first place.

The Find stage in action

Let us use as a test dataset one of the most popular spreadsheets released by the UK's Office for National Statistics (ONS). Published every summer, it shows the most common baby names in England and Wales for that year. Table 3.2 shows a few rows; I've slightly adapted the 2018 release to create this imaginary disaggregated dataset below.

The dataset comes from a reputable source, and it has been cleaned by the ONS already, so we can start analysing. The first thing we would do with a dataset like this is open Excel and create some pivot tables to pull out the top-level figures: the most common names for boys and girls in 2018 and the most common names by month and by region. Then we would download the same table for the last five or ten years, so we could compare 2018 to previous years. (If you're interested in this dataset, I'd recommend downloading the whole thing from the ONS website.)

Pretty quickly we'd get a sense of the overall shape of our data. This is usually something we assemble intuitively (and untidily), but if you prefer to approach the task more systematically, then it can be helpful to think in terms of the six categories that most data stories fall into:

- **Composition** – How does this dataset break down? How does each part relate to the whole?
- **Distribution** – How is the data distributed? Are all the datapoints close to the average?
- **Comparison (rank and magnitude)** – Which datapoint is the biggest? How much bigger? Which is the smallest?
- **Change over time** – How does the data compare to previous years?
- **Geospatial** – Are there regional or national differences?
- **Correlation** – What might have caused particular patterns and trends?

All of these categories overlap to some extent and often a story will contain many of these categories simultaneously, but there is usually one which dominates. You may prefer to devise different categories and subcategories, based on the data you work with most often.

The six main types of data stories

Here are some of the stories we would find in our baby names data.

Table 3.2 Most common baby names in England and Wales, 2018

Name	Gender	Month of birth	Year of birth	Region of birth	Mother's age in years
Oliver	Male	January	2018	London	24
Olivia	Female	January	2018	North East	37
Emily	Female	January	2018	South East	32
George	Male	January	2018	South West	29

Composition

- 657,003 babies were born in England and Wales in 2018.
- 51% were boys, 49% were girls.
- 33% of babies were born in London or the South East (67% in the other eight regions).

Distribution

- The average age of mothers at childbirth was 31 – with a standard deviation of 5 years (68% of mothers were between 26 and 36).[7]

Comparison

- The top five names for boys were Oliver (5,390), George (4,960), Harry (4,512), Noah (4,107) and Jack (3,988).
- The top five names for girls were Olivia (4,598), Amelia (3,941), Ava (3,110), Isla (3,046) and Emily (2,676).
- There are big differences between what older mothers (over 35) and younger mothers (under 25) call their children. For baby girls, Harper is ranked 5th for young mothers and 73rd for older mothers, whereas Charlotte is ranked 2nd for older mothers and 45th for younger mothers.

Change over time

- The top boys' and girls' names have remained static. Oliver has been number 1 since 2013. Olivia has been number 1 since 2016.
- Within the top 100, the biggest rises for boys since 2008 are Hunter (+1,042 rank change) and Grayson (+905). For girls, it is Harper (+1,365) and Aria (+1,094).
- Old-fashioned names are back in the top 100 for both boys (Archie, Reggie, Albert, Stanley) and girls (Ivy, Elsie, Nancy, Ada).
- Common 'baby boomer' names don't even feature in the top 1,000: Trevor, Keith, Nigel (boys) and Linda, Susan, Janet (girls). There

were only eight Nigels and six Susans born in 2018.

Geospatial

- For girls, Olivia is number 1 in every region, and Amelia is number 2 in every region except Wales (where Ava is number 2).
- For boys, there is much more variation. Oliver is top in five regions, Muhammad in four, Harry in one.
- London is an outlier. For boys, five names (Alexander, Adam, Joshua, David, Daniel) are in no other regional top 10s. For girls, Sofia (number 3) and Maya (number 5) are in no other regional top 10s.

Correlation

- Harper Beckham – the daughter of Posh Spice and David Beckham – was born in 2011. Between 2011 and 2018, Harper jumped from rank 858 to rank 27.
- Princess Charlotte was born in 2015. The name had been declining in popularity, falling from 9th place in 2005 to 25th place in 2015. By 2018, it was back up to number 12.
- The name Cameron was a popular boys' name in 2010 when David Cameron became Prime Minister of the UK, featuring in the top 50 for much of the previous decade. By 2018, it had fallen to 177th place.

Deciding which stories to pursue

Once we had a general sense of what the data contained, we would make a decision about whether there was enough there to interest our audience. We will assume that the answer is yes. The next stage is zeroing in on the stories that warrant further exploration. This is determined by

[7]The data range story is pretty bleak: it starts at a horrifying 12 years old and stretches to 59. The standard deviation used here is a rounded estimate, not an exact figure. (The range data is based on analysis for a Chemist4U graphic.)

several factors: a combination of audience need, their prior knowledge, their preferred format, project duration and project budget. For example, let us posit these four different audiences:

- You are making a ten-slide PowerPoint presentation for a company that makes bibs with babies' initials on them
- You are a journalist writing a story for a broadsheet newspaper like the *Guardian*
- You are a journalist writing a listicle for a website like Mental Floss or BuzzFeed
- You are the editor of the ONS website, writing a summary page for the baby names statistical release.

How might the **Find** stage differ in these situations?

A PowerPoint for a company

If you were making a PowerPoint for a company that makes bibs with single letters on them, you would probably focus primarily on composition stories – the size of the market – and how the company might maximise the number of bibs they sold. Stories might include:

- The total market in 2018 is 657,003 babies, 51% male and 49% female.
- The most common first letters for boys' names are A, J, M, R and L. These five letters represent 43% of the boys' market.
- The most common first letters for girls' names are A, E, M, S and L. These five letters represent 52% of the girls' market.
- Forget Q, U and X – these are the bottom letters for both boys and girls. Combined, these three letters are less than 0.2% of your market.
- Boys names beginning with J are almost five times more popular than girls' names beginning with J (31,841 boys and 6,753 girls).

This is the biggest discrepancy between the genders.
- If you produce genderless bibs, 22% of your total sales will come from two letters: A and M.
- Regionally, your biggest potential markets are London and the South East (33% of babies). Your smallest market is the North East (4%).[8]

You might also carry out more granular analysis of how first letters changed in popularity by region and season and whether long-term trends favoured some letters continuing to rise or fall compared to others. You would no doubt be combining this dataset with the company's own data on past and projected sales.

A broadsheet article

If you were a broadsheet journalist, you would perhaps spend more time on the comparison, change and correlation stories. These might include the following:

- The top 20 names for girls and boys and their change in rank from the previous year.
- The new arrivals in the top 20 for boys (Isaac, Theo) and girls (Ivy, Evelyn, Willow) and the biggest climbs/drops outside the top 20.
- Outside of this, you might focus on general trends and influences. For example, you might explore gender differences in more detail. Within the top 20, boys still seem to have traditional names, taken from kings (George, Henry, William) or religious leaders (Muhammad, Noah, Isaac, Joshua). In contrast, in the girls' top 20, four names are drawn from the natural world (Poppy, Lily, Ivy, Willow), and in the top 100, there are a lot of Disney and fantasy-fiction names (Aria, Aurora, Luna). Why are we are still giving our

---

[8]Note that these numbers are slightly off because the ONS dataset does not include names with a count of two or fewer. We have split the 'unknowns' proportionately among the 26 letters, relative to their popularity.

children such traditional, strongly gendered names?

- Another avenue to explore might be Britain's status as a multicultural society. In four regions (London, the West Midlands, the North West and Yorkshire), Muhammad is the most popular boys name. Sofia, the eastern European spelling of Sophia, is the third most popular girls' name in London and appears in no other regional top 10s.
- You might also focus on some of the quirkier stories – Holly suddenly appearing in the December top 10 (22% of Hollies are born in December), and Leo rising to number 2 in August for boys (presumably linked to the star sign).

If you were looking at the multicultural story, you might also use Census or ONS data to give you additional context on Britain's current demographics. Additionally you could spin out an entirely different second story about the rising age of new mothers and how/why women are postponing having children for longer.

A listicle

For a journalist writing a listicle for Mental Floss or BuzzFeed, the analysis stage would change again. Here the emphasis would be on finding an angle that grabs attention, and referencing popular culture. As well as touching on some of the stories above (in the broadsheet list), the analysis stage might involve looking at the influence of popular culture:

- For boys, these names all featured in the ONS list:
  - from the Marvel Universe, Loki (88 babies) and Thor (19)
  - from Harry Potter, Albus (7 babies) and Sirius (5)
  - from *Game of Thrones*, Tyrion (4 babies) and Theon (21)
  - from *Star Wars*, Anakin (10 babies) and Kylo (78).

Our angle could be: '17 names that were more popular than Clive' (there were three baby Clives in 2018).

- For girls, these names all featured:
  - from the Marvel Universe, Elektra (16 babies) and Rogue (19)
  - from Harry Potter, Bellatrix (6 babies) and Ginny (10)
  - from *Game of Thrones*, Khaleesi (56 babies) and Daenerys (4)
  - from *Star Wars*, Rey (18 babies) and Leia (140).

Perhaps our angle would be: '19 names that were more popular than Maureen' (there were three Maureens born in 2018).

An ONS article

For the ONS editor, your analysis of the data would be more comprehensive. You would no doubt talk about the most popular names that year, and changes from the previous year. But, with over 100 years of data at your disposal, you would be free to analyse longer-term trends. Your analysis stage might include:

- Examination of the number of births overall and how that affects the UK's population pyramid. For example, 5.9% of the population are between 0 and 4 years old. This is similar to other developed economies (e.g. USA, France), whereas in Zambia 16.2% of the population are between 0 and 4.
- Analysis of how many babies have names in the top 100. In 1996, most babies (67%) had a name that was in the top 100. By 2018, only a minority of babies (45%) did. We are experimenting more.
- Exploration of naming cycles. For example, Ada is in the girls' top 100 for the first time since 1924. Albert and Arthur dropped out of the boys' top 100 in 1954 but both are now back.

- Information about how the data was gathered. For example, the fact that only live births are counted, that different spellings of the same name are counted as different names, and that regional data is based on where the mother lives, not where the baby was born.

What all of this shows is that the context of your analysis (your role, purpose and audience) isn't something that you think about when you start making your presentation or graphic – it is hard-baked into the analysis process. Yes, you need to get an overview of everything first, but once you have mapped the kinds of stories you have, you need to adopt a more targeted approach. Even in a relatively straightforward dataset like this one, you can see that the number of stories is infinite. Parents, students, businesses, civil servants and journalists will all want different things. We all have names. Most of us have children. We all have opinions about other people's names: what they mean, whether they are trendy, embarrassing or somewhere in between. Appealing to every potential consumer of this dataset is not an option, and it's the same with almost any dataset, so understanding what it is in this data that your audience needs you to analyse is an essential characteristic of the **Find** stage.

What I've also tried to show here is that, regardless of our role and goal, our approach to the **Find** stage is similar. At this stage, we are not choosing the 'best' stories for our audience – that comes later – we are finding anything that might be important to them. We are not structuring these stories into a longer narrative – that also comes later – we note down stories as we find them. And remember that this is *noting down*. As we mentioned above, we avoid outputting visualisations during the **Find** stage, because it

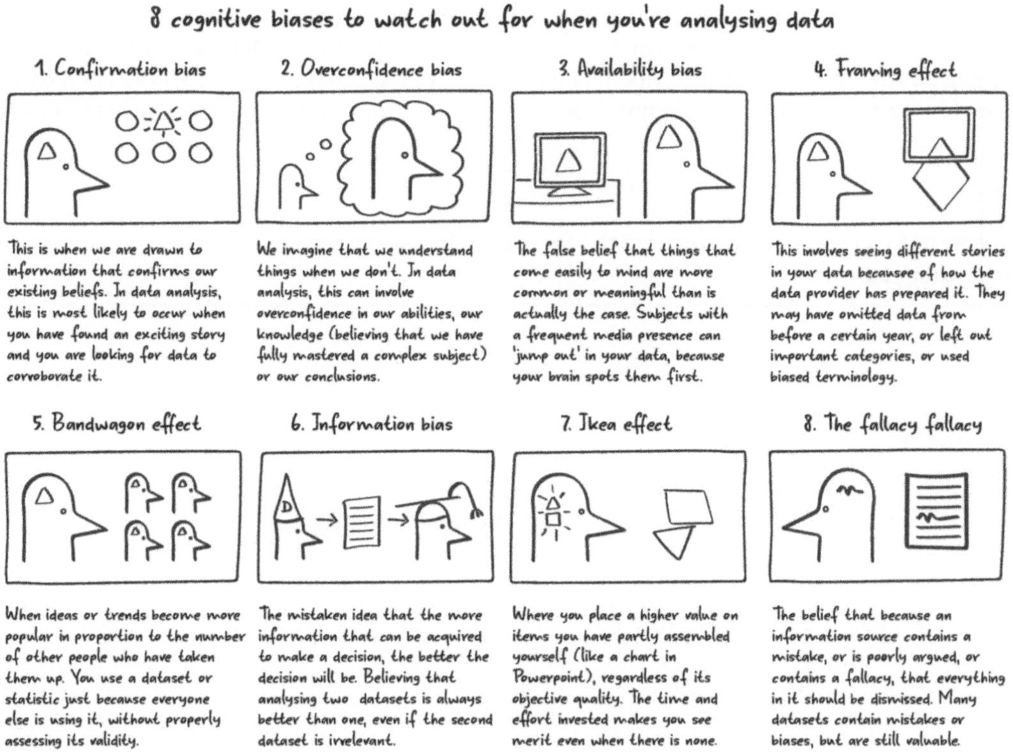

8 cognitive biases to watch out for when you're analysing data

1. Confirmation bias

This is when we are drawn to information that confirms our existing beliefs. In data analysis, this is most likely to occur when you have found an exciting story and you are looking for data to corroborate it.

2. Overconfidence bias

We imagine that we understand things when we don't. In data analysis, this can involve overconfidence in our abilities, our knowledge (believing that we have fully mastered a complex subject) or our conclusions.

3. Availability bias

The false belief that things that come easily to mind are more common or meaningful than is actually the case. Subjects with a frequent media presence can 'jump out' in your data, because your brain spots them first.

4. Framing effect

This involves seeing different stories in your data because of how the data provider has prepared it. They may have omitted data from before a certain year, or left out important categories, or used biased terminology.

5. Bandwagon effect

When ideas or trends become more popular in proportion to the number of other people who have taken them up. You use a dataset or statistic just because everyone else is using it, without properly assessing its validity.

6. Information bias

The mistaken idea that the more information that can be acquired to make a decision, the better the decision will be. Believing that analysing two datasets is always better than one, even if the second dataset is irrelevant.

7. Ikea effect

Where you place a higher value on items you have partly assembled yourself (like a chart in Powerpoint), regardless of its objective quality. The time and effort invested makes you see merit even when there is none.

8. The fallacy fallacy

The belief that because an information source contains a mistake, or is poorly argued, or contains a fallacy, that everything in it should be dismissed. Many datasets contain mistakes or biases, but are still valuable.

Figure 3.3 Cognitive biases – a visual summary by Adam Frost

can give a false sense of importance to pedestrian stories. More importantly, forcing yourself to distil what you have found into a sentence is a critical skill if you want to subsequently relay this insight to an audience. These sentences – and what they mean – will be the structural foundation of every chart you make and may even survive in their original form as titles or subtitles. For this reason, we tend to write down what we have found in complete sentences using pen and paper or in a Notepad app or a Google doc or anything else that is primarily designed for text and tables. The objective of the **Find** stage is to give the editors and designers everything they need to start the **Design** phase in as simple and as lucid a form as possible.

Try it yourself!

1 Download the most recent baby names data for your own country. It will probably be hosted on your government's statistics website. If it's not there, you could just use US or UK data. (https://www.ssa.gov/oact/babynames/ for the USA or https://www.ons.gov.uk/peoplepopulationandcommunity/birthsdeathsandmarriages/livebirths/ for the UK)
2 Using Excel or Google Sheets, spend an hour or so pulling out the main stories. If it's helpful, try to find composition, distribution, comparison, change-over-time, geospatial and correlation stories. Use sentences and tables of numbers to record what you've found.
3 Choose an audience type. Ideally this would be a group of people you often have to present to as part of your job. If you are a student, imagine that you are pitching to the editor of a student newspaper or presenting a research project to your supervisor. Look at the data again, pulling out the stories that would be most interesting to this audience. Once you've got a definitive list, move on to the exercise in the next chapter.

Extra resources

If you're new to Excel and data analysis, try the Excel exercises we've created at www.addtwodigital.com/book

Four

Designing static graphics

Adam Frost

Chapter contents

Once you've found everything that is potentially interesting for your audience and verified that it's all true, you have to fashion what you've discovered into a coherent and meaningful shape. We call this storytelling, but if you want to call it something else, that's fine – as long as you go through a similar process of selection, dramatisation and emphasis, throwing irrelevant things away and placing what's left into some kind of hierarchy, user journey or plot.

I've made this process sound simple, but in reality it isn't. It is usually the hardest part to get right. When we deconstruct charts that don't work (including our own), sometimes it is the numbers that are wrong, sometimes it is the visuals that are poor, but in the majority of cases, it is the storytelling that is broken – there is too much information, or too much at once, or the story is dull or incoherent or (most commonly) completely inappropriate for its intended audience.

So how do you design a great story?

Nobody knows.

This is why it's hard to do. In Chapter 3, we referenced statistical methods and data exploration techniques. These are all, to different degrees, teachable skills. The key concepts can be formalised, replicated by students and verified by teachers. If I ask you to find the median value in a dataset, as long as you use the correct methodology, you will obtain the correct answer. If I have data saying that a politician is liked by 45% of the population, and I ask you to calculate a margin of error with a confidence level of 95%, then your answer will be right or wrong. With patience, it is possible for anyone to pick up a statistics textbook and become, if not a statistician, then a proficient user of statistics.

This is not the case with storytelling. With apologies to colleagues who run creative writing courses, there is no textbook – and there never will be a textbook – that can turn someone into a storyteller. If there were, every book would be a bestseller, every film would be a smash hit, and every piece of data journalism would end up on the front page. 'If I knew where the good songs came from, I would go there more often', as Leonard Cohen put it. Even stories that are popular are rarely popular with everyone. Take a look at that Leonard Cohen quote again – 'If I knew where the good songs come from'. I think Leonard Cohen wrote good songs, but do you?

Another complicating factor is that great stories often work in the face of all logic or precedent or common sense. The script of *Star Wars* is, by most objective measures, terrible. As Harrison Ford reportedly said to director George Lucas during one scene: 'You can type this sh*t, George, but you sure can't say it!' (Buchanan, 2015). Yet in spite of criticism from Ford and many others, the script became the basis of the most successful film series in history.

So although we are going to talk about some storytelling principles in this chapter, I do want to be absolutely clear about the limits to their use. Storytelling is not a science, it is an art, and it is hard to define why one story is better than another, why one story fails in its own era but works hundreds of years later, or why multiple storytellers can tell an identical story but only one of them becomes a 'classic'. Having said this, there are plenty of great stories, and plenty of great data storytellers, so the lack of an instruction manual should not deter you. What we will cover in this chapter is some habits and techniques that good storytellers have adopted to give themselves the best chance of telling a great story when inspiration strikes.

Everyone has a novel in them

So why is it useful to think of data visualisation as storytelling? There is a huge literature on our tendency to structure experience as narrative, and I have put a longer discussion of the key arguments in Appendix E. You can find this at: www.addtwodigital.com/book

However, the key points are as follows:

- We still have the brains of nomadic hunter-gatherers who are used to quickly collecting information about our permanently changing surroundings.
- This information is not reliable (partly because of our flawed senses, and partly because of the speed at which we need to make effort-allocation decisions); it is simply 'good enough' to keep us alive.
- This flawed but 'good enough' information is shared with the rest of our band or tribe and exists as communal knowledge.
- This information becomes even more fictional over time, as we simplify it to remember it, and simplify it further each time we access it.
- These semi-fictional ideas and memories keep us sane and safe, we are protective of them, and we take in new information more readily that has a 'story-like' shape and structure.

But hang on – this is *data* storytelling, isn't it? The information we are passing on *is* reliable.

Yes, if you did your job properly during the **Find** phase. That is when you question the biases and errors of your storytelling brain and verify that those patterns and trends that you found are for real.

But now the purpose of the exercise has changed. Your audience has asked *you* to carry out the data analysis. Perhaps they didn't have the time or the expertise to do it themselves. Instead they trusted you to carry out the lengthy, painstaking work of data discovery, cleaning and exploration.

What they are asking you is what you found. In hunter-gatherer times, you might have been sent to check out a neighbouring village, but today you have been told to look at a dataset. But the underlying instruction is the same: *tell us what we need to know.*

This turns your credible, comprehensive dataset into something else. They didn't want any bias when you were analysing the numbers, but now they do. They want you to be biased against dullness,

confusion and irrelevance. They want you to be biased towards *them*, tailoring the information to their prior level of knowledge, their areas of interest, the amount of time they have, whether they like all their charts to be bright orange. They don't want you to lie, but they do want information in the same way that humans have always liked information: in small, coherent packages, in an order that makes logical sense, containing material that has obvious relevance, in a style that suits their taste, and in a format that is easy to pass on to others. Telling your audience everything you found is too much like life: messy, random, incomprehensible. What they want is for you to craft it. *Craft* suggests expertise but also *craftiness* – deception – and this is no coincidence, because there are elements of both when you start to package up information for an audience. The degree of craft depends on how fortuitously interesting and well structured the original data is, and the disposition of your audience. But conscious craft is inevitable. You are being asked to translate, to interpret, not to act like the archetypal Englishman abroad, repeating your native language in an increasingly loud voice in the hope that you'll eventually be understood.

For most of our projects, a different team usually takes over at this point. Our wireframes – a wireframe is a simple 2D outline of a graphic or webpage – tend not to be produced by analysts, but by editors, journalists, ex-teachers or digital producers who are accustomed to the compromises that you make when you are talking to an audience that knows less than you. Most analysts find it hard to construct narratives. It is not easy for them to pivot 180° and do the opposite of what they usually do. Don't be comprehensive, be selective. Don't equivocate, be clear. Don't be neutral, be emotional. Don't let the structure of the data determine the story; create a new structure, designed to keep the audience interested.

However, we are aware that many businesses do ask analysts to do exactly this, just as they often ask editors and journalists to become data analysts. This isn't ideal: it's like asking a lumberjack if they'd mind building the wardrobe too, or a farmer if they'd mind doubling up as a chef. But it is possible to do both, as long as you remember they are different jobs requiring a different mindset.

The heart of your story

So let's pick up where we left off, at the end of our **Find** process, with a long list of facts, stats, observations and insights that our audience might find interesting. How on earth do you narrow these down to the most useful and engaging?

I spoke briefly about emotion in the **Find** phase and how it is frequently unappreciated as an analytical tool. In the **Design** stage, emotion becomes even more central. It not only helps you to judge the value of a piece of information, but also gives you the drive to craft a sentence or chart or map that will reproduce that emotion in others.

Think about when you have information to share in your own life. What is it about that fact, that event, that story, that makes you desperate to pass it on?

It isn't just regular information, like what you had for lunch or what you said in a company meeting. It's exceptional, out of the ordinary. In fact, its extraordinary nature would have provoked an emotional response: perhaps fear, excitement, calmness, delight, disgust, surprise.

So here's an example. I was coming home from work and I got on the double-decker bus that takes me from the office to my house. I climbed up to the top deck and sat right at the front, where I always sit. There was no one else on the bus at first, but then a little old lady got on. She could have sat anywhere, but she chose to sit down right next to me. Then she turned round slowly and said: 'You made a mistake getting on this bus.'

Now if this had actually happened (it didn't), I would rush home to my partner and make them sit down while I told them about this bizarre thing that had just happened to me. I would *have* to. I would be compelled to tell this story and I would compel them to listen (they wouldn't be allowed to walk off half-way through). As I rushed home, I would have been playing the incident over and over in my head, removing some parts and emphasising others, not to be misleading, but to ensure my partner got a truthful sense of what it was like to have been there.

If I tell my story well, then something exceptional will happen. The next day at work, my partner will go into their office and tell their colleagues: 'You won't believe what happened to my partner yesterday....' The story will get passed on. My partner's colleagues will pass it on too, and each time, it will get slightly edited to accentuate the emotional truth of the original encounter.

This is the irresistible momentum that good stories have.

So, ideally, this is what you are looking for in your dataset – that novel or surprising or frightening or reassuring piece of information that you *have* to pass on.

Take a look at these (real) data stories below, and think about which ones you respond to most, and the emotions they provoke.

- One in six US women would rather be blind than obese.
- There are more African-American men in the US penal system today than there were slaves before Emancipation.
- There are more men called David heading up UK FTSE-100 companies than there are women in the same position.
- In 1900, there were an estimated 250,000 blue whales in the sea. Now there are fewer than 10,000.
- 44% of Republicans think Bill Gates wants to use Covid-19 vaccines to implant microchips in people.
- In 2019, two-thirds of Americans supported the legalisation of marijuana.
- 10% of Twitter users send 80% of tweets.

- At the end of World War II, 20% of Nazi admirals and 14% of Luftwaffe generals shot themselves.
- 42% of US adults believe that spiritual energy can be located in an object like a crystal.
- The number of British people saying that homosexuality is 'not at all wrong' rose from 11% in 1987 to 69% in 2017.
- Humans get almost half of their daily calories from just three crops: maize, rice and wheat.
- A storm cloud can weigh up to 1 million tonnes.
- To make the tunnels used in the 'great escape' from Stalag Luft III prison camp, the prisoners of war stole 90 bunk beds, 635 mattresses, 62 tables, 76 benches, 1,219 knives, 478 spoons, 3,424 towels and 1,700 blankets.

The sources – and more facts – can be found in the 'Favourite facts' section of https://www.addtwo digital.com/book

I'm sure you found some of these stories more interesting than others. But I selected all of them because when I first encountered them, I felt something. I experienced a jolt of attention that always reminds me of John le Carré's observation: 'The cat sat on the mat is not a story. The cat sat on the dog's mat is a story' (Barber, 1977). It's unexpected, and I want to know more.

Of course sometimes your data doesn't have this, but you still have to present it to an audience somehow. However, even in these circumstances, thinking in terms of stories and the emotions they provoke can be useful. The director Billy Wilder said: 'An actor entering through the door, you've got nothing. An actor entering through the window, you've got a situation' (Brandreth, 2013, p. 121).

Is there a way you can throw your data through the window? And create a situation around it?

For example, rather than saying 'The Bank of England kept interest rates at 0.25% this month',

you could say 'Britain now has the lowest interest rates in Europe.'

Rather than saying 'The world's eight richest people are worth $420 billion', you could say 'The world's eight richest people are worth the same as the poorest 50%.' If you put your data in a situation, then you have to get it out again. Your audience will keep listening.

Finding your rhythm

So, trust your feelings. But is that it?

Certainly, without that emotional hook, there is not much point designing an entire story. An audience has to care about what's going on, or they will quickly switch off.

However, there are plenty of emotionally compelling stories in the world, and not all of them reach a wide audience. It's also vital to structure your story in a way that holds the audience's attention. You need to release information little by little, partly so people can process it more easily, but also because those gaps and unanswered questions provoke curiosity.

A writer of fiction would call this the plot. However, many professions release information in a structured way to maintain audience interest. I have listed a few of them in Figure 4.1 and described the most common plot structures they use. This is a 'lying spectrum' with fiction writers at the bottom (obviously making things up), teachers and scientists at the top (who usually aim to tell the truth) and journalists, lawyers and the like scattered across the middle. The spectrum is based on how trustworthy each profession was judged to be in a recent Ipsos MORI survey.[1]

---

[1]The trustworthiness scores were: scientists 60%, teachers 52%, lawyers 25%, journalists 21%, advertisers 13%, politicians 9%; https://www.ipsos.com/ipsos-mori/en-uk/its-fact-scientists-are-most-trusted-people-world

TRUTH		
	Scientist / researcher	• Introduction • Methods • Results • Discussion • Conclusion • References
	Teacher	• Learning objectives • Intro to new material • Guided practice • Independent practice • Recap See also: cognitive load theory
	Lawyer	• Opening statement • Evidence • Witnesses (primacy and recency tactics) • Closing statement
	Journalist	• Headline • Subhead • Who? What? Where? When? Why? • Supporting information • Additional detail
	Salesperson	• Attention • Interest • Desire • Action
	Politician	• Opening (joke, anecdote, quotation) • Body (rehearsed points, heavy use of rhetoric) • Closing remarks (appeal to action)
FICTION	**Writer / director**	• Set-up • Conflict • Resolution See also: Seven basic plots

Figure 4.1 Story structures

these three story structures can potentially be useful when you are visualising data. They all have the same goal: to keep an audience's cognitive faculties at near capacity (more commonly known as immersion). If an audience is undertaxed, they get bored; if they are overtaxed, they get stressed. Plots help to manage this, and provide a rhythm of tension and release, disruption and resolution that is more likely to deliver 'moderate transient stress', which is what Robert Sapolsky has called every human's optimal state.

I mentioned that when we are creating charts, we borrow from all of these professional plots. It is usually the needs of the client and the purpose of the graphic that determine the plot type we draw on. For example, when we are working with civil servants, a legal approach can be useful. This is because civil servants are often trying to make a case: their department might be requesting extra funds or they might be lobbying for a particular project. Conversely, sometimes we are working with content marketing teams, who are essentially using an infographic to promote their brand. Advertising methods such as AIDA (attention, interest, desire, action) can be helpful in those situations. I would encourage you to draw on any and all of these ways of structuring information: they can all be useful in different circumstances.

However, I would also say we draw on some storytelling techniques more often than others, in particular, teaching, journalism and fiction-writing. This is because our goal is most commonly to educate, to inform and/or to divert. So I'm going to briefly look at these three storytelling structures here and tease out how they might help when you are visualising data.

Three useful story structures

Teaching

Teaching is the most useful model when you are talking to an expert audience, an audience that actively wants to know the information, or an audience that has come to you for 'official' or authoritative information. It is true that lessons are not commonly seen as 'stories' and, perhaps for this reason, people who visualise data from an academic or analytical background are often the most sceptical of 'data storytelling' as an idea. For them, teachers are not in the business of creating plots, story arcs and dramatic tension.

True, teachers are not storytellers in the conventional sense. However, they do often use narratives and anecdotes to illustrate their points and frequently speak in terms of broader stories ('the story of space exploration', 'the story of Earth's formation') to give their lessons a shape and direction. More generally, it seems to me that good teachers have one foot in the performing arts, and the way they structure their lessons bears comparison with the way playwrights and screenwriters time the release of pertinent information in order to keep an audience's interest.

Every teacher will approach this differently. Some may favour Gagné's Nine Levels of Learning, starting with gaining attention and explaining objectives, then guiding pupils through a lesson, and finally providing feedback and assessing performance. Others may be fans of Bloom's taxonomy, moving their students through knowledge, understanding, application, analysis, evaluation and creation (this is hierarchy one; there are two others). Others might follow William Blake's advice, creating their own system, rather than being 'enslaved by another man's'. But what comes across time and time again is that good teachers think in terms of plots and journeys, levels and ladders; they understand that information simply doesn't stick without respecting the human brain's affinity for narrative structure and progression.

Two theories in particular are worth exploring in more depth, because they are especially applicable to data visualisation. These are *cognitive load theory* and Daniel Kahneman and Amos Tversky's concept of *System 1 and System 2 thinking*.

To start with cognitive load theory, this has its roots in the work of Jean Piaget, but was formalised most expertly by John Sweller in a series of books and articles in the 1990s and 2000s. I explore the idea more extensively in Appendix E: www.addtwodigital.com/book.

Here I just want to emphasise its key insights:

- The world constantly bombards us with information. This information is messy, complicated and (usually) irrelevant.
- We have lots of useful, carefully organised information in our brains (known as 'schemas').
- We are protective of this information because, for whatever reason, it has earned its place in our long-term memories and helped us survive this far.
- We are extremely conservative about accepting new information. We need to ensure that important information is not overwritten or dislodged.
- As a result, our working memory imposes strict limits on how much new information it can hold at any one time. Our working memory is the 'gatekeeper' between the world and our precious long-term memories.
- How severe are these limits? Some believe that it's seven pieces of information (the famous 'Rule of Seven'); more recent research suggests that it is as low as three. The point is, it is incredibly low. For most people, even memorising a four-digit PIN requires effort, repetition and often a cognitive hook (like a date of birth) to make it stick. For four digits!
- What this means is that, when you are communicating new information, even your keenest student will be fighting against the strictness and stubbornness of their working memories: *Do I really need to know this? How important is this? Does it deserve a place in my long-term memory?*
- The only way to handle the conservatism of working memory is to respect its way of working.

- This means: (i) not too much new information at once; (ii) make sure each 'chunk' of information is coherent and self-contained; and (iii) make the relevance of each 'chunk' obvious so that it can be slotted alongside (or inside) an existing schema.

If you think about anything that you have successfully learned, whether it's a foreign language, or playing an instrument, or driving a car, it will have been because a kind teacher edited and structured the information in this way. Small amounts, in a logical order, tailored to your existing level of knowledge. (Certainly if every PowerPoint slide abided by these rules, there would be a lot less suffering in the world.)

The second theory I want to look at – System 1 and System 2 thinking – is rooted in the work of Daniel Kahneman and Amos Tversky and is best formulated by Kahneman in his masterly *Thinking, Fast and Slow* (2011). Here I just want to emphasise how well Kahneman and Tversky's work complements the other pedagogical theories outlined above. Like Bloom's taxonomy or cognitive load theory, Kahneman's book implicitly accepts how 'suboptimal' our brains are, how we actively resist difficult or complex information, and how we can only communicate effectively with people by working with or around our cognitive biases. He divides our thought processes into System 1 (quick, instinctive, error-prone thinking) and System 2 (slow, effortful, analytical thinking). System 1 is where we spend most of our time and seems to happen by magic: what is 2 + 2? Spell your surname. What colour is a stop light?

As an example of System 2, Kahneman suggests: what is 17×24?

Try to do the sum now. Seriously, stop reading and try it.

I bet you haven't. Or maybe you tried for a second, felt your brain grinding, and then stopped? And this is Kahneman's key insight. System 2 is *work*: it burns calories, your heart rate increases, your pupils' dilate. You are taken out of your surroundings – which

head and you have to concentrate. Unless there is a compelling reason to do this, we avoid it.

We might get better-quality information by using System 2, but we prefer the lower-quality System 1 stuff because it's easier and besides, in most cases, it's 'good enough'.

17 × 24 is 408, by the way. (And yes, I used a calculator.)

I can imagine Kahneman's work being useful in almost any field but, in data visualisation, it is invaluable. In most cases, you are taking System 2 information (a complex spreadsheet) and turning it into System 1 (a chart). Those endless rows and columns of abstract numbers are transformed into, say, five lines going up and one line going down. Wow! One of the reasons audiences respond so keenly to charts is because you have saved them so much System 2 *work*. They can respond quickly, easily, instinctively.

There's only one catch: you have to use a lot of System 2 thinking to create a chart that works on a System 1 level.

Furthermore, you often have to think about the members of your audience that will want more than just the 'basics', and construct charts that allow both System 1 thinkers to get the 'big picture' and System 2 thinkers to access the detail without their needs obscuring the clarity of your main visual.

There are many other useful insights to be found in both cognitive load theory and Kahneman and Tversky's work. However, what I find most useful about both of them is their unswerving focus on accepting people as they are, empathising with their weaknesses and biases. Everyone takes in new information in a similar way – slowly, haltingly – and everyone is resistant to analytical thought without a clear incentive. Slowing it down, breaking it down, is not dumbing it down; it is what smart teachers do. It is the only way to overcome 'the curse of knowledge': the often crippling cognitive bias that makes experts unable to empathise with novices.

Journalism

Journalistic story structures are also helpful, particularly when you are talking to a mixed audience of experts and non-experts, or a general audience. The best-known formulation of the journalistic 'plot' is the inverted pyramid (Figure 4.2).

The most important sentence in any article is the first one, and it usually contains some or all of the five Ws. For example:

- **Who:** Emmanuel Macron
- **What:** won the election
- **Where:** in France
- **When:** yesterday
- **Why:** by uniting moderates and the left against Marine Le Pen's National Rally party.

The body then gives the reader the critical details about this event, while the final paragraphs provide additional social or political context.

The reason it is called the inverted pyramid is because it takes the standard research pyramid and turns it on its head. An academic paper tends to start with an introduction to the project or topic, followed by a description of the methodology, a detailed account of the research or experiment, an explanation of the results along with any limitations or caveats, and finally after a hundred or so pages, you are told what the author's conclusions are. Smoking is bad for you, exercise is good for you, or whatever it might be.

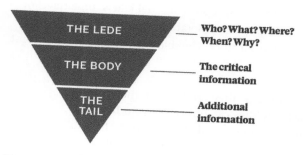

Figure 4.2 The inverted pyramid

Journalism turns this upside down and starts at the end. If you are more used to the world of scientific papers, I urge you to think about journalistic plotting and how effective it is at grabbing and retaining the attention of non-experts. Its message of 'most important information first' is particularly relevant when creating charts, as it encourages you to rank or prioritise the things you want your chart to say, and only then design a visual that makes the recommended read order clear. We will look at some examples of this in action later in this section.

The other element to note in the inverted pyramid is the fifth of the five Ws: *why?* This is the other key difference between research papers and news articles, and the part that our students from a scientific background find the hardest to incorporate in their own stories. Sometimes this is because they work for a government or research organisation and it is not their job to say why, just to present the data without comment. Sometimes it is because they are all too aware of the narrative fallacy, the human propensity to see cause and effect where there is none (see Chapter 3 for more on cognitive biases). However, journalists understand that without a why, or at least a possible why, audiences become frustrated. You have given them half a story, tension without release: 'There was a riot in London', 'The Statue of Liberty just caught fire.' OK, but why? What caused it?

Furthermore, if you don't suggest a why, audiences are likely to make up one of their own, or fall prey to those offering bogus but plausible explanations that accord with their pre-existing beliefs, for example: 'Don't worry about that chart showing record temperature rises; the temperature of the Earth has always gone up and down.'

Fiction

It might seem strange to draw inspiration from fictional plotting when the purpose of data visualisation is to convey factual information. However, as long as you have gone through the **Find** process, and ensured that all your data is credible, then borrowing from fictional plot structures to maintain audience interest is a smart idea, particularly if you are creating a PowerPoint or an animation or a long-format infographic, as these media types tend to be consumed more passively by audiences. They expect more of a 'show', and assume that the author will be thinking about structure and pace and narrative rhythm, because otherwise what is the incentive to get to the end? (Compare this to journalism, where all the key information is front-loaded, and few readers reach the end.)

It's also worth learning from fiction because of how much we love it, how happy it makes us and how our favourite books and films seem to be an integral part of who we are (our favourite news articles and scientific papers, less so). In any given year, the vast majority of the bestselling books and most popular films will be fiction. And when I say fiction, I want to stress how fictional this fiction is. Most of us aren't reading works of sober realism by Tolstoy or Zola: we are consuming stories that could never happen – utterly fantastical confections like Marvel superhero movies or *Lord of the Rings* or *Star Wars* or Harry Potter, books and films set in Tudor or Victorian England, or during the American Civil War, stories full of vampires or dragons, gangsters or serial killers, time travel or deep space exploration.[2] Very rarely does any popular story resemble 'normal life' in the present

[2] I suspect most of us know a surprising amount about vampires: they drink blood, they can't be seen in mirrors, they are repelled by garlic and crucifixes, they can only enter your house if you invite them in, they are killed by a stake through the heart (or sunlight) and so on. In fact, I suspect that most of us know more about this completely non-existent creature than about any one of the 8.7 million actual species that share our planet. *What the hell is wrong with us?*

day, and any student of the reading habits of previous eras (from the Epic of Gilgamesh onwards) will confirm that this has always been the case. When we get home from work, most of us like to read or watch total nonsense and nobody ever stops to ask *why am I doing this*? It's such a universal activity and, on some level, seen as 'good for us'. It starts with the fairy stories of childhood, and evolves from there, growing into a network of favourite books, plays, films and video games that often mean as much to us as our personal relationships.

I have put more information in Appendix E about our affinity for fictional stories: www.addtwodigital.com/book

With data visualisation, although all fictional structures can help to some degree, it is inevitably visual storytellers that have most to teach you: graphic novelists, illustrators and narrative artists (for presentations and infographics) and animators, film directors and video game designers (for motion graphics and interactives). When you compose, say, a static infographic, the way in which you indicate read order and maintain visual interest by balancing consistency and contrast is fundamentally no different from the way a narrative painter would have approached the same task in the eighteenth century (e.g. Hogarth creating *Marriage A-la-Mode* (1743–5)). Or, come to that, the way a graphic novelist would have taken on the same challenge in the twenty-first century (e.g. Alison Bechdel creating *Fun Home* in 2006).

We don't have space to look at these interrelationships in detail, but we've put more on the key techniques in the next chapter. The main point to stress is that if your job involves data visualisation, then you are fully entitled to read comics in company time and call it research.[3]

What does this look like in practice? Obviously you can't always crowbar 'the hero's journey' or a Hollywood three-act structure into a PowerPoint about sales figures. However, being aware of the rhythms of fictional stories and how they can artificially build and dissipate tension can make your audiences more responsive to your message. I've put a few of the classic story structures in Figure 4.3 – loosely based on Christopher Booker's *Seven Basic Plots* – and tried to show how they might be applied when you are telling data stories in a business context.

In your organisation, you will be vaguely aware that you tell similar stories again and again. What we always suggest is thinking more systematically about your company's main 'plots' and defining optimal ways of telling these stories. You might already do this for some of your more high-profile outputs (e.g. pitch presentations, annual reports), but a more thorough audit of your own 'seven basic plots' can stop you reinventing the wheel each time you create a new report or presentation and can also lead to greater consistency across different product types. Of course, you shouldn't stick to these templates too rigidly – that is creative death – but they are sometimes a more fruitful starting point than a blank screen.

Even if you just think about your *most* common plot – define the gold, define the dragon – this can provide a useful focus for presenters.

Select, dramatise, emphasise, present

Some of these story structures will be more useful to you than others, depending on who you are,

---

[3]Especially if the comic is by Randall Munroe. If you don't know it, check out xkcd – as well as brilliant comic strips, there are some excellent charts too. Also try Darryl Cunningham, who writes superb graphic explainers of complex subjects (like the 2008 financial crisis). The most useful writer on the theory of comics is Scott McCloud, whose *Understanding Comics* is an invaluable reference work for any visual storyteller.

Plot type	Summary	Examples	Business example
Overcoming the monster	A monster threatens the equilibrium of a community. A hero agrees to take on the monster and there is some kind of training or apprenticeship. The monster often wins the first few battles, and the hero comes close to death. But the monster is finally killed and the hero gets some kind of reward (love, money, power or all three).	*Jack and the Beanstalk* *Beowulf* *Jaws* *Dracula*	Company X moved into our sector last year and our profits dropped by 50%. So this year, we came up with a three-point strategy to restore our market share. After trialling this in China and India in Q1, we rolled it out globally in Q3 and Q4. Our market share is now back to 20% and it is predicted to increase to 22% next year. Meanwhile, Company X has announced store closures in at least six markets.
Voyage and return	A hero goes to a strange land. After an initial period of disorientation, they learn how to fit in and earn the respect of the people living there. At this point, they are allowed to go home. On returning, they realise they have learnt an important lesson about their own lives or home countries.	*Alice in Wonderland* *The Wizard of Oz* *Gulliver's Travels* *The Time Machine*	As part of our plan to enter the shampoo market, we carried out a huge research exercise in 24 markets. The results surprised us all. You probably picture the typical shampoo consumer as female, fashion-conscious, in her 20s or 30s. You're twenty years out of date! Instead we found that, in most markets, men are just as likely to be the main shampoo purchaser. The average shampoo buyer is now 47. These insights should change our product in the following ways...
Rags to riches	A child from a poor background, often with an evil parent or step-parent, overcomes a series of challenges to gain immense wealth. After their initial success, there is usually a temptation of some kind, but their moral qualities prevail and they end the story with a deeper understanding of how money alone can't guarantee happiness.	*Cinderella* *Aladdin* *Great Expectations* *Slumdog Millionaire*	Ben and Cindy Baxter made their first search engine in their garage in London in 1994. Although US corporation BadCorp offered them $10 million for their algorithm, they decided to stay independent, and kept their home offices in London. By 2000, they had 3,500 employees, but refused to pay themselves more than five times the salary of their lowest paid staff member. By 2010, their ethical search engine had become the most popular in the world. The company has been transformed in the last 25 years, but its values haven't changed since 1994.

Figure 4.3   Story structures in a business context

the stories you tell most frequently, and the audiences you tend to address. However, I'd like to emphasise what all of these different storytellers have in common, regardless of whether they are creating a screenplay, a sermon, a stand-up comedy show or something else. The process of turning random, unstructured events into a coherent, absorbing narrative involves going through the same fundamental stages every time. Turning a dataset into a series of charts is no different. The stages are as follows:

- **Selection**: identify the most emotionally resonant information and remove everything else.
- **Dramatisation**: build this information up, put it in context, create a world around it.
- **Emphasis**: structure the information into a logical, meaningful order with a clear narrative arc (i.e. your plot).
- **Presentation**: help your audience to 'get' this information using the clearest language and/or the most engaging visuals.

If you look at any successful example of data visualisation, you will notice that the designer has moved through these stages. I doubt they will have been conscious of it – most designers work instinctively – but they wouldn't have been able to create a successful piece of work without going through a version of this process.

When Sea Levels Attack!

Here is an example from David McCandless: 'When Sea Levels Attack!' (Figure 4.4). This was first published in McCandless's book, *Information is Beautiful* (2009), before being adapted by him for the *Guardian*'s Datablog in 2010. This version (number 3) is from 2014. It has featured regularly in infographic anthologies and is, in my view, a brilliantly executed piece of work.

Let's look at how McCandless moves through each of the storytelling stages mentioned above.

First, selection:

- He finds a dataset which provokes a clear emotional response (alarm, disbelief, anger) and which is relevant to his audience (climate change affects us all).
- He doesn't try to visualise the whole dataset (every town and city in every country), instead he selects 12 cities which his audience will have the closest connection with and deletes all of the others.
- He starts with cities (Venice, Amsterdam) that are famous for being close to sea level.
- For the two cities where many of his readers will be based (London and New York), he represents them twice. We have bars for London *and* South London, and bars for New York *and* Lower Manhattan.

Then, dramatisation:

- He adds contextual data to bring his story to life. As well as showing metres, he adds 'years' to his y-axis, giving his readers a very real sense of 'how long they have left' given current trends. For example, Venice has less than a century.
- He adds three small maps, showing what the whole world will look like in 80, 800 and 8,000 years.
- He also includes data on what is causing the sea-level rises (melting ice caps in the Arctic, Greenland and Antarctica).

Next, emphasis:

- Having assembled all of this information, McCandless now makes the read order clear.
- The title ('When Sea Levels Attack!') sets the scene, and then we are immediately drawn to the bar chart. Thanks to the clarity of the title and the overall design, we understand that we are looking at how different cities will cope with rising sea levels. We get the most important information at a glance.
- If we want further information, our eyes move left to the y-axis, where we also get an answer to the graphic's subtitle ('How long have we got?').
- If we are still interested, additional context is provided on the far right: longer-term trends and causes.

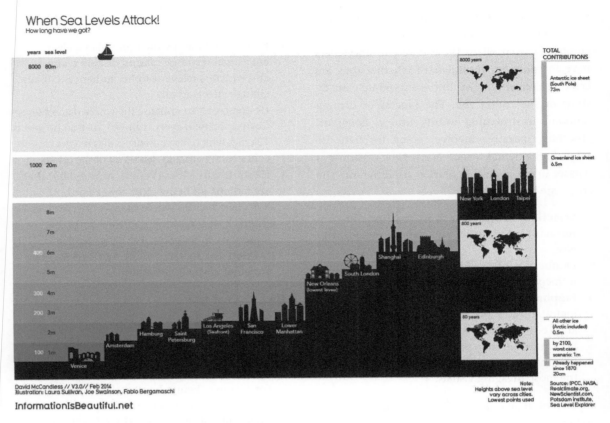

When Sea Levels Attack!
How long have we got?

Figure 4.4 When Sea Levels Attack, by David McCandless

- Credits and sources are at the bottom in a small point size, not intruding on the main graphic.
- This moves us through the story an intuitive way. It follows the classic journalistic template (Who? What? Where? When? Why?) but it is all rendered visually.

Finally, presentation:

- McCandless adds visual elements that make the human stories behind his bar chart more obvious.
- The tops of the bars are decorated with cityscapes. This makes the chart harder to read (are we measuring the top of the bar or the building?), but it helps us to see what those bars represent. They are metaphors for living cities, where millions of people live and work, and they could soon be underwater.

- There are horizontal strips of blue representing differing levels of inundation. This turns our chart into Atlantis, a drowned world worthy of J. G. Ballard. Even the boat at the top of the chart adds drama, suggesting a last few survivors floating above these lost civilisations.
- The *y*-axis has been broken in two places, at 600 and 1,000 metres. On one level, this is deceptive because it makes it look as if London, New York and Taipei will flood shortly after Shanghai and Edinburgh, when they won't. But on another, if the *y*-axis had been on an unbroken linear scale, it would have looked as if the story was about how safe London, New York and Taipei are. By using a broken *y*-axis, McCandless keeps us focused on all of these cities, how they are all at risk, and how the differences between them are negligible,

particularly once climate tipping points are reached. The fact that he doesn't have gaps between his bars (they are all in a single block) further underlines this message of interconnectedness and a shared destiny. They are all sitting on the same lump of space rock. At the same time, the bars become a series of steps – one leading to the next – and I always imagine refugees from one city seeking higher ground in the next city along. In this way, the emotions provoked by the original dataset – alarm, shock, a sense of urgency – are kept front and centre at all times. The kinds of nuances you would get in a more scientific chart – confidence intervals, an unbroken *y*-axis, technical language – are removed, because for a non-expert audience, these details are often counter-productive, suggesting that things aren't as bad as they seem (*there are a range of estimates; scientists don't really know for sure; some cities will be fine; there's still time to fix it*).

The True Size of Africa

Here is another example: 'The True Size of Africa' by Kai Krause (Figure 4.5).

Krause originally programmed synthesizers in the 1970s before becoming a successful interface designer (most data viz designers seem to have backstories like this). In 2010, he published this fantastic myth-busting map, created – in his words – to make 'a small contribution in the fight against rampant Immappancy'.

Let us look at why Krause's work is so effective.

First, selection:

- Krause's original dataset was a table showing the land area of every country in the world. But to make his point, he selected just a handful of these.
- The two biggest countries in the world – Russia and Canada – are not shown, because this would defeat his purpose. (Between them, Russia and Canada are almost the size of Africa – 27 million km².) In fact, he seems to choose countries for two reasons. Firstly,

population. The three countries with the highest populations (China, India and the United States) are all shown. This is smart, because it conflates our two measures for the 'size' of a country – land area and number of people. It makes us think: 'Wow, you could fit the whole of India – and its 1.4 billion people – into the Horn of Africa.' His second motivation appears to be audience. His chart is in English, most of his audience will be in Europe (so the whole of Europe is shown) or the United States (so the USA is shown) and they will have a Westerner's sense of the 'rest of the world' (so Japan is shown above Malaysia or Indonesia, for example). It is all perfectly judged.

Then, dramatisation:

- The title says it all: 'The True Size of Africa'. Krause turns this into a crusade, an attempt to correct 'inefficient geographical knowledge'.
- As well as the central map, he includes a table (top left) which makes the same point with slightly different countries.
- He adds further context, explaining his motives for making the graphic, referring to a survey of US schoolchildren which showed that they believed the USA was the largest country in the world.
- He also adds a table showing the top 100 countries by land area and 'small multiple' maps, showing Europe, the USA, India, China and Japan individually. So more data-literate readers are catered for too.

Next, emphasis:

- The read order could not be clearer. The Africa map dominates the page. After this, our eyes move left to the table and the contextual explanation. If we are still interested, we move to the right-hand margin, where there is additional information: the table – in a smaller point size – and the 'small multiple' maps. Its control of focal areas recalls narrative painting: there is such a clear beginning, middle and end.

The True Size of Africa

A small contribution in the fight against rampant *Immappancy*, by Kai Krause

Graphic layout for visualization only (some countries are cut and rotated)
But the conclusions are very accurate: refer to table below for exact data

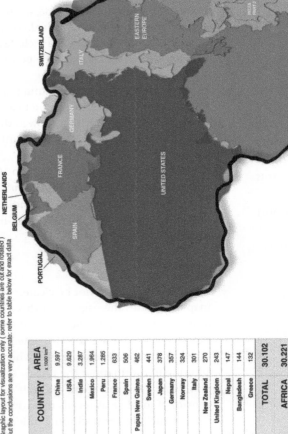

COUNTRY	AREA x 1000 km²
China	9.597
USA	9.629
India	3.287
Mexico	1.964
Peru	1.285
France	633
Spain	506
Papua New Guinea	462
Sweden	441
Japan	378
Germany	357
Norway	324
Italy	301
New Zealand	270
United Kingdom	243
Nepal	147
Bangladesh	144
Greece	132
TOTAL	**30.102**
AFRICA	**30.221**

In addition to the well known social issues of *illiteracy* and *innumeracy*, there also should be such a concept as "*immappancy*", meaning *insufficient geographical knowledge*.

A survey with random American schoolkids let them guess the population and land area of their country. Not entirely unexpected, but still rather unsettling, the majority chose "*1-2 billion*" and "*largest in the world*", respectively.

Even with Asian and European college students, geographical estimates were often off by factors of 2-3. This is partly due to the highly distorted nature of the predominantly used mapping projections (such as *Mercator*).

A particularly extreme example is the worldwide misjudgement of the true size of Africa. This single image tries to embody the massive scale, which is larger than the *USA, China, India, Japan and all of Europe......combined!*

Top 100 Countries

Area in square kilometres. Percentage of World Total
Sources: Britannica, Wikipedia, Almanac 2010

Figure 4.5 The True Size of Africa, by Kai Krause

Presentation

- The colours for the different countries are clearly differentiated. Krause reduces their opacity, so that they can overlap and still retain distinguishable borders.
- He rotates and positions countries so they are as recognisable as possible. For example, the UK includes Ireland – a completely different country – because the 'British Isles' are a more recognisable silhouette than Great Britain and Northern Ireland alone. He edits others so that they fit more snugly, chopping China in two and removing Alaska from the United States.
- He also uses the best-known map projection: the Mercator. This is arguably the least accurate map projection, and indeed Krause criticises it in his 'immapancy' rant. It is one of the main reasons why people misjudge the size of Africa: because this projection stretches the size of countries that are close to the poles and squashes countries that are nearer the equator. On a Mercator map, South America looks about the same size as Greenland, when it is over eight times larger. However, if Krause had used a Gall–Peters projection, for example, which is more accurate, the country outlines would have been less recognisable, and instead of focusing on his message, readers might have been distracted by the fact that all of the outlines looked (to them) distorted or poorly executed. For example, I want you to picture a map of Africa in your head, and then look at the map projections in Figure 4.6. Which one is closest to the shape of the continent that you imagined? When we ask our students this question, it's the Mercator – every time. So Krause had to use a map projection he disliked, because he wanted his work to be accessible to all, which meant accepting his audience's current (flawed) level of knowledge. These kinds of painful compromises will be familiar to any data viz designer.[4]

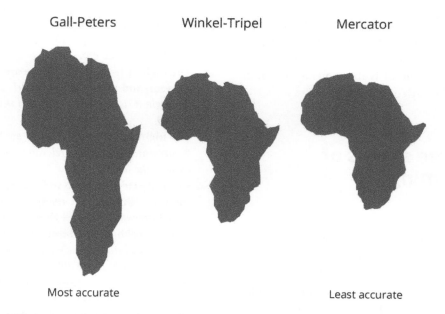

Figure 4.6 Different projections of Africa

---

[4]For a contrasting point of view, Kenneth Field has written a blog on how Krause's use of the Mercator projection is in fact unjustifiable: http://cartonerd.blogspot.com/2011/09/

- Where there is no need for a visual, Krause does not include one. His explanation of 'immapancy' is text; his list of the top 100 countries by land area is just a table. There is no need to include a map or chart unless they can justify the space they take up.

These are just two examples, but I've put some other best practice graphics here: https://bit.ly/data-viz-best-practice. They all approach the task of selecting, dramatising, structuring and presenting their stories in the same way.

Let's explore the practicalities now. How do you create work like this? What specifically is involved at each stage? Tobias will be discussing the presentation part in the next chapter; I am going to focus on how to select, dramatise and structure the elements of your story. This involves sketching and wireframing, usually with pencil and paper. I will be discussing static stories here; interactive story-telling will be covered in Chapters 6–10.

I should also re-emphasise: we call this design process wireframing, a term borrowed from interface design, even if we are making a static graphic. You may prefer to use a different term, but we'd suggest that the output is the same: a simple, 2D skeleton of the key content.

The three stages of wireframing

Selection

At the end of the **Find** stage, as I outlined in Chapter 3, you will have amassed a series of sentences and data tables, tailored for a particular audience, as well as a number of half-formed ideas and scribbles. In the **Design** stage, it is time to focus and prioritise. The most forensic researchers can still finish up with far too many stories at the end of the **Find** stage, even if they are continually aware of their eventual audience and any time, cost and software limitations.

Furthermore, it is easy to underestimate how much time and space you will need to tell even *one* of the stories you found. It's much better to be too selective – and then add more. Finishing a story and then being told to lose half of it is painful – and it's often easier to just start again.

For example, let us return to the baby names data we used in Chapter 3. I'm going to imagine that I am preparing a short PowerPoint presentation for a business. This time, the business will be selling bowls with babies' names on them, rather than just their initials. At the end of the **Find** stage, I have found a multitude of stories, and my first job is to select the most relevant. Or, to put it another way, to delete most of what I just found. For example, here is page 1 of my notebook at the end of the selection process.

- The total market in 2018 is 657,076 babies: 51% male and 49% female.
- These are the most popular boys' names: Oliver, George, Harry, Noah etc.
- These are the most popular girls' names: Olivia, Amelia, Ava, Isla etc.
- ~~The highest rising boys' names are Hunter, Grayson and Ezra.~~ *Not particularly relevant, as the highest riser – Hunter – is still not in the top 40.*
- ~~The highest rising girls' names are Summer, Bonnie and Hallie.~~ *Not relevant, none of them are close to the top 40.*
- ~~Celebrity culture seems to influence girls' names, with Charlotte rising after Princess Charlotte was born and Harper rising after Harper Beckham was born.~~ *Probably not relevant, as some celebrities cause names to become popular and some don't. Impossible to predict trends.*
- ~~There is a return of old-fashioned names like George and Edward (for boys) and Grace and Ivy (for girls).~~ *Probably not relevant, as many old-fashioned names haven't come back, and the company are likely to be more interested in which names are popular, rather than why.*
- The top three girls' names are pretty consistent across all regions. However, for boys,

Mohammed is the top name in four regions and not in the top 10 for the other six regions.
- ~~Oliver and Olivia have consistently been in the top three for over a decade~~. *Not relevant, unless it can be tied to a wider story of 'stable' v. 'unstable' names.*
- ~~Baby boomer names like Keith, Trevor, Brian (for boys) and Susan, Linda, Patricia (for girls) have completely vanished (fewer than 20 babies)~~. *They will not be interested in unpopular names – unless they were popular recently.*

Once I had gone through this editorial process, always keeping in mind the time and space I have been given to tell the story, I would be left with a core group of key stories. For a baby names business, it might be something like this:

- The total market in 2018 is 657,076 babies: 51% male and 49% female.
- These are the most popular boys' names: Oliver, George, Harry, Noah etc.
- These are the most popular girls' names: Olivia, Amelia, Ava, Isla etc.
- These boys' names are outside the top 20 but will probably enter it next year: Theo, Isaac, Theodore.
- These girls' names are outside the top 20 but will probably enter it next year: Emilia, Mila, Ada.
- These names are likely to drop out of the top 20: Alfie, Joshua (for boys); Jessica, Daisy (for girls).
- The top three girls' names are pretty consistent across all regions. However, for boys, Mohammed is the top name in four regions but not in the top 10 for the other six regions.

I have tried to put myself in my audience's shoes and focus on the stories that will provoke the clearest emotional response: *this is important, this is surprising, I need to know more about this.*

Dramatisation

Next, we need to dramatise. For example, let us look at our first finding:

- The total market in 2018 is 657,076 babies: 51% male and 49% female.

The next question for any business person is going to be: has my potential market grown or shrunk since last year? And what about before that? So I will need to find baby names data for perhaps the last decade to give them a sense of whether they even have a sustainable business. If the birth rate is rising or dropping sharply, it will affect every other part of my story.

So I find out that the birth rate has been dropping (3% since the previous year, 9% since a decade ago), but not enough to affect the company's direction. I add this context to my first story.

Is that enough? I'd argue we need to add more. Because telling a business that 657,076 babies have been born this year (a drop of 3%) only tells them what their potential market is. Is their target 100% of this market? Unlikely for any business, but particularly a business like this one, given that 7% of girls and 6% of boys have unique names, not shared by any other babies. For the sake of this exercise, I'm going to assume that this business is realistic and wants to target only 20% of the available market and that its products are equally popular with boys and girls. So ultimately the figures to share with them will be total market (657,076) and target market (65,707 boys and 65,707 girls). (I'm rounding down to 'whole' babies). This gives you the spine for the rest of your story too.

Notice that we can only build up and dramatise our story because we have forced ourselves to be selective. This gives us the space to add context.

Let us look at the next part of our story.

- These are the most popular boys' names: Oliver, George, Harry, Noah etc.
- These are the most popular girls' names: Olivia, Amelia, Ava, Isla etc.

This is a little flat at the moment. But remember – we know what this business is targeting 20% of the market. So this is how we could frame our top boys' and girls' names: These 18 names represent 20% of the boys' market. These 29 names represent 20% of the girls' market. This also lets them know that girls' names are more diverse, and they will need to create a wider range of bowls to get the same market share.

You would work through all of your stories in this way, making it dramatic for your audience by thinking about what this data signifies for them.

Emphasis

The next stage is emphasis or plotting, putting the information in an order that makes logical sense.

There are various ways to approach sketching or wireframing your information, depending on what you are making. For an infographic, I use a sketchbook before working it up in Illustrator; for a report or article, a combination of a sketchbook and a word-processing tool like Google Docs. Because in this example we're making a PowerPoint, I'll be using paper sticky notes because this forces you to break up your stories and keep them concise. You can then easily move around your paper sticky notes as you work out the most intuitive beginning, middle and end. But you need to choose tools that suit you best: whatever stops you from just dumping the output of the **Find** stage directly into a presentation.

On each Post-it note, I'd be adding the slide title, the key data and usually a rough sketch indicating the kind of chart that might work. This should not be too prescriptive; what you're trying to show the designer (even if this is also you) is which information is best conveyed by the presenter speaking, which by text on the slide, and which by a visual of some kind. I have put more about these essential tools of the trade (speech, text and visuals) in Appendix E (www.addtwodigital.com/book). What you are trying to work out in your wireframe is how these three media can best complement each other.

If a visual is required, then you will also be sketching the type of visual metaphor that might suit this dataset and this audience best. Tobias will be covering visual metaphors in the next chapter too, because designers will tend to extend these metaphors across whole reports or presentations. But designers take their cues from the wireframe, so it's good to think about metaphors as early as possible.

For example, let us take the first story we've selected for the baby names company.

- 657,076 babies were born this year, 3% less than the previous year, and 9% less than a decade ago.

We have data for the last 10 years to make this point.

The first question is: should we visualise this? After all, we could just keep the information as a sentence. However, it's a pretty dull sentence: it leaves out 2010 to 2016 and the degree of change is hard to picture.

Our second option is to present the numbers for 2009–18 in a clear, neat table. This approach works for the music charts, football league tables, and bus and train timetables. Leaving the data in (essentially) a spreadsheet has not stopped these charts from reaching wide audiences. (In fact, I suspect that visualising the Premier League – covering it with bars and bubbles – would lead to riots.) However, tables work best in very specific circumstances, in particular when readers need to find one datapoint quickly ('When's my train leaving? Where's my football team?') and where they need a sense of having direct access to objective data, with little 'spin' or framing. When readers need to actively compare different values in a table, or when they need help understanding the magnitude of these differences, then visuals become much more useful. I'd argue that my baby names company falls into this latter category.

So let's visualise. But which kind of visual? We are trying to convey how many babies were born this year, and how this number has changed. This sounds like a change-over-time story. The simplest metaphor for this would be a line moving left to right across the page. But line charts suggest continuous, constant change – and here we want to compare this year to previous years. We also want to convey that this is the numbers of babies born in this self-contained year, so a shape enclosing this number (657,076 for 2018 versus 679,106 for 2017) would work better as a metaphor than a continuous line or a dot on a floating line.

But which shape? Circles are popular, as we discussed in Chapter 2, but they are hard to compare with each other, and this is a business audience, who will almost certainly want charts that can be accurately compared. Side-by-side circles can work better when there are big differences between datapoints, but that is not the case here. More fundamentally, side-by-side circles are not an intuitive metaphor for the passing of time – they are such distinct, closed-off shapes, perfect when you want to compare different countries or categories – but rarely the right answer when you are talking about months or years.

This leaves us with a standard bar chart, which would allow us to show all ten of the previous years separately, but also (if we wanted) to highlight and compare the most recent year with the year before. So the next question is: should these bars be horizontal or vertical?

Horizontal bars are often the default in 16:9 PowerPoint, because you have a lot more horizontal space than vertical, particularly when you allow for titles, subtitles and mandatory brand detritus at the top and bottom of each slide. Vertical bars can seem squashed when they are dropped into the letterbox content area in the middle of a standard corporate slide, and the main thing in their favour (the drama as they defy gravity to soar into the sky, getting more precarious as they grow taller) is often lost if all the bars look like tree stumps. Another upside of using horizontal bars in PowerPoint is that the labels are easier to read, particularly if you have long labels, and particularly if they all have to

be a minimum of 24-point which is a common requirement in many style guides.

However, in spite of all these positives, a horizontal bar would be entirely the wrong metaphor here. Horizontal bars suggest a race across the screen, progress towards an end point. They are often arranged largest to smallest to emphasise this sense of rivalry between the bars. What they don't suggest is change over time. We scan them like rows of a table, reading top to bottom, and time metaphors (in the West, at least) are left to right.

So it is looking like vertical bars. They are separate shapes – and that suggests different years – but, unlike horizontal bars, the fact that they are rooted to the 'ground', side by side, suggests a kinship, like buildings in a city, or wooden posts in a fence, or even people standing shoulder to shoulder. That is what we want here – a balance between separateness and interconnectedness.

We also want our audience to have an immediate sense of one year having more or fewer babies than another. On a metaphorical level, we think of 'more' as up and 'less' as down, rather than 'more' as right and 'less' as left. The clue is in our likely slide title: the birth rate has *gone down* or *fallen* or *declined*. The position in vertical space metaphor will be used to characterise the number of babies that year. If the birth rate had gone sideways, it would have a very different meaning. (I have put more about how metaphors structure almost all of our thoughts in Appendix E – visit www.addtwodigital.com/book.)

One other advantage of using vertical bars is that it is easier to compare the tops of vertical bars than to compare the ends of horizontal bars (Munzner, 2014, p. 118). We also see differences in height as more *important* than differences in length, and for a baby names company, those taller bars are indeed more important.

One other option here could have been turning these bars into isotype charts. This is when you replace a bar with a repeated icon so, for example, 650,000 babies would be represented by 65 or 6.5 small baby icons. But isotype charts work better horizontally (which we've already dismissed as a metaphor for comparing individual years over time). In addition, they tend to be used to communicate to the wider public, rather than to a business that wouldn't need to be reminded that the number 650,000 represents 650,000 babies.

As Figure 4.7 shows, it's a good idea to sketch all of the available options because sometimes it is not clear, until you see it, what the most appropriate metaphor is. Not only do different shapes suggest particular stories, but the shape of those shapes (a jagged line versus a straight one, a tall rectangle next to a short one) convey distinct emotions, and only by sketching can you become aware of all these connotations.

A single straight flat line can be reassuring ('unemployment has remained at record lows') or alarming (on a heart monitor). Equally, you can have a shape that looks alarming – a company's stock rising and falling – but which you know is completely ordinary. So sometimes you need to be aware of context: which shapes your audience expect. And sometimes you need to adjust chart scales or add comparators so that people understand that an alarming-looking shape is ordinary and vice versa.

You would work through the 'plot' of each slide in this way, deciding on the right text and visuals for your story. Sometimes a single metaphor can sustain a whole presentation; sometimes the metaphors need to shift. For example, in our baby names presentation, after we have talked about the 650,000 babies born this year, we would go on to discuss the fact that the company wanted to

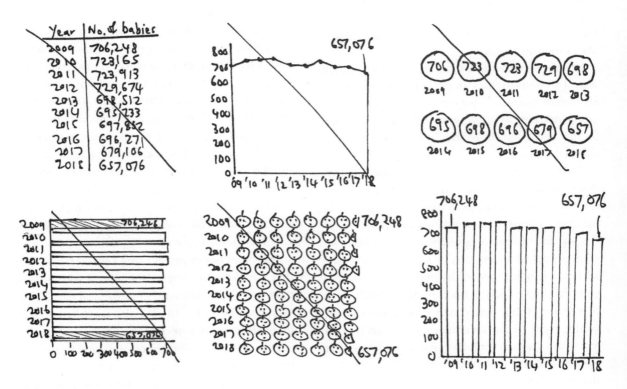

Figure 4.7 Keep sketching till it works

target 20% of this market. Vertical bars would not work for this next slide. When we want to suggest a world or a market or any self-contained population, the most intuitive metaphor is a circle. If we want to convey a business's 'slice' of a market, then pie charts and doughnut charts are one obvious solution. But it wouldn't have to be pies; it could be a different shape, provided there was a clear visual break from the previous slide. That was about *change over time*, this is about *composition* at a single point in time. The shapes should make this distinction clear at a glance.

Metaphorically speaking

Getting into the habit of thinking of charts as visual metaphors is perhaps the single most important part of the **Design** stage – and arguably the **Make** stage too. Charts only exist because, at some point, someone thought 'This group of numbers would be more understandable if I turned it into this shape.' The choice of which shape to use is often deep-rooted in our biology – circles look friendlier than squares, or going up is (usually) good, going down is bad. Sometimes there is a clear link to something in nature (a family tree, an alluvial flow) or the built world (a pyramid chart, a funnel chart), but often it is harder to articulate why one group of shapes feels like a good fit for a story and another feels wrong.

The key thing to remember is this: the closer your visual metaphor is to the story in your data, the more accessible it will be. A row of ten bananas labelled January, above a row of nine bananas labelled February, with a key indicating that each banana represents 1,000 bananas being sold, is so clearly a metaphor for banana sales over time that you'd barely need to give it a title. When William Playfair first invented the bar chart, he made a similar point:

Suppose the money received by a man in trade were all in guineas, and that every evening he made a single pile of all the guineas received during the day, each pile would represent a day, and its height would be proportioned to the receipts of that day; so that by this plain operation, time, proportion and amount, would all be physically combined. (Playfair, 2005, xi)

His new invention – the bar chart – is a scaled-down outline of those stacks of coins on a table.

The only caveat to make is that sometimes accessibility is not your top priority. For example, as I sketched my baby names wireframe, I assumed a no-nonsense business audience who prefer simple charts, with each chart making a single clear point. However, let us imagine that the business is owned by an ex-market researcher who prefers charts that deliver 'the greatest number of ideas in the shortest time with the least ink in the smallest space' (Tufte, 2001, p. 51). Just as advanced readers of novels prefer more sophisticated metaphors, so advanced readers of charts can cope with shapes having multiple meanings. Edward Tufte, for example, celebrated the moment when William Playfair moved away from bar charts and line charts, and started to visualise multi-dimensional data. He 'broke free of analogies to the physical world and drew graphics as designs-in-themselves' (p. 44). This ultimately led to 'the greatest of all graphical designs … the scatterplot and all its variants' (pp. 46–7). If you were presenting to an extremely data-literate businessperson, you might also want to consider a chart that is a 'design-in-itself' like a scatter chart or a Marimekko chart or another analytical chart where the shapes are able to represent three or more dimensions of the data, and therefore by definition cannot act as a clear visual metaphor for any one of them. They are to be *studied* – like a literature student poring over the symbols in *The Waste Land* or a film student scrutinising an Ingmar Bergman movie – rather than simply read.

However, what I would say is that, even in these situations, where your audience has a higher tolerance for charts that superimpose multiple meanings onto a single shape, it is still a good idea to either build the chart gradually across several slides or isolate the most relevant parts of it. For example, let's say that during the **Find** stage, you assembled a five-dimensional scatter chart, where each shape represented a child's name; its position on the x-axis was its count; its position on the y-axis was percentage change since the previous year; its colour was gender; its shape type was name origin (Biblical, royal, celebrity, etc.); and its fill type was whether it ended with an 'A'. Wow! A density of symbolism worthy of Rimbaud or Verlaine. However, if you decide that your data-literate audience would find this useful, it might still be worth starting simply, as Figure 4.8 shows, with just one of these stories, before moving through the extra dimensions in successive slides, so that you can explain to your audience what the more complicated encodings add to the story, and so that each stage can be annotated with your principal insights.[5] In other words, even when presenting to analysts, a wireframe is sensible, because it forces you to verify that each of those extra dimensions does indeed add depth to your story, and isn't you overlaying variables just because you can. (If it works, you might find that you can use a single chart – deconstructing and then reconstructing it – for your whole presentation.)

Another thing to remember when presenting to more expert audiences is that they can find simple, accessible metaphors either boring or suspicious. Boring because there just isn't enough going on, or suspicious because they are wondering what you have left out. It is always a good idea to build up a comprehensive appendix of more detailed charts when presenting to experts. These are usually the charts you will have made anyway when isolating your story, so it is often just a question of dropping (tidied-up) versions of these more analytical charts into the back of the presentation or report in case more detail is requested. For example, in the baby names presentation, perhaps one of your stories was showing that the average age of mothers in the UK has been increasing. Even for an expert audience, you would probably start by showing this simple story on a line chart. However, you might then be asked to show the distribution of data around that average: how closely do most mothers cluster around the median? In the **Find** stage, you might well have charted this – perhaps on a box plot or (for even more detail) on a violin plot. Or, at the very least, you will have the information in a table. If you keep these tables and charts in your appendix, you can jump to them if a statistical arms race breaks out among your learned audience ('I need more detail!', 'Well, I need even *more* detail!'), but leave them out of sight if nobody interrupts your story.

For now, I'm going to return to my original assumption, which is that I'm presenting to a business audience that prefers simple and accessible charts. So I would work through my baby names wireframe with this in mind, always trying to tell the story in the clearest way – moving my audience from speech to text to visuals and back again, using the most appropriate visual metaphors for each section of my story. Then I would work out how each of these slides should fit together, to ensure that there was a logical connection between them.

Finished wireframes

I have put the first eight slides of my wireframe for the baby name company in Figure 4.9. This would have begun life as a poorly-drawn sketch

---

[5] As a general rule, I would say that making a multi-dimensional chart is a bit like jazz: it's more fun for the person making it than for the people watching.

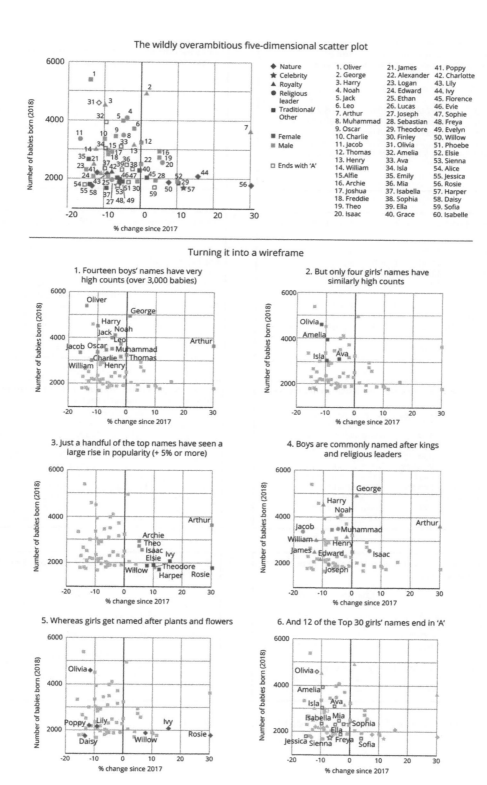

Figure 4.8 Walking your audience through a more complex chart

1.

657,076 babies were born in England and Wales in 2018, a drop of 3% since last year.

[This data in column chart]

2009	706248	2014	695,233
2010	723165	2015	697,852
2011	723913	2016	696,271
2012	729674	2017	679,106
2013	698,512	**2018**	**657,076**

2.

Let's assume you want 20% of this market. What are the best ways of getting it?

65,707 boys   65,707 girls

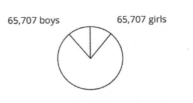

3.

These 18 names represent 20% of the boys' market.

OLIVER	5,390	JACOB	3,350
GEORGE	4,960	THOMAS	3,243
HARRY	4,512	HENRY	3,172
NOAH	4,107	WILLIAM	3,015
JACK	3,988	ALFIE	2,977
LEO	3,721	ARCHIE	2,950
ARTHUR	3,644	JOSHUA	2,922
MUHAMMAD	3,507	FREDDIE	2,838
OSCAR	3,459		
CHARLIE	3,365		

4.

These 29 names represent 20% of the girls' market.

OLIVIA	4,598	POPPY	2,226	PHOEBE	1,883
AMELIA	3,941	CHARLOTTE	2,202	ELSIE	1,875
AVA	3,110	LILY	2,184	SIENNA	1,834
ISLA	3,046	IVY	2,104	ALICE	1,827
EMILY	2,676	FLORENCE	2,062	JESSICA	1,812
MIA	2,490	EVIE	2,052	ROSIE	1,808
ISABELLA	2,369	SOPHIE	2,007	HARPER	1,796
SOPHIA	2,344	FREYA	1,921	DAISY	1,769
ELLA	2,326	EVELYN	1,902	SOFIA	1,728
GRACE	2,301	WILLOW	1,900		

5.

For girls' names, you can use a single distribution strategy.

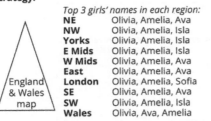

Top 3 girls' names in each region:

NE	Olivia, Amelia, Ava
NW	Olivia, Amelia, Isla
Yorks	Olivia, Amelia, Isla
E Mids	Olivia, Amelia, Isla
W Mids	Olivia, Amelia, Ava
East	Olivia, Amelia, Ava
London	Olivia, Amelia, Sofia
SE	Olivia, Amelia, Ava
SW	Olivia, Amelia, Isla
Wales	Olivia, Ava, Amelia

6.

But for boys' names, you will need to distribute different names to each region.

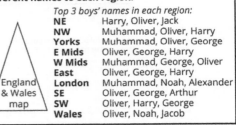

Top 3 boys' names in each region:

NE	Harry, Oliver, Jack
NW	Muhammad, Oliver, Harry
Yorks	Muhammad, Oliver, George
E Mids	Oliver, George, Harry
W Mids	Muhammad, George, Oliver
East	Oliver, George, Harry
London	Muhammad, Noah, Alexander
SE	Oliver, George, Arthur
SW	Oliver, Harry, George
Wales	Oliver, Noah, Jacob

7.

These boys' names are outside the Top 18 but may enter it next year.

Rank	Name	Change since 2017	Change since 2008
19	THEO	+2	+39
20	ISAAC	+4	+19
29	THEODORE	+9	+99
44	HUNTER	+34	+1042

These names are most likely to drop out:

15	ALFIE	-3	-9
17	JOSHUA	-2	-12

8.

These girls' names are outside the Top 29 but may enter it next year.

Rank	Name	Change since 2017	Change since 2008
34	EMILIA	+2	+63
49	MILA	+25	+661
65	ADA	+49	+634

These names are most likely to drop out:

25	JESSICA	-10	-20
28	DAISY	-10	-3

Figure 4.9   A wireframe for a baby names merchandising company

and then it would have been turned into a digital version once I was happy with the sketched version.

I've also included wireframes for entirely different audiences (Figures 4.10 and 4.11). Figure 4.10 is a wireframe for a double-page spread in a broadsheet newspaper. Figure 4.11 is an article – a mixture of text and images – for a market research company website. You will notice that I've drawn on the stories I found for these audiences in Chapter 3. To create each wireframe, I used the principles outlined above: selecting only relevant stories, adding contextual drama, and then emphasising some stories over others in a clear information hierarchy. However, you will see that even though I adhered to the same process each time, the three wireframes could not be more different. There are as many right answers as there are audiences.

Wireframing tips and tricks

I'd like to end this chapter with some additional guidance on structuring your wireframe. Just as it's a good idea to give the designer an indication of appropriate visual metaphors in each section of your story, so it's a good idea to give them a general sense of which layout type might suit the overall narrative. You can see that I've tried to do this in the baby names wireframes. For the newspaper wireframe (Figure 4.10), I'm suggesting that the two pages should mirror each other, indicating that the two pages are showing similar data and have equal importance, and that the reader can start on either side and then read *down* to read more about names for that gender or read *across* to compare that story (e.g. change in girls' names) to the same story for the opposite gender (e.g. change in boys' names). For the article on the market research website, I'm suggesting which information should be text, which should be a chart, and where in the flow the images should be placed.

I've put a selection of the most useful structures in Figure 4.12, along with a sense of the kinds of story they are most commonly used for.

There are a few general points to make about wireframing in each of these different instances. Although wireframing is always highly recommended, it is absolutely essential for more ambitious graphics (those numbered 1–5 on Figure 4.12). In fact, I would recommend treating the wireframe as a separate mini-project with its own timeline, so that the content can be checked and stakeholders or the client can sign off the visual approach before designers get started.

Here are some other suggestions:

- **Canvas**: Make sure the canvas size of your wireframe (e.g. a 16:9 PowerPoint, an A4 infographic, a 1024 × 512 animation) is the same size as the eventual product. Remember to allow for any margins, gutters, subtitle areas or any other no-go areas on your canvas.
- **Font**: Try to use the (approximate) font size that will be used in the final graphic so that you understand both how much text is appropriate and where abbreviations and edits will be required. If possible, use the right typeface too as fonts take up radically different amounts of space on the page (try typing the same sentence in **Impact** and then in Verdana).
- **Optional content**: Give the designers some room to manoeuvre. I often include instructions such as: 'If space please include this' and 'Delete this line if not enough space' to make it clear which parts are truly essential.
- **Visual guidance**: As mentioned earlier, where there is a single chart that will work, then include a simple version of the chart (with crude shapes), sized roughly to scale. Where more than one specific chart would work, just signal in text the kind of visual metaphor to be used: 'Change-over-time chart here', 'Composition chart here'.
- **Extra text**: If the graphic requires annotations or footnotes, either these should be included in the wireframe or it should be made clear that a specific amount of space will be needed for them (by using Lorem ipsum dummy text – a site like https://www.lipsum.com/ will generate this for you).

Top 100 girls' names 2018

When Oliver met Olivia:
Girls

Top 10 girls' names

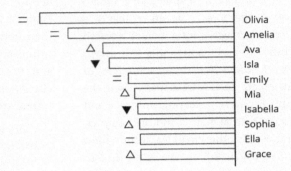

	Name
=	Olivia
=	Amelia
△	Ava
▼	Isla
=	Emily
△	Mia
▼	Isabella
△	Sophia
=	Ella
△	Grace

Biggest risers in Top 100 (since 2017)

Margot   Ada   Delilah   Mila   Hallie   Bonnie   Summer

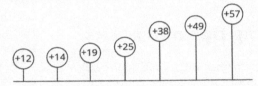

(+12) (+14) (+19) (+25) (+38) (+49) (+57)

Biggest drops: Martha (-18), Sara (-16), Lucy, Darcie (-12)

[If space?] Generation gap?

For Mums under 25, Harper is ranked 5th and Charlotte 45th.
For Mums that are 35+, Charlotte is ranked 2nd and Harper is 73rd.

Flower power

[Flowers or image
from the natural world]

Unlike boys, girls are still named after flowers and trees. The Top 30 includes Poppy, Lily, Ivy, Willow and Daisy. In December, Holly (56th overall) becomes the 8th most popular girls' name.

Name of thrones

[Illustration
from Marvel or Game
of Thrones?]

Names inspired by favourite books and films include: Khaleesi (56 babies), Rey (from Star Wars) (18), Elektra (16) and Bellatrix (6).

[Icon?] **Name graveyard:** There were only 10 Joans, 6 Susans and 3 Maureens born in 2018.

Figure 4.10   A wireframe for a newspaper

Top names in England & Wales

Boys

Top 10 boys' names

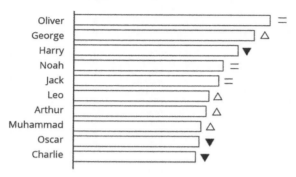

Oliver	=
George	△
Harry	▼
Noah	=
Jack	=
Leo	△
Arthur	△
Muhammad	△
Oscar	▼
Charlie	▼

Biggest risers in Top 100 (since 2017)

Hunter Grayson Ezra Sonny Dominic Jesse Rowan

(+34) (+24) (+22) (+15) (+15) (+15) (+14)

Biggest drops: Luke (-18), Matthew (-15), Riley (-15)

[If space?] Generation gap?

For Mums under 25, Logan is ranked 6th and Jack 29th.
For Mums that are 35+, Jack is ranked 3rd and Logan is 46th.

MO-mentum

[UK map with W. Mids and Yorkshire shaded. London and NW lightly shaded.]

Muhammad is the top name in these four regions. The West Midlands and Yorkshire also have a second spelling of the name (Mohammed) in the Top 10.

Marvel-lous names

[Illustration from Marvel or Game of Thrones?]

Names inspired by favourite books and films include: Loki (88 babies), Kylo (78), Theon (21), Thor (19) and Albus (7).

[Icon?] **Name graveyard:** There were only 13 Keiths, 8 Nigels and 3 Clives born in 2018.

Top 100 boys' names 2018

Baby names in England and Wales: 2018

Most popular first names for boys and girls according to registered births

	Boys			Girls	
Rank	Name	Change vs 2017	Rank	Name	Change vs 2017
1	Oliver	0	1	Olivia	0
2	George	+1	2	Amelia	0
3	Harry	-1	3	Ava	+1
4	Noah	0	4	Isla	-1
5	Jack	0	5	Emily	0
6	Leo	+1	6	Mia	+1
7	Arthur	+12	7	Isabella	-1
8	Muhammad	+2	8	Sophia	+3
9	Oscar	-1	9	Ella	0
10	Charlie	-1	10	Grace	+3
11	Jacob	-5	11	Poppy	-3
12	Thomes	+1	12	Charlotte	0
13	Henry	0	13	Lily	-3
14	William	-3	14	Ivy	+11
15	Alfie	-3	15	Florence	+4
16	Archie	+2	16	Evie	-2
17	Joshua	-2	17	Sophie	-1
18	Freddie	-2	18	Freya	+2
19	Theo	+2	19	Evelyn	+3
20	Isaac	+4	20	Willow	+6

There was no change at the top in 2018, as Oliver kept its top position for the sixth year in a row, and Olivia remained the top girls' name for the third year running.

The biggest riser in the Top 20 for boys was Arthur, jumping 12 places from to 7. The name was last in the Top 20 in the 1920s. The two new entries to the boys' Top 20, Theo and Issac, have never been in the Top 20 before.

James dropped out of the Top 20 for the first time in over 200 years.

The biggest jump in the girls' Top 20 was Ivy, which jumped 11 places to 14. Ten years ago, Ivy was ranked the 322nd most popular girls' name. The other two new Top 20 entries are Willow and Evelyn. Willow is a new name that first entered the Top 100 eight years ago. Evelyn's rank of 19 is its highest ever, beating its previous high of 28 in 1914.

Hunter	+1042	Harper	+1365
Grayson	+905	Aria	+1094
Arlo	+531	Margot	+1078
Jaxon	+511	Mila	+661
Ezra	+441	Ada	+634
Albie	+289	Aurora	+570
Reggie	+236	Luna	+537
Ralph	+218	Penelope	+379
Teddy	+202	Delilah	+318
Carter	+198	Ivy	+308

The names in the Top 100 that have jumped the most places in the last 10 years are Hunter, Grayson and Arlo for boys and Harper, Aria and Margot for girls. None of these names featured in the Top 100 before 2015.

The influence of popular culture seems particularly apparent on female names, with Harper beginning to rise after the birth of Harper Beckham in 2011 and Aria rising after the success of Game of Thrones (although note that the character's name is spelt Arya). Names from Disney (Aurora) and Harry Potter (Luna) also feature.

For boys, it seems that 'alternative' or counter-cultural figures are more of an inspiration, with the best-known Hunter being Hunter S. Thompson, the most prominent Grayson is the artist Grayson Perry and Arlo is possibly influenced by protest singer Arlo Guthrie.

Figure 4.11 A wireframe for an online article

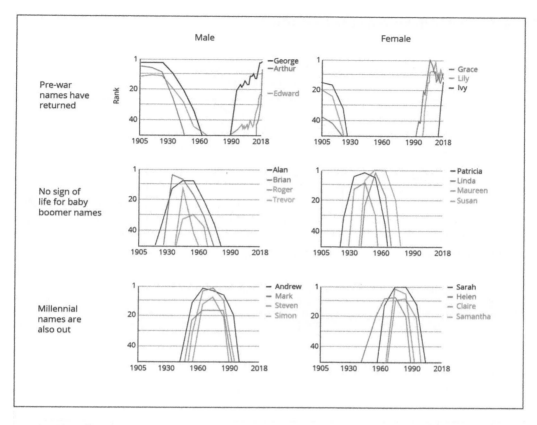

More generally, we have seen changing tastes affect both the names that appear in the Top 50 and the names that don't.

In particular, there seems to be fondness for names from three or four generations ago, and a clear rejection of names associated with the baby boomer and Millennial generations. As well as the names charted above, there is little sign of a return of boomer names such as Keith, Trevor or Derek (for boys) or Carol, Christine or Barbara (for girls), nor are the Millennial names Darren, Neil or Wayne (for boys) or Natalie, Lisa or Nicola (for girls) showing any signs of life.

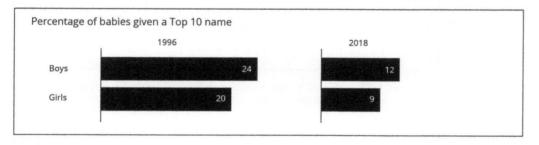

This is all the more surprising when you consider that there is far more experimentation and variety today than even 20 years ago, with parents less inclined to 'follow the crowd' and more likely to give their children unusual names.

Baby girls in particular are less likely than ever to have one of the most common names. There are also a large number of babies with unique names, with 7% of girls and 6% of boys having a name that only appears once in 2018.

9½ ways to wireframe a static graphic

1. One large chart

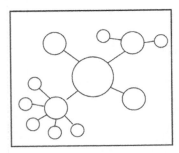

'The worldwide paperclip industry'

- Good for exploring the detail of one large dataset
- Could be a conventional chart, map, timeline or something more bespoke

2. One large chart - with supporting charts

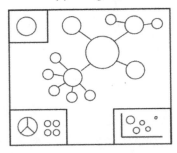

'The paperclip industry in context'

- Good for when your 'hero' dataset begs further questions
- The smaller charts are not an integral part of the story, but give detail to those who want it

3. Two mirrored charts

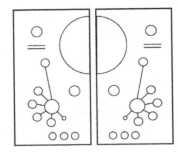

'The paperclip industry: US v China'

- Useful for comparing data on two places or from two time periods
- Can also mirror horizontally

4. Lots of small charts

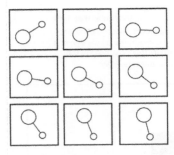

'Paperclip sales in all 50 US states'

- Great for comparing the same data from different places or time periods
- Also known as 'small multiples' (via Edward Tufte)

5. A linked series of charts

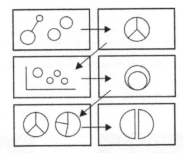

'How the "paperclip bubble" caused a stock market crash'

- Ideal for explaining an issue or process
- Allows for a mixture of story and chart types
- Also the structure for most PowerPoint presentations

6. A random list

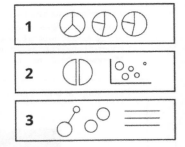

'10 fun facts about paperclips'

- Useful for a superficial introduction to a topic
- Perfect when you effectively have bullet points rather than a clear narrative thread
- Easy to repurpose for social media

Figure 4.12 Wireframe structures

7. Charts to support an article

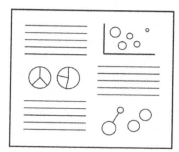

'An article about paperclips'

- Charts are solely to support the copy
- Preferred option of many data journalists

8. Just numbers with photos or icons

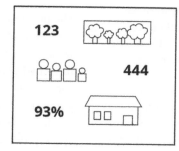

'Paperclips in numbers'

- No charts at all
- Just a collection of key stats
- Photographs are well-chosen and integrated with the content (not just stock shots)

9. One small chart

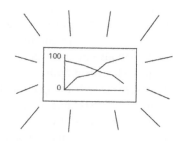

'Paperclips overtake staplers to become world's top paper fastener'

- A single freestanding chart, ideal for social media
- Allows for little exploration or contextual detail but can be powerful in its simplicity

Novelty corner 1: A very long chart

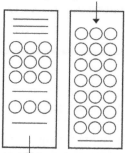

'How many paperclips does the world use every day'

- Online only: good when your data is about long distances or large differences in scale
- Works best when the scrolling offers a reward (greater detail or a surprise ending)

Novelty corner 2: Riffs on 'classic' charts

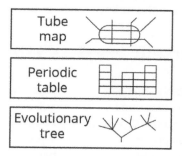

'The tube map of office supplies (paperclips = Kings Cross)'

- Tend to get shared but rarely taken seriously
- Content has to be both appropriate and brilliant to work

Who wireframes?
Editors, producers, project managers, designers

Using which tools?
Pencil and paper first, then transferred into Illustrator or Photoshop. But you can use anything (e.g. Word, PowerPoint) with simple shapes and text boxes.

How long does it take?
For the most ambitious graphics, the sketching and wireframing takes as long as making the final graphic (between 1 and 2 weeks). For simpler charts, it can take less than a day.

- **Read order**: Even if the final product doesn't have numbered sections, it's often worth numbering the content 'blocks' just to make it clear to anyone reading or approving the wireframe what the intended read order should be. It will also help the designer when they come to lay the graphic out.
- **Multiple sizes**: If the graphic does not have a single fixed size (e.g. there is a PowerPoint version, an A4 print-out and a mobile version), then you need to create separate wireframes for each. Minimum font size will be different in each case, and the most appropriate charts and illustrations will vary depending on the canvas size and orientation.
- **Multiple solutions**: If you think that there are two approaches that could possibly work for the story, then you will need two wireframes. The client will not understand the strengths and weaknesses of each approach unless you show them. Furthermore, it is best to keep any narrative experimentation to the wireframing stage when edits are quick and easy, rather than

waiting till the **Make** stage, when significant edits can mean starting again.

The phrase I tend to keep in my head when I'm wireframing is *don't kick the can down the road.* Because it's *so* tempting to kick it. I suspect that most bad graphics end up that way because at some point someone looked at an incomplete wireframe and thought, 'we can work that bit out later'. If it's about the story, and how much space it takes up, then you should work it out now. This might well be challenged or overturned during the **Make** stage: clients change their minds; new technology appears; crazy experiments are successful. Iteration and change are an inevitable part of making data visualisation. But the output of the **Design** stage should be your best guess at the right answer *at that moment*. That way, everyone in the team understands the story that is being told, and this gives them the freedom to think more creatively about the best way of telling it.

Try it yourself!

1 Return to the sentences and data tables that you created at the end of Chapter 3. This was using baby names data from your own country. Or you can use your own data stories if you prefer.
2 Create your own wireframe for one of the audiences mentioned above: a business selling merchandise, a broadsheet newspaper or a market research company website. Use pen and paper initially and then transfer this into a digital format. This can be carried out in Illustrator, Inkscape, PowerPoint or whichever software you have access to.

For those who want more:

3 Create an infographic based on your wireframe. Depending on your level of familiarity with and access to professional graphic design tools, this will either be in Illustrator/Inkscape (if you have them) or, if you are just starting out, a templating tool like Venngage, Canva or Infogram.
4 If you are using Illustrator for the first time, have a look at some of Adobe's online tutorials before you start: https://helpx.adobe.com/uk/illustrator/tutorials.html. You can also check out '10 things I wish somebody had told me about using Illustrator for data viz' at www.addtwodigital.com/book
5 If you are using a templating tool like Venngage, Canva or Infogram, I have included a walkthrough of how I turned a wireframe into a graphic using Venngage in the teaching resources section of www.addtwodigital.com/book. At this URL, you can also find a sample wireframe in png, ai and Google Doc formats, which you can use if you don't have a finished wireframe of your own.

Five

Making static graphics

Tobias Sturt

Chapter contents

Making a start

Figure 5.1 A stock photo, a poster and a fresco

Three completely different pictures, right? Three completely different *types* of pictures, in fact (Figure 5.1):

A photo of a horror movie clown

A metal poster of 1940s propaganda icon Rosie the Riveter, exhorting women to join the workplace

A Renaissance Italian fresco showing Judith decapitating Holofernes.

Different times, different subjects, different media, each with its own meanings and interpretations, but placed in sequence, one after another, they tell a story:

A scary man menaces us

A strong woman rises up

And cuts his head off.

In the early years of the last century, in the very first glimmerings of cinema, the filmmaker Lev Kuleshov tried an experiment. He took a single sequence of the film star Ivan Mosjoukine staring directly down the lens and intercut it with other, random shots: a bowl of soup, a child in a coffin, a woman lying on a divan.

The extraordinary thing about this was not the film, but the audience. What they saw was not a random collection of odds and ends of footage but instead a brilliant performance by Mosjoukine: his sorrow at the death of the child, his lust at the woman on the couch. Whatever strong emotions he felt about soup.

The point is that they couldn't help but see a link between the pictures. They were looking at exactly the same frames of Mosjoukine repeated over and over again, but what they were seeing was story. The context in which those frames were placed changed how they interpreted them. The Kuleshov effect became the basis of film storytelling through editing: by placing images and scenes in juxtaposition and sequence we can make an audience see a story, even if there isn't one there.

Images expand beyond their inherent meanings. We see not just what is depicted, but also the manner of depiction, the intentions and the assumptions behind that depiction. Images are full of stories. Placed into context with other images, with text, with meaning, those stories multiply. It is inevitable.

Humans tell stories, even just to themselves. We can't help it. We look out from the solitude of our skulls at the world around us and we conjecture cause and effect and relationships and theories of mind.

Presented with images, human beings see stories.

Which is lucky, because that's what we want them to see.

We just have to make sure they're the right ones.

Three goals

This book is about data visualisation as an act of communication, of deliberate storytelling. In this case, we are trying to achieve three things:

- **Truthfulness**: making sure that our data is represented truthfully, that we are not misleading the audience but also not confusing them
- **Clarity**: showing our story in a way that our audience can read, making sure they can grasp our information hierarchy and read down into the complexity of our data
- **Persuasion**: presenting the data in such a way as our audience wants to look at it and continue looking at it, being visually

persuasive, convincing[1] them that our work is worth their attention.

Obviously doing all three things at the same time is a hard balancing act, and if it is impossible, we must prioritise a clarity of expression over everything else. Think of it like a pyramid with clarity at the top.

Clarity is the pinnacle and the most important element. But truthfulness and persuasion are fundamental. By understanding the point of our data and drawing that out in a way that makes it easy to read, that is, showing our story clearly, we are both expressing our data truthfully and persuading our audience to read.

In practice our process tends to run clockwise round the triangle, while always keeping the other considerations in mind:

Start with the charting: does it represent the data well? The meaning as well as the detail?

Does it then make it clear how to read? Can you emphasise and structure within the visuals? If not, you might have to reconsider your chart.

Does it make you want to read? Is the chart nice to look at? Can you improve it with colour choices or illustration?

But have those persuasive choices affected the truthfulness? Does your visualisation still work?

And round we go.

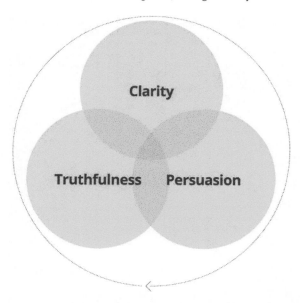

Figure 5.2 Clarity, truthfulness and persuasion in a mystical conjunction

Two parts

The reason why we have to think about these three factors simultaneously is that our audience thinks about our data in a very different way than we do.

They are not going to start with the detail, they begin at the other end. The first thing they see will be our visual persuasiveness: does this look interesting? Then they will engage with the structure of the storytelling, as long as it clearly

[1]The terms Clarity and Persuasion are swiped from Scott McCloud's excellent *Making Comics* (2006), the best book on visual storytelling I know of.

indicates how and what to read. Only then might they actually get to the data itself: the detail that underlies our story.

Of course we need to show our data and show it well, but we have to remember that a good proportion of our audience may never even read it. They may, if we're lucky, read the story and take it on board. Some of them may only ever see one main point (which is why we should always make sure that we're making one main point). And some will never engage at all.

This is why we have to try to do everything all at once, so that that first glance contains information, expressed with the data itself. This is why clarity is the most important element of our triad: it is through a clarity of expression that we can communicate in a glance and also be persuasive, because that clarity invites engagement: 'Here is an interesting thing: it might be worth your time to read more.'

Many designers and artists have a habit, when they are working, of standing back from their work and cocking their head to one side to look at it. They do this to reset how they are looking and to see the work afresh, to move away from the details and take in the piece as a new whole.

As a practice, data visualisation concentrates on the *detail*, but we must balance that with the *overview*.

Think of how a city map works (Figure 5.3). The detail is all important: which street connects to which, which turning leads where. But we need the overview to orient ourselves, to get the sense of the landscape, identify that landmark there, so we must be here and we want to go there, so .... Both overview and detail are equally intrinsic to how it works, what it is. And what is a map, after all, other than a chart?

So our charts work the same way, by turning complex numbers into instinctively understood visuals, giving our audience a comprehensive overview of the data, helping them discover the detail below.

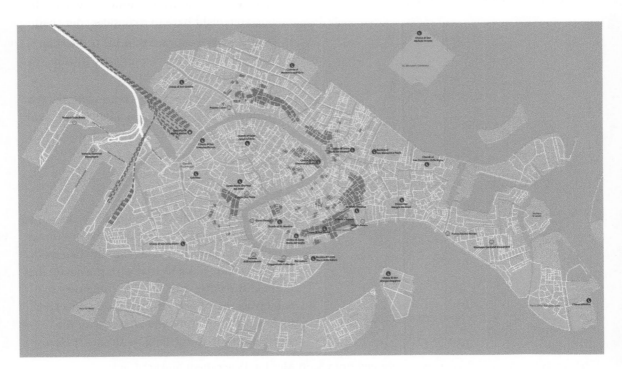

Figure 5.3 Venice, one of the most wonderful (and smelly) cities

Visual appeal lies in balancing a harmonious whole in overview with interesting and rewarding detail.

And any act of communication needs a comprehensible, cohesive theme that tells a strong message in overview as well as the all-important detail that adds colour and, more importantly in our case, context and evidence.

At every stage of working towards our three goals we are going to be thinking about how we balance and maximise both our overview and the detail.

One tool

The bad news is we have only one visual tool with which to accomplish all these things. The good news is that it's a versatile one: *contrast*.

Using visual contrast means setting up a consistency of visual language and then introducing change.

Human beings are easily startled. Our world is full of dangers and they make us nervous: we like order and predictability, we like the patterns and symmetries it creates. *Consistency* is visually pleasing and reassuring (Figure 5.4).

On the other hand, it also quickly gets boring. A *change* is as good as a rest, after all. It is stimulating: catching our attention, making us interested (Figure 5.5).

But because each change is a call on our attention, it can quickly get noisy and overwhelming. Too much change stops being restful and gets agitating, upsetting and confusing.

Figure 5.4   An inoffensive row of dots

Figure 5.5   One of these things is not like the others

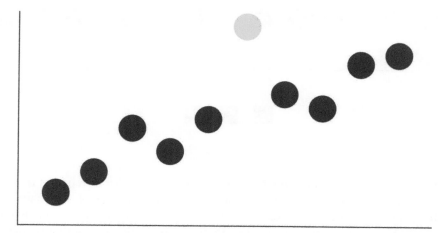

Figure 5.6   I think they're trying to tell us something

Change needs consistency to work, otherwise it's no change at all. And by placing meaningful change within a context of established consistency, we can create structure. By bolding or italicising a bunch of words in a paragraph, for instance, to show importance. Or moving around dots in a space to create a chart (Figure 5.6).

The process

In the next few pages we're going to be looking at each of our three goals in the order in which we work at them:

- **Truthfulness**: everything starts with the data and therefore with the basics of chart making.
- **Clarity**: ensuring that our data is communicating clearly and that we have told our audience a story they can read.
- **Persuasion**: making sure that our visuals are appealing, that they make the audience want to read and want to continue reading, but without obstructing the clarity or obfuscating the truth.

And at each stage we'll be looking at how we use our key visual tool of *contrast* to manage that balance between *overview* and *detail* and so help our audience engage with our story and discover our data.

Making data visible

Truthfulness

So we visualise data by setting up a consistent visual language and then introducing meaning through change, altering that pattern to show our data. This means we have to figure out how to make that change and what it is that we are changing.

Jacques Bertin – one of those looming figures who dominate the data visualisation landscape like distant giants – in his classic *Semiology of Graphics* (1967) has a list of seven basic visual properties, the visual variables, which we might summarise as in Figure 5.7.

All of these attributes are processed 'preattentively', that is, 'at first glance', before we're consciously aware of what we're looking at. However, as you can probably see, we have different kinds of attributes here. Bertin evaluates them in terms of what kind of visual representation they're best suited to, what we might summarise as *quantitative* and *differential*.[1]

The properties that we might call 'quantitative' (and thus the properties we tend to use for visualisation) are position, in two-dimensional

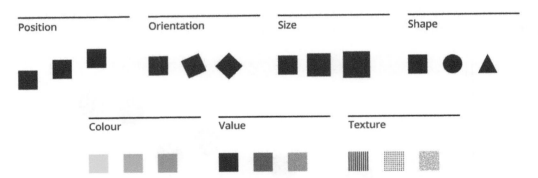

Figure 5.7 The visual variables

[1]Bertin talks about 'The Properties of Z' (which sounds like a magical realist novel); that is, we start with the x and y position on a plane and then add z-axis visual variables of size, shape, value, orientation, colour, texture – all things that add further information to that initial point. In practice, some of these (as we shall see) are suited to the representation of quantitative data, and some aren't, so I've chosen to divide them up along those lines as it felt more practical.

space (the *x*- and *y*-axis), size and value (the brightness, density of colour, etc.). We also tend to use orientation in charting, although usually in conjunction with size and position, as a qualifier. The lines on a line chart join points that show the data by position; the orientation of the lines shows us the rate of change between the datapoints.

The other 'differential' properties describe qualities of the object: shape, colour and texture (pattern and so on). They tend to be used for qualifying (meta) information: categories in different shapes on a scatter, emphasis in changes of colour, similarity in common patterns.

These are the properties that we're going to use to layer context onto our charts to create emphasis and hierarchies of information, making similarities and differences.

We're going to concentrate on the 'quantitative' attributes for the moment, because they're the ones we use most as the fundamentals of our charting.

Column and bar charts operate largely through a combination of size and position (Figure 5.8). The position of the top of the bar is what gives us the value, measured off against the *y*-axis. This is amplified by the area of the bar: the larger the area, the higher the value. Note how the area is made easier to compare by changing just one dimension – the height or width.

Line charts are a mixture of position and orientation. As with the bar charts, the position of the datapoint in a 2D plane against a common axis

gives us the value. By joining those datapoints with lines we also get orientation – the steepness of the slope giving us an indication of the degree of change between the two points.

Pie charts are a mixture of orientation and size. The angle of the segment is essentially giving us value, marking off against a notional axis that runs round the perimeter of the circle, while the size amplifies this value, especially when there are significant differences (and particularly when there are only a few datapoints being visualised).

Note how all of these use multiple attributes to achieve the visualisation – this is pretty common, but the key thing to remember about it is that they're doubling up – using different attributes to show the same thing. Clarity over complexity, after all.

The quantitative display of detail

In their seminal paper 'Graphical Perception: Theory, Experimentation, and Application to the Development of Graphical Methods', William Cleveland and Robert McGill (1984) tested a range of what they called 'elementary perceptual tasks' in order to assess how they affect our ability to extract quantitative information from charts.

As a result of their explorations, they theorised that charts could be ranked by accuracy of the representation of data – that is, how accurately a

Figure 5.8 Simple charts: column, line and pie

viewer could estimate, by the eye, the values shown in the chart (Figure 5.9):

1 position along a common scale
2 positions along non-aligned scales
3 length, direction, angle
4 area
5 volume, curvature
6 shading, colour saturation.

Note how the first four on that list are position, orientation and size, the 'quantitative' visual variables we spoke about earlier as working best for data visualisation.

Different visual languages have an effect on how we see the data. The simpler the relationship between the shape and the number – the height of a bar as opposed to the angle and area of a wedge in a pie chart, for example – the easier it is for readers to grasp the detail.

However, as Cleveland and McGill point out: 'One must be careful not to fall into a conceptual trap by adopting accuracy as a criterion .... The power of a graph is its ability to enable one to take

in the quantitative information, organize and see patterns and structure not readily revealed by other means of studying the data.'

This is important: we must be careful not to let our desire for truthful detail blind us to the need for a clear overview. The overview of the data that a chart gives us is a core element of its power, helping us see the data in ways mere tables cannot achieve.

However, that overview must be based on truthful charting because otherwise the insight it gives us is not true. And I'm not sure which is worse: a reader who has been misled by reading a chart more carefully and discovering they have been lied to, or one who just wanders off into the world with a completely erroneous idea of it in their head.

In practice

Sergio has designed a report (Figure 5.11) from the wireframe Adam produced for an article being published by a research company, so the audience is expecting clear, clean data communication.

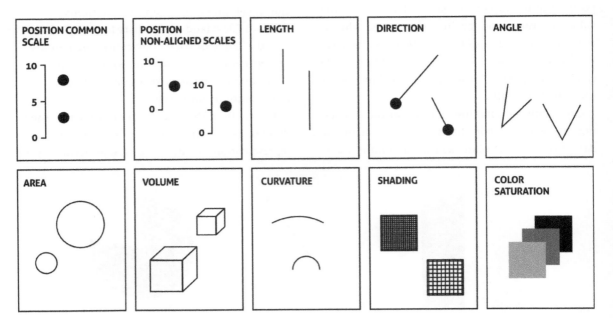

Figure 5.9 The example visualisations from the Cleveland–McGill paper

The first charts (Figure 5.10) are bar charts, using what Cleveland and McGill called 'position along a common scale' to show the data. That is, the data is shown by position (the end point of each bar, as placed along a horizontal axis common to all the bars) This is, of course, what allows us to make meaningful comparisons between the bars: a consistent shape changing against a consistent measure.

It shows us the detail admirably, but notice how much it does in overview, how much it tells us, even at a glance. We get an immediate sense of the dataset as a whole: the highs and lows (Arthur and Jacob), the smaller trends (William and Alfie) within the larger ones (more red in the lower half than the top half). The flagpole arrangement of the chart tells us we're dealing with positive and negative differences, even if we might not know what they are until we read the label. We even get a secondary dimension of data: they are ordered by ranking, so we can understand the context of that growth.

Notice how Sergio has not included that horizontal axis on this chart. It's not actually needed to understand the data. All the bars are labelled, it's perfectly easy to understand what they mean without it, and by removing it we remove just one more visual element cluttering up the chart.

We can think of data visualisation as happening in layers of information. At the base is the visualisation layer, the visuals that represent the numbers – those basic visual attributes that are giving us meaning.

To this we add the layer of text and chart elements that elucidates that meaning. The key to making this layer is to think of it as the explanation layer. The information that is going to explain the visuals: what does the audience need to know to understand this chart?

Our job is to show them what they need but no more. The data is already complex; they don't need us to layer on any more complexity. We need to give them detail, but not in a way that clutters up the overview. Equally, we have to make sure that the overview from the visualisation layer delivers the audience cleanly to the detail.

Then we have the annotation layer, in which we add in the elements that will emphasise the importance of the data: highlights, notes and graphics. But we'll get to that.

The framing power of overview

However, by giving us these immediate, instinctive ideas about the data, the overview

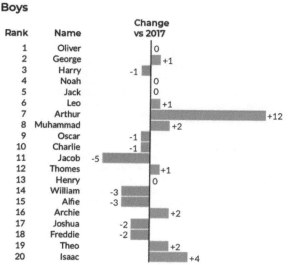
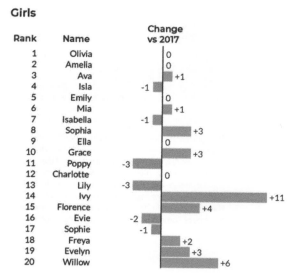

Figure 5.10   Two charts showing change in rank

Baby names in England and Wales: 2018

Most popular first names for boys and girls according to registered births

Boys

Rank	Name	Change vs 2017
1	Oliver	0
2	George	+1
3	Harry	-1
4	Noah	0
5	Jack	0
6	Leo	+1
7	Arthur	+12
8	Muhammad	+2
9	Oscar	-1
10	Charlie	-1
11	Jacob	-5
12	Thomes	+1
13	Henry	0
14	William	-3
15	Alfie	-3
16	Archie	+2
17	Joshua	-2
18	Freddie	-2
19	Theo	+2
20	Isaac	+4

Girls

Rank	Name	Change vs 2017
1	Olivia	0
2	Amelia	0
3	Ava	+1
4	Isla	-1
5	Emily	0
6	Mia	+1
7	Isabella	-1
8	Sophia	+3
9	Ella	0
10	Grace	+3
11	Poppy	-3
12	Charlotte	0
13	Lily	-3
14	Ivy	+11
15	Florence	+4
16	Evie	-2
17	Sophie	-1
18	Freya	+2
19	Evelyn	+3
20	Willow	+6

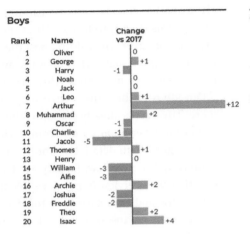

There was no change at the top in 2018, as Oliver kept its top position for the sixth year in a row, and Olivia remained the top girls' name for the third year running.

The biggest riser in the Top 20 for boys was Arthur, jumping 12 places from to 7. The name was last in the Top 20 in the 1920s. The two new entries to the boys' Top 20, Theo and Issac, have never been in the Top 20 before.

James dropped out of the Top 20 for the first time in over 200 years.

The biggest jump in the girls' Top 20 was Ivy, which jumped 11 places to 14. Ten years ago, Ivy was ranked the 322nd most popular girls' name. The other two new Top 20 entries are Willow and Evelyn. Willow is a new name that first entered the Top 100 eight years ago. Evelyn's rank of 19 is its highest ever, beating its previous high of 28 in 1914.

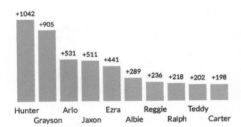

The names in the Top 100 that have jumped the most places in the last 10 years are Hunter, Grayson and Arlo for boys and Harper, Aria and Margot for girls. None of these names featured in the Top 100 before 2015. The influence of popular culture seems particularly apparent on female names, with Harper beginning to rise after the birth of Harper Beckham in 2011 and Aria rising after the success of Game of Thrones (although note that the character's

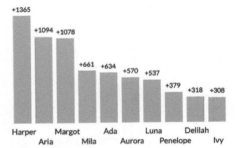

name is spelt Arya). Names from Disney (Aurora) and Harry Potter (Luna) also feature.

For boys, it seems that 'alternative' or counter-cultural figures are more of an inspiration, with the most well-known Hunter being Hunter S. Thompson, the most prominent Grayson is the artist Grayson Perry and Arlo is possibly influenced by protest singer Arlo Guthrie.

Boys

Pre-war names have returned

No sign of life for baby boomer names

Millennial names are also out

Girls

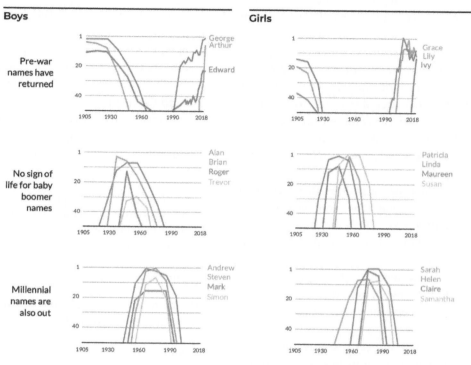

More generally, we have seen changing tastes affect both the names that appear in the Top 50 and the names that don't. In particular, there seems to be fondness for names from three or four generations ago, and a clear rejection of names associated with the baby boomer and Millennial generations.

As well as the names charted above, there is little sign of a return of boomer names such as Keith, Trevor or Derek (for boys) or Carol, Christine or Barbara (for girls), nor are the Millennial names Darren, Neil or Wayne (for boys) or Natalie, Lisa or Nicola (for girls) showing any signs of life.

Percentage of babies given a Top 10 name

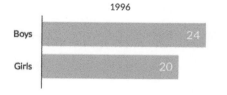

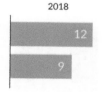

This is all the more surprising when you consider that there is far more experimentation and variety today than even 20 years ago, with parents less inclined to 'follow the crowd' and more likely to give their children unusual names.

Baby girls in particular are less likely than ever to have one of the most common names. There are also a large number of babies with unique names, with 7% of girls and 6% of boys having a name that only appears once in 2018.

Figure 5.11   An illustrated article for a research company

also starts to frame how we think about and approach it.

In their paper 'Bars and Lines: A Study of Graphic Communication', Jeff Zacks and Barbara Tversky (1999) set out to investigate how different visual representations of data can affect not just how we see the data but how we read and interpret it.

In one of their experiments they showed participants two different graphs of the same data – in this case the average heights of men and women (Figure 5.12). What they discovered was that the participants who saw the column chart were more likely to describe the data as a discrete comparison: 'The average male is taller than the average female.'

However, if they saw a line chart, they were more likely to see it as a trend: 'The more male a person is, the taller he/she is.' This even though, in the terms of this dataset, gender was not a spectrum but a binary choice.

And when they reversed the experiment and asked people to draw charts based on data, they discovered that people instinctively draw column charts for comparison and line charts for trends.

Tversky and Zacks suspect that this might come from a combination of our instinctive readings of visuals, reinforced by associations with particular chart types. Whatever the reason, visuals are intricately and intimately tied with meanings and framing in our minds.

The fact is that the 'standard charts', customary as they are, play to all our strengths in the perception of data in shape and also how we understand the meaning of data, both intrinsically and in how we have learned to read certain charts.

This means that in choosing a chart type, we need to think how that visual is going to frame the data for our audience – how those shapes are going to tell them a story. This matters because we have a story to tell, so we need to make sure we're using the right chart language to tell it.

Generally we're telling one of these four stories (Figure 5.14):

- comparing datapoints or sets to each other
- seeing change in a dataset over time
- showing composition – the relationship of part to whole in a dataset
- plotting correlation between two datasets or variables.

(There are also geospatial and distribution stories, but we'll cover those in Part II.)

In practice

In Figure 5.13 we have line charts showing the change over time and bar charts to compare percentages.

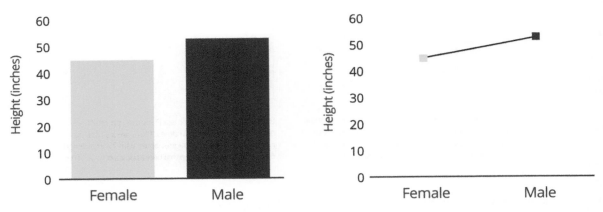

Figure 5.12 Difference in height between males and females

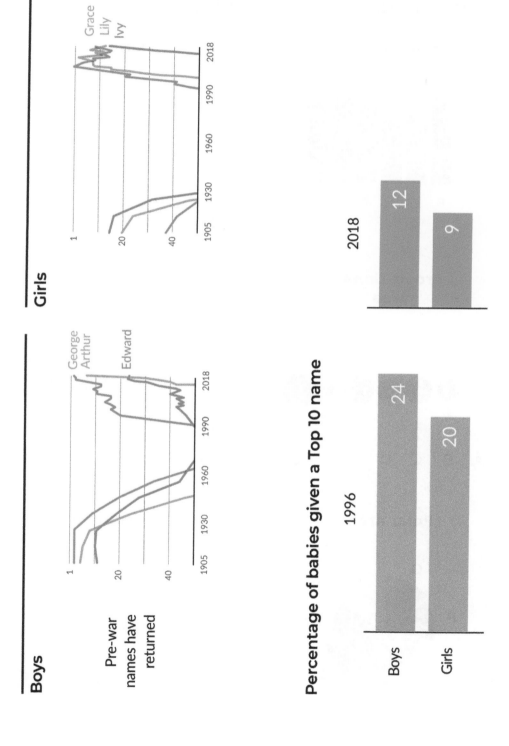

Figure 5.13 Line and bar charts

Comparison

Column/bar

Proportional area

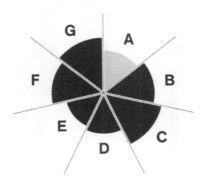

Polar area

Change

Line

Area

Bar/column

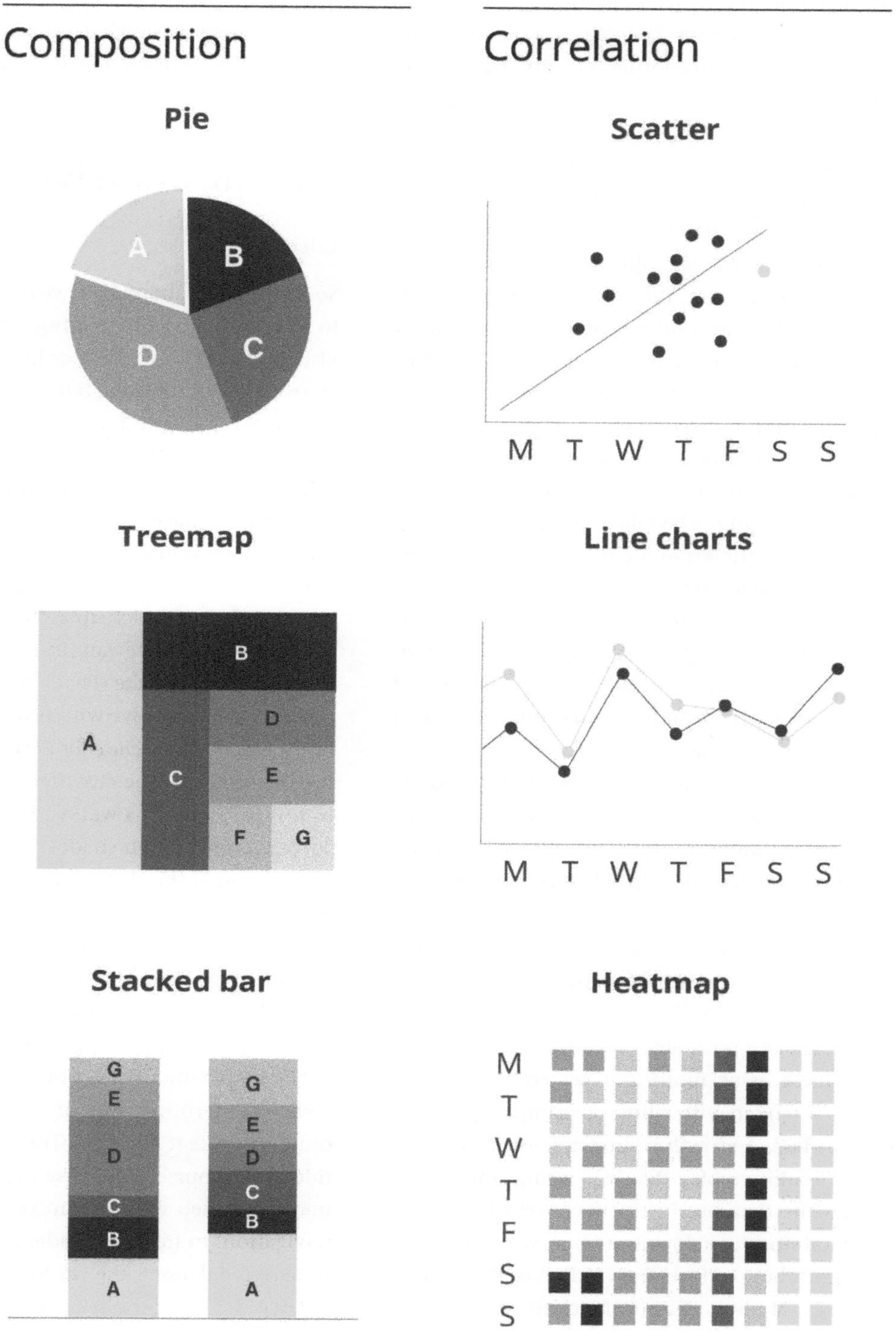

Figure 5.14 Every chart tells a story

In a line chart, each datapoint is joined to the next, each one leading us on to the next, along the axis and through time. It creates a relationship from one datapoint to another, a chain of causation or reaction. It describes a trend across the page, in our heads.

We might have expected the percentages to be displayed as pie charts. Pie charts take a complete whole (or, perhaps, hole), a circle, and then divide it up into constituent parts, illustrating in the visuals the nature of the data: the composition of a total.

Here, though, we want to compare those values with each other, and bar charts are perfect at that. As we have seen, they work by positioning values against a common axis. They align their bars and then ask us: Who's gone further? Who's fallen behind? Who's longer, who's shorter? Who's winning? Who's losing? The relationships between the datapoints are shown as a contest, a comparison.

Of course, there are more complex associations with shape: we tend to think of number lines as progressing, either 'up' or 'along' (left to right in Western perception), so we talk of values 'rising' and 'falling'. Amounts of things can be piles or poured into containers, so they can 'grow' or 'shrink'.

These associations can feel obvious, but it's easy to become distracted by charting visuals. Time progresses; in European language text this is often left to right, the progress of a line chart or flow diagram. But units of time are cyclical, they recur regularly: hours, weeks, quarters, years. We need to consider whether we are talking about patterns in time or distinct periods: a line chart for the latter, but possibly something like a polar area chart for the former.

And these associations can get emotional, too. There is a tendency to think of rising as good and falling as bad. A growth in unemployment is a bad thing. Should we plot that as a rising line, which matches the data but instinctively tells the wrong emotional story, or a downward line, which matches the import, but confuses our reading of the data?

The answer always lies in the clarity of our communication. How well will our audience understand what we're saying? With a rise in unemployment, there's very little chance of an audience misunderstanding a rising line on a line chart and failing to grasp the emotional and cultural meanings.

Making ourselves clear

Clarity

So in thinking about how we chart data, we need to be considering not just how accurately the visuals display the details or how well they give us an overview of the data, but also how that overview is going to frame how we think about and explore that data.

It's no coincidence that we use the word 'chart' in English to mean both graphs and maps.

Let's go to Venice.

There are many different ways we might explore Venice. We could pick up a tourist map in St Mark's Square, so we can find the Rialto Bridge or San Giorgio Maggiore (Figure 5.15).

If we're sensible, we will have remembered to bring J. G. Links' *Venice for Pleasure* (1966) – easily the best guide to the city there is – and are going to follow one of his walks round unexpected corners and through shadowy alleys where the only sound is the slap of water on stone and a distant voice in an upper room somewhere.

But later on, we're going to need a complete street map of Venice, if we're ever going to find that little bar in the Dorsoduro with the tramezzini and the Aperol spritz (Figure 5.16).

The map, famously, is not the territory. Maps stylize the territory, simplify it, emblematise it, in order to make it readable. They have to do so with fidelity, of course, otherwise they are useless as maps, but their whole point is to facilitate navigation, to help the reader explore the underlying dataset: the world.

Anyone who visualises data needs to read *On Exactitude in Science* by Jorge Luis Borges (2004), in

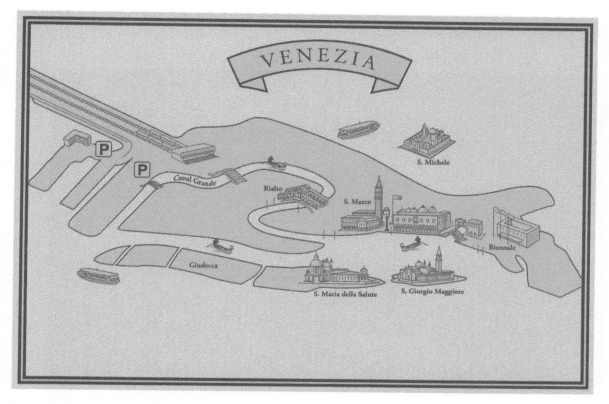

Figure 5.15 Make sure you remember where you parked the car

which an obsession with accuracy in cartography leads to the making of a map the exact size of the empire it depicts. Gradually time and weather wear it away until only scraps are left in desolate places, under which beggars shelter.

The point is, all these maps use a different visual language, and that language is going to change the way we explore the city: from main point to main point, or along a designated route, or simply wandering to see what we can find.

The visual language the maps use gives us different ideas of the city: the city remains the same (albeit possibly closer to sea level), but the reader's experience of it changes.

In order to achieve different goals, the maps give us different visions of the city, which in turn means that while we may walk down the same streets, our approach to them changes. We think about the

actual, physical city differently because of the way a map structures our experience of it.

The design of a chart doesn't just visualise data to make it easier to read, or to show us a particular point, but also will influence the way we think about the underlying data, even if we end up drilling down to the data table beneath.

The map may not be the territory, but it is how we think about the territory.

If we are going to be clear in showing our audience how to explore our data, we need to make sure that our overview is giving them clear indications of starting points and goals and the detailed legible directions to follow.

Laying out the overview

The key to constructing structure within our visuals is our old friend contrast. Just as we can

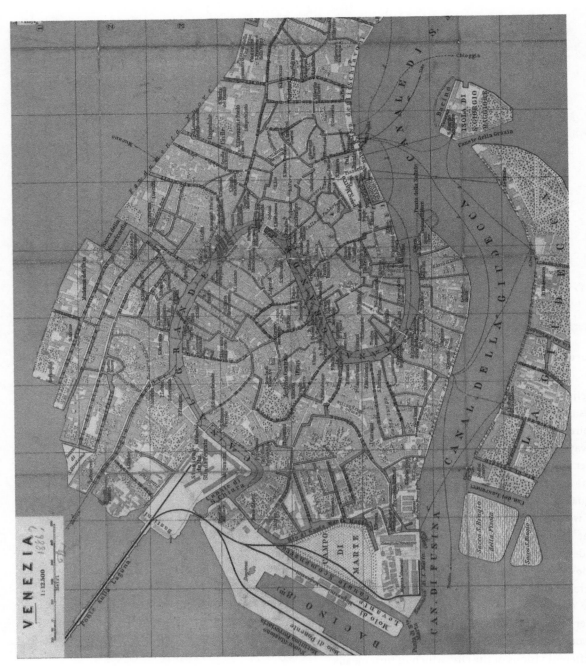

Figure 5.16 Streets full of water, please advise

use change within consistency to show meaning in our charts, so we can use it to show higher-level groupings.

This sounds more complicated than it is, but fortunately for us, humans are very simple beings. As we have noted before, humans tend to swerve away from complexity and will almost always look for ways to minimise the amount of information they have to deal with. Equally, we are all adept pattern-finding creatures. Pareidolia, the tendency to see a meaningful image where one does not necessarily exist (e.g. seeing faces in anything with two equally spaced dots in such as plug sockets, knots in wood, car headlights), is a side-effect of our deep programming to look for recognisable patterns, even when they're not intended.

However, we can intend them, and use these instincts to look for patterns and to simplify visuals to create groupings in our visuals by – you guessed it – making changes in visual attributes.

These principles of grouping were defined by Gestalt psychologists to show how humans tend to instinctively group elements depending on various visual signals. The important thing to realise is that this happens unconsciously, whether you intend it as a designer or not. Your audience will see order and structure in your visuals whether or not it is there. This is why we have to consider these effects carefully as we work up and lay out our visuals.

All these features use a combination of consistency and difference to create groupings within visuals, and by creating groups we create emphasis (this element is not like the others) and thereby structure and information hierarchy. (I've simplified the principles here (Figure 5.17) a little from their original definitions, just for the sake of space.)

Similarity shows how we tend to group by visual similarity. In these examples similarity of shape, also size, colour, value, texture and position divide the visuals up into two immediately distinct groups.

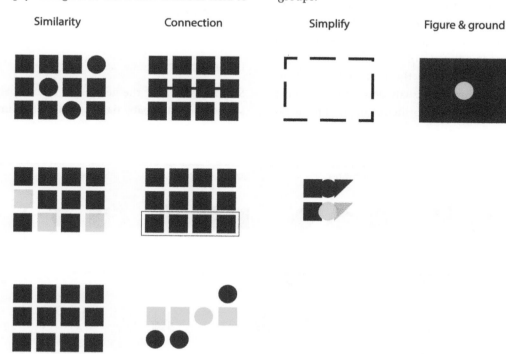

Figure 5.17 Gestalt groupings (simplified)

You'll notice that these are basically Jacques Bertin's elements of visual vocabulary (Figure 5.18) that we discussed earlier. As we saw, it is similarities and differences in size and position that we use to create data visualisations. It is our tendency to group elements by these attributes that means we see trends and patterns within our visualised data. This then leaves us with colour, value, shape and texture to layer other groupings on top of our data.

Connection shows how elements can be grouped together by joining or by enclosure to create a connection between otherwise potentially disparate elements. The latter you'll hopefully be very familiar with after you've circled all kinds of important facts in Adam's chapters to separate them from the rest of the information.

But there is also a connection of movement and direction. This gives us two principles: *good form*, in which we tend to mentally complete shapes hidden 'behind' other shapes (so we see the line of dots pass 'in front of' a line of squares in that last example) and *common fate* (we see the line of dots moving up at an angle, although this tends to apply more to animation).

Simplification refers to the human tendency to conceptually simplify visuals down to their most basic reading, as in the principle of good form. So

in the first example in Figure 5.17, we don't see a set of unrelated short lines, we see a rectangle with a dash outline. We instinctively complete the shape of the rectangle. In the second example we read the complex shape as a combination of simple shapes: square, circle, triangle.

Figure/ground refers to the fact that people have a tendency to separate elements into a key figure against a background – usually they see the smaller element to be the 'figure' and the larger element to be the 'ground'. Often the figure will be seen to be 'nearer', literally standing out against the background.

Although they can both be useful in structuring layouts, indicating ways to enter and read a visual, both the latter two are probably more important to bear in mind as ways in which audiences may 'misread' visuals, particularly charts, if these phenomena are in play.

These are really just descriptions of how people tend to read visuals, but we can reverse-engineer them and use them to guide our readers through our information.

In practice

Sergio has laid out the newspaper double-page spread about the baby names data that Adam

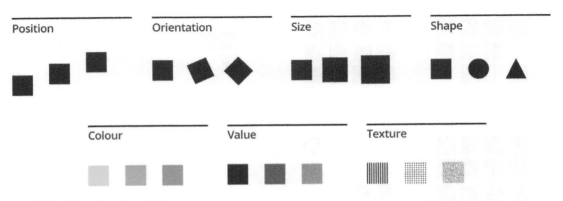

Figure 5.18 The visual variables

wireframed (Figure 5.19). It's a big canvas and there's a lot of information on it, but you can see how he's used changes in those fundamental visual attributes to signal changes in the information structure:

- **Space**. This most obviously plays a role right down the centre of the spread – the gutter either side of the fold that serves as the axis across which the content is mirrored.
- **Enclosure**. Most obviously we have the dark boxes at the bottom corners, but because of how we tend to simplify shapes, the rules dividing the blocks become outlines enclosing the content.
- **Colour**. Notice how the colour background to the titles matches the charts underneath, helping us see the meaning, but then the colours change for the different data of the growth charts.
- **Texture**. The complexity of outline of the photography and illustration explicitly distinguish them from the clean lines of the data visualisation.
- **Weight**. Weight plays a vital part in the text formatting, showing levels of importance, but the heavier weight of the quotation also serves to single it out from the rest of the text.

The changes in these elements play on the pattern-seeking that guides the Gestalt groupings. They simplify the content from uncountable amounts of data down to eight blocks, repeated in a symmetrical layout – a consistent layout partitioned by change within that consistent layout, showing out readers where and how to read.

But then we have to think about what they read.

Note that this spread uses a symmetrical, mirrored layout. This works well when you want to compare and contrast two things or two stories. Just the symmetry alone is appealing.

The most common layout is the sequence of boxes of content that can be read as a comic strip, effectively, reading from one box to the next. You can see this effect if you look at just one half of the newspaper spread (Figure 5.20).

Each section is clearly demarcated with borders and spaces, assuming that you will read in a 'z' order, left to right, top to bottom. These best suit a story of development, from one point to the next – a beginning, middle and end, essentially.

They also work well for lists, of course, although in that case you'll want to make sure that each segment is clearly independent of the others. This is most often the case online where the infographic tends to become a tower of panels, one on top of the other, read downwards as the reader scrolls.

Another common layout is the single large chart, either on its own or with small charts around it as context. This is best suited to composition stories, where there is no particular read order, but instead a variety of key points all drawn from or about the core visual.

People are still likely to read clockwise, however, so bear in mind that you'll need some kind of individual visual attraction in each section, like icons or highlighted elements, to keep them moving round.

This works best as a poster (Figure 5.21) and is hard to make work on smaller screens.

Delineating the detail

As above, so below.

Even within an individual chart there is a visual hierarchy. The chart itself – the graphics that represent the data – is usually the visually dominant element, simply because of size, complexity or density of ink. But there are a lot of other elements that we need to consider (titles, subtitles, legends, axis labels, and so on), and all of these need to be placed within a hierarchy so that they're not fighting each other for attention.

When Oliver met Olivia:
Top names in England & Wales

Girls

Top 100 girls' names 2018

1. Olivia	51. Eleanor
2. Amelia	52. Lola
3. Ava	53. Violet
4. Isla	54. Bella
5. Emily	55. Rose
6. Mia	56. Emma
7. Isabella	56. Holly
8. Sophia	58. Molly
9. Ella	59. Thea
10. Grace	60. Ellie
11. Poppy	61. Lucy
12. Charlotte	62. Hannah
13. Lily	63. Lottie
14. Ivy	64. Nancy
15. Florence	65. Ada
16. Evie	66. Maria
17. Sophie	67. Lilly
18. Freya	68. Zara
19. Evelyn	69. Aurora
20. Willow	70. Amber
21. Phoebe	71. Georgia
22. Elsie	72. Robyn
23. Sienna	73. Gracie
24. Alice	74. Summer
25. Jessica	75. Jasmine
26. Rosie	76. Annabelle
27. Harper	77. Abigail
28. Daisy	78. Darcie
29. Sofia	79. Hallie
30. Isabelle	80. Amelie
31. Matilda	81. Bonnie
32. Ruby	82. Iris
33. Eva	83. Maryam
34. Emilia	84. Beatrice
35. Scarlett	85. Anna
36. Chloe	86. Heidi
37. Maya	87. Orla
38. Esme	88. Arabella
39. Eliza	89. Clara
40. Millie	90. Delilah
41. Imogen	91. Edith
42. Aria	92. Aisha
43. Luna	93. Francesca
44. Layla	94. Martha
45. Harriet	95. Ayla
46. Maisie	96. Zoe
47. Elizabeth	97. Lyla
48. Penelope	98. Sara
49. Mila	99. Margot
50. Erin	100. Felicity

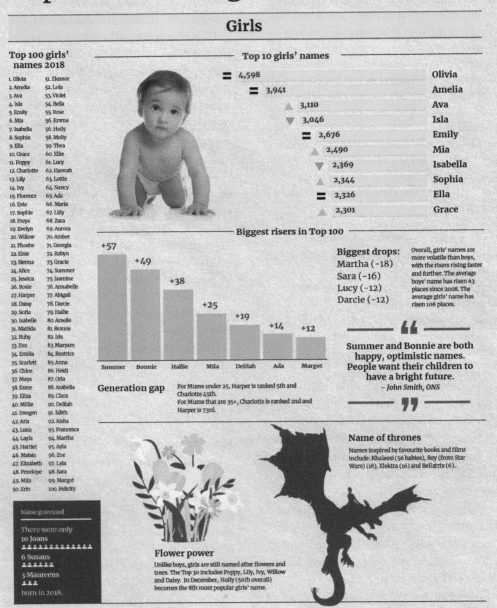

Top 10 girls' names

= 4,598	Olivia
= 3,941	Amelia
▲ 3,110	Ava
▼ 3,046	Isla
= 2,676	Emily
▲ 2,490	Mia
▼ 2,369	Isabella
▲ 2,344	Sophia
= 2,326	Ella
▲ 2,301	Grace

Biggest risers in Top 100

+57 Summer
+49 Bonnie
+38 Hallie
+25 Mila
+19 Delilah
+14 Ada
+12 Margot

Generation gap
For Mums under 25, Harper is ranked 5th and Charlotte 45th.
For Mums that are 35+, Charlotte is ranked 2nd and Harper is 73rd.

Biggest drops:
Martha (−18)
Sara (−16)
Lucy (−12)
Darcie (−12)

Overall, girls' names are more volatile than boys, with the risers rising faster and further. The average boys' name has risen 63 places since 2008. The average girls' name has risen 106 places.

" Summer and Bonnie are both happy, optimistic names. People want their children to have a bright future.
– *John Smith, ONS* "

Name graveyard
There were only
10 Joans
▲▲▲▲▲▲▲▲▲▲
6 Susans
▲▲▲▲▲▲
3 Maureens
▲▲▲
born in 2018.

Flower power
Unlike boys, girls are still named after flowers and trees. The Top 30 includes Poppy, Lily, Ivy, Willow and Daisy. In December, Holly (56th overall) becomes the 8th most popular girls' name.

Name of thrones
Names inspired by favourite books and films include: Khaleesi (56 babies), Rey (from Star Wars) (18), Elektra (16) and Bellatrix (6)..

Figure 5.19   Sergio's design for Adam's newspaper wireframe

This year, there's no change at the top for both boys and girls. The long, unchallenged reign of Oliver and Olivia continues for another year. Other firm favourites like Emily and Amelia for girls, and Harry and Jack for boys, remain in the Top 10.

Where there is change, it's a strange mixture of old and new. Yes, there are novel names in the Top 100 like Luna and Aurora (for girls) and Grayson and Jaxon (for boys). These are often taken from books, films or celebrity culture.

But most of the new names and high risers aren't new at all. For girls, old-fashioned names like Ava and Grace have risen further into the Top 10 and the highest-rising names include Edwardian favourites like Ada and Margot. For boys, what to make of the appearance in the Top 100 of Reggie (at 51), Stanley (at 67) and Ralph (at 81)?

Cultural differences are also a factor for boys' names. Muhammad is the seventh most popular name, and two other spellings (Mohammed and Mohammad) also feature in the Top 100. The influence of religion and culture is less apparent for baby girls, although Eastern European names like Mila and Sophia feature in the Top 20 and are particularly popular in London.

Boys

Top 10 boys' names

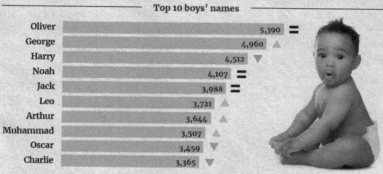

Name	Value	
Oliver	5,390	=
George	4,960	▲
Harry	4,512	▼
Noah	4,107	=
Jack	3,988	=
Leo	3,721	▲
Arthur	3,644	▲
Muhammad	3,507	▲
Oscar	3,459	▼
Charlie	3,365	▼

Top 100 boys' names 2018

1. Oliver	51. Luca	
2. George	52. Albie	
3. Harry	53. Hugo	
4. Noah	54. Zachary	
5. Jack	55. Albert	
6. Leo	56. Jude	
7. Arthur	57. Toby	
8. Muhammad	58. Riley	
9. Oscar	59. Ezra	
10. Charlie	60. Carter	
11. Jacob	61. Gabriel	
12. Thomas	62. Roman	
13. Henry	63. Frankie	
14. William	64. Harley	
15. Alfie	65. Frederick	
16. Archie	66. Ronnie	
17. Joshua	67. Jake	
18. Freddie	68. Elliot	
19. Theo	69. Louis	
20. Isaac	70. Jenson	
21. James	71. Mohammad	
22. Alexander	72. Stanley	
23. Logan	73. Bobby	
24. Edward	74. Michael	
25. Ethan	75. Jesse	
26. Lucas	76. Finn	
27. Joseph	77. Jayden	
28. Sebastian	78. Harvey	
29. Theodore	79. Caleb	
30. Finley	80. Jackson	
31. Max	81. Charles	
32. Mohammed	82. Matthew	
33. Samuel	83. Grayson	
34. Harrison	84. Blake	
35. Benjamin	85. Liam	
36. Arlo	86. Elliott	
37. Daniel	87. Ellis	
38. Adam	88. Ralph	
39. Teddy	89. Jasper	
40. Mason	89. Rowan	
41. Elijah	91. Alex	
42. Reuben	91. Ryan	
43. Dylan	93. Felix	
44. Hunter	94. Luke	
45. Reggie	95. Dexter	
46. Jaxon	96. Ollie	
47. Rory	97. Leon	
48. Louie	98. Tobias	
49. David	99. Sonny	
50. Tommy	100. Dominic	

Biggest risers in Top 100

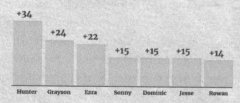

+34	+24	+22	+15	+15	+15	+14
Hunter	Grayson	Ezra	Sonny	Dominic	Jesse	Rowan

Generation gap For Mums under 25, Logan is ranked 6th and Jack 29th. For Mums that are 35+, Jack is ranked 3rd and Logan is 46th.

Biggest drops:
Luke (-18)
Matthew (-15)
Riley (-15)

The reason for the rise in popularity of particular names is often hard to pin down. Hunter could be linked to the maverick US author Hunter S. Thompson and Grayson could be connected to Grayson Perry, the British potter and TV presenter. But the reason for the popularity of Ezra, Sonny and Rowan is not immediately obvious.

Furthermore, none of these names appeared in the Top 100 before 2010 so it's not as if they are a revival of a previously popular name or the name of a great-grandparent.

These newer names appear to be more popular with younger mothers. For example, Hunter is ranked 122nd for mothers over 35, but is in 10th place for mothers under 25. Grayson is ranked 57 for younger mothers, but 118 for mothers over 35. Dominic is ranked 100 overall, but 76 for younger mothers and 126 for mothers over 35.

MO-mentum
Muhammad is the top name in these four regions. The West Midlands and Yorkshire also have a second spelling of the name (Mohammed) in the Top 10.

Marvel-lous names
Names inspired by favourite books and films include: Loki (88 babies), Kylo (78), Theon (21), Thor (19) and Albus (7).

Name graveyard
There were only
13 Keiths
🧍🧍🧍🧍🧍🧍🧍🧍🧍🧍🧍🧍🧍
8 Nigels
🧍🧍🧍🧍🧍🧍🧍🧍
3 Clives
🧍🧍🧍
born in 2018.

Instinctively we tend to distinguish these elements using differences of position, size and density: titles are at the top, big and bold; labels might be body copy size and a regular font face; sources are probably small and thin, tucked away at the bottom.

The position is dictated by read order, of course, but we can play with the structure using the other attributes. We might have a small section header at the top, followed by a large title – showing the hierarchy within an information structure.

This is something that we all do naturally, indeed something we expect all word processors to do for us, with text. We understand that the order of importance between titles, subtitles, text, captions, footnotes, and so on is all delineated by changes in density: altering size, value, texture to signal structure.

We're often doing this with text in visualisations too, but it's also what we're doing with all our visuals – using changes in density to signal changes in hierarchy.

This can only work when we have a consistency of visual language showing the structure: that elements are placed consistently in the same places, that fonts are sized consistently for the same purposes, that colours are used to indicate meanings consistently. By using a consistent visual language we can clearly signal to our readers how to read what we're showing them; otherwise we're making them puzzle out how to read, even before they've tried to understand what they're reading. For a lot of people, that's going to be a challenge too far.

The crucial thing to remember, however, is that our aim here is clarity. We need to be wary of any choice that might confuse our audience. We might say: always use the same colours to mean the samething, except for when we suddenly discover we've defined all the colours to mean different kinds of road vehicles and we've got nothing left to use for railways. What we need is consistency. If colours don't have set meanings then we need to avoid using them in a way that suggests they do: if red is our highlight colour, we should never use yellow.

A fundamental consistency to our visual language matters, however, because part of being clear is reducing the amount of work the reader has to do to understand. We are doing work so they don't have to – until we need them to. Data visualisation is by its nature a practice that requires concentration from the reader: but on the data. Defining our structure, and the visual language that shows it, is a vital part of our doing our job of getting the reader to the numbers with as little friction as possible.

Figure 5.20 One side of the double-page spread

Figure 5.21 A big wheel of numbers

In practice

You can see in Figure 5.22 how Sergio is using those changes in density to signal differences in importance.

Throughout we can see a consistent font size and display for subtitles: 14 point and bold. This is complicated though – one of these subtitles is the title for the whole block, two of them subtitles within the block. Rather than disrupt that consistency, however, Sergio has placed the block title within the line that separates off the whole block – using positioning to signal its difference from the other subtitles.

Meanwhile the pull quote has exactly that font size and weight, but is itself carefully sectioned off with enclosure within the top and tailing lines and quotation marks.

You can see how the consistency of visual language and the weight and size of the font face are just as important as the changes that indicate difference in nature, and it is the two working together that give us a clear sense of information hierarchy.

Visual storytelling

If storytelling is, as Adam claims, a matter of selection, dramatisation and emphasis, then charting represents the first two parts, selecting and dramatising the subject-matter, and this stage is the emphasis.

This is where we put our information into an order to show the information hierarchy and give our audience a clear sense of what they're looking at.

Doing this means being ruthless. We must kill our darlings in the wireframing process, making definite decisions about which piece of information is more important than another. Relegating one interesting fact even as we elevate another. This is hard to do, but if we don't, there's no way we can meaningfully use contrast to indicate that order clearly.

And clarity is our goal. We want to give our audience a clear idea of what we're trying to say, a clear (usually single) way in and a clear path to follow to the detail.

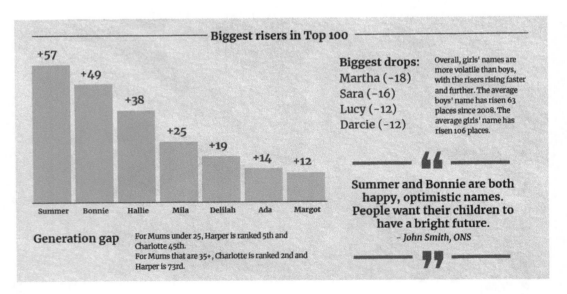

Figure 5.22   Biggest risers

Only once we have established our map can we start to draw big sea monsters in the empty bits.

Let's get dramatic.

Making an impression

Persuasion

One of the biggest problems with making something that looks attractive is taste. People like different things. One person's delicate and balanced minimalism is another person's boring and featureless empty space; one person's exciting and exuberant composition is another person's gaudy and childish mess. Finding a visual expression that everyone likes is incredibly difficult.

However, there are some basic principles we can bear in mind when we try to make something that looks nice.

And what do you know: they are our old friends, consistency and change.

Visual consistency in design is comforting, relaxing: a rhythmic pattern, a harmonious colour palette, a predictable layout. These things don't stress us, don't overwhelm us with information, and show us visually the presence of a calm and considering mind.

Visual change is, of course, exciting. Change attracts our attention and we like that; it's stimulating. It relieves the boredom, keeps us stimulated and engaged in the world.

Using the two together allows us to create visuals that interest and please, that are aesthetically satisfying. But they're more than that – this is also the visual language that we use to show data and information structures and meaning. Data visualisation is a kind of design, and in design form follows function (this isn't always true, but for the sake of this discussion I'm going to arbitrarily rule that design is functional and art is not, which is also not true – no definition of art ever is).

What something looks like depends on its function, and our function is communication –

it is how well we communicate that determines our design. So even as we try to make everything look nice, we need to be considering the effect our choices are going to have on our communication.

Fortunately, though, communicating well is – in itself – attractive. Often just having a clear point well made is enough to draw an audience in, without needing any bells or whistles.

Harmony

Harmony is agreement, having elements working together. In music this can be thought of as a process, where dissonance resolves into harmony. Or harmony can be thought of as the balance or relationship between forces otherwise in tension. Resolving that tension produces harmony, a resolution that is aesthetically pleasing and emotionally fulfilling.

In design, this resolution lies in how we reconcile figure and ground, the focus and the context, the drama and the world. Or, to be slightly less sententious: consistency and change.

'Figure and ground' refers to the background and the object in focus. In general, viewers will separate visuals into figure and ground (whether we intend them to or not), assuming that the larger visual element is the ground and anything contrasting against is the figure, the object of focus.

We have already insisted on how consistency gives us visual appeal: order, symmetry and pattern are all things that audiences find appealing, or at least non-threatening – they give us ways to be not unappealing, at least.

The basics of our visual design therefore become setting up those rules of consistency, laying out a grid to align the layout to, picking a font or two and sticking to them, composing a coherent colour palette, and choosing an icon style and photography approach.

All of which is to say that I know you are bored with your corporate brand guidelines and the brand police who won't let you do anything interesting, but they are important. Not because of all that vapid verbiage about values that the management insist gets put in the handbook, but because they give us that consistency of visual language.

It's that consistency that also allows us to create contrast: and contrast is interest, excitement, drama. In order to build a harmonious design, however, that contrast still needs to sit within the rules of consistency. A contrasting colour still has to work within our palette; placing something on a third only works because it plays against the symmetry of the composition while respecting the grid. We are creating contrast within consistency, which is what gives us our harmony.

Drama

When we talk about drama in design, we generally mean it in the sense of excitement, unexpected developments, emotionally fraught events. The bright green of a 'go' traffic light creates a thrill of impulse, the red of a fire alarm signals alertness, the bright yellow of a 'sale' sign piques our curiosity.

What is noticeable in those examples is how the other meaning of drama lurks in the background. How a play takes those moments of emotional intensity and strings them into a structure that creates a story. That kind of drama. The barbeque we buy in the sale is later going to set fire to the garden shed, fire engines running the lights in full blues and twos towards smoke billowing upwards over suburbia.

A useful way to think about this is by thinking about filmmaking and what is called mise-en-scène – the way all the visuals (camera framing and movement, the blocking of actors in the frame, costumes and set dressing, motion and animation) in a film come together to tell a story.

Movement in the frame of a film is inherently interesting, and filmmakers can use it to create sequences that are stimulating, but ultimately empty – multiple planes of complex motion that tell us nothing, that move no plot along, that develop no character.

On the other hand, we could watch the opening scenes of Steven Spielberg's *Raiders of the Lost Ark* (after all, why shouldn't we?). Throughout the first few sequences the camera barely moves. Instead characters walk through a static shot. And we're not yet quite sure what we make of this mysterious man in the slouch hat. His face is frequently hidden from us. He seems dangerous, unpredictable. What is he doing in this jungle? Where is he leading us?

Everything changes when we discover the answer. Indiana Jones has entered the ancient temple and brilliantly avoided its traps, and now he stands before a golden idol, weighing a bag of sand in his hand, expertly trying to judge its weight.

And the camera finally moves – it dollies. Physically moving in towards Dr Jones and taking us with it until we are right up at Harrison Ford's face, giant on the movie screen, right with him as he makes his decision. And gets it wrong. He makes a mistake and everything goes bad very, very fast.

That single camera move puts us right into the head of and into identification with the character at the crucial moment – at the moment he shows that he's just like us: he makes mistakes. And then he shows us that (often unlike us) he can always escape just by the skin of his teeth, and now we're barrelling along with him on his wild ride because now we love Dr Indiana Jones.

This is what is termed motivated camera: movement that is happening not just to be interesting (although it is still that) but in service of the story. Likewise, what we need is motivated design, creating moments of stimulating, exciting and engaging visual design that also serve to show our data and communicate our insight.

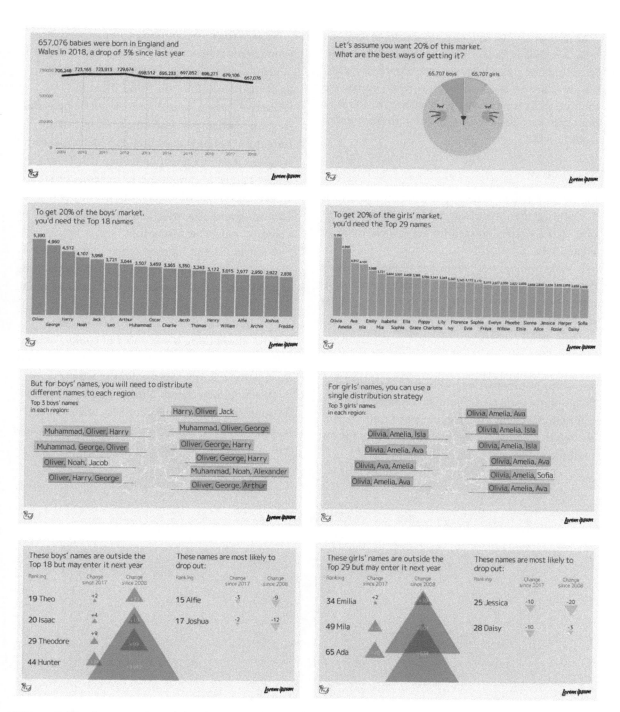

Figure 5.23 Presentation slides for a clothing manufacturer

Attractiveness doesn't just attract. In making us look, it makes us look in a particular place. It directs. So in thinking about how we make attractive visuals, we also have to think about how those visuals are framing what we are saying, what they're showing our audience and how they're going to make them think and feel.

In practice

Figure 5.23 shows Adam's presentation slides for a clothing manufacturer. Take a closer look at one of the panels created by Sergio, enlarged in Figure 5.24.

It looks simple, but Sergio has done a lot using colour, font and illustration to make this approachable and appealing, and it's worth thinking about in depth.

Colour

It's worth noting that as part of this process I made Sergio some truncated brand guidelines for each of our fictional clients, to give him some rules to work to. Figure 5.25 shows the brand guidelines for our clothing company.

Perhaps the most common complaint we hear from clients is how much they hate their brand guidelines: they're bored with them, they never liked the hero colour, they find them too restrictive. Now colour is undoubtedly a powerful weapon, particularly when it comes to making something visually appealing. But like all powerful weapons it can be horrifying when it falls into the wrong hands. It's important to remember that, as we have seen, visual change can quickly get confusing and upsetting, and this is just as true of colour as any other visual tool.

A restrained and harmonious colour palette is an extremely useful element in making something visually attractive. You can see that in those brand guidelines there are more colours available than Sergio has used; he has stuck with a limited palette. Restraining the number of colours and adhering to the guidelines are often the safest way of creating a harmonious colour scheme.

Of course, he's chosen pink and blue for other reasons: colours have meaning too. Brands have colours; countries have colours (some combination of red and blue stripes, usually, maybe with a bit of

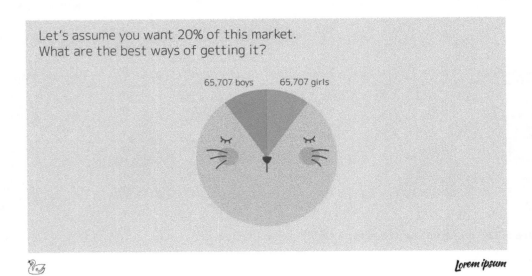

Figure 5.24 Look at the likkle pie chart and his boopable nose!

Primary colours

R253, G185, B169
fcb9a9

R86, G204, B206
56ccce

Secondary colours

R255, G189, B108
ffbd6c

R238, G233, B230
eee9e6

R132, G214, B154
84d69a

Illustrations

Lorem Ipsum has a library of custom illustrations. Icons are solid, preferably on a coloured background

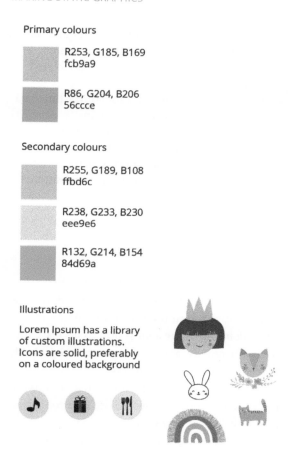

Logo

Lorem ipsum
fashion boutique

Lorem ipsum

Fonts

Brand Font   Kaushan Script

System font   M PLUS Rounded 1c

Powerpoint template

Figure 5.25   (Very) simple brand guidelines

white or yellow for variety; politics has colours (red menaces, green new deals) emotions have colours (feeling blue about being called a yellow belly, I'm browned off and in a black mood) – let alone the endless theories about how blue is cool and calming and red is hot and energising. And many of those meanings have cultural inflections, any of which can confuse our communication.

And all this is before we get to questions of legibility and accessibility. Eight per cent of men are red–green colour blind. That's a lot of people. It has to be a consideration in picking our palettes; they still tend to retain a distinction between blue and yellow, which is a much nicer colour combination, to boot. Then there are questions of contrast and readability, especially when we're

projecting a presentation on a clapped-out projector in a sunny meeting room where the blinds don't work.

So colour has to be used with care. Not least because, like all our other visual tools, it tells stories, too.

Even in a simple colour wheel we can see how different combinations of hues suggest different kinds of framing – how the oppositional difference between complementary colours makes us see a stark contrast, while the gradual change in a monochromatic series shows us a close relationship (Figure 5.26). We can use these colour relationships to show the structures within our data.

In constructing a palette and thinking about its use, it can be helpful to think about how humans interact and talk about colour. Languages are most likely to have words for black and white and then, in decreasing order (Berlin and Kay, 1969):

- red
- yellow and green
- blue
- brown
- pink, orange, purple and grey.

Red appears to have a very special importance for humans; red ochre pigments are, in fact, one of the surest signs of early humans in the archaeological record. In fact the most pared-down palette imaginable, black and white and red, is also one of the reliable and consistently effective (and gives everything a nice bit of Bauhaus flair, too).

It's attractiveness means that red works best as a highlight colour, so we might use a blue or yellow as our main base colour to contrast red against and be sure that these colours are recognisable and clear to most audiences.

Of course, not all of us have the time or the ability to generate our own colour palettes. In case it is helpful, we have made an example palette for you (Figure 5.27). It is made of six core colours, from which we have created:

- a range of tints and shades (lighter and darker versions of the core colours) which are useful for heatmaps and closely associated datasets
- a set of diverging palettes for contrasting data or highlighting one dataset against another, including one in the viridis style, blue–green–yellow, which is a better alternative to traditional red–amber–green schemes
- a set of contrasting colours for compositional stories.

Font

The advent of desktop publishing and the squeezing of every font face in the world into the little 'font' menu in the ribbon on Microsoft PowerPoint has done a great deal to decrease the sum of happiness among designers. And probably increase it among everyone else.

Everyone loves playing with font, and everyone needs to get a grip on themselves. Like colour, font feels like an easy option in making something attractive and like so many easy options it is often the path to ruin.

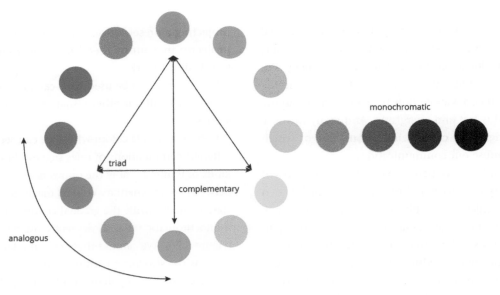

Figure 5.26 A simple colour wheel

Of course, as with colour, our brand guidelines have a preferred font, and again, as with colour, Sergio has followed them. The restraint itself becomes part of the appeal. But there are other considerations, too. Look at another slide from the presentation, shown in Figure 5.28.

There's a lot of information here: the map, the different colours, the labels, the explanatory text. And the visual change of a different font face in the middle of all this would be yet another call on our reader's attention. An unnecessary call, at that.

Of course, we need to prioritise legibility and make sure that our font can be easily read at all the font sizes we are using (you can go quite small in print, but not so much on screen, and definitely not if it's a presentation) – this usually means sticking to more common serif and sans-serif fonts and not using display fonts or anything too showy.

We also need to think about how we are using the font. Naturally text is information, but our font choice gives us meta-information. The way we use styles to give emphasis or distinction through bold or italic faces, or size and weight to show importance, gives our reader an immediate sense of information hierarchy.

But like all our visual tools, our font choice also frames reading, not just in structure, but also in tone of voice. For example, in their research with the *New York Times*, Errol Morris and David Dunning found that people instinctively trusted information given to them in Baskerville. It's hardly surprising, given its a good, serious-looking serif font – very much the kind of type face you'd expect to find in a print reference book (as a rule of thumb, serif for print and sans serif on screen).

On the other hand, in data visualisation, we're often using sans serifs, partly because they tend to render numbers in a more legible format, but also because they put less character into the communication. They are less strident, less present, more suited to a neutral, considered piece of communication.

Figure 5.29 shows some recommended fonts.

Using a single font face across a whole piece is the easiest way to ensure everything is legible and easy to parse. Digitally we might use a serif font for titles and a sans serif for body copy, or in print – like this very book – we might use a serif in body copy (as it's easier to read in physical print) and a

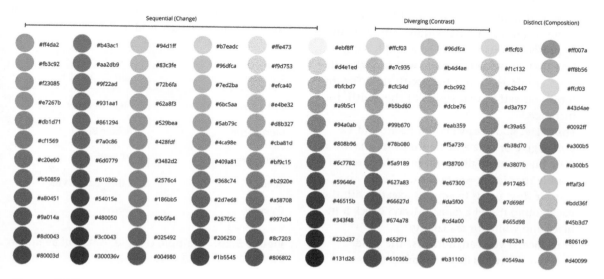

Figure 5.27 Some example colour palettes

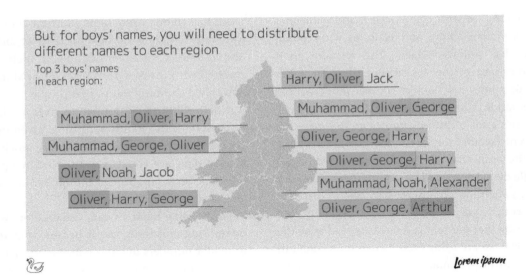

But for boys' names, you will need to distribute different names to each region

Top 3 boys' names in each region:

Harry, Oliver, Jack

Muhammad, Oliver, Harry

Muhammad, Oliver, George

Muhammad, George, Oliver

Oliver, George, Harry

Oliver, Noah, Jacob

Oliver, George, Harry

Muhammad, Noah, Alexander

Oliver, Harry, George

Oliver, George, Arthur

Lorem ipsum

Figure 5.28 A map of names

sans serif in the visualisations. But a maximum of two font faces at a time, thanks.

Once we have chosen a good font for our communication, we then have to lay it out in a way that is legible. These are some hints for text use:

- **Word count**: Generally aim for line lengths of around 60 characters (give or take 10) – that's about the length of a line in a paperback book, for instance. Shorter lines will tend to give us solid blocks of text rather than distracting widows and orphans. In presentations we tend to avoid having text that runs the complete width of the slide (the templates do not help with this). Try to limit yourself to two-thirds of the width, for instance.
- **Font size**: Body copy should be around 12 point (give or take a little) for print, maybe a little bigger for digital, and probably around double that for presentations.
- **Colour**: Text needs to contrast clearly with the background it's set against. Always check it in black and white for readability.
- **Font face**: If you can, don't use the 'bold' and 'italic' settings in your word processor,

but instead find a font that has those faces specifically designed. They'll look better.

- **Hierarchy**: Use bold to add weight for importance; use italic to add emphasis. Have at least 4 point difference in font size between different levels in the information hierarchy – generally, the higher up the information hierarchy, the bigger the font size.

In the end, though, all that really matters is – of course – can the reader read it?

Sans Serif	Serif
Open Sans	Merriweather
Montserrat	Roboto Slab
Source Sans	PT Serif
Roboto	Libre Baskerville
Raleway	Alegreya

Figure 5.29 Example Google fonts (all available online and free to use)

Iconography, illustration and photography

Come on now, though, what's the most appealing thing about the slide in Figure 5.30? The cute animal face, of course! Admit it, you love it.

Illustrative elements are obviously one of the more powerful elements we can add to our visualisation to make them more visually appealing, but they are hugely varied and have hugely varied effects.

We're going to look at them in three sections:

- **Iconography** – the small symbols that stand in for concepts and words
- **Illustration** – more complex drawings and artwork that embellish content
- **Photography** – images of the real world that provide concrete references and connections.

Iconography

Iconography is a microcosm of data visualisation, as it is the use of visuals to communicate an often abstract concept – an icon is information in its own right.

Now, obviously an icon is part illustration and partly serves a role as decoration (and sometimes that's what we're using it for: just a little visual fillip). It's certainly more eye-catching to put in a little icon alongside (or instead of) text, but they need to be read as clearly as text, especially when they are standing in for navigation elements or chart labels.

The secret to good iconography is leaning into visual cliché. Icons work because they are clichés, and to interfere with the clichés is to interfere with the icon working. We may object to the 'female' icon wearing a skirt, but to alter the traditional iconographic man and woman is to risk confusing the audience, which we don't want to do, especially if they're desperate for the lavatory.

Obviously these clichés can be fairly broad – an iconographic stick figure might work for 'staff members', 'personal details' or 'filter by demographics', for instance. The crucial thing is not to try to be too cute. Your little voter doesn't need to be holding a pencil. The aim is clarity, not accuracy. Tip – if an icon doesn't spring immediately to mind, then there probably isn't one. Try using text or a more complex illustration instead.

This is not to say we can't create icons to represent concepts of our own. We just have to be aware that it will take multiple exposures for our readers to learn what our icon means and to understand it as quickly as they do text (research by Jon Puleston and Satsuki Suzuki suggests the users have to see the icon accompanied with a label at least eight times before they recognise the visual as quickly as the word).

On the whole, when it comes to creating iconography, it's usually best to err on the side of the conceptual rather than the literal. Think of the

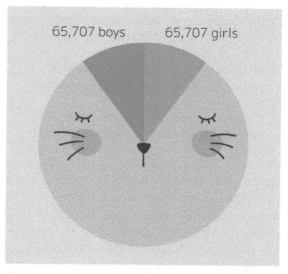

Figure 5.30 Some nicely deployed illustration – good work, Sergio! (There, I finally said it in print)

iconography we deal with everyday – the three lined 'hamburger' of the menu icon, the pierced circle of the power icon (Figure 5.31). Both of those examples use a degree of simile and metaphor to express the idea: the hamburger represents the rows of choices in the menu, the power button the 1 of binary 'on' and the 0 of 'off'. But those meanings don't actually matter. You've probably never even thought about what that circle and line might mean and neither do you care. You know it's the power switch. By being visually simple and essentially conceptual, they avoid confusing us with literal and potentially misleading depictions and complicated illustrations.

Figure 5.32 shows some icons illustrating age ranges: child/adult/elderly. They vary in style and approach.

- **Simple**: the most common form of icon, designed to be read as quickly as a word
- **Complex**: more detailed than a common icon, adding more identity
- **Illustration**: more realistic depictions, although still simple enough to work at small sizes, adding a personality
- **Object**: using a representative object rather than a direct depiction (of an individual, say), often useful to avoid stereotyping (the woman in a skirt, for instance)
- **Metaphor**: Adopting a visual metaphor, particularly useful when avoiding cultural references
- **Conceptual**: creating an abstract depiction of the concept to escape any specific depiction.

The more complex an icon becomes, the more specific it is: the more it tells us something very particular about the content (and starts to introduce cultural biases, like an indication of gender or ethnicity). Objects can be effective, but they rely on context – the representation of age here only works because the baby bottle is a clear stand-in for babies. With both the metaphorical and conceptual approaches you're

Figure 5.31 Hamburger on!

avoiding these possible confusions but introducing a different one: effectively asking the audience to learn the iconographic language from scratch, as they read – not the most economical means of communicating.

Illustrations

There are essentially three kinds of illustration that we tend to need, what we might call *diagrams*, *descriptions* and *decorations*.

Diagrams are often really just a branch of data visualisation, or at least information structuring, and most of the rest of this book applies to them – most specifically, the need to clearly determine what the point is. We need to know what our main point is, and to find a visual metaphor to make that plain. A process will often travel left to right or top to bottom, an organisation might be a tree or spider out from a centre. We often end up using conceptual landscapes (the map metaphor) to place elements within. Once we have that basic process, we can see how we can structure and layer up more information in that metaphor, discarding anything that gets in the way of understanding (Figure 5.33).

Diagrams have a specific purpose that will determine their content and layout. The only issue is sometimes having to balance a style guide against the technical detail that needs to be illustrated. As a rule of thumb, the content ought to override any stylistic considerations.

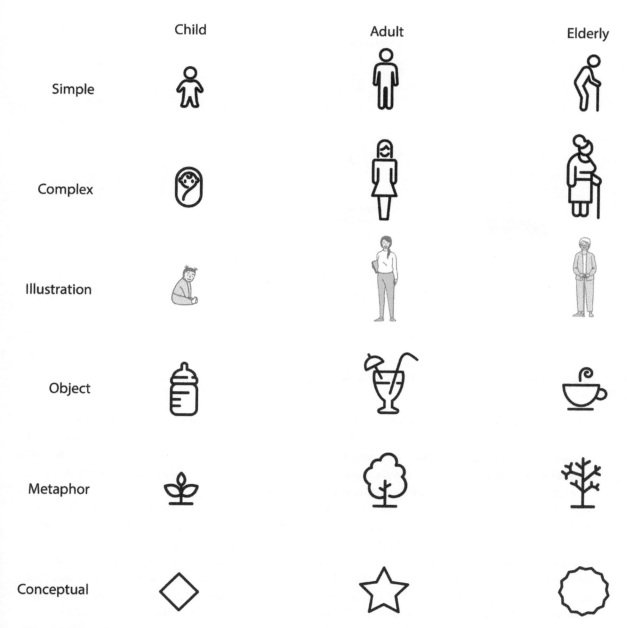

Figure 5.32 Different icon styles for the same concepts

Descriptions are probably what we think of when we think of illustrations, visuals that give an example of or context to an idea, like the illustrations in a picture book or illustrated encyclopaedia.

The crucial thing to remember is that in illustrating something you are being editorial, giving a specific instance and concrete example, often of something quite conceptual and broad (Figure 5.34).

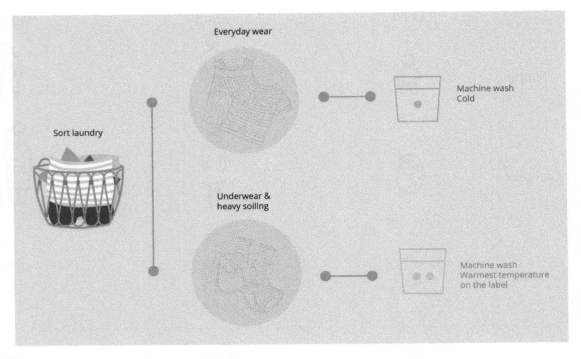

Everyday wear

Sort laundry

Underwear &
heavy soiling

Machine wash
Cold

Machine wash
Warmest temperature
on the label

Figure 5.33 A diagram of washing instructions

For this reason we often err towards the metaphorical, rather than the literal, to try to make sure that we aren't misleading the audience or making them think about a general issue in very specific ways.

Descriptive illustrations amplify or augment the content. The illustration can help give a concrete reference to an otherwise entirely notional concept.

Even when we're illustrative simply for decorative purposes of *decoration*, just to have some visual content on the page, we need to be sure that what we're doing isn't going to mislead or confuse the audience, and also that we're not going to overwhelm the content with what is a largely disposable visual.

Even in purely decorative illustration we are often thinking about the content (Figure 5.35). The subject-matter – babies – gives us the opportunity to have a cute decoration, and the circle of the pie chart gives us the perfect round shape to drop a face onto.

When we illustrate, we are often very deliberately framing how the reader will think about the content, so we need to consider what frame it is that we are creating: what is the tone?

A looser, more cartoony style will often feel more playful, but allow us to be more general, while something more photo-real can feel more serious but also appear more specific. Dark colours are more sombre but can feel dull and worthy, bright colours are more eye-catching but can drown out other content and feel trivial. Simple illustrations can feel a lot more straightforward, but can also be seen, particularly by expert audiences, as dumbing down. More complex illustrations, on the other hand, can feel very technical and overwhelming. As with all our visuals, we have to think about framing as much as we do the actual content.

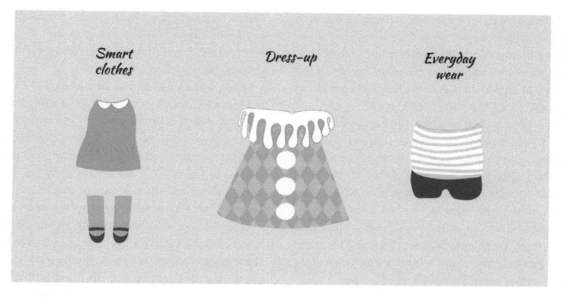

Figure 5.34 Illustrations of kinds of clothing

Photography

Photography can be a great way to grab an audience's attention: it is visually dense and full of interesting detail, it gives us images of recognisable and relatable things that the audience can comprehend in an instant, and when it comes to pictures of human beings, there is no better way of capturing the attention of social apes than pictures of their fellow simians.

On the other hand, attracting attention means distracting it from something else. The density and interest of photography means that it can easily overwhelm more complex and less visually interesting data visualisation. We also run the risk of being overly specific, of making our story about this particular person in the photo, rather than a population, potentially giving the audience the wrong interpretation. And, particularly when it comes to photos of people, we can have an emotional impact on the audience that can frame our story in unexpected ways.

And then, when we come to look for photographs to use, all we can find is staged stock photography of women smiling at salads (https://www.thehairpin.com/2011/01/women-laughing-alone-with-salad).

Like all powerful tools, we need to use photography carefully, especially around data visualisation.

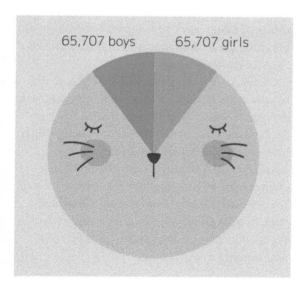

65,707 boys   65,707 girls

Figure 5.35 Purely decorative illustration, but that's not a bad thing

It is best used to set a mood or context, rather than as a specific example. Look for atmosphere rather than particular elements – photographs where people's faces are hidden, not the main feature of the frame, or where there is more than one person so that we're not being too literal.

And it's also best used as a feature rather than just an element on the page or slide. In fact, particularly in presentations, a full-bleed photograph can be a splendidly dramatic moment.[2] If you need to add content, then make sure it is on a featureless part of the photograph, or on a solid colour background overset on the photography. Make sure you have sufficient contrast between text and background. The more complex the content is, the simpler the photograph needs to be.

Given the visual power of both photography and data visualisation, combining them to stage photographs dramatising data is always an effective approach (Figure 5.36). This, of course, means following the whole process for creating any kind of data visualisation, plus the considerations required for photography: staging, lighting and so on.

When used alongside data visualisation, photography can very quickly become a problem. Not only does it often start to force our layout in unhelpful ways but even the simplest photographic element can quickly detract and distract from our data (as in Figure 5.37). The photography is so visually dense and stimulating that the data becomes barely noticeable, let alone informative.

Where it does work well is alongside simple and direct content, such as titles or key points, so that the information and the photograph aren't competing for attention and the photograph can do its job of bringing in the audience (Figure 5.38).

Figure 5.36 Making a chart in a photograph (61% of the toast is missing)

Making do

Here is a hack for making data visualisations that are visually stunning: hire a professional designer.

Seriously. This is why we stress teamwork: because different people are good at different things. If design isn't your thing, concentrate on planning good wireframes and find someone else to make them for you.

Of course, this is easier said than done. And it usually takes money, or time, or money and time, everyone's least favourite combination.

So, here are some actual hacks for making things look nice, if not actually stunning. First, a *consistent visual language*: establish a grid that elements are aligned to pick fonts that work well together use a harmonious colour palette and stick to rules about what kind of assets (chart types, iconography, illustration, photography) you're going to use.

[2]'Full bleed' means an image or background that runs right out, across the margins, to the edge of the page/screen.

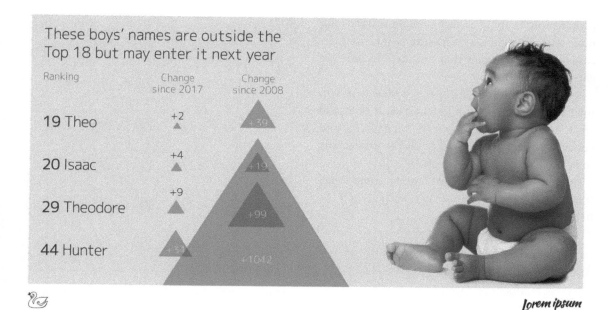

These boys' names are outside the
Top 18 but may enter it next year

Ranking	Change since 2017	Change since 2008
19 Theo	+2	+39
20 Isaac	+4	+19
29 Theodore	+9	+99
44 Hunter	+33	+1042

Lorem ipsum

Figure 5.37 Photo and chart – note how the photo takes up both physical and conceptual space

Second, *contrast*: use visual change to create drama, but only when it's motivated by the content. Use the contrast to direct the audience's attention where you want it to go.

Third, *maintain harmony*: the balance between consistency and contrast, ensuring that the two work together, that the contrast is dramatic within its context and does not become a clashing, distressing fracture.

The key to the balance is more consistency than contrast. Way more. Ideally you want a sole point of focus, clearly singled out. This alone makes

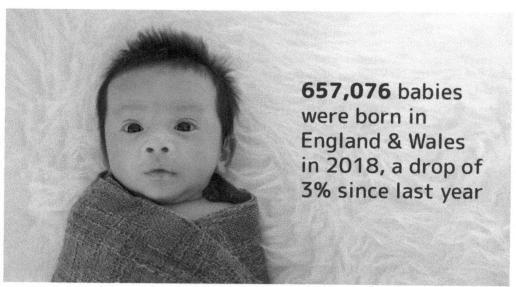

657,076 babies
were born in
England & Wales
in 2018, a drop of
3% since last year

Figure 5.38 Text on a photo (which needs photography with convenient blank spaces in)

people more likely to engage because it stands out more and also signals a clear entry point – a single, easily understood point that can then become the gateway to complexity.

One easy way to do all this is to adhere to a minimal design route. A simple chart with bold and clear highlights advertises its readability and encourages engagement. Clarity is the easiest way to be attractive.

However, sometimes we just have to primp something up a bit. Add some touches. Make it 'pop'. So here are...

Twenty-five design tricks that almost always work

Stuck for ideas? In a rush? Can't be bothered to read the rest of the book? In no particular order, here are some visual tricks that we use (usually on slide 121 of an interminable and meaningless corporate PowerPoint) that almost always work ('almost' is doing a lot of work there):

1 **Polar area charts**. Polar area charts are uncommon, which is a shame, because they're excellent, but also a blessing because it makes them very attention-getting (Figure 5.39). They're for comparison, preferably where there's a large range between the highs and lows in the data. Each segment has the same angle, but then extends out from the centre to give a different area. They're hard to make, though – Highcharts is the only charting engine I know of that provides them (and even that doesn't size them by area, which is bad and wrong and means you have to at least square-root all your values before you chart them).

2 **Icon in a doughnut**. Just got a single percentage to visualise? '87% of people don't even look at statistics'? Whack it in a doughnut chart and put a nice icon in the blank space in the centre (Figure 5.40). It's like a flower arrangement on a dining table:

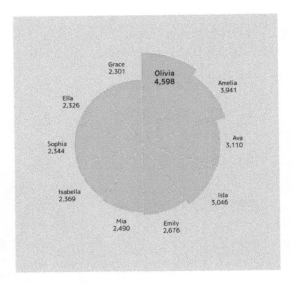

Figure 5.39 A polar area chart (sized by area; note – not by radius)

it doesn't do anything for the food, but it looks nice and everyone likes it.

3 **Text on a photo.** Got a statement that needs to be made exciting? Stick it on top of a photo (Figure 5.41). This requires, of course, having a photo with lots of blank space in

Figure 5.40 Icon in the centre of a doughnut chart

it on which you can add text, but that's OK because you're going to want a photo with plenty of contrast in it anyway. No obvious subject for a photograph? Use a city at night: either the skyline or a street scene. Maybe timelapse lights, or lens flare, or bokeh, or rain on a windshield. They nearly always work – they suggest people, community, technology, networks, modernity, development, and so on. The other alternatives are a city street in sunlight with silhouettes of pedestrians, countryside with a clear sky (and maybe some shallow-focus elements, like an out-of-focus flower in the foreground) or a starry sky, maybe with some timelapse streaking of the stars in their courses.

4 **Photo of a person.** People like people (in the abstract – there are plenty of specific, individual people I don't actually like). People also like big pictures of people. The trick here is to avoid ineptly posed stock photography – you will certainly be using stock, and it will almost certainly be posed, but you need to avoid heavy handed clichés, flat angles and stolid poses. Look for odd, dutch angles, dramatic shadows and people caught unaware. You don't even need to see faces (Figure 5.42): they can be

Figure 5.42 People doing things! Two-thirds of the way across the frame, too! Fascinating!

obscured, or we might just be looking at hands or specific features – it's all attention-getting for our fellow social apes.

5 **Positioning everything on thirds.** If you've ever done a photography course, or studied art, you'll know this one: position your key bit of content one-third of the way across the canvas. The rule of three is a powerful one and it gives us a nice fundamental trick of making something the focal point (centring also works, but thirds is more … curious).

6 **Angled stripes on a background.** Take a lesson from Adidas: stripes are a nice, simple, effective way to make a little dynamic decoration without being too distracting. It doesn't have to be full Tim Burton trousers; just a couple of stripes across a corner of a frame, like the ribbon on a chocolate box, works nicely (Figure 5.43).

7 **Text in a curved shape.** Blah, blah, blah. Just a big ol' block of boring text. Blah blah blah. Well, let's snuggle it down in a nice circle (Figure 5.44). Especially if that circle is clipped off the edge of the frame, so we just have a swathe of colour in a shallow curve. Nice. The text is still boring, but at least it looks interesting now.

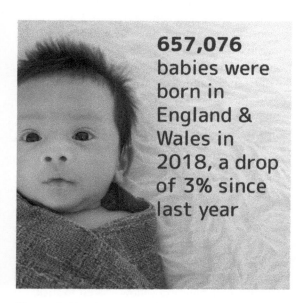

657,076 babies were born in England & Wales in 2018, a drop of 3% since last year

Figure 5.41 Text on a photo

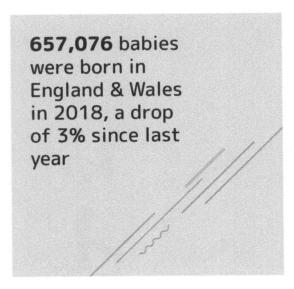

Figure 5.43   Inspired by a mid-1980s hair gel ad?

8   **Brightly coloured circles.** People like circles, people like bright colours: there you go. An easy little touch that can brighten up a dull corner.

9   **Block colour backgrounds to separate content.** Having lots of panels of content can start to feel

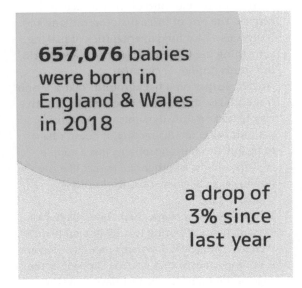

Figure 5.44   Using a brightly coloured curve to separate out text

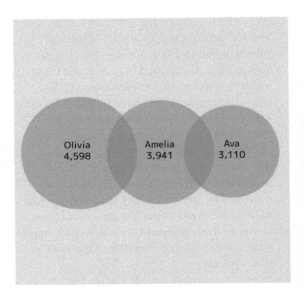

Figure 5.45   Think pink!

very fussy and samey, like a business dashboard. Try giving them each a different solid colour background – reversing out most of the content to white on block colour. This makes the page a lot more of an exciting patchwork than just another grid of charts.

10   **Bubble chart.** People like circles, so give 'em circles. A line of bubbles is an interesting change to a bar or column (Figure 5.45). They work best, mind, where there are some clear visible differences between the data values (they're particularly good at emphasizing big differences) and you have to remember that they're not as visually accurate as columns or bars. If you want to get really cute, do them with a less than 100% opacity and let them overlap a little bit (if you think purists hate bubble charts, wait until you find out how much they hate overlapping bubbles).

11   **Dark backgrounds with white text and charts.** Stuck with a bar chart that's perfectly legible, accurate and clear but, ultimately, looks boring? Reverse it out (Figure 5.46): make the background dark and the content bright and light (any contrasting pair of colours: black and white, dark blue and yellow – safest to stick to just a pair though). The dark background

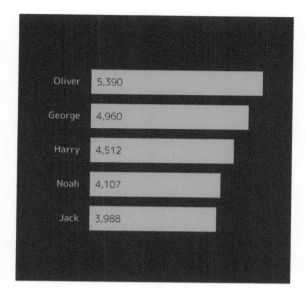

Figure 5.46   Neon in the night

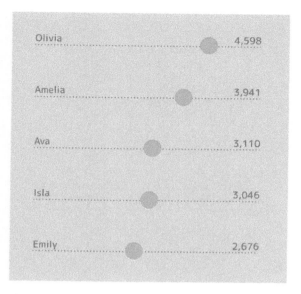

Figure 5.47   Abacus chart with aligned labels

will make brighter colours really stand out and the whole thing becomes a great deal more interesting.

12 **Abacus charts**. Used with restraint, there's something very appealing about the 'beads on a string' effect of an abacus chart (Figure 5.47). I suspect because they can make a nice minimalist pattern. It can be very tempting to get over-excited with these, though, and keep adding lots of dimensions and meaning. Keep it simple.

13 **Align text left and right to make straight lines and frames**. One trick I use a lot, especially when I have a circular chart like a pie or polar area, is to put the chart in the middle and then right-align text (labels, say) on the right and left-align on the left so you get these two straight vertical lines either side, making a box for the chart to sit in. In general, aligned text gives us nice straight lines that we can use to frame and guide the eye

14 **Minimal colour palette**. Colour is hard. Fortunately, keeping it easy means keeping it nice. One easy trick is to bring your palette right down to monochrome. Maybe add a contrasting colour. There, that's all you need: nice. It helps avoid any unpleasant clashing or

confusing contrast, and it's visually pleasing. Perfick.

15 **Subtle keylines to guide the eye**. Keylines are really useful for dividing content up, but they can also join it together. If you have, say, columns of content or a row of icons, running a keyline between them all helps guide the eye down the read order, as well as helping arrange them nicely on the page (Figure 5.48).

16 **Small text**. Oh, I know, designers hate words and deliberately make all the text tiny because it makes it into unreadable graphical blocks that they can then just shove about at random. It's true, but have you ever stopped to wonder whether it's because they know that there are equally effective ways of communicating purely visually? But you know what, it works.

17 **Short line lengths**. I said earlier that line lengths should ideally be about 60 characters in length. This helps readability. But keeping your line lengths short also helps keep things looking nice – rather than having a single long sentence just floating out there like a studio logo adrift in the cosmos, you can wrap it a couple of times and suddenly you have this identifiable block of content that you can then arrange neatly with all the other content.

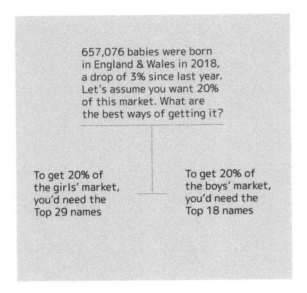

Figure 5.48 Keylines dividing up blocks of text

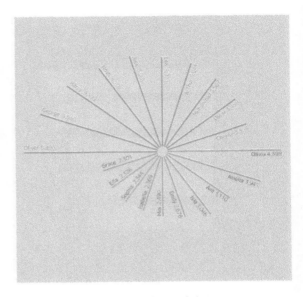

Figure 5.49 Mirrored fans of data

18 **Reflect the content around the vertical or horizontal axis.** Ah, symmetry, the secret to a beautiful face, a beautiful house, a beautiful garden, a beautiful … data visualisation! Now, obviously, as I've outlined above, reflecting elements has implications for meaning and relationships, but it also looks nice, and if you're at a loss as to how to arrange a bunch of disparate elements, reflecting them around a vertical or horizontal centre isn't a bad idea (Figure 5.49).

19 **Urchin charts.** That's my name for them, but you'd know them if you saw them: bars or lines of dots and shapes all splayed out in a halo around a central hub; a bar chart where the x-axis has been bent into a circle, concentric rings of symbols and lines; nested doughnut charts. This is an easy way to turn something potentially pedestrian into a work of data art. Even just arranging a series of charts into a circle will do it. It plays havoc with being able to read the data but if your aim is to make a visual splash rather than tell anyone anything useful, then that's your trick, right there.

20 **Big, simple line illustrations.** This is really just a cheap way of getting round sourcing good, custom-drawn illustrations. All you need is an icon relevant to the subject, but you need it in line style, rather than filled. Just the outlines (if you've only got solid icons, try outlining them and removing the fill – doesn't always work, but sometimes you get lucky). Then scale it up nice and big. You'll probably want to tweak the line width to keep it visible, but don't make it too thick (Figure 5.50). Effectively we're leaning into the minimalism: a nice big, simple statement.

21 **Cropping illustrations off the side of the canvas.** Cropping is a powerful tool for making photographs and illustrations interesting by highlighting important bits or hiding elements; and using the actual page, screen or slide to do the cropping, pushing parts out of view beyond the frame, is a neat way to do it. That missing bit of the illustration just makes it more intriguing and interesting.

22 **Icon charts.** Another one of those tricks for when you're stuck with yet another boring old bar chart – icon charts are a magic alternative. Essentially you replace the bar with a line of icons, repeating the icon to reflect the data (Figure 5.51). These work best when you have a nice simple icon, preferably with a clear

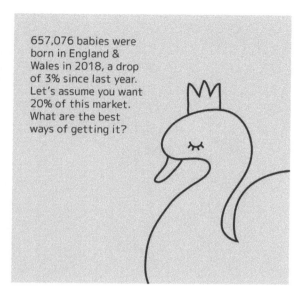

657,076 babies were born in England & Wales in 2018, a drop of 3% since last year. Let's assume you want 20% of this market. What are the best ways of getting it?

Figure 5.50 A line illustration escaping the canvas

solid fill and not much detail (you're going to want simple visuals because you're going to be repeating them). They also work best with low numbers – too many icons can feel crowded – but keep it under 10 or so and it should work fine. I say this, but it's also a hot tip for waffle charts, particularly percentages: a 10 × 10 grid of icons, a proportion of them coloured to represent a percentage. Nowhere as easy to read as a pie or stacked bar, but it looks great – another useful solution if you're stuck visualising a single percentage with no other context to add.

23 **Box or panel over a photo with 80–90% opacity**. Finding a photo with appropriate blank space in it in which you can fit your content is hard, so why bother? Because it works nicely. It is, however, a pain. Instead, whack a solid filled box over the top, make it slightly opaque so you can still just about make out the photo underneath, and put your text in the box (Figure 5.52). It doesn't even have to be just a small panel – make the picture full bleed and then make most of the page or slide a slightly opaque panel over the top – the margins will still be full of photographic imagery.

24 **White space to isolate elements**. This is one of those techniques where we get to use the problem to solve itself. Say we have a single bold statement, or just one simple little chart, and a whole PowerPoint slide to fill (Figure 5.53). Use the simplicity of the visuals to make them bold. Just put them on their own against white space. Isolate them and so make them stand out. Trust them to make their own impact without extra decoration or adornment. It's one of those approaches that is really its own style: a minimalism of presentation that lets the content do all its own work.

25 **Align and distribute**. And here she is, the mother of all tips: align and distribute. It's something so fundamental that pretty much any visual design package will have tools to help you do this, and even PowerPoint these days will offer up little visual hints for alignment and spacing as you drag elements around the screen. Listen to it. Line things up, space them out evenly, group them into grids – at the very least we can order a messy canvas and give it structure. If this is the very least we can do, it is something.

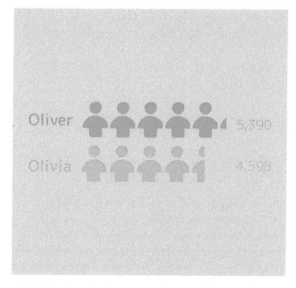

Figure 5.51 Check out the work of the Isotype movement for further inspiration on icon charts and on life in general – it's wonderful stuff

657,076 babies were born in England & Wales in 2018, a drop of 3% since last year. Let's assume you want 20% of this market. What are the best ways of getting it?

Read me

Figure 5.52 Putting a background over a busy photo

Figure 5.53 Empty your mind. Embrace the space. Nothing is freedom.

Try it yourself!

Visual truthfulness (charting)

Take the dataset in Table 5.1 and try to visualise it in seven different ways, using Bertin's visual variables:

1 position
2 orientation
3 size
4 shape
5 colour
6 value
7 texture.

You will see how some of them work pretty well – there's a reason why we often use position and size in data visualisation (they are, after all, how we judge height and size in the real world). But while something like the angle of a line might tell us a lot about change, it does nothing for a single value (unless, of course, that value is 'How many minutes past the hour is it?').

Now let's start from the other end, with the visual metaphor. Since we're using the baby name data for examples, I want you to list five visual metaphors for babies.

An easy way into this is to think about what we would use as an icon – how we might indicate the baby clothes department in a store or what we might use to illustrate a 'baby on board' sign in a car rear window. We could then go beyond a literal baby to think about objects related to babies, like bottles or bibs, nappies or sleep suits. Or the kind of equipment that surrounds them: cradles and prams and high chairs.

Then there are the even more abstract objects that either symbolise babies or have become related to them in popular iconography. The stork, for instance, or perhaps birds in a nest. There are toys like teddy bears, or mobiles, or rattles, or maybe more generic symbols of celebration: balloons and bunting and cake.

Table 5.1 Most popular first names for baby boys and girls in 2018 using birth registration data, England and Wales

Boys' names		Girls' names	
Name	**Count**	**Name**	**Count**
Oliver	5,390	Olivia	4,598
George	4,960	Amelia	3,941
Harry	4,512	Ava	3,110
Noah	4,107	Isla	3,046
Jack	3,988	Emily	2,676
Leo	3,721	Mia	2,490
Arthur	3,644	Isabella	2,369
Muhammad	3,507	Sophia	2,344
Oscar	3,459	Ella	2,326
Charlie	3,365	Grace	2,301

And now things get difficult, because I'm going to ask you to think about how well those metaphors could work to show data. Take each of your five visual metaphors for babies and figure out how you might use them to visualise data, preferably using one (or more) of those seven basic visual attributes, especially the main three: size, position and orientation. Do you scale a rattle in proportion to the values, or raise or lower balloons? Do you just shade icons different colours or just write big numbers in the middle of them?

What we now have to do is shift our thinking from the clarity of the communication of a concept, to the accuracy of the communication of data, looking at our visual ideas from a completely different angle and requiring different things from them.

Visual storytelling

We start with the text of a single story – so a wireframe or part of one, preferably in a digital format. Make sure you strip any text formatting out of it, to begin with.

Here's an example, if you need one.

These girls' names are outside the top 29 but may enter it next year:

Rank	Name	Change since 2017	Change since 2008
34	Emilia	+2	+63
49	Mila	+25	+661
65	Ada	+49	+634

These names are most likely to drop out:

Rank	Name		
25	Jessica	–10	–20
28	Daisy	–10	–3

Now go through that wireframe, structuring the text in order of importance using just the typography. Establish a baseline body copy size and weight (try 12 or 10 point). Now vary text size, weight and face (making it bold or oblique) to see how it distinguishes different parts of the text.

(Continued)

The thing to keep an eye on, as you do this, is how busy the text looks. It can be tempting to try to emphasise a lot of the information, but you'll quickly discover that the text will become messy and unreadable. You'll have to be discerning and ruthless. In this way we're refining our information hierarchy, figuring out precisely what we want to emphasise and in what order.

Now we're going to double down on that structure by reproducing it with graphics. The first thing to do is to visualise the data, of course (but if you're this far into this book, that shouldn't be a problem), since that is going to be the core visual on the page after all, and will likely have a significant effect on the layout. Then we need to look at all the content and figure out its structure.

You might divide the content into sections with:

- White space – gaps between blocks of content
- Boxes – putting enclosures round content or fills behind it
- Lines – putting rules between sections (different thicknesses might show different orders of distinction).

You might join content together with:

- Lines – linking elements together, or showing flow from one element to another
- Similarity – using the same visual language (colour or shape, for instance) to signal that different elements are equivalent
- Positioning – using the natural read order (top to bottom, left to right) to show your reader how items relate to each other (horizontal arrangement can create a sub-hierarchy within the vertical order).

Our aim is to arrive at a visual emphasis that makes itself entirely evident at first glance, which we can see how to read long before we understand what it is that we're reading.

Visual persuasion

Before we start creating our visuals, we need to know our guidelines. So we're going to create some.

We're not going to do a full set of brand guidelines, because that's a whole book in itself, but we are going to cover the basics, so that once we actually start working we know the tools we're using:

- Typeface: pick a font pairing. This generally means finding a body font first – the typeface that's going to show most of the content – and so will need to be legible at lots of different sizes. Then we need to find a headline font – usually something with more character, so that the headlines stand out. Google Fonts (https://fonts.google.com) is a good place to find fonts, and it will even offer possible pairings for each font (but there are plenty of resources online to discover font pairings).
- Colour: pick a core palette of five colours. With a brand palette this usually starts with a key brand colour; in our case we might want to think about both the overall look and feel (the tone we want to have for the whole piece) and how we want to signal highlights (a contrasting colour that will stand out against the rest of our palette). But we also have to consider data visualisation, of course. There are never enough colours in a set of guidelines to cover charting. It is often safer to start from the needs of visualisation and determine the palette from there. Have a look at a tool like Coolors (https://coolors.co) to see palettes designers have uploaded. Check the colours you want to use against something like Elijah Meek and Susie Lu's Viz Palette tool (https://projects.susielu.com/viz-palette).
- Iconography and illustration: determine a style for your imagery. Again we need to consider the look on the page and the density of visual content. Traditional solid icons have a lot more presence than line art ones, but that means they can also get a little too

emphatic. On the other hand, they can feel a little old fashioned next to something a little more subtle. Be aware of how fashions in design might date your work. The Noun Project (https://thenounproject.com) is a great source of iconography. If you want to use photography, Unsplash (https://unsplash.com) is a reliable source of generally good quality stock images.

Remember: our aim here is purely to give ourselves some guidelines. We are almost certain to start needing more and different tools once we start working, but this will give us something to begin with.

One thing that might be useful to do at this stage is to lay out a grid to work to. Lay out a series of equally sized and equally spaced columns (try http://gridcalculator.dk). These will provide the vertical rules to align your content to. A 12-column grid is a good place to start, as it gives us lots of ways to divide it up.

Given all the preparation we have done – figuring out our information hierarchy and the basics of our layout, planning our design tools – we are now free to concentrate on the actual execution: how we are going to apply those design tools in the service of our content.

1 Apply your font choices, checking to see if spacing and size require any changes to your layout, making sure everything is still legible.
2 Apply colour. Start with the visualisations, since they are the most important visual element. Only once they're done should you think about how the rest might be coloured.
3 Once these elements have been done and you can check to see how clear your story is, start thinking about all the other decorative elements you might use, like iconography, illustration or photography. With each choice you need to be sure that they are not detracting from the charts, of course.

You can find resources to help with all these exercises online at: www.addtwodigital.com/book

Six

An introduction to interactive stories

Adam Frost

When Tobias and I first started working in data visualisation in around 2005, the air was thick with talk of interactive charting. This, we were told, was the future. Within a few years, most charts would be interactive, drawing in live, constantly changing data, allowing users to access a multitude of stories and to control what they saw and how they saw it. There were even people saying that if it wasn't interactive, it couldn't really be considered data visualisation at all.

This was very much linked with the advent of 'Big Data': the idea that governments and companies were collecting more data than ever, from a greater variety of sources, and at greater speed. Surely any static chart would be unable to do justice to such volume, variety and velocity – and would be out of date as soon as you made it. Only with an interactive did you stand any chance of extracting insights from this deluge of data.

At the same time, a growing number of tools appeared on the market that sped up the process of creating interactive charts, from JavaScript charting libraries to dashboarding software such as Tableau. As the years passed, the number of tools increased further – Spotfire, Qlik, Power BI – as well as 'scrolly-telling' tools such as Shorthand and Strikingly, all of them offering users easier and faster ways of turning huge datasets into dynamic, engaging visuals.

So where has all of this innovation left us? Is interactive data visualisation now the norm?

There is no question that interactivity has transformed the **Find** stage of the process, both speeding up and broadening the scope of data analysis. A well-made dashboard can make you feel lucky to be alive at this point in history, because it gives you an almost god-like power over your data: you can travel anywhere, find out anything, in an instant.

However, when it comes to presenting stories and insights to others, we have seen far less take-up of interactive tools. PowerPoint still seems to be the primary communication tool in most businesses; the majority of charts produced for news websites are static; school and university teachers who attend our seminars tell us that they almost exclusively use static charts and maps (and occasionally, animations). Reports of the death of static graphics have been greatly exaggerated.

This is a shame, as the best interactive storytelling does seem to expand the potential of data visualisation in new and unique ways. However, in our discussions with clients, a range of reasons have been given for sticking with static graphics, many of which are legitimate:

- Author preference. The author or designer wishes to present a specific set of facts, or explain something in a linear order, and interactivity would distract from this.
- Audience preference. The audience is keen to learn or understand from an expert presenter, and they don't have the time or inclination to click or 'drill down' to find out more by themselves.
- Project constraints. Creating an interactive version of a story often takes longer, costs more and usually requires a team with a diverse range of skills.
- Limitations of the form. Interactive storytelling is still in its infancy and as a result there are fewer best practice examples and templates than there are with static charts, which have had hundreds of years of history in which to develop.

So this leads me to my first point about interactive storytelling. Before you start, it's always worth asking if you are creating an interactive because it's new and exciting and the company down the road has got one, or because it genuinely is the right way of telling the stories you've found. In general terms, I would say that although the default way of *finding* a story is interactive (a dashboard of some kind, or a spreadsheet with filters and formulas), the default way of *telling* a story is more often a one-way street. Books, plays and movies don't generally require you to click on anything or jump around to different points of the story. Teachers giving a lesson are happy to answer questions, but usually at specific points, and only if they are on-topic.

The fact is, an interactive is only suitable for certain types of story and certain types of audience. Above, we listed the reasons why clients often stick with static graphics. If you turn those reasons upside-down, you have the usual situations when an interactive solution is a sensible one:

- Author preference. The author has found a multitude of stories and static graphics can't possibly encapsulate them all.
- Audience preference. Each member of the audience will need something different from the data (relating to their location, interests, gender, nationality, etc.) and there is no way that a single story is going to suit everyone.
- The right team and tools. You have a team of people who get how interactive stories work and who have expertise in the most appropriate tools.
- Data that suits an interactive treatment. When data is dynamic and continually changing, any static graphic will be out of date before you have even finished it. Think of real-time election maps or the dashboards created during the Covid-19 pandemic.

For the purposes of this chapter, we will assume that you have a dataset, a skillset, a story and an audience that justify an interactive approach.

What we mean by interactive stories

Next, we should unpack this word 'interactive' because it tends to get used very broadly to describe anything from an animation in a museum (where visitors just click Play and Pause) to a bespoke operational dashboard in a multinational company. What the builder of the animation and the dashboard have in common is:

- a wish to pass more control to users, so they feel more ownership of the stories they discover

- an understanding that by making charts move and transform, users feel that the end product is somehow more 'alive' and 'human' than a static graphic would be
- a belief that they have a dataset that is important or interesting enough to warrant the extra time and cost that adding animation or interactivity will entail.

Everything else is just a question of degree. How *much* control and autonomy do you want to give to your audience? How much should this interactive feel as if *they* and not *you* are the author? Figure 6.1 shows that there are in fact a range of solutions, and (usually) the more interactivity you introduce, the further you move away from a fully controlled narrative.

I've used the baby names data referenced in Chapter 3 for these example wireframes, but I've also added some 'real world' best practice examples of each type down at the bottom. One note of warning: interactives don't always date well, and can get killed by browser updates or taken down by their authors or otherwise become unusable. So there will almost certainly be better examples of each type by the time you read this. I try to keep this Google doc up to date with extant and recent examples: https://bit.ly/data-viz-best-practice.

Developing interactive narratives

The range of interactive types in Figure 6.1 might look daunting: so many different tools and techniques, so many possible solutions. Certainly it is common to find data visualisation practitioners who specialise in just *one* of these kinds of output – for example, people who only produce animations or who make nothing but JavaScript charts. However, what I would say is, whichever interactive approach you decide is right for your story, the process outlined in Chapter 1 should still be applicable. When we make any

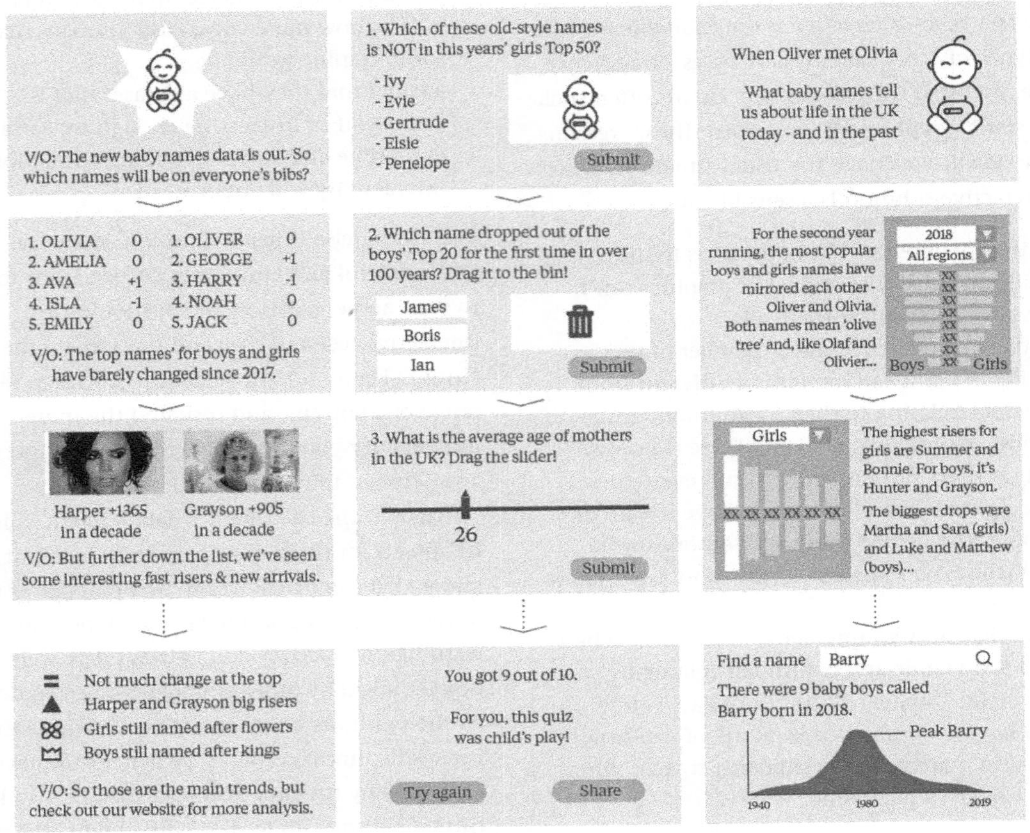

1. An animation

V/O: The new baby names data is out. So which names will be on everyone's bibs?

1. OLIVIA	0	1. OLIVER	0
2. AMELIA	0	2. GEORGE	+1
3. AVA	+1	3. HARRY	-1
4. ISLA	-1	4. NOAH	0
5. EMILY	0	5. JACK	0

V/O: The top names' for boys and girls have barely changed since 2017.

Harper +1365
in a decade

Grayson +905
in a decade

V/O: But further down the list, we've seen some interesting fast risers & new arrivals.

= Not much change at the top
▲ Harper and Grayson big risers
� Girls still named after flowers
♔ Boys still named after kings

V/O: So those are the main trends, but check out our website for more analysis.

Goal is to introduce or explain a subject.

Author maintains full control. Perfect for when your audience are novices.

Tools to create it include:
• Photoshop (for wireframes)
• Illustrator (for assets)
• After Effects (for animations)

Good practice examples include:
• Real World Visuals, 'New York Carbon Emissions'
• Neil Halloran, 'The Fallen of World War II',
• Patrick Clair, 'Stuxnet'

2. Quiz or simulation

1. Which of these old-style names is NOT in this years' girls Top 50?
- Ivy
- Evie
- Gertrude
- Elsie
- Penelope

Submit

2. Which name dropped out of the boys' Top 20 for the first time in over 100 years? Drag it to the bin!

James
Boris
Ian

Submit

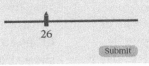

3. What is the average age of mothers in the UK? Drag the slider!

26

Submit

You got 9 out of 10.

For you, this quiz was child's play!

Try again   Share

Goal is to introduce or test current knowledge of a subject.

Author maintains high level of control. Perfect for when your audience are novices.

Tools to create it include:
• Google Forms (for quizzes)
• Flourish
• custom HTML/JavaScript

Good practice examples include:
• BBC, 'The Great British Class Calculator'
• *New York Times,* 'Can You Live on the Minimum Wage?'
• Periscopic, 'Inequality.is'
• Google Project Sunroof

3. Interactive infographic

When Oliver met Olivia

What baby names tell us about life in the UK today - and in the past

For the second year running, the most popular boys and girls names have mirrored each other - Oliver and Olivia. Both names mean 'olive tree' and, like Olaf and Olivier...

2018
All regions

Boys   Girls

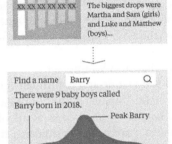

Girls

XX XX XX XX XX XX

The highest risers for girls are Summer and Bonnie. For boys, it's Hunter and Grayson.

The biggest drops were Martha and Sara (girls) and Luke and Matthew (boys)...

Find a name   Barry

There were 9 baby boys called Barry born in 2018.

Peak Barry

1940   1980   2019

Goal is to describe or explain a subject, and allow (limited) exploration.

Author maintains moderate level of control. Ideal for when you have a mixed audience.

Tools to create it include:
• Shorthand/ Google Sites/ Carrd (for simple sites)
• HTML/JavaScript/Flourish/D3

Good practice examples include:
• Josh Worth, 'If the Moon Were One Pixel'
• R2D3, 'A Visual Introduction to Machine Learning'
• *Der Zeit,* 'A Nation Divided'
• Angela Morelli, 'Water'
• *The Guardian,* 'Firestorm'

Figure 6.1   Different types of interactive data visualisation

4. Interactive chart with walkthrough

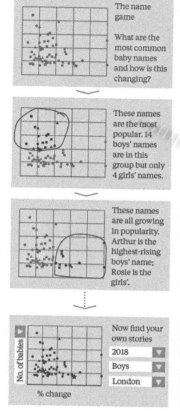

The name game

What are the most common baby names and how is this changing?

These names are the most popular. 14 boys' names are in this group but only 4 girls' names.

These names are all growing in popularity. Arthur is the highest-rising boys' name; Rosie is the girls'.

Now find your own stories

2018

Boys

London

Goal is to explain a subject and allow deeper exploration.

Author hands more control to audience. Perfect for when you have a mixed audience.

Tools to create it include:
- HTML/JavaScript
- Highcharts (for simple charts)
- D3 (for more complex charts)

Good practice examples include:
- Bloomberg, 'Red Meat & Cancer'
- *New York Times,* 'Income Mobility Charts'/'Punishing Reach of Racism'
- *National Geographic,* 'Clash of the Canines'
- *Washington Post,* 'America's Housing Divide'

5. Interactive chart (data explorer)

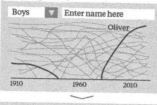

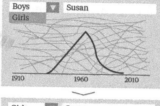

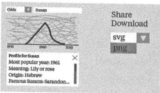

Goal is to allow users to explore a dataset.

Author is almost invisible. Ideal when your audience are more expert.

Tools to create it include:
- HTML/JavaScript
- Highcharts (for simple charts)
- D3 (for more complex charts)

Good practice examples include:
- *The Guardian,* 'Gay Rights State by State'
- Periscopic, 'Gun Deaths'
- Gapminder
- Every Noise At Once
- *New York Times,* 'Mapping Segragation'
- Histography (histography.io)

6. Dashboard (many charts)

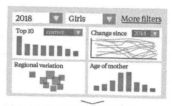

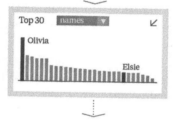

OLIVIA	4,598
AMELIA	3,941
AVA	3,110
ISLA	3,046
EMILY	2,676
MIA	2,490
ISABELLA	2,369
SOPHIA	2,344
ELLA	2,326
GRACE	2,301
POPPY	2,226
CHARLOTTE	2,202

Share
Download

csv
xls

Goal is to allow users to explore a large and complex dataset.

Author is invisible. Stories are discovered by users. Perfect for an expert audience.

Tools to create it include:
- Power BI
- Tableau
- HTML/JavaScript/D3 (if custom)

Good practice examples include:
- Mostly found in corporate environments (so not publicly accessible) but *Makeover Monday* by Andy Kriebel and Eva Murray (2018) contains some great examples.
Also *The Big Book of Dashboards by Steve Wexler* et al. (2017)

kind of interactive visualisation, we are still finding, designing, making and refining; we are still selecting the most relevant datasets, structuring them in an intuitive information hierarchy and using aesthetic techniques to increase usability and engagement. It invariably takes longer than making a static graphic, and requires a lot more testing and refining, but if you are able to make a clear, interesting static chart, then there is nothing to stop you applying the same principles to the task of creating an interactive version.

Let's recap those core principles and see how interactive storytelling relates to more traditional kinds of narrative. In Chapter 4, I talked about how the inverted pyramid of a journalistic article or the explanatory structures of a teacher's lesson plan can be helpful in those telling data stories. Here I'd like to focus more closely on fictional models because they are in many ways the archetypal story type and, when you are allowing users to cocreate stories with you, understanding the purpose and structure of narrative at its most primitive level will help you build both content and an interface that allows users to quickly orient themselves and assemble coherent stories of their own. (See Appendix E for more on how humans unconsciously use narrative as a way of mediating reality: https://www. addtwodigital.com/book/)

I'm going to use as examples perhaps the most famous novel and the most famous movie of all time. We'll start with Chapter 1 of the novel:

It was a bright cold day in April, and the clocks were striking thirteen. Winston Smith, his chin nuzzled into his breast in an effort to escape the vile wind, slipped quickly through the glass doors of Victory Mansions, though not quickly enough to prevent a swirl of gritty dust from entering along with him.

The hallway smelt of boiled cabbage and old rag mats. At one end of it a coloured poster, too large for indoor display, had been tacked to the wall. It depicted simply an enormous face, more

than a metre wide: the face of a man of about forty-five, with a heavy black moustache and ruggedly handsome features. ... BIG BROTHER IS WATCHING YOU, the caption beneath it ran.

George Orwell, *Nineteen Eighty-Four* (2013)

I want to briefly consider why George Orwell's opening is so effective. We start with perhaps the most powerful opening sentence ever written: 'It was a bright cold day in April, and the clocks were striking thirteen.' Immediately we know that we are not in the present day (clocks don't strike – and have never struck – thirteen) so this is set in the future or in an alternative reality of some kind. After generally establishing time and place, Orwell puts us outside a large apartment block – Victory Mansions – which narrows the setting down further: the name 'Victory Mansions' implies that we are in a town or city in an imperial or totalitarian state. Next, we zoom into our protagonist, Winston Smith, entering the glass doors of this mansion. His name suggests that he is an Everyman figure: 'Winston' like Winston Churchill and 'Smith' being the most common surname in the UK. We follow him into the hallway, which smells of 'cabbage and old rag mats', suggesting that Winston – and the population generally – live in unpleasant, even squalid, conditions. In the hallway, Winston is confronted with the poster of an enormous face – 'more than a metre wide' – with a caption underneath it: BIG BROTHER IS WATCHING YOU. Our protagonist and antagonist come face to face for the first time.

As well as the emotional resonance of the scene – it paints a bleak, unsettling picture – it is worth thinking about how Orwell guides us into his narrative. As deftly as the writer of a fairy tale, he starts with a 'Once upon a time' sentence, establishing the general setting, before pointing us at his castle ('Victory Mansions') and then moving us through the door of the castle with his hero,

Winston. From the general to the particular in just two sentences. Then we get even closer – *inside Winston's head* – as our hero looks into his own version of an enchanted mirror: Big Brother's face looking back at him. All of this happens without the reader even being conscious of the narrative telescoping – it is just what stories do. They start with an overview, we are placed in a particular location, then we are shown a select group of characters, we move inside their heads, there is interaction or conflict, and then we zoom out and the process starts again.

A different kind of story now. We are in outer space and a giant spaceship is chasing a much smaller one. The way that the giant spaceship is shot – it looms above our heads and seems to go on for ever – implies that it is the antagonist in this story. As a huge blast hits the smaller spaceship, we zoom inside it and there is a medium shot of two droids – a tall, gold, human-looking one and a short blue-and-white one with a revolving head. Around them, soldiers prepare to defend the ship. *Pew pew*. There is a close-up of the taller droid who says: 'We're doomed! They'll be no escape for the princess this time.' We are inside his head: he is anxious and pessimistic. We are also given information: there is a princess aboard the ship who has escaped before, but maybe not 'this time'.

Star Wars – of course it's *Star Wars* – is famous for starting *in media res:* in the middle of the story, like *The Iliad* or *Hamlet*. We join an epic space battle half-way through and we are rushing to catch up. Who is everyone? What just happened? But notice how the underlying structure keeps us anchored. As with Orwell's *Nineteen Eighty-Four*, we start with a clear 'Once upon a time' establishing shot. We are in outer space. There is clearly a battle – in fairy tale terms, a castle is under siege – and it is apparent whose side we are meant to be on. Then we move inside one of the 'castle' corridors. We overhear the conversation of a couple of 'courtiers': the princess is going to be taken prisoner. Although the action may be frenzied, the rhythm of the narrative could

not be more predictable – mirrored by the movement of the camera through wide, medium and close-up shots. If it were a breadcrumb trail on a website, it would look something like this:

Outer space > Large spaceship chasing small spaceship > A corridor in the small spaceship > C-3PO and R2-D2 talking > Inside C-3PO's head

This is repeated throughout the movie, every time we start a new sequence. The droids escape from the besieged ship – with a rescue note from the princess – and land on Tatooine. We have a (very) long shot of their crashed ship and two tiny figures walking away from it across the sand. The camera zooms in and holds on a medium shot, and then we have a close-up of C-3PO lamenting: 'How did we get into this mess?' The two droids have an argument, and go off in opposite directions. In less than a minute, we completely understand the nature of where they have landed, what they each think about it and what they plan to do about it. It is because, as well as the story being engaging and visually innovative, George Lucas has structured the scene in a way that moves us seamlessly from overview to detail.

This universal structure is something we all use without thinking too much about it. Say we are walking across the market square in a small town, and we suddenly say: 'You see that church opposite, my sister got married in there. Did I ever tell you about what happened half-way through the ceremony?' We discard all the other buildings in the town square and focus on the church, then we are inside the church, then we are thinking about a specific day in the church, then we are going to hear about one person's experience in the church. We remember an emotionally resonant event that we think our audience might find interesting, then we rapidly and intuitively start the process of assembling our 'inverted pyramid' structure: we set the scene, assemble our protagonists and then dive in deeper. Once upon a time … A long time ago, in a galaxy far far away …

Thinking about the different kinds of interactive story outlined in Figure 6.1, it is easy to see how this structuring principle helps to shape the more explanatory approaches on our diagram. Motion graphics are essentially short films, and interactive infographics need a strong central narrative on which to hang their optional explorable elements. Even a quiz tends not to pose random questions in a random order, but starts with simple or general questions before getting more difficult or granular as the user progresses.

However, I'd argue that even the most open and exploratory approaches on our diagram – the inter-active charts and dashboards – draw on the same narrative conventions (or at least the more success-ful examples do). It is sometimes expressed in different terms; perhaps the most celebrated is Ben Shneiderman's 'Overview first, zoom and filter out, then details-on-demand' (Shneiderman, 1996), of which more later. Other examples include the (dubious) three-click rule for drilling down into online content and getting the information you need. But what sits behind all of these mantras is the fact that our brains like information to be structured in a very particular way, and we favour information sources that either do this work for us, or allow us to effortlessly assemble story-making apparatus for ourselves.

To take a general example, let's imagine I visit DataShine, a UK site which has turned all of the results from the 2011 England and Wales Census into an explorable heatmap.

When you first arrive on the site, a random dataset is served up – I got 'Method of travel: on foot' for the centre of London (Figure 6.2). This was already quite interesting – it showed me how people who lived in the middle of London or in Docklands were more likely to walk to work – but, more importantly, it also told me what the site contained and how it could be used. It clearly stated: 'Once upon a time, in England and Wales, there was a Census. People were asked lots of detailed questions about their lives. Here is how they answered just one of those questions. But you can see the answers to any question you like.'

So off I went. I explored all the possible datasets that could be loaded onto the map. There were hundreds of fascinating options, but I started with

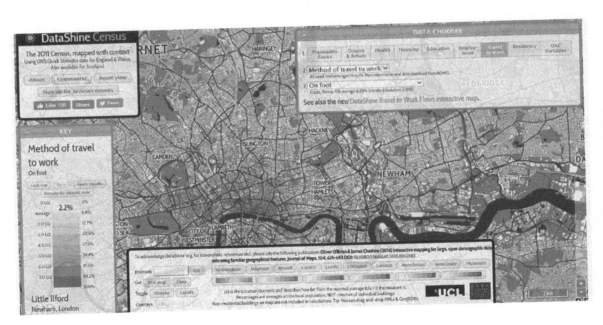

Figure 6.2   DataShine landing page

Figure 6.3 The gender ratio in my part of town

the gender balance story, and selected Sex > Females to see which areas had an equal percentage of men and women and where there was more of an imbalance. Inevitably, I moved the map to my area – Wanstead in East London (Figure 6.3) – and discovered that it was 68.1% female and 31.9% male, or 2.1:1, one of the most unequal ratios in the city.

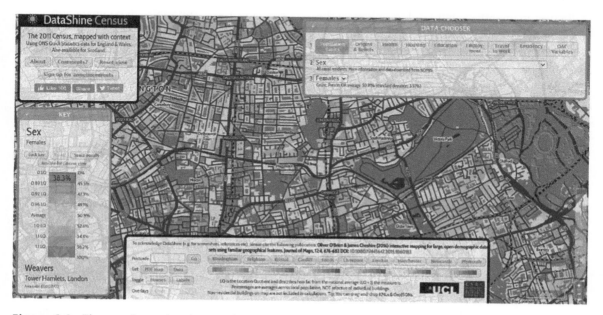

Figure 6.4 The gender ratio where Tobias lives

Intrigued, I panned the map across to where my esteemed coauthor Tobias Sturt lives, in London's fashionable Hackney (Figure 6.4). There, the data showed that the population is 38.3% female and 61.7% male – an unequal ratio of 1.6:1 in the other direction. (Note that there were only two gender options given in the 2011 Census. Hopefully this will be modified in future surveys.)

Now, having been to Tobias's part of Hackney, I can confirm that the data broadly accords with my own observations: there are an awful lot of men living there, mostly young men with large beards and small dogs, eating artisanal crisps and vaping.

However, I can also assure Tobias that if he decided to up sticks and move to my part of town, in the hope of being surrounded by a sea of female faces – perhaps something akin to the Castle of Maidens in Galahad's Grail Quest – then he would quickly discover that the reality was a lot more prosaic. There are dozens of nursing homes in the area, and most of the residents are female, and it is this which produces our 2.1:1 gender ratio.

So that was the end of the first story. I went on to discover many others, but I did so following the same logic each time, resetting the view, choosing a topic that I was interested in, zooming in, and comparing the data I found about my area with other areas. Sometimes I would download the final image as a pdf or grab the raw data (a csv file) for that particular section of the map.

How authors shape interactive narratives

DataShine works because the authors understand the rules of storytelling: interesting, relevant content, progressively disclosed in a logical and coherent order. Yes, I control the pace of it, and which specific content to drop into this predetermined structure,

so in that limited sense, I am 'finding my own stories'. But DataShine are the creators of DataShine as surely as George Orwell is the creator of *Nineteen Eighty-Four*, and it's important to remember this when you are making interactives, *particularly* where the user is given more control. There is a reason why the average user of DataShine hasn't downloaded the full Census spreadsheet from the Office for National Statistics. Instead, what they want is all the pleasures of data exploration with none of the frustrations – and that means that an intelligent designer must make hundreds of decisions about where freedom is a benefit and where it is a burden. (I am a tourist when it comes to this data, and therefore I want lots of maps, signposts and artificial trails in my national park.)

So, when we arrive at DataShine, we notice that the Census questions have been divided into eight topics for us to choose from: population basics, origins and beliefs, health and so on. The site authors take on work that would be dull and onerous for us to do ourselves (establishing an information hierarchy) and they also respect the limits of cognitive load (see Chapter 4) by not giving us too many topics to compare and choose from. We then choose a specific question within one of these topics, thereby mirroring the familiar 'overview to detail' route into content that we outlined above as the way most archetypal stories are structured. When it comes to representing the data we choose, the DataShine authors again make a lot of choices on our behalf. The data is represented on a heatmap. They have clearly decided that this visualisation type is likely to appeal to the widest range of people (people do love maps) while also being highly efficient (lots of information is visible at a glance) and effective (people can find specific streets if they need them). Offering different chart types would involve a lot more work for the site developers but little obvious benefit to users other than a more complicated interface and a steeper learning curve. Instead, for those who have a problem with heatmaps, there is the option to download the data and make their own charts. Perfect.

What users do get is freedom where it matters. We can enter our postcode to jump to a specific location. There are shortcut buttons to the major cities of England and Wales. We can pan across the map and zoom in or out. We can toggle houses and labels on or off to change the appearance of the map. If we don't want the default red–amber–green heatmap colours, there are five other palettes to choose from.

DataShine won't let us change or break anything that will impede the site's ability to generate intuitive, relevant stories.

I'm not saying DataShine is flawless. It is not the most polished site in the world and it doesn't work well on mobile. But I'm not sure either of those things is relevant for a typical user of this site. Does the kind of person who likes exploring Census data need a slick, polished, responsive site, or rather one that's functional and easy to use? Spending weeks optimising this site for mobile feels like a sub-optimal use of resources, given only a minority of users are likely to use a Census exploration tool on their phones (unless the site analytics suggest otherwise, of course).

The point about DataShine is that it is a data exploration tool. The site authors are not telling specific stories; indeed, there is no way that they can be aware of even half of the stories that this Census tool can tell. However, what I would like to re-emphasise is that, even when you are allowing users control over the particular content they see, you are likely to get better results if you think of yourself as an author or even storyteller. Yes, you are sharing this role with your audience, but you are still the *principal* author, deciding on the subject of the story (e.g. a Census), the levels of your story (the topics and sub-topics), how to move through these levels (the interface), how the story will be told (e.g. a heatmap) and the story's narrative style (titles, annotations, instructions). The best interactives may well make it feel like there is 'no author', that the user has found everything themselves, but it takes a highly skilled author to give users this illusion of total control. If you delegate the role of principal author to your audience, giving them authority over every last detail of how to access content, how to display it, how to navigate through it, then you are essentially suggesting that this data is (literally) uncharted; no map currently exists. This is fine when you are making an analysis tool – a tool that could work for *any* data rather than *this* data. In fact, users of business intelligence dashboards are used to overloaded interfaces and lengthy tutorials: that is the price you pay for flexibility. But when you are creating an interactive focusing on a particular dataset for a particular audience – which is what we are covering in this book – then users expect a structure, an interface and a visual approach which suits the data, which stops them getting lost, and which makes the whole experience, well, *fun*. That won't happen unless an author takes charge.

We are now going to work through two of the interactive types in Figure 6.1 in detail (animations and interactive infographics) and try to give you a sense of what 'good' looks like and how (we think) the most successful interactives consistently draw on the storytelling principles we discussed in Chapter 4 – selection, dramatisation, emphasis, presentation. We will also talk more about how we wireframe each type and how it's a good idea to research the (often free) tools that are available before you begin wireframing, because the data viz community is a wise and generous one and, by drawing on their expertise – and GitHub repositories – you can often be very ambitious indeed. Finally, we will discuss how you make what you have wireframed, and how and where the tools and techniques you use differ from making static graphics and PowerPoints.

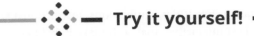 **Try it yourself!**

Find a dataset that will lend itself to interactive treatment. This will usually contain several or all of the data story types that we mentioned in Chapter 3:

- change over time
- comparison
- composition
- geospatial
- correlation
- distribution.

Good places to find complex datasets include the following websites:

- World Bank
- Our World in Data
- Gapminder.

You could also use a large study of opinions on social or political subjects. For example, the Wellcome Global Monitor – a study of how people around the world view science – is a fascinating and freely available resource.

Seven

Designing motion graphics

Adam Frost

.... Chapter contents

Motion graphics are an extremely powerful way of telling data viz stories. However you want to measure it – by number of visitors, completion rate, social sharing, return visitors, or 'buzz' (I have no idea what this means) – the most successful products we have made have all been motion graphics. Is it because we are better at making animations than interactives, infographics or print products? Possibly, but I don't think so. Most agencies that we know tell a similar story. Animated explainers or walkthroughs tend to do *really* well. No matter how much we data viz geeks might extol the virtues of fully interactive, explorable charts, it turns out that for most people, clicking Play, Pause, Subtitles On/Off, is all the interaction they need and there is something uniquely comforting in sitting back and watching a gifted data storyteller putting on a show.

They are the gift that keeps on giving. Clients frequently tell us that successful animations have a long afterlife. As well as being used in their original context (often to accompany a particular report or release), they also get used in conferences to introduce delegate speeches, deployed in portfolios and pitches, and repurposed for social media, and screenshots are dropped into PowerPoint presentations.

Moreover, audiences seem to be particularly forgiving of animations. We have had motion graphics utterly obliterated by client feedback until they are nothing but a blizzard of bland corporate slogans, meaningless icons, and stock photographs of cities at night, and people still watch them. The same content as an infographic would (and does) sink without trace.

However, before you start enthusiastically teaching yourself After Effects, just a few notes about what is involved at each stage of the production cycle. Here I am assuming that you are making a 'typical' data viz explainer animation lasting 2–3 minutes. I'm also assuming that this is a mixture of voiceover (or subtitles) and visuals, rather than the text having to appear as a graphical element on screen (which takes up space that could be more profitably used for charts and illustrations).

To keep things simple, I'll use the baby names dataset that we've been drawing on throughout the book.

Find

This stage tends to take longer with animations, just because the goal is usually to condense a large amount of complex information and then walk people through a coherent explanation. To do this well, you need to immerse yourself in the subject-matter, which requires time and patience. If an average single-page infographic requires around a week of dedicated research time, an animation is at least a fortnight, and usually a lot more. For the baby names data, for example, it won't be enough to just look at the dataset in front of you: you will also need to be aware of longer trends, the cultural context and demographic patterns in the UK.

Design

To illustrate what's involved at the design stage, I've included an example script (Table 7.1).

I've assumed that the audience for this animation is *Guardian* readers. It focuses on a story – *maybe we are not as progressive as we think* – designed to intrigue and perhaps challenge them. As I move through the design stage outlined below, I will be keeping this audience in mind.

You will see that, just as the **Find** stage involves more finding, so the **Design** stage requires thinking more rigorously about selection, dramatisation and emphasis.

Selection

The biggest surprise for most of our clients when they make animations is how much content they

Table 7.1   Example animation script

Voiceover/subtitles	Supporting data (to be used in visuals)
Looking at the top baby names for 2018, this generation has some clear winners.	Boys' top 5: Oliver, George, Harry, Noah, Jack. Girls' top 5: Olivia, Amelia, Ava, Isla, Emily
Oliver is number 1 for boys – and has been for the last five years.	Line chart showing Oliver persisting at the top as names swap round below it.
Olivia is number 1 for girls – and has been for the last three years.	Line chart showing Olivia persisting at the top as names swap round below it.
Other names – like Amelia and Emily for girls and Jack and Harry for boys – have been in the top 10 for at least a decade ...	Line chart showing persistence of Amelia and Emily in top 10 for 10 years. Same with boys – Jack and Harry.
and represent this generation as surely as Sarah and Chris did in the 1980s ...	Top 3 girls' names 1984: 1. Sarah, 2. Laura, 3. Gemma Top 3 boys' names 1984: 1. Christopher, 2. James, 3. David
and Margaret and John in the 1950s.	Top 3 girls' names 1954: 1. Margaret, 2. Patricia, 3. Christine Top 3 boys' names 1954: 1. John, 2. David, 3. Michael
So names have changed. This generation has its own identity, right?	
Actually, it's not that simple. Yes, we've dropped the boomer names, but replaced them with names that were popular four or five generations ago.	Line charts showing Grace and Ivy (girls) and Arthur and Edward (boys) as top names in the 1910s, then disappearing from the top 100 and returning in the 2000s.
They are retro chic. And even when the names have changed, the attitudes certainly haven't.	
Girls are still named after flowers and plants.	Top 30 names include: Poppy, Lily, Willow, Rosie, Daisy
Whereas boys are named after kings and religious leaders.	Top 30 names include: George, Henry, Noah Muhammad, Isaac
For girls, we are influenced by celebrities and fantasy movies.	Rank change since 2008: +1365 Harper +570 Aurora +537 Luna
Whereas boys – well, let's just say, don't mess.	Rank change since 2008: +236 Reggie +50 Ronnie [Kray twins?]
Which begs the question: when we give our children a name, are we really thinking about what their future might be? Or are we stuck in the past?	
Read more about our baby names coverage at: www.theguardian.com/baby-names-2019	[URL, Guardian logo and any legal/disclaimer text]

have to cut. First of all, the data. Think of all the fascinating trends and surprising insights you found as you analysed the baby names dataset (Chapter 3). Remember how difficult it was to cut it down to just six or seven key points (Chapter 4). Now have a look at the script in Table 7.1. There's barely *any* data in it: the top 5 for boys and girls some change-over-time data, a handful of flower names for girls and the royal names for boys, the two or three biggest risers. And that's it. There's no point including any more because the audience simply won't see it. In fact, it will just create a headache for your animator as there will be too much *stuff* on screen.

In fact, it could be argued that there is too much data in our example script. Often motion graphics are more like explainers, slowing things down, per-haps even walking through a single chart. For example, our two-minute animation could just look at the top 3 for boys and girls, one name at a time. We would explore how long these names have been popular, why they are popular and who they are popular with (older or younger mothers? urban or rural mothers?). Just six datapoints.

In some ways, it's best not to think of motion graphics as data viz, but as a trailer for the data, an attempt to sell it to readers, so they get to the end and feel motivated enough to discover more for themselves. Think of the Gapminder animation, which I referenced in Chapter 2 (it's on Youtube https://www.youtube.com/watch?v=jbkSRLYSojo, or just google 'Gapminder 200 countries 200 years'). Here Hans Rosling talks about an overall trend – countries growing healthier and wealthier – and picks out the occasional datapoint along the way – China, India, countries hit by HIV and civil war. But ultimately the objective of the motion graphic is for the audience to feel so swept away by the potential stories *they* can dis-cover in this bottomless dataset, that they go and start playing with the Gapminder Trendalyzer straightaway (which is at gapminder.org – brace yourselves).

So in the first part of the selection process, you'll be deleting perhaps 99% of the data stories you found. Then, there's the text itself. In Chapters 3 and 4, I talked about the importance of using clear, succinct sentences. With animation scripts, you have even less time and space for copy. Your text will either be read out by a narrator or rendered as subtitles or perhaps both. Either way, people need time to take in your copy, and then absorb the accompanying visuals. For a two-minute animation, you are looking at a maximum of 15 short sentences, containing no more than 250 words. After writing the draft of any script, we frequently read it out loud and time it, adding a few seconds for any logos or stings at the beginning and end, to check that we're not overrunning. Usually we are – and we need to cut more.

In the example script above, notice that each sentence is as lean as we could possibly make it. Sometimes this means you lose nuance (it's clarity v. accuracy again – see Chapter 2) or even impact (the bolder statement just takes too long to say). You have to be economical, because if you take too long to make point 1, then there's no longer any space to make points 4 and 5 and your animation loses its narrative rhythm.

- Oliver is the number 1 name for boys – and has been the top name for eight of the last 10 years.
- Oliver is ~~the~~ number 1 ~~name~~ for boys – and has been ~~the top name for eight of the last ten years.~~ for the last five years.

The other point to make is that you need to be continually mindful of what your visuals will be showing. You can say less, because you will be showing more. You don't need to duplicate what your visuals are already doing, and this should be the focus of your editorial efforts. At the same time, you can't cut too much text, and expect your visuals to sustain narrative momentum by themselves. It's about balancing the two media – text and visuals, each doing what it does best

Table 7.2 Text v. visuals

Parents still seem to be influenced by the natural world – flowers and plants – when it comes to naming their girls, going for names like Poppy, Lily, Willow, Rosie and Daisy.	Top 30 names with names highlighted: Poppy, Lily, Willow, Rosie, Daisy	*Textual clutter*
Girls' names are influenced by these things.	Text on screen: Flowers and plants Icon of: Flower and tree Names: Poppy, Lily, Willow, Rosie, Daisy	*Visual clutter*
Girls are still named after flowers and plants.	Top 30 names with names enlarged/ highlighted: Poppy, Lily, Willow, Rosie, Daisy	*A good balance*

(see Appendix E for more on the importance of balancing verbal and visual elements: www.addtwodigital.com/book).

Dramatisation

After you have selected the datapoints you want to show, you need to dramatise them. This is when you build a world around your data. In screenplay terms, this is when you make your audience identify with your characters and demonstrate why they should care about what is happening. Likewise, with data viz animations, you need to make those datapoints human, relatable, meaningful.

In our baby names script above, we have made it clear from the first sentence that we are talking about a wider story than just the 2018 data: 'Looking at the top baby names, it feels as if this generation has some clear winners.' We will be discussing generational differences, and everyone belongs to (and identifies with) a generation.

Once we have established the Generation Alpha names (Oliver, Jack, Harry, Olivia, Amelia, Emily), we compare these to the top names from the 1980s (Chris and Sarah) and 1940s (John and Margaret). This invites viewers to compare their own generation's names with the current crop, and is designed

to provoke an emotional response, whether that's nostalgia, surprise, disbelief or something else. As in Chapter 4, to achieve this effect, we had to look beyond our original spreadsheet and bring in historical data. We are, in effect, creating our data's backstory.

Likewise, when we talk about the fastest-rising names, we need to step outside our dataset and research cultural trends. In fact, you won't even be able to *select* the most relevant names without understanding what has driven their popularity. Your chosen audience will of course affect which names you end up selecting and dramatising.

In our example, we are primarily talking to a UK audience (*Guardian* readers), so we will be using celebrity references that British people will get

Table 7.3 Adding context

For girls, we are influenced by celebrities and fantasy movies.	Rank change since 2008: +1365 Harper +570 Aurora +537 Luna
Whereas boys – well, let's just say, don't mess.	Rank change since 2008: +236 Reggie +50 Ronnie [Kray twins?]

(e.g. Posh Spice creating a generation of Harpers; see Table 7.3). But, at the same time, the *Guardian* has a global reach, so it can't be too parochial. We know that Posh Spice is also well known in the rest of the world, as is Harry Potter, so Luna (after Luna Lovegood) is also safe to include. Everyone knows Disney, so we can add Aurora too. With boys' names, we could have gone with Grayson as a fast-rising boys' name, but are Grayson Perry or Larry Grayson familiar to non-UK audiences? Our final choice (Reggie and Ronnie, after the Krays) should have wider reach. These two affable psychotics have frequently featured in 'Swinging Sixties' documentaries, not to mention countless TV and film adaptations. Once again, the visuals will do the explaining for us, so the text does not need to mention 'Harper', 'Aurora' or 'the Kray twins'.

If our audience had been different, we would of course have selected and dramatised differently. A two-minute motion graphic at the start of a conference for businesses selling baby names merchandise would not have bothered with the top names from 50 or 80 years ago, because nobody is buying merchandise with those names on anymore. And it would have focused on the top 5 or 10 fastest-growing names (rather than choosing a handful with obvious pop cultural relevance). And, in fact, if the overall count for these top risers was still low, our animation may not have included those names at all. The overall theme for the motion graphic would most likely be something like the increasing variety of names and the impact this has on profit margins. The contextual statistic at the beginning might be something like: 'In the Victorian era, one in eight boys were called John. Today, there are no Johns in the top 100 and the top boys' name (Oliver) is shared by just 1.6% of boys. And this is shrinking all the time.'

Emphasis

You have chosen the most meaningful data, and you've found contextual data that will bring it to life. Now you have got to work out how to frame and arrange those elements in a way that will spark your audience's curiosity and hold it for 3 minutes.

The frame

The frame for your story is one of the most important decisions you will make at the scripting stage, as it will affect which and how much data you select and (later) the visual treatment of your story. I've put it here in the emphasis stage but in reality, it will be on your mind throughout.

By frame, I mean the kind of story I alluded to right at the start: *this year's baby names data shows that we are not as progressive as we think*. This was my chosen angle for *Guardian* readers. I will be arranging all of the elements in my story to make this fundamental point.

However, this is just one frame that could work. I have included some alternative 'hooks' in Table 7.4 and how each story might then be framed by its opening sentence and consolidated by succeeding sentences.

But or however

Once you've chosen your frame, and set the scene, you need to introduce tension. In my script (Table 7.5), it occurs just before the half-way point.

In most animations (as in most short narratives), this 'however' moment is about halfway through, once you have set up your premise and the audience's attention is naturally beginning to wane.

If you go for a 'myth-busting' approach, these 'howevers' are positioned throughout the animation, after every statement: 'You might think this [myth 1]. However the truth is ...', 'You might believe this [myth 2]. However in reality ...'.

Likewise, with a personal story. 'Phil and Susie thought this .... However, the reality was that .... Therefore they did this .... However, this led to ....'

Table 7.4 You've been framed

Story type	Hook	Framing sentence	Consolidation
List	Baby names in 7 charts	The new baby names data is just out and there are some big surprises in the Top 20.	Oliver and Olivia are still number 1, establishing them without doubt as *the* most popular names for Generation Alpha.
Myth-busting	6 myths about baby names	A lot of boys get named after their fathers, right? Not any more. Those Generation X names – Andrew, Chris, Mark – are gone for good.	Today boys are more likely to be called Arlo or Reuben than Philip or Richard, and girls are more likely to be called Willow or Matilda than Claire or Alison.
How to	How to choose the right name for your baby	Choosing a name for your baby is definitely not child's play.	Do you want to give them a top 10 name so they blend in? Or a rare or unique name so they stand out? Or something in between?
Topical (current affairs)	The impact of Brexit on baby names	After Brexit, there were worries that Britain had become a more insular place. But the baby names data suggests otherwise.	Yes, 'traditional' British names like George and Charlotte feature in the top 20, but there are also names from eastern Europe and the United States, and from Jewish and Muslim culture.
Topical (pop culture)	The rise of celebrity baby names	What do Marvel movies, *Game of Thrones* and Posh Spice have in common? They have all affected what we call our children.	In 2018, there were babies called Thor and Loki, Khaleesi and Tyrian, and Harper has jumped over 1,300 places in a decade.
Personal story	Why we took six months to name our baby	When Phil and Susie Jones had a baby boy this year, they downloaded the latest baby names data, expecting to see their favourite names in the top 100: John, Peter, Andrew, Paul. But they had all vanished.	If Phil and Susie want their baby boy to have a 'regular' name, they'll need to consider Noah, Leo or Oscar – all top 10 names in 2018. None of these names has ever appeared in the top 100 before, let alone the top 10.

With more personal stories, you are in effect creating a condensed version of a standard movie script, positioning moments of conflict and resolution, tension and release, along the spine of your narrative: 'It's 1936. Indiana Jones is happy teaching archaeology at university. *However*, a group of army officers visit him and tell him that the Nazis are about to find the Ark of the Covenant. *Therefore* Indiana has to go to Nepal and get the "Staff of Ra", an artefact that will help him locate the Ark first. *However*, when he gets to Nepal, he discovers that the Staff of Ra has been stolen and its owner has been killed. *Therefore* he joins forces

with the owner's daughter, Marion (who is also an old flame of Indiana's). *However*, she is tied up by a sadistic Nazi and *therefore* Indiana has to rescue her.' And so on: *however* and *therefore*, for two hours, until the good guys win and the bad guys get their faces melted off.

In our example script, there is just one hinge, when we say: 'Actually, it's not that simple.' Because in our story (*We are not as progressive as we think*) we want a straightforward thesis and antithesis before we synthesise everything at the end. This is the most common structure for the animations we make, perhaps because for most

COMMUNICATING WITH DATA VISUALISATION

Table 7.5 The 'however' moment

Text	Visual
So names have changed. This generation has its own identity, right?	
Actually, it's not that simple. Yes, we've dropped the boomer names, but replaced them with names that were popular four or five generations ago.	Line charts showing Grace and Ivy (girls) and Arthur and Edward (boys) as top names in the 1910s, then disappearing from the top 100 and returning in the 2000s.
They are retro chic. And even when the names have changed, the attitudes certainly haven't.	
Girls are still named after flowers and plants.	Top 30 names include: Poppy, Lily, Willow, Rosie, Daisy
Whereas boys are named after kings and religious leaders.	Top 30 names include: George, Henry, Noah, Muhammad, Isaac

companies and non-governmental organisations, there is just one main point they need to make in the few minutes they have, and they want to build the whole animation around it. The main point usually follows the 'however', as this is when the story bites, this is the part when the author explains *why* they are telling you all of this: '250 million children in the world are Vitamin A deficient. *However,* we can combat this by encouraging breastfeeding and distributing vitamin supplements' or 'Between 30% and 50% of all food grown is never consumed. *But* here at Food Waste International, we are launching a Lovely Leftovers campaign, designed to save food, water and energy.'

In our baby names example, the 'however' is the emotional heart of our story, the moment when our audience is jolted out of their belief that society is inevitably becoming more liberal and tolerant. In fact, across the UK, girls called Daisy and Poppy are still dressed in pink princess outfits, and boys called Rex and George are dressed as superheroes. This data is sociological gold dust and every *Guardian* reader should read it! Now!

Wrapping things up

This is usually where you tell your audience what to do with this alarming or exciting information

that you have just given them. You've created a situation, you've introduced disruption or tension, and now you are going to tell them where to go or what to download or who to email. It tends to be teed up with: 'You can help us by …', 'You can take part by …', 'Find out more by …'. There is usually just a single, simple call to action. If there is more than one (e.g. 'There are three ways you can help'), then it is best to treat this as a section of the animation (like a 'however' moment) and give your multiple calls to action space to breathe, rather than squeezing your three or four points on to a conclusion screen.

As well as a clear message, many companies include a campaign URL (so marketing types can track clicks), although nobody types URLs any more and you can't click or copy and paste them from an animation screen anyway.

There are usually lots of logos to tag on to the end of your animation, as well as disclaimers, footnotes and so on. It is important to include all this information in the script if you can, because it counts in your run time, there are usually important legal reasons for including it, and it means you won't forget to request (or make) the necessary assets in good time.

Keys to good animation design

Be flexible

In Chapter 4, we talked about how your wireframe was usually your best guess at what the final content would be. During the **Make** stage, there are inevitably edits and changes, because some elements might not fit, others might not work, and the client might change their mind about what they want.

For animations, you need to be even more flexible. Once things start moving, you will inevitably notice that parts of your copy have become redundant, or there are visuals that don't make sense without extra explanation. We have never – *never* – produced an animation which has stuck entirely to the script.

Gaps are good

For people new to scripting animations, the hardest thing to learn is how readily audiences will fill in any gaps. In static graphics, you tend to walk people through each stage of your journey. 'This datapoint increased [chart], which led to this social impact [photograph], and these possible solutions [icons].' It is the same with any static or text-based story.

But take the following sentence: 'John closed his bedroom door, crossed the street, opened the door to his office, and sat down on a park bench.'

Er, what now? John's bedroom leads directly to the street? Is he in a bedsit? And then is his office on the other side of the road? And there's a park bench in his office?

In a movie, this would be a perfectly ordinary sequence. The man walks out of his bathroom, dressed in his suit; we cut to him crossing the street outside his house, maybe heading for the station; we cut to him arriving in his office and perhaps hanging up his jacket, and then we finally see him sitting on a park bench (still jacketless), eating a sandwich at lunchtime, where we assume someone of significance will sit next to him and move the plot of the movie forwards (unless it's a French film, in which case he'll just think, sit there, thinking deep thoughts).

It's not only that we can leave out all our conjunctions: 'Afterwards', 'Meanwhile', 'Later that day', 'In another part of the city'. In a movie, we can leave out *reams* of explanatory content that we would need to include in a novel or news article.

In other words, you can animate a chart representing an increase in wealth inequality and then cut to footage of Occupy Wall Street, and then cut to a chart showing that 60% of Democrats under 30 supported Bernie Sanders' presidential bid.[1] Not a single word is necessary – just the titles and labels on your charts and perhaps some dramatic, royalty-free music in the background. Your audience will do the rest.

Clever copy

Where you do use copy, you need to think of it as an entirely different exercise from writing copy for a report or infographic. With an infographic, everything is sequential: *read text,* then *view image,* then back again. If they complement each other well, your mind will fuse the disparate media as one fact or memory.

With animation voiceover, the audience experiences words and images simultaneously. It is like the narrative voice in a film noir, framing what we are looking at, giving the kind of abstract

---

[1]https://nymag.com/intelligencer/2020/02/this-one-chart-explains-why-young-voters-back-bernie-sanders.html

or contextual information that images can't give. So at the beginning of *The Third Man* (which the British Film Institute recently crowned the greatest British film ever), we have a narrator's voice accompanying shots of Vienna in the late 1940s:

I never knew the old Vienna before the war, with its Strauss music, its glamour and easy charm. Constantinople suited me better. I really got to know it in the classic period of the black market. We'd run anything – if people wanted it enough and had the money to pay.

The voiceover tells us when and where we are, so the visuals can focus on atmospheric shots of snow on statues, bootleggers furtively exchanging money, and dead bodies floating in the Danube.

However, notice the language of the *Third Man* voiceover too. In particular:

- It is superbly paced, switching from evocative, poetic sentences ('I never knew the old Vienna before the war') to terse, cynical asides ('We'd run anything – if people wanted it enough').
- It has a personality and a perspective: just a few words ('Constantinople suited me better') summon up an Englishman of a particular type, class and era.
- It is designed to be performed. It sounds like speech, not writing. This makes it easier for the actor to invest it with energy and emotion, and means it is a perfect partner for the visuals, giving different information, but with equal intensity.

When you are writing copy for animations, it's a good idea to think about these elements too. Write with an awareness of what is easy to perform, think about the natural rhythms of speech, and give your language personality so that it is not marginalised by the visuals. More specifically:

- Use metaphors and figures of speech that suit the topic. Adding wordplay to copy can make it feel more inventive. However, your

puns and metaphors need to be used sparingly (or it all gets a bit tabloid) and they need to complement the visuals. In our examples above, we use occasional wordplay that emphasises the subject-matter (e.g. 'Choosing a name for your baby is definitely not child's play').

- Alternate between sentences of differing lengths. Here is option 1: 'Boomer names like Andrew and Susan are out and pre-war names like Stanley and Ivy are in, which suggests that parents across the country are increasingly choosing hipster names.' Here is option 2: 'Boomer names like Andrew and Susan are out and pre-war names like Stanley and Ivy are in. We are all hipsters now.' If you follow a long sentence with a short sentence, it will hold your audience's attention more effectively. It just will. (There I go again.) But be warned. Avoid lots of short sentences. They sound odd. Like a telegram. Like everything's important. And it usually isn't. And when there's something important. Like really important. This fact won't stand out. It will just fizzle out.
- Alternate between different kinds of language: poetic and direct, formal and informal.

Take a look at the section towards the end of our script, shown in Table 7.6. The change in register in the last few sentences is designed to be a jolt for the viewer: 'For girls, we are influenced by celebrities and fantasy movies. Whereas boys – well, let's just say, don't mess.'. The use of slang ('don't mess') is also meant to suit the story – it is the kind of thing that British gangsters in movies say. Alternating between formal and informal language gives your copy energy and elasticity, and helps it to 'keep up' with the visuals.

But it isn't just about changing the tone, it's also about moving between different types of sentence. We use rhetorical questions such as: 'What do Marvel movies, *Game of Thrones* and Posh Spice have in common?' These sentences directly address the viewer and ask them to

Table 7.6 Different types of language

Girls are still named after flowers and plants.	Top 30 names include: Poppy, Lily, Willow, Rosie, Daisy
Whereas boys are named after kings and religious leaders.	Top 30 names include: George, Henry, Noah, Muhammad, Isaac
For girls, we are influenced by celebrities and fantasy movies.	Rank change since 2008: +1365 Harper +570 Aurora +537 Luna
Whereas boys – well, let's just say, don't mess.	Rank change since 2008: +236 Reggie +50 Ronnie [Kray twins?]

ponder a situation or dilemma. But then we might switch to sentences that are simple and factual ('Girls are still named after flowers and plants') or more descriptive ('When Phil and Susie Jones had a baby boy this year, they downloaded the latest baby names data, expecting to see their favourite names in the top 100'). I should stress: none of this is variety for its own sake, it is about finding and exploiting the natural rhythms of your story, so your text is as fluid and immersive as the visuals.

When you have finished your script, it is time to start making the animation, which Tobias will cover in the next chapter.

 — **Try it yourself!**

1 Take the dataset you found at the end of Chapter 6 or, if you prefer, you can return to the baby names data we used in Chapters 3–5.
2 Isolate a story that would work best as a motion graphic for a general audience. Remember that motion graphics are usually explainers, so it's a good idea to choose a story that involves you walking the audience through an unusual or intriguing element of the data.
3 Create a two-minute script. Remember to include some suggested visual elements too.

4 Once you've finished, work through this checklist:

- Is your script less than 250 words?
- Have you cut any text that duplicates information contained in the visuals?
- Have you given your story an obvious hook or frame?
- Is there a gear change part of the way through? A 'but' or 'however'?
- Have you provided a clear conclusion? Is it obvious what the audience can do if they want to find out more information?

Eight
Making motion graphics

Tobias Sturt

We are doing precisely the same thing with motion graphics that we are with static ones: trying to communicate data through visuals. We have the same goals (truthfulness, clarity and attractiveness), and we have the same visual mechanism (contrast through consistency and change). We also have much the same visual vocabulary: lines and shapes, colour and position, images and font.

What we are adding is time, and with time come two more visual tools:

- **Movement** – moving objects in the frame by changing position and other attributes (shape, size, colour, etc.). This gives us:

  ○ **Direction**: going forward and backward, increasing or decreasing
  ○ **Relationships**: things moving in synchrony or opposition, one thing becoming another
  ○ **Character**: how does the thing move? Eagerly? Reluctantly? This adds an emotional dimension for the audience.

- **Transition** – moving from frame to frame through editing or motion of the camera (or more correctly 'viewer', as we are unlikely to have a camera, real or virtual). This gives us:

  ○ **Structure**: arranging moments in time, from point to point
  ○ **Meaning**: as the Kuleshov effect shows, audiences see two sequences edited together as related in causation, space or emotion
  ○ **Drama**: edits can create surprise in contrasting visuals or create unexpected connections.

Like our other tools, movement and transition also have complex overlapping roles – we can use them to represent elements of our information, to elucidate the structure and flow of our communication, and also to have a metaphorical function in how they frame the viewer's experience and add character to the telling.

Moreover, animation is, in itself (as Adam has already intimated) attractive. Moving things grab our attention. *Anima* is the Latin for 'soul'. When we animate something, we give it a soul, bring it to life.

Process

This is why the **Design** and **Make** parts of the process tend to overlap a lot more in animation than they do in static design. We want to do as much visual work as we can before we start animating, because reanimating a scene takes a lot longer than rewriting a script or redrawing a storyboard.

So we have to start thinking about visuals as soon as we have a script, long before we would with a static visualisation. We want to be able to concentrate on animating when we're animating, instead of still thinking about the basic visuals. We start by thinking about our basic visual storytelling approach and then elaborate on the applications through a series of stages, from scenario, to storyboard, to animation:

1 **Visual approach**: what best suits our content – an animated presentation, slide by slide, or something more dramatic?
2 **Scenario**: writing a script that describes everything that happens on screen so the client gets a sense of our visual ideas before we draw anything.
3 **Storyboard**: drawing that scenario so we can begin to put visuals and motion on paper and test how well they are communicating.
4 **Graphics**: establishing the look and feel, usually in conjunction with the storyboard so we can get an idea of how the finished animation might look, providing the visual assets for the animation.
5 **Audio**: if we're having voiceover or music then we need it recorded before the animation starts, as it's going to give us rhythms to animate to.
6 **Animation**: finally things start actually moving, as we take the assets and the audio and animate them based on an approved storyboard.

Visual approach

There are four basic visual approaches to motion graphics. These are the motion equivalents of page layouts in print infographics. I have taken Adam's baby names story to show how each approach could be applied in Table 8.1 here, from simple slideshow style to full scene-by-scene animations.

Scenario

I'm using the term 'scenario' here to distinguish this process from the scripting of the on-screen text or voiceover on the one hand, and the more conventional screenplay composition on the other. It is traditional in screenplay writing to concentrate on the dialogue and actions and not to describe the visuals. This is the absolute opposite of what we want to do. We want to take the approved text and content and then describe in detail how we are going to animate them.

Our aim is to describe how the motion and transitions are going to help show our story. As with a wireframe, we're less concerned with the substance of the actual visuals and more with how they will work. Be aware that it is often hard for readers to imagine the movement when simply described in words. We do need to be as descriptive and emotive in our language as possible, to make sure that the audience gets the sense of the effect of the visuals, even if they can't picture them exactly.

The scenario isn't always a necessary step. Sometimes we might go straight to storyboard, particularly if we're animating based on assets that have already been created. If you have made a load of charts for a report, for example, and now want to introduce that report with an animation, you will be making a slide-by-slide animation of the pre-existing charts and you can more easily storyboard that than write it. Some animators

may also find it easier to move straight to the visuals of the storyboarding process rather than spend a lot of time typing something they could draw more quickly.

However, writing a scenario does mean that we get to try out several different visual approaches and start to make some preliminary decisions about which one might work best, before we spend more time on drawing a storyboard.

For our baby names, for instance, we could have a single chart – say a line of icons to represent babies – and then animate different settings around it to show the passage of time, or maybe use clips of famous people with the appropriate names to dramatise how names have changed over time.

You can see an example scenario for Adam's script in Table 8.2.

Storyboards

A storyboard is a series of illustrations, showing frames from the animation so that a reader can see how the visuals will flow from one to the other. Storyboards are generally hand-drawn, partly for reasons of speed of production but also to ensure that the viewer does not mistake them for finished frames. This is because they are essentially wireframes for the animation.

We want the reader to be able to see what happens without being distracted by the look and feel. The illustrations don't have to be amazing, but they do need to show everything in frame and to indicate, with annotations if necessary (arrows, captions and so on), what's happening.

Ideally a storyboard should include a frame for every line or point in the script, and frequently more, especially for more complex movements and arrangements.

The storyboard should also be accompanied by the script and description from the scenario, just to ensure that there's as little confusion as possible about what's happening on screen.

Table 8.1

Approach	What is it?	When should I use it?	Example
Slideshow	A presentation with (much) fancier transitions. You move from set frame to set frame through a series of animated transformations. Each frame can contain movement and loops; but the story is in the frame, rather than the movement between frames.	Use it when you have content that is very presentation-like (as you might expect): a lot of charts and visuals that you need to move through, one by one, to explain your story. This animation type is probably the easiest to describe, the easiest for a client to envisage and often the easiest to animate. We tend to use it when we have complex stories and not much time.	Each point in the baby names story gets its own chart and we then transition between those charts. It also means that individual sequences of the charts could be sectioned out for social media.
Bird's-eye view (or rostrum camera)	We are travelling over an image, zooming in and out of a single big visual or moving through a landscape. The story evolves as we move.	Best suited to stories where you have a single big metaphor or graphic that you want to explore (a timeline, for example). It also works for those animated visual notes you get where the 'camera' travels over a piece of paper as ideas are drawn on it.	We have a big line chart that shows all our data. We then move back and forth across it, highlighting and calling out key elements, zooming in and out of details.
Changing scenery	We have a single chart, which we update as the story progresses, changing the surroundings to reflect the changing content. This is a sort of animated version of a scrollytelling interactive, updating chart surroundings and decorations to reflect change in the narrative.	Works best where we're investigating a single dataset – say, popularity of baby names over time (see next column) or survey results where we're looking at what different segments of a population think and feel about something and we want to shift between (for example) what 'young people' think and what 'older people' think.	We have a single chart – say, a row of 10 icons for babies, representing the 10 most popular names. The scenery around them changes, adding annotations and highlights, as well as more fun things, such as changing the background to match time periods. This gives us the potential for a nice, simple, core visual while having some more active elements around them.
Scene-by-scene/ montage	Otherwise known as filmmaking. This is your basic motion picture, where we're transitioning between scenes in which elements move. They might be talking heads in a documentary, animated data visualisations or accident-prone coyotes (*Carnivorous Vulgaris*) who just want to eat.	This approach is used a lot in explainers, when we have complex stories to tell, with lots of separate elements that need distinct visual elucidation before being linked into an overall narrative.	We concentrate on the people rather than charts, personifying the parents and babies in a two-parent family with twin babies. This allows us to refocus the story onto the people who give and have the names and so place this data properly within its human context. It's likely to be very visually appealing with animated characters, but that is also what would make it the hardest work.

Table 8.2 Animating between key visualisations

Voiceover/subtitles	Visuals on screen
Looking at the top baby names for 2018, this generation has some clear winners.	Two mirrored bar charts (top 5 names for girls and boys) grow from the centre of the screen, both starting from the bottom.
Oliver is number 1 for boys – and has been for the last 5 years.	We highlight Oliver at number 1 and fade out the girls' bars, shrinking the boys' bars down to a square for each name and moving the names to the right. Lines grow back left across the screen to show the ranks for the last 5 years.
Olivia is number 1 for girls – and has been for the last 3 years.	Cross-fade to a similar line chart for the girls but only showing 3 years.
Other names – like Amelia and Emily for girls and Jack and Harry for boys – have been in the top 10 for at least a decade …	The line chart extends out to 10 years and grows to be a top 10, highlighting Amelia and Emily. We then cross-fade to the same chart for boys, highlighting Jack and Harry.
and represent this generation as surely as Sarah and Chris did in the 1980s …	The camera pushes left, the names disappearing off to the right, the lines crossing and fading as the x-axis years tick back towards 1984. By the time we get there the line chart has disappeared entirely and another mirrored bar chart appears, showing the top 3 names for girls and boys.
and Margaret and John in the 1950s.	The mirrored bars transform to show the top 3 in 1954.
So names have changed. This generation has its own identity, right?	The bars animate away and the axes of four line charts appear, the x-axes all labelled 1900 at one end and 2018 at the other.
Actually, it's not that simple. Yes, we've dropped the boomer names, but replaced them with names that were popular four or five generations ago.	Each line chart traces the same pattern: popular in 1900s, disappearing, reappearing again in the 2000s; they are labelled Grace, Ivy, Arthur and Edward.
They are retro chic.	The line charts fade away, leaving the names highlighted. Then they fade.
And even when the names have changed, the attitudes certainly haven't.	The screen starts to fill with 30 dots.
Girls are still named after flowers and plants …	25 dots fade away, leaving 5 that then grow to become sized bubbles and are labelled: Poppy, Lily, Willow, Rosie, Daisy.
whereas boys are still named after kings and religious leaders.	We cross-fade to the same chart for boys: George, Henry, Noah, Muhammad, Isaac.
For girls, we are influenced by celebrities and fantasy movies …	The boys' bubbles fade away and a dot chart grows from the bottom of the frame showing rank change since 2008: +1365 Harper / +570 Aurora / +537 Luna.
whereas boys – well, let's just say, don't mess.	The dot charts shrink back and fresh ones grow for the boys, showing rank change since 2008: +236 Reggie / +50 Ronnie. Illustrations of Reggie and Ronnie Kray appear in the dots.

(Continued)

Table 8.2 (Continued)

Voiceover/subtitles	Visuals on screen
Which begs the question: when we give our children a name, are we really thinking about what their future life might be?	The dot charts shrink away and two sized bubbles appear on screen, labelled Oliver and Olivia. The bubbles are then filled with illustrations of babies' faces.
Or are we stuck in the past?	The babies morph into illustrations of Oliver Cromwell and Olivia de Havilland – the labels update to match.
Read more about our baby names coverage at: www.theguardian.com/baby-names-2019	Logo and URL on screen

We need the storyboard to be as complete a record of the animation as we can manage. We need to make sure that the visuals match the script, that the motion tells our story, that we can follow everything that is going to be happening on screen as in Figure 8.1.

Assets: Graphics

Once we have an agreed storyboard we can start producing the assets for the animation. We've probably already started thinking about this process, but now we are beginning the more thorough process of gathering together all the assets that the animator will need.

This means working to the storyboard to make sure that everything depicted is created, which also means that we usually have some of the key frames fully designed. This gives us a precise idea of what the final animation will look like.

If we're working for a client then we share these flat designs along with the storyboard so they can understand how they work in context and to enable us to have the more detailed discussions about representation (whether that square should be brand red, what a farmer should look like, will the boss like the way we've drawn the factory?) before we embark on any actual animation.

One further step we sometimes take, particularly with more complex animations, is to use the storyboard (and sometimes the designed assets) to produce a crude animation often called an 'animatic'. This rarely includes any detailed animation but rather transitions elements and scenes in the general way they are intended to move in the final product. The aim is to get a more coherent sense of the motion, and sense-check any storytelling decisions.

The crucial thing to remember with these assets is that when we move into the animation phase of the process it can get a lot harder to make changes to visuals, especially to more fundamental look-and-feel decisions. The more of those choices we can make now, the happier the animation process will be.

Assets: Sound

If you're going to need audio in the animation – voiceover, music, sound effects – then it's also preferable to have these in place before animation begins. Particularly with voiceover and music, it helps to be able to animate to the audio rather than sync them up later.

Both music and voiceover should be as professionally sourced as possible.

- **Music.** Often the choice of music can be a matter of taste, but bear in mind that it sets pace (and gives a rhythm to edit to), mood (upbeat, serious, propulsive) and tone (classical might feel serious but highbrow, folk approachable but lighthearted). Licences cost money and even while there are plenty of

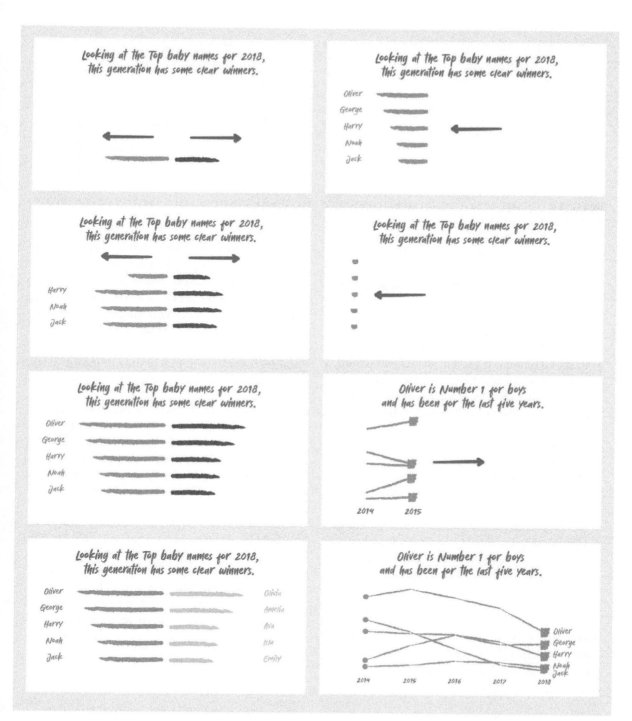

Figure 8.1 Example storyboard graphics – note the annotations reinforcing directions of movement

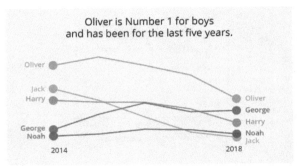

Figure 8.2 Designed layouts for the animation assets. Unlike the storyboard, we only design up a single representative screen, and often make look-and-feel decisions while we do so

reputable licence-free sources (such as https://filmmusic.io), it still takes more time than you might expect to search and review appropriate pieces.

- **Voiceover.** You should be ready to direct and explain the pronunciation or timing of any technical terms or brand phrases. It's a good idea to ask for multiple takes, and alternative versions, just to pre-empt any client feedback about problematic sentences. If you haven't directed actors before, then consider using a professional recording studio that can direct the actors for you.
- **Sound effects.** We use sound effects sparingly, as they can come across as cartoonish, but they can, particularly in explainers, lend useful character to animated sequences. More abstract sounds (swooshes and chimes, for instance) can help accentuate movement but we tend to reserve more specific sound effects for when they have a deliberate meaning: white noise to match static on screen, animal sound effects to match a character, and so on.

One thing to note when considering whether to have music or voiceover (or just to have text on screen, perhaps) is that sound costs money and takes time, to research, to gather, but also to process for the final animation.

Animation

We are animating our data visualisation for a reason: because animation is going to help us to communicate more clearly. Just as with our static visualisations, our visual choices have to be motivated, they must be rooted in the information we're trying to get across, and this goes as much for movement as it does for images. Every action in our motion graphic should mean something.

There are some rules of thumb that we usually start with (and then, like all rules of thumb in data visualisation, subsequently ignore entirely):

- **Charts.** Generally they will build out from the zero point of the axes, and the shapes that represent the data will animate away from the axes or origin points (so columns grown up or down from an *x*-axis, lines animate left to right across the frame, pies build clockwise from 12 o'clock).
- **Numbers and titles.** Numbers will count up, especially if it's an important or big value; bubbles and dots in a scatter will grow in, often with a 'pop'; and often we'll fade in elements like titles and labels, just to give a smoother appearance than just switching things on.
- **Moving objects.** We tend to assume certain meanings until our story requires something different:

  o Objects 'grow' up and/or right across the frame and 'shrink' down and/or to the left.
  o Left is back and right is forward, both in the sense of direction but also in time. It should be borne in mind that as the 'camera' moves right, the objects in frame will move left – in fact in most

animation to give the effect of moving right, we just move everything on screen left – but this is still a move 'forward'.

- ○ Up is growth and down is decline – just as it would be in a chart.
- ○ Up and down can also be a move higher in a hierarchy, up to an overview, or down into the detail.
- ○ 'In' is a zoom and so a move into detail, to 'dig into' elements on screen. This usually involves simply enlarging everything.
- ○ Conversely, 'out', shrinking everything, is a zoom out to an overview.

Transitions

Transitions also have meaning. Most fundamentally, as we noted with the story of Lev Kuleshov right at the beginning of Chapter 5, editing makes meaning: viewers see a cut as a relationship between the two sequences on either side of it.

Essentially an edit in video is an elision of time and often space, but as viewers our personal experience of both is usually seamless, so we assume a connection across those changes. Some transitions heighten this: a dissolve, fade or match cut will emphasise direct relationships between objects, and camera movements will put the objects into the same physical space, even if we cut during the move, making them directly related.

All transitions between sequences tell stories, but different edits tell different stories – some keep meaning flowing, like dissolves and wipes, while some create contrast and drama, like smash cuts.

- **Fades and dissolves**. A fade to white or black is a gentler way to remove elements from the frame instead of just dramatically vanishing them. Cross-fading – or dissolving – between sequences creates a sense of continuity between different parts of the animation.
- **Match cuts**. Match cuts cut between matching frame contents, highlighting the similarity. A straight cut between two similarly laid-out frames highlights that they are intended to

convey the same kind of information – as two similarly laid out slides in a presentation would.

- **Wipe**. Wipes are the kinds of transitions you get in presentation software like PowerPoint: sliding one frame in over the top of another, or revealing it in a clockwise sweep. They give us a sense of motion in the edit, but they're considered old fashioned in cinema these days. More often we're using hidden wipes, where an object passes in front of what's on screen, revealing a new scene in its wake.
- **Jump cut**. Jump cuts jump in time, within the same scene, causing elements to then jump around the frame. It's as if we've cut a few frames out of the sequence, missing a period of continuous action. Jump cuts can be very disconcerting, but are dramatic too.
- **Smash cut**. The 'smash' in 'smash cut' is more descriptive of the effect than the technique – a cut between two contrasting elements, creating drama through that contrast (i.e. the opposite of a match cut).

Character and emotion

In their book *Disney Animation: The Illusion of Life*, two Disney animators, Frank Thomas and Ollie Johnston (1981), laid out 12 basic principles of animation. These principles are, as you might expect, primarily focused on animating characters for Disney films, but I still feel that they can give us a really good guide to thinking about how we make motion graphics engaging and appealing. The 12 principles are as follows:

- **Squash and stretch** – the way that the weight of an object will redistribute as it moves
- **Anticipation** – that characters will prepare for action, either to make it or receive it
- **Staging** – this is the mise-en-scène we spoke about in Chapter 5: laying out the frame so that the focus and meaning is clear
- **Straight ahead versus pose to pose** – technical animation choices: do you draw frames one by one, or lay out key frames and then animate the frames in between?

- **Follow through and overlapping action** – how bodies and objects move in space: limbs will move at different, overlapping, rates, while things like hair will carry on moving after the body has stopped
- **Slow in and slow out** – the physics of movement mean that objects generally have to accelerate when they move, starting slowly and speeding up, and then slow to a stop at the end
- **Arc** – objects tend to follow an arcing trajectory, rather than moving in straight lines
- **Secondary action** – complementing your main action (someone walking, say) with another movement, like arms swinging or whistling (or both)
- **Timing** – this is partly about physics, allowing the right amount of time for an action, but also about mood and character (how quickly or slowly an object reacts, for example)
- **Exaggeration** – what we think of when we think of 'cartoony' action: exaggerating the movement to make it more visible
- **Solid drawing** – partly just about drawing well, but is also about preserving the 'realism' of the graphical assets you're working with
- **Appeal** – the purely aesthetic part of the list: do our assets look attractive?

These principles break down into three more general categories: physics, character and visual style, each of which needs to be considered in animating motion graphics.

Physics

Real-world physics can seem like an unlikely consideration when we're talking about motion graphics depicting purely symbolic images in a notional space, but our perception is so used to dealing with the actual world that it can be key in selling movement as convincing and, more importantly, interesting.

We are very rarely dealing with a complex walk cycle of an animated character, where all the different body parts are moving at different speeds in different ways. Usually what we're doing is moving elements into place, or transforming shapes or colours in response to changes in the data and the meaning. But even in just moving a dot across a frame, we need to consider the details of the animation.

In most motion graphics, we are generally taking a 'pose to pose' approach: moving elements between rest states and letting the software fill in the frames in between – what is called 'tweening'. It is in that tweening that we need to at least consider the 'slow in, slow out' rule, which is usually generally applied using 'easing'.

A regular tween will simply divide the distance an object needs to move by the number of frames it has to move it, and move it an equal distance in each frame. Easing changes this. Easing in moves an object more slowly at the beginning and thus more quickly at the end (slower movement takes more frames, so it has less to play with at the end). Easing out starts quickly and slows down at the end. Easing in and out on the same tween gives us our 'slow in, slow out' from the Disney principles.

Generally animation software like After Effects will let you finesse the easing, often by manipulating a curve to give yourself different options, from the subtle to the most cartoonish bounces and wobbles. These more extreme eases will also give us a degree of anticipation and follow through as objects draw back, preparing to move and settle into place at the end of their animation.

Some effects we use more sparingly – arcs in movement, for instance. Because direction in movement has meaning, we have to make sure that any finessing is not confusing the viewer. If it makes sense, most animation software will allow us to set motion guides for our tweens, so that we can tweak the way an object travels.

This meaning in movement is our primary deciding factor in what techniques we use. Because size frequently has meaning in data visualisation, we tend to be sparing in using effects like squash and stretch (the way an object will bunch up at take-off or landing, and stretch out as it moves), simply because it means altering shapes as they move. Moreover, it is so effective at adding physical reality and character it can often be distracting from visualisations about more serious topics. After all, we don't want anyone to mistake the bubbles in our scatter chart for balls or faces.

In Figure 8.3 you can see three sequences showing the frames of a tween between two positions over seven frames. The top example has no easing – the circle travels exactly the same distance each frame. The other examples have easing on the in and out of the tween, meaning that in the middle example the circle travels less distance between frames at the beginning and ending and more in the middle. This means it will appear to move more slowly at the start and finish and quicker in the middle of the tween. In the bottom version the reverse is true: the circle will appear to move faster at the beginning and end and slower in the middle.

Adding a similar tween to the bars in our bar chart in the example storyboard, for instance, would make their appearance that little bit more natural and appealing.

The sequence in Figure 8.4 gives an example of exaggeration and secondary action in a motion graphic – in this case a dot appears by growing, expanding out, then shrinking to its final size – this will give a slight bounce to the animation. Then we've added in little motion lines that explode out of it in combination with that bounce to give it a 'pop' as it appears. These might be, for example, the markers on our line chart in the example storyboard, popping into existence as the line extends back through time.

Character

Character is something that is often neglected by people making motion graphics, often because they are trying to avoid being too lighthearted. However, I would argue that character is an intrinsic part of making shapes appealing.

As with the physics effects mentioned above, we are rarely animating actual 'characters' in a motion graphic, which means that if we want to introduce charisma into our shapes and objects, we have to work the animation a little bit harder.

The exaggeration of physical effects is a basic part of animation, so much so that we refer to exaggerated gestures and actions as 'cartoony' and

Figure 8.3 Different speeds of animation

Figure 8.4 A dot pops into existence

more often than not our visual appeal lies in the simplicity of our graphics, rather than in inventive or attractive character design. This means that if we are going to add squash and stretch or follow through to a simple graphic, we will need to exaggerate them for that effect to be properly visible.

More common is the use of secondary action: a little halo of motion lines that spreads out and disappears when an icon pops onto the screen, or drawing of an outline to emphasise an element. These little additions serve a useful double purpose of drawing attention to objects, as well as just adding a fillip of movement to the frame.

Visual style

For the most part our visual style in our staging and drawing is going to be decided the same way as it is in static graphics: by our story (and any brand guidelines, of course).

The one thing to note about visual style in animation is the extra element of timing. The speed at which the animation moves is also going to frame how to read the information (as well as how easy it is to read as it flashes by). Slow and deliberate tends to read as sober and calm, but can also quickly descend into something not much more complex than a slideshow. Quick and slick feels energetic but also antic (and hard to read). Picking a pace is as important to the mood of the piece as it is to readability.

On the whole, it's safer to default to a faster animation than a slower one. Quick animations move more smoothly and are more likely to keep a viewer's attention, particularly when the subject (i.e. data) might not be immediately appealing for a general audience.

 **Try it yourself!**

Start with a script for an animation (possibly the one you wrote for the exercise at the end of the previous chapter, if you did that). Now rewrite it as a scenario:

- Decide whether you are going to have text on screen, voiceover or both (or neither).
- Divide up the script into discrete blocks of meaning (usually sentences).

- For each block, write a description of what is happening on screen (include any text from the script).

Once you have a scenario, draw a storyboard from it:

- Decide on your aspect ratio, as this will affect how much screen space you have (essentially a

- choice between widescreen 16:9 and square 1:1).
- Create a template with frames of the correct ratio and space beneath each one to write notes (you should be able to find plenty of templates online to download).
- Now take each of those blocks from the scenario and draw a sketch of what is on screen:

  - Draw everything, including any text on screen.
  - Indicate movement, either within the frame or of the 'camera'.

- You will probably find that:

  - Some sentences will need several frames to illustrate clearly.
  - Some things you've described in words can't be drawn and you have to come up with something else (this happens more often than you think).

Once you have a storyboard you can think about designing up the assets and animating them – this will require an image editing application (usually a vector editing tool like Adobe Illustrator) and animation software (like Adobe After Effects, or even dear old Adobe Animate, which is just our old friend Flash in mufti). Any professional animation tool should have plenty of tutorials to help you.

You can find resources to help with all these exercises online at: https://www.addtwodigital.com/book.

Nine

Designing interactive infographics

Adam Frost

Chapter contents

The first thing to establish is what to *call* the storytelling medium that we will explore in this chapter. The animations we discussed in Chapters 7 and 8 have been around for over a century; exploratory dashboards such as DataShine (mentioned in Chapter 6) were first used decades ago as a data analysis tool, but the hybrid kind of storytelling that we are discussing here is a relatively new development, something that didn't really take off until browsers like Internet Explorer began to support scalable vector graphic (SVG) effects in the early 2010s.[1] But when they took off, they took off in a big way, unleashing an explosion of creativity and quickly becoming embedded in the mainstream of data journalism and science communication.

From pioneering work like Angela Morelli's 'The Water We Eat' (2013) and the *Guardian*'s 'Firestorm' (Henley et al., 2013), through to brilliant investigative journalism like the *New York Times*'s 'The Punishing Reach of Racism' (Badger et al., 2018) and 'Who Gets to Breathe Clean Air in Delhi?' (Wu et al., 2020), the best examples of this new storytelling medium fuse animation and interactivity with static elements like illustrations or photography, and create something that is more akin to a digital exhibition – a multimedia experience in a museum or gallery that has a strong central narrative pathway, but lots of side rooms to explore, objects to pick up and buttons to press.

The placeholder term for this new kind of storytelling is (deep breath) 'scrollytelling'. It's not clear who first invented the term, possibly because they are now so ashamed they have retired from public life. We'll be using the term *interactive infographic* instead, which isn't exactly elegant either, but at least it is broad enough to cover every type of interactive data story, rather than just the ones that rely on scrolling to trigger particular transitions and effects. It also differentiates what we are doing – creating information graphics and charts – from scrollytelling more generally, which includes stories that have no data component at all. For examples of scrollytelling with no data viz, have a look at the *Washington Post*'s superb article on the making of 'Walk this Way' ('The inside story of when Run-DMC met Aerosmith and changed music forever' (Edgers, 2016)) or the *New York Times*'s 'Shark and Minnow' (Himmelman, 2013).

When you are making an interactive infographic, your goal is usually to describe or explain a subject, and allow limited exploration. It tends to be for a mixed audience, skewing slightly towards novices, and uses bold visuals to reinforce key points. Outside of this, there is no single template that works for all subjects and audiences.

Three general approaches

To simplify, the three most common approaches are stepped, stacked or focussing on a single complex chart.

- **Stepped.** Some are more like presentations, for example Maarten Lambrecht's 'How Belgium is Heating Up' (2016) or Bloomberg's 'How Americans Die' (Klein, 2014). The audience is 'stepped' through the content, usually by clicking on Previous/Next or a similar pagination device that clearly demarcates the end of one story chapter and the beginning of the next. This approach suits stories that need a clearly visible author, walking the audience through a complex subject one step at a time.
- **Stacked.** Others are more like reportage, for example *Die Zeit*'s 'A Nation Divided'

---

[1]Before this, there was Flash. But this tended to be used for self-contained explorable charts (like Gapminder) or animated walkthroughs, rather than story-led interactive infographics. As a plug-in, it was frowned upon by most web developers, which is one of the reasons why it has ceased to exist.

(Borgenheimer et al., 2014) or the *New York Times*'s 'Greenland Is Melting Away' (Davenport et al., 2015). Here content tends to be 'stacked up' – text, image, text, map, text, chart or whatever it might be. The copy carries the emotional weight of the story, and any charts are there to provide context or additional evidence.

- **Single complex chart**. Sometimes the end product is more of a lecture or an explainer. Here there is usually a single hero dataset or chart that is held on the screen for most of (or all) of the infographic. Scrolling reveals a new aspect or dimension of this dataset. For example, the *New York Times*'s 'How the Recession Reshaped the Economy, in 255 Charts' (Ashkenas and Parlapiono, 2014). Visuals rather than copy tend to be the narrative driver in these infographics.

These three approaches overlap to some degree, and often time or technical constraints will determine your chosen solution. Stacked content, for example, is usually easier to template and test, and this is probably why it is often used for data journalism, particularly for topical stories that need to be turned around quickly. Most free tools (e.g. Shorthand, Strikingly or Google Sites) make it easy to generate stacked sites, whereas single complex charts that deliver additional content on scroll almost always require custom coding.

But whatever your situation, the storytelling principles that we have referred to throughout this book should also help you build a clear and compelling interactive infographic. It is still a question of selection, dramatisation, emphasis and presentation. What has changed is that there will be several levels of your story and you have to apply these principles to each of them. In some ways, you will be doing this already when you tell stories in a professional setting. Most presentations, lessons and even blog posts are multi-level.

- If you are giving a presentation, there will usually be the content in the main presentation, supplementary content in an appendix (or hidden slides) and then the contextual context that you might anticipate in a Q&A session at the end.
- In a lesson, you will differentiate information. The main lesson will cover the key objectives, but you will also have extension material for the able students, and possibly different types of stimulus for students with different learning styles.
- If you are writing an online article, you will often put extra content and references into footnotes or rollovers and usually add links to contextual material on other web pages.

With an interactive infographic, you simply formalise this split-level approach, consciously marshalling the content into lanes, and ensuring that the rewards for clicking through and drilling down are worth the expenditure of cognitive effort. Frequently a clickthrough or mouseover can just reveal a data dump – unedited and unstructured, a computer-generated replication of every field in the database, slapped into a tooltip with default styling. (For me? Really, *you shouldn't have*.) Given that the people who request more information are usually your keenest readers, I'd argue that you should take more, not less, care over the stories you give them.

Let's return to our baby names dataset now and think about how we might design an interactive infographic for a particular audience. I'm going to assume that we have been commissioned by the UK's Office for National Statistics (ONS), the publishers of the data, to produce an interactive infographic about this dataset – which is one of their most popular annual releases. They want it to appeal to everyone but, at the same time, as the Office for National Statistics, they have to be mindful of their reputation as providers of accurate, reliable data.

Find

The **Find** stage when you create an interactive infographic is usually lengthy (on average, 6–8 weeks), because you need not only to research your dataset, but also to be aware of contextual datasets that you will be drawing on in the deeper levels of your story.

In a static graphic there is usually a defined audience, often a specific demographic, but with interactive infographics the audience is usually broader, partly because that is one way of justifying the additional time and cost that is involved in making them, but also because the entire purpose of an interactive is to offer differentiated content for a much wider range of people.

For my baby names interactive, I would analyse the latest release as I outlined in Chapter 3, drawing out any interesting stories and, if necessary, thinking about those top-level story types: change over time, comparison, composition, distribution, correlation and geospatial. But as well as the newest release, I would also be exploring other kinds of datasets:

- **Historic data**. The ONS has baby names data going back over 100 years and I would want to draw on some of these generational stories. For example, some names have stayed permanently in fashion and others have not. The following boys' names have been in the top 100 since records began: James, George, Thomas, William, Joseph, Edward and Daniel. But for girls, only one name has persisted since 1900: Sarah.
- **Other datasets owned by the organisation**. We might look at other contextual ONS data, partly because there would be no licensing or ownership issues, but also because the ONS would presumably be keen to use the interactive graphic to showcase some of the other datasets that they have in their collection. For example, we might look at their monthly employment statistics and economic indicators to explore whether people have fewer babies in a recession. (In the 2008 recession, research from Pew in the USA suggested a correlation (Livingston, 2011).
- **Datasets published by other organisations**. As in Chapters 3 and 8, where we are

discussing making a static infographic or animation, we would be looking at cultural trends, examining a variety of datasets, ranging from the bestseller lists (*Hunger Games* and Harry Potter names) to box office data (Marvel and *Star Wars* names), and of course newspaper and magazine articles.

- **Qualitative data**. One of the biggest differences between an interactive graphic and a static graphic is the opportunity to use qualitative data in a much more integrated way. Indeed, qualitative data – interviews, descriptions, anecdotes, opinions – often sit at the heart of interactive infographics, particularly for a piece of data journalism. For my baby names interactive, it would make for a more immersive experience if I could interview parents who had given their baby the most popular name (perhaps twins called Oliver and Olivia?) as well as others who had chosen celebrity names (Loki or Thor) or given their baby a unique name. Qualitative data is often better at explaining the 'why' of a story than quantitative data. Why would anyone call their baby L (there were three boys called L in 2018) or A (four boys)?

It is often sensible to begin an interactive graphic with a human story too, rather than starting off with a chart. For example: 'When Oliver Smith was born in 1945, he was one of only 95 Olivers in the country. "It felt like it was just me and Oliver Hardy", he says, of the name that has been the top boys' name for most of the last decade.' You could then return to this interview throughout the article and draw on it again to wrap things up.

Qualitative data also allows you to change formats, and introduce visual variety to your graphic. If you have interviews, you can drop them in as audio or video files; you can bring in photographs of interview subjects; you can add pull quotes. Even if you decide not to feature them in your main story, these kinds of materials work well as optional extras that can be clicked on by those who want to dig deeper.

Design

There are three big differences between wireframing a static graphic and wireframing an interactive infographic:

- the initial briefing stage
- the number and complexity of the wireframes
- the number of people involved.

Let's explore these one by one.

The briefing stage

We sometimes get a written brief for a static infographic. But more often, it's just an email with a spreadsheet attached. Even when the brief is written down, it's usually no more than a general description of intended audience, preferred format (e.g. double-sided A4, double-page spread in a report) and a few success measures. There is rarely any specification of *how* we make the infographic (e.g. 'you must use Illustrator, but it must be possible to open the source files using CS3').

For an interactive, these kinds of precise specifications are critical. Indeed, the first task is usually coercing the client (even if it is an internal client) to create a proper brief. As a minimum, you will need to understand the nature of the content, the intended scope, the exact deliverables, any technical constraints, which browsers and devices they expect you to support, where the interactive will be hosted, and how they wish to track and measure visitors. Figure 9.1 shows a fictional brief for our baby names interactive graphic. This is a skeletal version; in reality, a comprehensive brief should be several times this length.

This is all information you will need before you get started, and arguably before you even decide to pitch for the work, because almost every interactive

brief we have seen starts by wildly overestimating how many interactive charts can be made in the available time. It's hard enough to get a single custom-made interactive chart working across every browser and device, let alone ten or twenty charts. This is also why we ask that final question – tell us what other interactives do you like? – because then we can say: 'Well, if you want one like the *New York Times*, that will involve a team of 10 and cost about $———.' This invariably leads to a conversation about how we can reduce the scope. The most common outcome is that we drop the number of bespoke elements and take advantage of excellent off-the-shelf charting libraries such as Flourish and Highcharts. This element (number of custom charts v. number of off-the-shelf charts) then gets reflected in the brief.

One final point: this brief reflects the questions we ask now (autumn 2020). It changes all the time, and by the time you read this, you might need to build something that is compatible with virtual reality headsets, haptic legwarmers or another yet-to-be-developed technology. The point is: get it all down in writing.

The number and complexity of wireframes

Static graphics are usually designed for a specific use case: as a PowerPoint slide, or a double-page spread in a newspaper, or an A4 printout. They might be adapted later, and reused in other contexts, but they rarely stray too far from the look and feel of the original. One wireframe is usually enough for most static graphics.

For an interactive, you will have a minimum of two wireframes: mobile and desktop. Sometimes you will have a tablet view as well. At the time of writing, it is seen as good practice to start with the mobile wireframe first, just because it is easier to start simple and scale up, rather than to start with the

Subject	Description
Name of project	Baby names interactive infographic
Who we are	The Office for National Statistics is the UK's largest independent producer of official statistics and the recognised national statistical institute of the UK, reporting directly to the UK Parliament.
Aim of this project	We wish to turn our annual baby names data release into an interactive infographic that reaches the widest possible audience. This is part of our wider 'The ONS is for Everyone' initiative which aims to establish the ONS as the first port of call for anyone who seeks interesting social, political or economic data about the UK.
Key message	This dataset offers a fascinating cross-section of British social and cultural life in 2018. It also shows how naming trends and conventions change with every generation.
Key audiences (in order of importance)	• The general public in the UK • The UK media • The international media • The data visualisation community • Statistical bodies in other countries
Principal sources	The 2018 baby names release: https://bit.ly/babies-data-viz
Supplementary sources	Previous releases of baby names data (our collection goes back to 2001).
Content length	3,000–5,000 words, depending on the amount of copy used in animations, charts and 'hidden' content
Content tone	The information presented should be accessible enough for an educated 12-year-old to understand, and language should be free of jargon and clearly presented. See the ONS content style guide for more details.
Expected media types	Around 9–10 interactive charts, 1 motion graphic, 1 quiz or poll
Licensing guidelines or restrictions	Any photographs, icons or other third-party content should be either free-to-use or purchased by the supplier. The same applies to any code used in charts and graphics.
Design guidelines	The interactive should comply with all of the ONS's design guidelines, which can be downloaded here.
Accessibility	The interactive should meet the international WCAG 2.1 AA accessibility standard. It should be designed to work with assistive technologies.
Browser support	The interactive should work on the latest two versions of these browsers: • Chrome • Firefox • Safari • IE • Edge The site should be built using the principles of progressive enhancement.4
Mobile support	• iPhone 5 and above • Samsung Galaxy S6 and above • Pixel 2 and above • iPad 3 and above
Deliverables and hosting	Full project files to be supplied to the ONS. Site will be hosted on our servers, and must be built to work with our CMS-Sitecore 9.2.
Tracking solution	Google Analytics Event tracking
Budget	£20,000–£25,000 + VAT
Launch date	October 2019
Similar interactive infographics that you like	*New York Times* – 'The Punishing Reach of Racism' *The Guardian* – 'The Counted'

Figure 9.1 An example brief for an interactive infographic

desktop view and work out how things will be shunted around on mobile.

It is also seen as good practice to embrace the responsive era and serve up identical content and visuals for both mobile and desktop users. Whatever you make just expands or contracts to fill the available space in the most intuitive way. Another powerful motivation for doing this is that Google moved to a 'mobile first' model for all new sites in 2016, which means their algorithms will evaluate your site based on its mobile version. Anything that *only* features on desktop will potentially not be seen by Google's crawlers. (Of course, this might change, so always be aware of current search engine protocols.)

In reality, with data visualisation, fully responsive sites are always desired but seldom achieved. Charts are complex syntheses of text and image, and deciding how much text to show is complicated enough on a static graphic, let alone when the same chart is expected to deliver the same information on two entirely different devices – one that is huge (e.g. 1920 × 1080) and one that is tiny (e.g. 360 × 740), one that is in landscape mode (desktop) and one that is portrait (mobile), and one that supports mouseover (desktop) and one that doesn't (mobile).

So, although responsiveness should be your ambition, don't feel too despondent if you can't exactly mirror content across all screen sizes. It happens to the best of us. When the *New York Times* published: 'How the Recession Reshaped the Economy, in 255 Charts', they created a much simpler mobile version, and prefaced it with this message: 'The full interactive version of this graphic requires a larger screen. Trust us. It will be worth it' (Ashkenas and Parlapiano, 2014). Of course that was in 2014 and they would no doubt attempt something more responsive today. But the fact remains: some charts just don't work well on mobile; others look bizarre on desktop.

Fortunately, in the case of my baby names interactive, I think I should be able to create something

close to a responsive site, with perhaps a handful of compromises. So we should start with the mobile wireframe. I've put the first page in Figure 9.2.

The desktop version would then take the same content and scale it up, trying to minimise any content or functionality changes. There are a few tricks you can use to keep the desktop version as close in appearance as possible to the mobile version:

- **Keep the content area narrow and centred, with a wide margin.** If you look at the desktop version of a data-led article from the *New York Times* (e.g. 'The Punishing Reach of Racism' (Badger et al., 2018)) or the *South China Morning Post* (e.g. 'The History of the Forbidden City' (Arranz et al. 2018)), you will notice that the article copy has a wide margin on each side. The font size is usually pretty large too, and certainly never less than 16 point, which is good practice for readable on-screen text. All of this keeps the basic article structure – long and narrow – pretty close to the mobile layout.
- **Choose background images and illustrations intelligently.** I have a background photo at the top of my interactive, covering the screen. Choose images that will work equally well in landscape or desktop format. Go online and look at the photos that the *Guardian* chose for their 'Firestorm' article (Henley et al., 2013) and compare the site *across* desktop and mobile. Or the illustration at the top of the *South China Morning Post*'s 'How Bruce Lee and Street Fighting in Hong Kong Helped Create MMA' (Arranz et al, 2019). In each case, they have chosen images that work in both landscape and portrait crops.
- **Choose charts that are easy to adapt.** Wherever possible, you should use the same chart in the same aspect ratio on both desktop and mobile. Two charts stacked up on mobile might become side-by-side charts on desktop, but otherwise not change their shape. However, sometimes preserving a chart's dimensions ends up

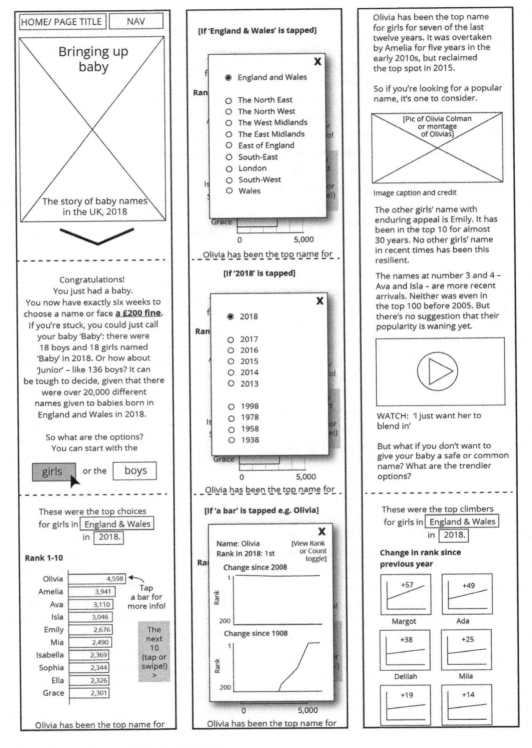

Figure 9.2 Baby names mobile wireframe

torturing the content. This is why it's a good idea to choose simple visuals that can be easily rotated or resized without significantly altering what the chart means. One example would be a timeline, which you would usually position vertically on mobile but rotate on desktop so that it is horizontal (see the *SCMP*'s 'How Bruce Lee and Street Fighting in Hong Kong Helped Create MMA' for a good example of this). In my baby names wireframe, I might consider a similar approach to my horizontal bar chart of girls' names, rotating it on desktop so that it becomes a vertical bar chart. Yes, the visual metaphor has shifted, but the desktop audience gets a more readable chart.

Next, there are elements of the desktop wireframe that can and should change as part of good responsive design:

- **Navigation.** Your mobile navigation will probably be a hamburger menu or something similar. On desktop, you are likely to have a more traditional horizontal nav bar.
- **Interaction types.** This will vary for each interactive infographic, but a swipe left/right on mobile might become clickable arrows on desktop; a modal window on mobile might become an on-screen drop-down menu on desktop; pinching to zoom in and out of a map on mobile will become something controlled by buttons or the mouse wheel on desktop. This is all to be expected; you just have to remember to give users clear signals about interaction differences if they aren't obvious from the interface. For example, take a look at the *National Geographic*'s excellent 'Atlas of Moons'. There is a section where the Earth's moon fills the screen and you can rotate it to explore the Moon's geographical features. On mobile, the instruction is: 'Drag two fingers to rotate.' This is sensible as you would not know you could rotate the Moon otherwise, or perhaps you might try to spin it by swiping with a single finger. On desktop, this instruction simply becomes: 'Drag moon to rotate.'

Finally, there are the extra elements that you will add to the desktop version, or the elements that will just be *better* on desktop. There's no way round this. As I said above, users understand that mobile and desktop are not the same thing, and they are less concerned with getting a 100% responsiveness score than you might be. They just want content presented in a way that suits the capabilities of the device.

- **Content that works better in landscape format.** Some content just suits landscape format and there is no way it can be easily repurposed for mobile. Take videos, for example. Unless they are deliberately shot in mobile portrait format (perhaps for a social media site), then most professionally shot films are widescreen and therefore work better on desktop. On mobile, users need to rotate their phones to go full screen, which is annoying half way through a portrait format story, and even then the experience tends to be less rich and immersive.
- **Maps also tend to come into their own on desktop,** particularly world maps and maps of the USA, which suit landscape format. (If you live in the UK or Chile or another long, thin country, then this is less applicable.) Furthermore, extracting 'detail on demand' from maps is usually easier on desktop – think of the way you might hover your mouse over US states on a heatmap to glean a specific percentage.
- **The desktop experience of a map is usually more compelling.** even when there is no data on mouseover, and it's more of an animated walkthrough, Take a look at the *New York Times*'s 'Sizing up the 2018 Blue Wave' (Watkins et al., 2018) on your mobile phone and then open it on a desktop and compare the ease and speed with which you can grasp both an overview of the story and extract granular detail.
- **Detailed charts.** In fact, it's not just maps. Any charts with multiple dimensions or a high level of detail – think scatter charts or an alluvial diagram – tend to struggle on a small screen in portrait format. Above, I suggested using

simple charts to avoid this predicament, but sometimes you can't: a scatter chart might be the best way of telling your story (Gapminder is just one example). With these complex charts, functionality that you might have hidden or limited on mobile can be restored in a desktop wireframe.

- **Interface expectations**. Above, I talked about how you should turn mobile interface elements (hamburger menus, tap and swipe functionality) into desktop interface elements. But there is some functionality that you can add to desktop that you can't or shouldn't attempt on mobile. The obvious example is content revealed on mouseover. Sometimes this content is a preview of what happens when you click – think of mousing over a link to an article and getting a preview of the content in a styled tooltip (e.g. Wikipedia does this on desktop, but disables it on mobile). Sometimes it is an extra content – you might get detail about a datapoint on mouseover, but clicking will do something different: perhaps highlight the datapoint or drill down into a more detailed chart. Often mobile simply cannot support all these options without making the experience unintuitive (having to double-tap on the same element, use multiple fingers, etc.). As long as this 'bonus' desktop content isn't central to your story, then there is no reason not to give desktop users all the functionality they would naturally expect.

- **Performance**. This is less of a concern these days, as smartphones often have more processing power than desktop computers, particularly given that people are more likely to update their phone to the latest model, but live with the same old laptop for years (unless that's just me). Nevertheless, there is still a presumption that the mobile version of any interactive graphic should be lighter than the desktop equivalent. This isn't a bad habit to get into, because most surveys suggest that users do expect information to be faster and simpler on mobile (An, 2017). This might mean that your desktop wireframe would add elements that might slow down your mobile version.

For example, at the top of my mobile baby names wireframe, I have a static image. Perhaps on desktop, I might make this a looping film, just to add a bit of dynamism to my splash page. On mobile, any movement would be less visible and would probably not be worth the performance cost. Similarly, there might be illustrative or decorative elements that I would include on desktop but choose to simplify or omit on mobile.

Once I had worked through all these decisions, the first section of my desktop version might look a little like Figure 9.3.

Most of the time, we create our wireframes in Photoshop or Illustrator, just because they are tools we are used to, and they give you a lot of freedom. But there are a wide range of wireframing apps out there that can help you speed things up. They tend to give you drag-and-drop options for common interface elements like navigation, scroll bars, drop-downs, images and so on. I like Pencil Project, which is free and easy to use. Other producers I've worked with prefer Balsamiq, which isn't free, but is more fully featured. All of these tools encourage you to concentrate on the basics of your website – layout, information hierarchy, functionality and intended user responses. How it looks comes later.

In terms of how much detail to include in your wireframe, this depends very much on the project and the client. Key decisions include:

- **How much should you describe its functionality?** When I first started wireframing websites in the late 1990s, you had to use extensive annotations. Even a link needed a call-out explaining what would happen when a user clicked on it. Now there is widespread understanding of what happens when you interact with standard interface elements. Unless I am using new or innovative features, I tend to keep annotations to a minimum. In my baby names example, I have decided that the affordances on offer – what each interface element suggests to the user – are all fairly self-evident. If my client were to need drop-down

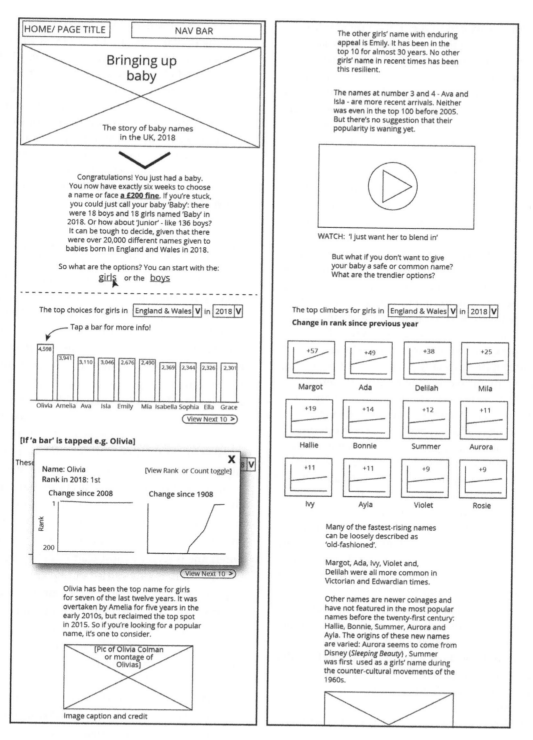

Figure 9.3 The desktop version of the wireframe

menus explained to them, then there is little point showing them any kind of wireframe. Instead, it would be better to use a wireframe for internal purposes only. The client would be given a Word doc with just the content in, and once this was approved, we would show them the content in a more 'designed' version of the wireframe (usually called a mock-up).

- **How much content should you include?** In standard website design, you tend to use lorem ipsum for any text. This is because the content is dynamic and constantly refreshed. In these situations, including sample text just encourages the client to start arguing about the copy and that is not what is being decided in a typical wireframe. However, in an interactive infographic, the content is usually fixed and is the sole reason for the infographic's existence. In fact, you or your client may already have a series of assets – interviews, videos, reportage, illustrations – and the interactive infographic is usually just a way of showcasing and structuring this pre-existing material. So leaving it out and using dummy content is pointless. Arguments about particular wording or chart types or interface options are exactly what you need to be having at the wireframing stage of these projects. Should we use a sticky nav? (Usually not.) Should we use an image carousel? (Well, do *you* like them?) Should it scroll horizontally, not vertically? (Depends if you want anyone to read it.) Things might change as you make the interactive, but the key content decisions need to be resolved before the designer starts laying the information out.

- **How much should you specify the technical solution(s)?** It all depends on the client. Some clients are developers (or ex-developers) and want to know how you are going to deliver that ambitious animated scatter chart. But most of the time, detail about whether you are going to make a particular chart in Highcharts or D3 or WebGL is irrelevant. Likewise whether you will get text on to the site via JSON or a content management system or whether the whole interactive graphic will be built in Squarespace.

Of course, *you* need to be aware of how you are going to make the graphic, and you will have discussed this with the team – probably before even sending in a proposal (see 'The number of people involved' below). In many cases, you will even be preparing a separate technical specification document (although sometimes this happens piecemeal in project management tools like Jira or Trello). But the content wireframe should focus on what, not how. Its focus should be defining the ideal shape and structure of your story.

The number of people involved

The final big difference between a static and interactive infographic is the size of the team. If you think of a project like the *New York Times*'s 'Punishing Reach of Racism' (Badger et al., 2018), this had four named authors – two journalists and two graphics editors – plus four authors named at the Equality of Opportunity Project, the article's main source. For an infographic that features audio, video or extensive photography, like the *Guardian*'s 'Firestorm' (Henley et al., 2013), the number of contributors will typically be even higher (18 people are named in the credits).

Of course brilliant solo projects are possible, but they are less common, and if collaboration is the norm for static infographics, this is doubly true of interactive projects. Just the process of making a wireframe is seen by most teams as a separate and distinct skill, usually carried out by an experienced web producer, data journalist, or UX professional. This wireframe might then be presented to the client by someone else – perhaps an account manager, who will also deal with any client feedback and edits. Static mock-ups will then be produced by a graphic designer and, if necessary, an illustrator. These go back to the account manager for any client feedback on these designs. Only once the designs are approved can the build start. This will involve developers and testers and a scrum master (or someone else in a project management role) to coordinate everyone's time and priorities. And once it's built, how will anyone know about it? Even if another team (or your client) is responsible for the marketing of the product, they still need to be factored into any project plan and feedback cycle.

Furthermore, all of these people are involved *all* of the time. When a UX professional creates a wireframe, they don't just finish it by themselves and email it across to the client. They get the feedback of everyone who is going to make it – designers, developers, quality assurance teams – to check that everything on the wireframe can be built on time and within budget. Ideally, we test it at this point too. This is often an informal process, asking a few members of the target audience to read through the wireframe and check that they understand it. But it gets us into the habit of building what Daniel Kahneman would call the 'outside view' (Kahneman, 2011, pp. 245–54) into every phase of the project, and it irons out any content kinks before they become permanent features.

I should stress at this point that the size of your team and the difficulties of coordinating this team should not deter you. In fact, the rewards of creating an interactive graphic are so great that the pain of creating it is easily outweighed by the pleasure you will feel once it is out in the world and your audience starts reading, sharing and reacting to it.

Selection, dramatisation, emphasis

Back to the specifics of our wireframe. Above, I mentioned that the process of making an interactive infographic tends to be longer and more complex than making static visuals. However, as with creating any other kind of visual story, we can return to the process I have outlined in previous chapters. You are still crafting a narrative, and therefore you still need to select, dramatise and emphasise. Once this is done, you need to work on the interface and aesthetics, which Tobias will cover in the next chapter.

Selection

As soon as interactivity is involved, there is a temptation to select less, just because you can include more. It is true that an interactive infographic requires more content, but you will have gathered a lot more material during the **Find** stage (see above). If you typically throw away about three-quarters of the stories you find for a static graphic, it should be roughly the same proportion for an interactive graphic. Most of the stories you have gathered will not be relevant for your audience, and skim-reading and rejecting unnecessary information is time-consuming and onerous for them; your job is to minimise the number of times they have to do this.

So, as always, the first stage of storytelling is deciding what to leave out. Looking at the first chart in my wireframe – the bar chart – here are some of the stories I decided to omit (Figure 9.4).

I have decided to allow users to change the regional drop-down: the default is England and Wales, but they can choose from one of nine individual regions if they wish. Note that I am *not* allowing them to drill any further down than this – into sub-regions, constituencies, wards and so on. I am also letting users change the year but only to choose the last 5 years, or data from 20, 40, 60 and 80 years ago. Why not every year? Because I don't want users to get *too* lost in the data at this point. At the end of the infographic, I will leave them with a chart where they can explore *everything*, but right now, I need to signal clearly that this is a detour in a story – the story of girls' names in 2018 – and the job of any drop-down list is to illustrate this main story, rather than to begin a completely new story. So the available years are limited to options that will contextualise the 2018 dataset. The alternative is a list with 120 years to choose from, which would

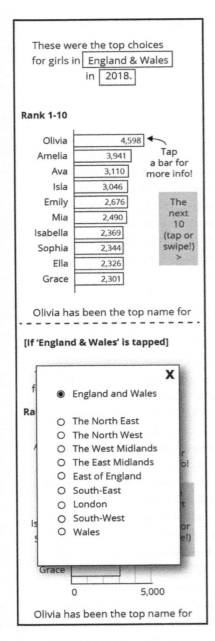

These were the top choices for girls in [England & Wales] in [2018.]

Rank 1-10

Olivia	4,598
Amelia	3,941
Ava	3,110
Isla	3,046
Emily	2,676
Mia	2,490
Isabella	2,369
Sophia	2,344
Ella	2,326
Grace	2,301

Tap a bar for more info!

The next 10 (tap or swipe!) >

Olivia has been the top name for

[If 'England & Wales' is tapped]

- ● England and Wales
- ○ The North East
- ○ The North West
- ○ The West Midlands
- ○ The East Midlands
- ○ East of England
- ○ South-East
- ○ London
- ○ South-West
- ○ Wales

X

0   5,000

Olivia has been the top name for

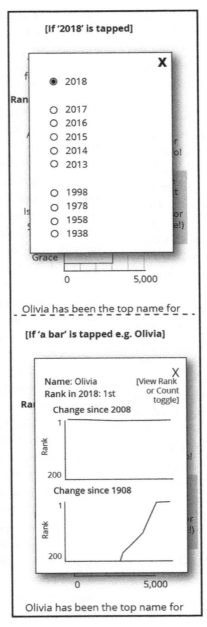

[If '2018' is tapped]

- ● 2018
- ○ 2017
- ○ 2016
- ○ 2015
- ○ 2014
- ○ 2013

- ○ 1998
- ○ 1978
- ○ 1958
- ○ 1938

X

0   5,000

Olivia has been the top name for

[If 'a bar' is tapped e.g. Olivia]

Name: Olivia
Rank in 2018: 1st

[View Rank or Count toggle]   X

Change since 2008

Rank: 1 — 200

Change since 1908

Rank: 1 — 200

0   5,000

Olivia has been the top name for

Olivia has been the top name for girls for seven of the last twelve years. It was overtaken by Amelia for five years in the early 2010s, but reclaimed the top spot in 2015.

So if you're looking for a popular name, it's one to consider.

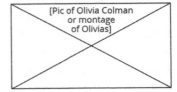

[Pic of Olivia Colman or montage of Olivias]

Image caption and credit

The other girls' name with enduring appeal is Emily. It has been in the top 10 for almost 30 years. No other girls' name in recent times has been this resilient.

The names at number 3 and 4 - Ava and Isla - are more recent arrivals. Neither was even in the Top 100 before 2005. But there's no suggestion that their popularity is waning yet.

WATCH: 'I just want her to blend in'

But what if you don't want to give your baby a safe or common name? What are the trendier options?

Figure 9.4 The first part of the story

cause both story and interface challenges, and would be more appropriate on a data analysis dashboard. For the same reason, I am suggesting limiting the number of bars on screen to 10, to emphasise that this section is about the most popular names. Users can swipe (or click on desktop) to see the next 10, but only 10 at a time. They cannot view 50 or 100 at once. Because this is not a dashboard; this is not a chart about everything. Curiosity should be encouraged but within the limits of the current topic: popular girls' names. Similarly, we do not have a drop-down that allows users to change the top 10 girls to the top 10 boys. When a bar is clicked, users can see the trend over time for each name, but only for the past 10 years or the past 100 years. They can't change this to see the past 50 years or the past 114, because again, this would require more interface, more choices, and more cognitive effort on the user's part. The master version of this bar chart may include all this functionality (displaying more bars, filtering every variable), but on this chart you would be selecting which options to remove to ensure that your readers don't get overwhelmed or distracted. In any testing, you would want to sense check these assumptions. Are there still too many choices on this chart? Or not enough?

This process of selection would then be applied to every sentence, every dataset, every chart in your graphic.

Dramatisation

In an interactive infographic, most of the dramatisation comes from the copy you write and supporting visuals like photography, audio and video. This is how you build a world around your data. In the case of this dataset, I have used:

- a photograph or looping video on the landing page of a parent and baby to make the topic clear and to emphasise that these numbers represent living, breathing human beings making life-changing decisions

- an introduction that puts the reader in the position of a parent ('Congratulations! You just had a baby!') and which underlines the urgency of the task (choose a name, or face a £200 fine) and how difficult it is (there are over 20,000 names to choose from)
- supporting copy after every chart, suggesting why parents might (or might not) choose particular names
- an image after every chart, showing famous people with the same name(s)
- a video after every chart, bringing in ordinary members of the public who either have one of the names in the preceding chart, or have given their baby one of these names.

These aspects are like your data's supporting cast – your Olivia datapoint doesn't mean much on its own, but copy explaining its durability as a name, photos of famous Olivias, and video footage of parents with a new baby Olivia will amplify that single statistic (4,598 Olivias in 2018) and help your readers to care, to identify with the numbers and to understand that this is data that affects their everyday lives.

Emphasis

The plot of your interactive infographic will be simultaneously more structured and more fluid than its static equivalent. More structured because you will be thinking about the multiple tiers in your story, the points where users can choose to access more information. More fluid because you will be testing your wireframe, your prototype and the finished graphic with a user acceptance team, and this will inevitably lead to changes in content, design, functionality or all three.

We try to keep both of these things in mind when creating an interactive wireframe. Initial sketches tend to be more like a flow chart, with a particular emphasis on:

(1) **The central narrative spine.** This is the non-negotiable content, the story that you want to tell as an individual or organisation, the

content that every user needs to engage with and understand. Testing will focus more on the effectiveness of the content and visuals than on whether chapters should be substituted or replaced.

(2) **The second- and third-level stories.** This is the content that can only be accessed by a user action of some kind. It provides valuable context for your main story. These are the elements that will require more extensive testing, to make sure that the interface elements are clear, that the number of user choices is manageable, and the information accessed is of an expected quality and density. These stories are more likely to be modified, because you will inevitably get the balance wrong in some places – too much is surfaced, or too much is left out.

(3) **Optional extras.** This is the additional content that you *could* include, allowing an even more granular exploration of the data, but testing would be essential to ensure that the increased interface complexity was justified by the quality of the additional content. These bonus elements would also take time and money to build, and you need to be sure that the tiny minority of users who access this kind of content are valuable or important enough to justify the increased workload. Sometimes this material doesn't survive the wireframing stage, but it's still good to reference it in any early sketches, if only so that the decision not to include it is documented.

My top-level flowchart for the baby names interactive might look a little like Figure 9.5. I have just put the first page here. We often create a story map like this in tandem with the wireframes shown in Figures 9.2 and 9.3 so that we have both a bird's-eye and worm's-eye view of the same content.

This is just one way of mapping the content; you might prefer to approach it differently. It's whatever helps you to demarcate your content hierarchy. And it's whatever helps you create these three critical elements:

- a central narrative that is engaging and comprehensible even if a user doesn't do anything except scroll
- relevant and well-signposted secondary content that enriches your main narrative
- third- and fourth-level content that offers additional breadth or depth without disrupting the momentum of the central narrative.

Best practice for interactive infographic design

If the Moon Were Only One Pixel

If you look at interactive infographics produced by the world's best information designers, you will see how they all share this disciplined approach to selection, dramatisation and emphasis. They all maintain a perfect balance between explanation and exploration. Let's start with a fun and simple example from Josh Worth (n.d.): 'If the Moon Were Only One Pixel' (see Figure 9.6).

Worth takes us on a trip across the solar system, where everything – the planets and the distances between them – is to scale. We start at the Sun and then we scroll. And we wait. And we wait. Every now and again, Worth has comments appearing on screen: 'That was about 10 million km', 'Pretty empty out here…'. Eventually, after a lot of scrolling, we reach planet 1 of 8: Mercury!

A single, barely visible orange pixel in a sea of black.

On we go, scrolling through more blackness, eventually reaching Neptune (if we make it that far). Try it out now, and then come back and continue reading. You can google 'Josh Worth one pixel' or go to https://joshworth.com/dev/pixelspace/pixelspace_solarsystem.html

Selection

At first glance, Worth looks like he is satirising selectiveness. His point is that most visualisations of the solar system minimise cosmic distances and

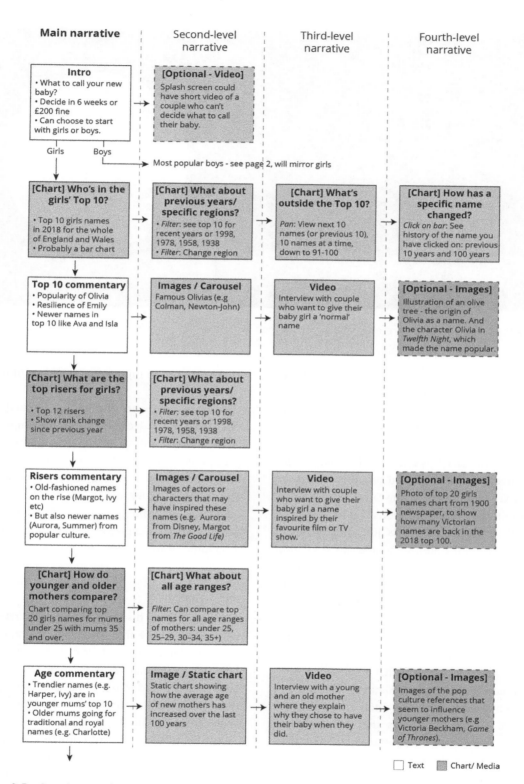

Main narrative

Intro
• What to call your new baby?
• Decide in 6 weeks or £200 fine
• Can choose to start with girls or boys.

Girls   Boys

[Chart] Who's in the girls' Top 10?
• Top 10 girls names in 2018 for the whole of England and Wales
• Probably a bar chart

Top 10 commentary
• Popularity of Olivia
• Resilience of Emily
• Newer names in top 10 like Ava and Isla

[Chart] What are the top risers for girls?
• Top 12 risers
• Show rank change since previous year

Risers commentary
• Old-fashioned names on the rise (Margot, Ivy etc)
• But also newer names (Aurora, Summer) from popular culture.

[Chart] How do younger and older mothers compare?
Chart comparing top 20 girls names for mums under 25 with mums 35 and over.

Age commentary
• Trendier names (e.g. Harper, Ivy) are in younger mums' top 10
• Older mums going for traditional and royal names (e.g. Charlotte)

Second-level narrative

[Optional - Video]
Splash screen could have short video of a couple who can't decide what to call their baby.

Most popular boys - see page 2, will mirror girls

[Chart] What about previous years/ specific regions?
• *Filter*: see top 10 for recent years or 1998, 1978, 1958, 1938
• *Filter*: Change region

Images / Carousel
Famous Olivias (e.g Colman, Newton-John)

[Chart] What about previous years/ specific regions?
• *Filter*: see top 10 for recent years or 1998, 1978, 1958, 1938
• *Filter*: Change region

Images / Carousel
Images of actors or characters that may have inspired these names (e.g. Aurora from Disney, Margot from *The Good Life*)

[Chart] What about all age ranges?
Filter: Can compare top names for all age ranges of mothers: under 25, 25–29, 30–34, 35+)

Image / Static chart
Static chart showing how the average age of new mothers has increased over the last 100 years

Third-level narrative

[Chart] What's outside the Top 10?
Pan: View next 10 names (or previous 10), 10 names at a time, down to 91-100

Video
Interview with couple who want to give their baby girl a 'normal' name

Video
Interview with couple who want to give their baby girl a name inspired by their favourite film or TV show.

Video
Interview with a young and an old mother where they explain why they chose to have their baby when they did.

Fourth-level narrative

[Chart] How has a specific name changed?
Click on bar: See history of the name you have clicked on: previous 10 years and 100 years

[Optional - Images]
Illustration of an olive tree - the origin of Olivia as a name. And the character Olivia in *Twelfth Night*, which made the name popular.

[Optional - Images]
Photo of top 20 girls names chart from 1900 newspaper, to show how many Victorian names are back in the 2018 top 100.

[Optional - Images]
Images of the pop culture references that seem to influence younger mothers (e.g Victoria Beckham, *Game of Thrones*).

☐ Text   ▨ Chart/ Media

Figure 9.5 Stay in your lane

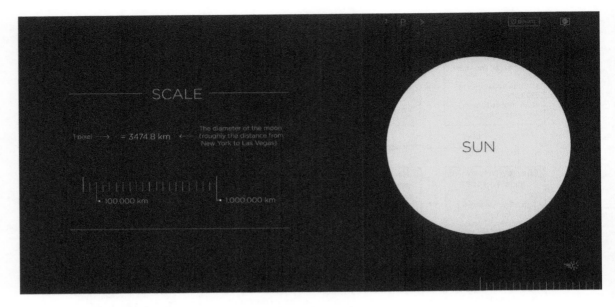

Figure 9.6 If the moon were only one pixel, by Josh Worth

give us a false sense of how large the planets are (for example, picture Jupiter in your head). Worth seeks to rebut this, promising a 'tediously accurate scale model', with all the endless nothingness of space included.

But wait. To make this simple and brilliant point, Worth does have to select and simplify. Planets are not a fixed distance from the Sun: depending on their orbit, they vary by millions of kilometres. For example, sometimes Pluto is just over 4 billion kilometres from the Sun, sometimes it's 7.5 billion kilometres. Worth doesn't include this variation in his visuals, because it would make his graphic cluttered. Likewise, he has the planets all sitting on one single horizontal line, on the same side of the Sun, ordered left to right, like they never are in reality. But of course this makes it easier for us to compare them. Thankfully for us, Worth is not being 'tediously accurate'; he is being (slightly) inaccurate in order to make a truthful and interesting point.

Indeed, Worth emphasises this in one of his on-screen comments: 'The distance between planets really depends on where the two planets are in their orbits around the sun. So if you're planning

on taking a trip to Jupiter, you might want to use a different map.'

There are also plenty of other space visuals he could have added. He could have superimposed manned missions data, or the current position of space probes. Or he could have just added illustrative elements – flying saucers, shooting stars and the like. But instead he held back, leaving out everything except the size of the planets and their (approximate) position. It makes his graphic clean, and his message clear.

Dramatisation

Worth also makes his story relatable and relevant. As we scroll, we see that the default measure of distance is kilometres. But we can change this to miles, AU, light minutes, buses, blue whales, Great Walls of China and so on. It may not be hugely useful to be told that the Earth is 5 billion blue whales from the Sun, but it did make me smile.

Likewise, as we scroll, Worth inserts comments on screen every few seconds. Sometimes these are jokes ('When are we gonna be there?'); sometimes they are fun facts (the *New Horizons* spacecraft took 13 months to get to Jupiter); at other points he puts the distances in context (you could watch 2,000 feature films on the flight from Earth to Mars).

All of these additional elements have the same effect. They turn a story about nothingness into a story about something.

Emphasis

Worth also times everything perfectly. The comments I mentioned above appear just as our attention is beginning to wane. Worth seems to know exactly when scrolling through blackness becomes monotonous and when we need to be rewarded for our perseverance.

He also allows us to travel at various speeds through his graphic. The default is that we scroll and are encouraged to continue every few seconds by another joke or insight.

However, there is also a navigation bar at the top of the page – a kind of 'warp speed' option – which lets us jump to particular planets. This helps us if we're wondering about particular features of the solar system. Are any of Jupiter's moons large enough to feature on this graphic? What about the asteroid belt in between Mars and Jupiter?

Best of all, we have a 'light speed' option. It's a little *c* in the bottom right of the screen. The joke here is that this is the *slowest* option. The screen auto-scrolls left-to-right at a glacial pace, *much* slower than it does when you scroll yourself. Again, it emphasises Worth's key point: the distances between planets are huge, and even when moving at the fastest speed in the universe, it takes for ever to get anywhere.

A Nation Divided, by *Die Zeit*

In 2014, *Die Zeit* published a fantastic piece of data journalism on the state of modern Germany (Borgenheimer et al., 2014). They argued that in spite of all the hard work Germany had undertaken to erase division, 'East Germany's legacy remains visible in statistics'. They then go on to use 'images, graphics and statistics to tell the story of German unity – or its continued division'.

Selection

Die Zeit's editorial intelligence is obvious as soon as we arrive on the landing page. We are shown a photo of Berlin at night (see Figure 9.7). We

Figure 9.7   A Nation Divided

instantly see that East and West Berlin are different *colours*. In the West, the lamps are white; in the East, they are orange, as the sodium vapour lamps installed under Communism are still mostly functioning. It is the perfect photo to start the story with: showing that Berlin is clearly a single, connected city, but that on closer inspection, the history of separateness is everywhere.

Die Zeit's ability to select the right content for their story continues with the data they choose to visualise. There are an abundance of datasets showing how differences between East and West Germany have persisted. But *Die Zeit* do not try to overwhelm us with numbers. Instead they zero in on around 20 datasets where the trend is clearest or most interesting, and they deliberately choose a *range* of sources – drawing on economic, retail, sport, tourism and linguistic data. This gives us a 360° view of every aspect of German life. Here are just a few of the datasets

- average farm size (up to five times larger in the former East Germany)
- gun ownership (much higher in the former West Germany)
- flu shots (East Germans take them, West Germans don't).

They also look at motor home ownership, the use of day care (much higher in East Germany) and the popularity of the name Ronny (East Germans love it). They end by looking at the way that East and West Germans have different words for things like stapler (*Tacker* in the West, *Klammeraffe* in the East) and roast chicken (*Hähnchen* in North West Germany, *Gockel* in South West, *Broiler* in the East).

There is explanatory text in between each of the visual elements, but it is concise and *Die Zeit* essentially let the charts do the talking. Here is just one instance of this – about half way down the story, we have this text: 'A quarter of a century later, differences both small and large divide Germans hailing from the two halves of their country. One quick example? They prefer different vacation destinations.'

They then show a chart that visualises how East Germans are far more likely to holiday in Germany, while West Germans go to Spain and Italy. There is no other explanatory text. There is no verbal summary of what's in the chart, no laborious recitation of the key datapoints (the kind of thing you might get in a market research presentation: 'Italy is on 8.9%, Turkey is on 6.6%, Greece is on 5.0%'). *Die Zeit* simply introduce the chart – Germans prefer different holiday destinations – and then they trust the chart to do the rest (see Figure 9.8).

The article feels long and rich and detailed, but there are fewer than 600 words of copy.

Dramatisation

The copy also takes every opportunity to emphasise the human stories behind the numbers. In the introduction, they tell us: 'Germans worked hard to make their decades of division disappear. Only a few metres of the Berlin Wall remain standing.' They continue: 'The Wall's death strip has become a place to picnic. These days, tourist buses park where trigger-happy guards once patrolled.' Just a few well-chosen words conjure up the new peaceful Germany: residents having picnics in urban squares, and visitors arriving in tourist buses (Figure 9.9).

These human stories are further amplified by two videos. The first shows before-and-after images of identical locations in Berlin, comparing the bleak, deserted streets of the divided capital with the open, bustling streets of today. The second video shows aerial footage of where the East German–West German border used to be, soaring above miles of fields and farms, and showing that a scar remains – a grey strip of unused land – where the fences and towers were built. This video emphasises the old border's astonishing length, makes us marvel at the manpower that must have been required to police it, and helps us understand why pulling it down cannot possibly create unity and harmony overnight.

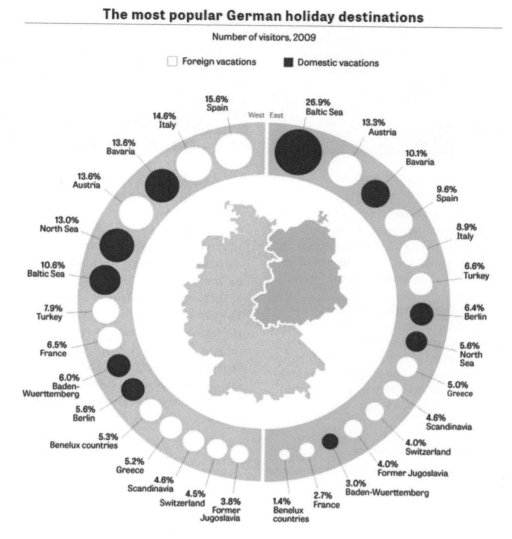

The most popular German holiday destinations

Number of visitors, 2009

☐ Foreign vacations   ■ Domestic vacations

Figure 9.8   Holiday destinations for East and West Germans, by *Die Zeit*

Emphasis

The story is so well structured, you barely notice that it has a structure. But it is there all the same.

- An introduction introduces the subject of Germany's continuing divisions.
- Four hexmaps show data that clearly emphasises the persistent differences between the two former countries.

- A video emphasises how much has changed superficially – the Wall has gone, two countries have become one.
- More datasets show how different the habits of East and West Germans continue to be, from holiday destinations to child care.
- Another chart explains why East Germans might have such a different outlook: they survived the traumas of the last days of Communism.
- Two final datasets illustrate the downsides and upsides of East Germans embracing a capitalist

Figure 9.9 Before and after shots of Berlin

lifestyle. On the downside, their football teams can't compete with their wealthier western counterparts. On the upside, the ownership of basic domestic appliances – washing machines and dishwashers – has rocketed in the former East Germany.

- A conclusion ties everything together. It accepts that deep differences between the two former countries remain, but posits that this is an important part of modern German identity: 'The dividing line is still there. Is that a bad thing? Do all the differences have to be plastered over, all the scars removed?'

As well as having a strong overall structure, the team at *Die Zeit* are also skilled at telling stories within individual charts, framing their data so that the who, what, where, when and why flows naturally.

The line chart in Figure 9.10 is one example. The title tells us that we are looking at children per woman in Germany. We notice the precipitous drop in the blue line, helped by the decision to start the *y*-axis at 0.5 and the *x*-axis at 1979. The designer makes sound colour choices for the lines: blue and orange are complementary

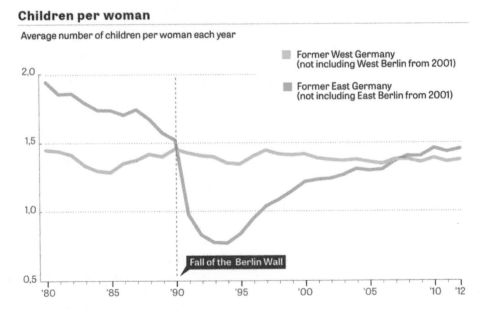

Figure 9.10 Children per woman in Germany, by *Die Zeit*

colours, meaning that the lines stand out against each other clearly, but in a more appealing way than if the designer had chosen, say, red and green, which are complementary in an aggressive way (think Christmas). Furthermore, blue and orange are easier for colour-blind readers to differentiate than red and green. In addition, the line weight (around 3pt) and the light grey (almost invisible) gridlines help us to see the story in these two lines quickly.

Next, we glance at the legend and see that the blue line is East Germany. The key is where we expect it to be – top right. The designer uses squares of colour for the legend rather than lines (which is often a software default). This is a good choice, as the squares are easier to make out.

We hardly need to be told why the blue line has plummeted, but an explanation is there for us anyway: another subtle dotted line, and an annotation in a different style: Fall of the Berlin Wall, white on a black background. The East German economy collapsed in 1990 and most civilians feared for their lives.

We might then notice that the blue line starts to climb in 1993 and by 2008, it has overtaken West Germany – an interesting secondary story. This might then provoke us to look at the whole chart again: to reflect on how high the birth rate was in East Germany under Communism: almost two children per woman. Also, how the rising birth rate since 1993 in the former East Germany still hasn't come close to equalling what it used to be in 1980. This in turn echoes the wider story told in the main article: that there are still differences between how East and West Germans behave, but there are historical reasons for this, and they are not always of major significance, and in fact these persistent differences might be a cause for celebration.

This, for me, is what good story design looks like. Dozens of brilliant small choices, barely noticed by the reader, that encourage a certain read order and facilitate understanding. Imagine what just one mistake – thick black gridlines or starting the chart at 1945 – would have done to this perfect story.

Keys to good interactive design

When you come to create your own interactive infographic, it is worth beginning by studying best practice examples like *Die Zeit*'s 'A Nation Divided', or any of the other graphics we mention in this chapter. There are further examples here: https://bit.ly/data-viz-best-practice. What you will notice is that, in spite of the diversity of subject-matter, the authors of these graphics approach the task of telling data stories in the same way. Zeroing in on the most interesting and relevant parts of their dataset, deleting anything dull or redundant, releasing information progressively, and using the most engaging words and pictures to tell their stories.

Yes, they differentiate their stories for different audience types and allow their readers freedom to choose where and when to dive into second- and third-level narratives. The task of establishing an information hierarchy is more challenging. But if you can tell a story – and we all tell stories all of the time – then you have the ability to design an interactive graphic. After all, in daily life, aren't all of the stories we tell interactive to some degree? I might relate the story of a terrible car journey to a friend. I choose the parts I know she'll find most dramatic or amusing, and release this information gradually to maintain tension. If she reacts strongly to one of the incidents, I might dwell longer on it, build it up some more (the bit where I had to change a flat tyre in a blizzard). If she asks questions about another incident, then I'll provide more detail (the part where a flock of sheep blocked the road for two hours). But if she doesn't, if she just listens, I will simply tell my main story until it's over. And if she asks for more information about an irrelevant part of my story ('What happened when you stopped for petrol?'), I won't provide her with information for the sake of it: 'Nothing happened. That bit was boring.' This to me is what interactive storytelling is: anticipating and reacting to an audience's needs in real time, just like human beings always have when they tell each other stories. That's also why I think good interactive storytelling feels so immersive and rewarding for an audience, because in spite of the addition of interface elements and technical wizardry, it feels closer to the oldest form of storytelling there is: oral storytelling. In both oral and interactive storytelling, the author is *right there*, listening and reacting to an audience; the narrative is fluid and grows or shrinks depending on an audience's level of interest, and both the author and their story feel like they belong to the audience, and even if this is an illusion (the author knows the story backwards),

a good author can always make the most familiar yarn feel new, personal and spontaneous.

I suspect that more and more data stories will become interactive, not just because they are modern and state-of-the-art, but because they feel curiously traditional. They have an affinity with the first stories we are ever told, and with the stories we still enjoy telling the most in our daily lives – the face-to-face, in-person kind, where storyteller and audience are on the same level.

Of course, the interactive story you are telling can't just be interesting. It also needs to be clearly presented and visually engaging. Tobias will cover these critical aspects in the next chapter.

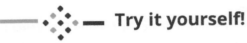

Try it yourself!

1 If you are not a developer, research at least two of the key templating tools that can help you to make your own interactive charts and infographics. Here are three of our favourites: Flourish, Datawrapper, Beam from Venngage.

2 If you are a developer, research JavaScript charting libraries such as D3 and consider whether it is worth learning some of the basics. If so, Scott Murray's book *Interactive Data Visualization for the Web* (2017) and his website alignedleft.com can help.

3 Next, consider how you are going to frame or structure your charts. Will you need a site templating tool? If so, research some of the

possibilities. Our favourites include: Shorthand, Strikingly and Google Sites. These tools all allow you to create simple websites where you can embed interactive charts, animations and other visuals.

4 Now you're aware of what's out there, design a wireframe for the dataset that you found in the Chapter 6 exercise. Remember not to propose anything that you can't create in your chosen tool. Start by sketching your wireframe and then translate it into digital format when you're happy with the basic information structure. For example wireframes and more information, visit: https://www.addtwodigital.com/book

Ten
Making interactive infographics

Tobias Sturt

Story is inescapable in visual communication. The visual metaphors we use to communicate data bring with them implications and connotations that have a profound effect on how our audience reads and understands. They frame meanings. They tell stories.

Animation tells stories too. Motion and transition imply agency and purpose, and build relationships and chains of causation, as Lev Kuleshov discovered.

So you won't be surprised to learn that interface tells stories too.

Interface describes the tools we use to interact. The world is full of interfaces, some of them so common we barely notice them at all. Just looking round the room I'm sitting in, I can see plug sockets that have switches, a light fitting that has a dimmer, a sound system with a power button. All of them interfaces. Even the door has an interface: a knob that helps me work it, helps me open and shut it, latch it closed and unlatch it again. But in doing so, it frames how I interact with, and think about, that door.

There are a lot of things I could do with that door. I could unhook it from its hinges and use it as a table; I could paint it with *trompe l'oeil* and use it as an art work; I could simply paint it shut and seal myself in with a seamless wall. But the interface directs me to a certain relationship with it, to swing it back and forth on its hinges, using it as a means to pass through from one room to another while keeping those two rooms separate.

Interfaces direct as well as facilitate. Or rather they direct as they facilitate. That dimmer knob on the light fitting means that in switching it on, the light levels travel through stages of brightness rather than just switching straight to full glare. The nature of the interface changes how I experience the functionality (in fact I almost never use it because it's irritating and, more importantly, I'm one of those people who never switches the overhead light on and instead has numerous lamps dotted about the place – but that's another story).

And this is also true of digital interfaces, of the virtual buttons and sliders and clicks and rollovers that we use to interact with online interactives. The nature of the interface tells us what we can do. A selection of empty circles declares itself as a list of radio buttons – click one and the others will deselect themselves – while a list of squares are checkboxes, and we can click multiple options at once.

The interface tells us what we can do, it gives us options for action, but in doing so it constrains that action: you may only pick one of these things, you may pick many things but only from these options. And these choices then constrain our thinking about the content: these things are mutually exclusive, while these other things can be combined.

Interaction creates engagement, but in doing so it frames that engagement. So even in our interface design we need to think about our storytelling.

But now we have added multiple new elements that we have to consider:

- **Interactive charting** – interactive charts behave differently to static ones and add new layers of complexity to our data storytelling.
- **Interface** – the tools that allow us to interact with the data and, in doing so, create new ways of engaging and understanding the data.
- **Integration** – interactive charts rarely stand alone; they are part of fuller interactive experiences and we need to consider how we tell stories in that larger context.

Interactive charting

A line chart like the one in Figure 10.1 immediately frames the story as being about change over time – we instinctively see how we should be interpreting the data.

We can see that the chart still gives us some degree of overview. We can glean some key

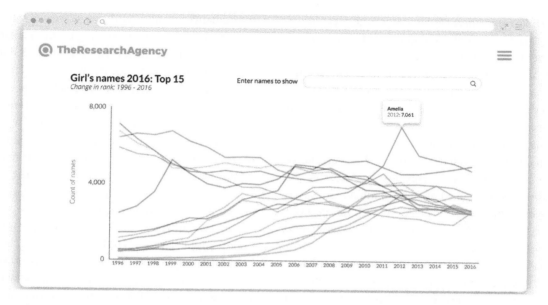

Figure 10.1 Well, those are certainly some lines

insights: we can see a general trend where the most popular names are new, and some names stand out – the big peak for Amelia, for example, or the general stasis of Olivia (just taking the lead at the end there).

However, the main mass of data is simply a mess – even with only 15 lines showing, this is tending towards unreadability – and particularly towards the end the chart starts to become distressing (or annoying) in its complexity.

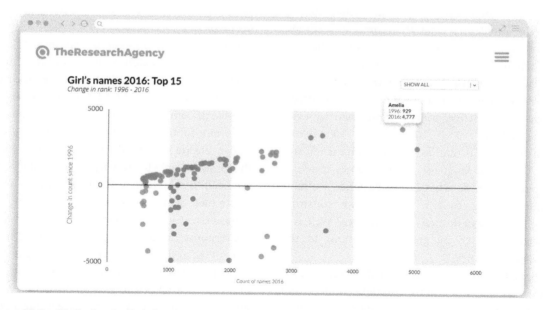

Figure 10.2 Well, that's slightly easier to … wait, what?

While a line chart clearly frames the meaning of the data for us, it also complicates it and makes it harder to read as it gets denser in content.

A scatter plot is a lot easier to read at scale: Figure 10.2 shows the top 100 names from 2016, and they're much less of a challenge than even just 15 lines.

But what do they mean?

The title might tell us that this is showing change over time, but this actually just complicates the reading, as we don't have any natural association between this kind of position and trend. Even where we might expect the x-axis to be time, we'd be wrong in this case.

We do get a clear overview of the shape of the data. We can see a general trend upwards towards the top right with some clear outliers. But what does that pattern mean? Answering that will take some careful study of the axes and come considered thought about what the relationship between the two values means.

While the chart itself might adapt better to the density of data we're likely to have in an interactive, it does not help us make that density any more inviting, clearer or easier to explore.

The core problem with interactive charting is not that there is more data: that is what visualisation is for. The problem is that there are more stories. There are, of course, always more stories than we can tell in any dataset, but the difference with interactive visualisation is that we can tell more, and we are opening up the dataset to our audience so they can discover more – more than we even know are there.

The problem is that, as we know, charts tell stories: the visual language we use frames how our audience reads. So what do we do when we have multiple stories to tell? How do we construct graphics that can do everything at once? Well, fortunately, interactivity gives us solutions to the problems it creates.

Interactivity allows us to create visualisations that exist in time, both through motion and through revelation. They can animate and change, and they can animate and change in response to the audience's desires. This means we can build palimpsests of meaning, layering up information without obscuring the layers. And it means that we can allow the audience to discover stories rather than having to reveal them all at once.

Of course, we still have to consider the framing effect of the visuals, but here we are thinking not about a single story, but about a kind – or kinds – of story. This still requires a degree of editorial rigour: we need to pick a set of stories of the same type to concentrate on, but we have a wider choice than with static visualisation.

Moreover, interactivity and animation allow us to build multiple layers of kinds of story: a bar chart race, for example, takes a story of comparison and then allows it to change over time. What we have to recognise is how that prioritises one kind of framing over another. The attractiveness of the animation in that bar chart race will make us see the change over time first, and only when we pause the movement will we be able to compare the values usefully. Most importantly, the addition of animation and revelation over time means that we can now start considering all kinds of more complex charts that we might treat with more suspicion in static visualisation: scatter plots and treemaps and polar areas.

This means that they can be repurposed through the interaction of the user to tell different stories. The key is that this is an active process. They don't start out detailed: they are merely capable of complexity. Indeed, it is even more important for us to be clear and to not confuse the reader. We are inviting them to interact, therefore they must be able to see why and how they do so. We need to give them a simple invitation to create their own complexity.

Too often I see interactive visualisations where the response to the problem of deciding what story to tell in the default chart is: none (Figure 10.3). Just some blank axes and, if you're lucky, a bit of text telling you to select a dataset to start. But why would you? If an interface is like a door, this is a shut door, with curtains drawn and the lights off and someone inside wondering why no one's coming in. We don't just need an open door; we need a clearly visible and welcoming interior, and quite possibly a big selection of those rubber dinners that Japanese restaurants have in the window so that passers-by know exactly what they're getting if they come in.

And this is why it's difficult, of course, because as well as having to create a chart that can help the audience explore, we also have to make the thing communicate just as a static chart would. So we're going to have to take that chart we've chosen to tell multiple kinds of stories and use it to tell just one (at least, hopefully, that one story will be of the same kind).

This means taking that probably more complex charting language and stripping away as much complexity as we can to reveal the single, simple story we want to tell. We have to remember that this still needs to work as a static chart: a casual reader, who merely looks and does not interact, still needs to understand the data and see the point of it.

This is why the advantages that interactivity and animation give us are so important. Interactivity means that we can strip out detail, knowing that it can still be discoverable.

In our hectic line chart of the top 100 baby names of the last 20 years, for example, we can make everything a faint grey except Olivia, knowing that the reader can mouse over to highlight, or

Figure 10.3   No, why should I?

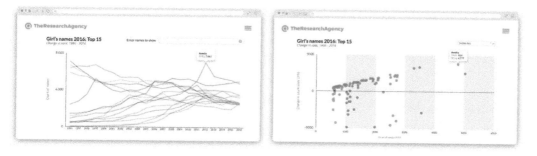

Figure 10.4   Alarming but comprehensible versus incomprehensible but bearable

filter to reconfigure the chart, once they've grasped the data and understood what they're looking at: the change over time of the rankings.

Or we can animate a bar chart race, making that change over time even more dramatic, ensuring that the reader understands what's important about this dataset, while still maintaining that highlight, focusing them on the rise and rise of the Olivias.

This stage – applying everything we have discussed in earlier chapters about static visual storytelling to interactive charts – is probably the most important part of this process and why we spend so much time on those basics. Because that engaging story is what tells our reader what they are engaging with, why they should engage with it and how they should explore it further.

While our scatter plot is a lot less of a challenge to read than the line chart, it is a lot more obscure when it comes to the overview of the story: change over time, something that the line chart frames perfectly (Figure 10.4).

So the line chart does the better job of showing the kind of story, even while it's doing a terrible job of showing us an actual story. If anything, it's working very hard to put off any potential readers.

We need to give our readers a way in by telling them a coherent and easily comprehensible story from that overview. The easiest way to do this, if we don't have a specific story in mind, is to start from the kind of story and define the data that might best typify it.

In this case, we want to show change over time, so why not pick out the names in the 2016 top 100 that have changed the most (Figure 10.5)? This is immediately clearer and less threatening as a visual, giving us a comprehensible story in overview (the way those lines cross over, Hannah and Chloe becoming deeply unfashionable as Amelia and Isla rise to the top) and the clear indication of the kind of data we're looking at (change over time).

In this way we can immediately tell a casual reader something in a first glance while also presenting clear paths by which to explore the data.

Interface

Just as visuals can quickly get overwhelming and confusing, so can interface. In fact, every interface element is a call to action, and thus a challenge

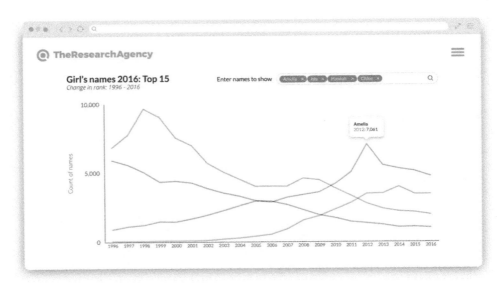

Figure 10.5   Hey, this seems to actually mean something!

to our decision-making. An excess of interface quickly leads to a paralysis of choice. Faced with an aircraft control panel of teeming knobs and switches, those of us who are not trained pilots will quickly freeze. I probably shouldn't be up here, I'm going to go and sit back down in Economy and watch the bad movies, thanks.

Our first task in designing interface is deciding what interface we don't want. Fortunately this first task is made all the easier because we've already decided what kind of interactions we're going to want our audience to be able to perform – because we've already decided the kinds of stories they're going to be looking for. If the kind of interface we encounter determines the kinds of the stories we discover, then the kinds of stories we're looking for must require specific kinds of interface in order to be found.

So we need to look at what stories we want the audience to discover and give them the interface that will allow them to do that and nothing else. If we want the audience to be able to discover how the popularity of the top 100 baby names has changed over the last 20 years, and we've chosen a line chart, then they're probably going to need a way to change the names they are seeing, possibly some way to search for names, need some way to change the time-scales they're looking at, and maybe, at a pinch, some way to tweak the value axis for when they're looking at names with very small changes.

While it might be interesting to be able to sort the names by cultural origin, or gender, or mean-ing or whether they end with a vowel, every single one of those options is another drop-down, another set of checkboxes or search field, another set of choices and challenges we're handing to our audience. Every tool is also a potential obstruction, another thing they have to learn how to use and what it does before they can interact with the data, so we need to think very carefully about how nec-essary it is and whether its usefulness outweighs its difficulty.

But as with all our visual storytelling, we have to consider not only that job of selection, but also emphasis. Even within this smaller set of interface elements we're going to use, we have to judge and prioritise. We have to create a visual hierarchy of interface too, making it as easy as possible for our audience to grab hold of the most important element, and pushing less important features to the background.

As with our structure in static design, we have to think about how we use read order, grouping and visual density to make a hierarchy of interface, making sure that the most important controls are the most visible and inviting.

With our line chart of 100 names, for example, we might put the filter for names directly above the chart, as the most prominent feature after the lines themselves, and relegate tools for manipulating the axes to sitting by the axes themselves, tucked out of the way. The name filter might be big and bold, the axis tools thin and grey, so that the audience might only discover them later in their explorations.

In fact, one of the most useful features interactivity offer us is the ability to hide the interactivity completely. We can push information into tooltips, right-clicks and press-and-holds (for touchscreens), so that the audience isn't bombarded with information, but can still find it when they look for it.

Affordance

'Affordance' is the term for the opportunities for interaction that the world affords us. What can we see about us to do? Of course objects everywhere offer us all kinds of affordances: a chair might give us something to stand on to harangue a mob, or to brandish to ward them off when they get feisty, or to throw and break a window with to escape their riled frenzy; but what we're interested in, as we saw earlier, is what the great Don Norman called 'perceived affordance':

the affordance we most readily perceive when we look at the object – in the case of the chair, to have a sit-down after all our adventures.

In interface design this means using interface elements that clearly advertise themselves and their purpose.

Interactive design of course offers us a huge range of choices when it comes to the visual display of our interface. A button can be a button, or an icon, or a word. 'How about we title our visualisation of baby names over time "20 years of Olivia" and then the user can click on the name Olivia and change it to be any other name?' Fine, but how will they know to click? The word will have to be styled some way to let the audience know it's interactive. We need to clearly declare our interactivity, and give the audience clear indications of where they can start interacting (even if some, deeper interactions are hidden in subtler forms of interface).

And how will they know that they can change that name? Just making it blue and underlined will just make it look like a link, a link that will take you away from the chart, not deeper in. It would need to look something more like a drop-down. In fact, what not just make it a drop-down?

Using conventional interface elements like drop-downs, radio buttons and checkboxes can feel like giving up, not being inventive enough, but it's not our job to be inventive here. We're in the business of helping our readers be inventive. Using interface elements with which our audience will have perceived affordance will remove just one more layer of friction from their interaction. The interface elements tell them there is the opportunity of interaction and also what interactions are possible. They will not have to puzzle out whether that is a button and what it might do; it will clearly declare its presence and function, and now they can concentrate on puzzling about the data instead.

This is where visual consistency becomes really important in our interface design. We have to use a visual language consistent with accepted design practice (Figure 10.6). For instance a checkbox (where you can select more than one instance in a list) needs to be a square box, while a radio button (where selecting one item in a list deselects all the others) should be a circle.

And those elements then need to be visually consistent throughout the whole interactive. All our checkboxes need to look the same and all our radio buttons need to behave in the same way, because this is vital to making it as easy as possible for our audience to identify and use the tools we are giving them.

Affordance doesn't just tell the user what an interface element is and how it works, it also frames how they will then use it to explore. The kind of interface element we use is going to have a profound effect on how the audience approaches the data.

This is not just a case of a checkbox allowing them to select more than one filter or a radio button restricting them to a single choice. That difference then changes how they think about the data: the checkboxes show that the variables can be compared, a radio button insists that they are distinct. This will then change how the audience explores the data and the kinds of meaning they look for in it.

Moreover, the display of the interface is also going to have an effect on how the audience interacts. While the affordance might help the audience understand the interactions on offer, we also need to make it as easy as possible for them to take them. For our 100 top baby names, for example, a list of 100 checkboxes is going to be either far too long or clipped off in a scrollable frame that hides most of the content, making it increasingly unlikely a reader will ever look at a name starting with 'S' (Figure 10.7).

On the other hand, a search field takes up much less room and gives a clear indication of how much content there is (so much you have to search) but is much more obscure (Figure 10.8).

Tools

Checkboxes
For lists where you can select more than one option

Radio buttons
For lists where you can only select one item at a time

Toggle switches
For switching between distinct options (on/off, for example)

Dropdown
Opening up a long list from which you can choose one or more options
Date pickers are often dropdowns that open a calendar interface so you can choose a specific date

Buttons
Like all interface elements, buttons need to be designed with clear visual signals of interactive options and states

Search
The magnifying glass icon is used universally now. Individual containers for search terms allow them to be easily removed.

Range finder
Useful for zooming in on chart axis, so you can quickly set outer limits by dragging on ther handles.

Information

Tooltips
For contextual information - particularly useful for separating the detail from the overview.

Dialog box
For contextual information - generally something you want the user to have to read.

Navigation

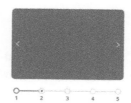

Carousel
Carousels or slide shows need to show progress as well as allow quick navigation

Progress indicator
Scrollytelling sites or complex pages need to have an indication of how far you have read (& how much more there is to put up with)

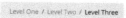

Breadcrumbs
In multi-page/state dashboards breadcrumbs are really important in helping you understand the page structure and find your way back to where you began.

Figure 10.6 Various common interface elements

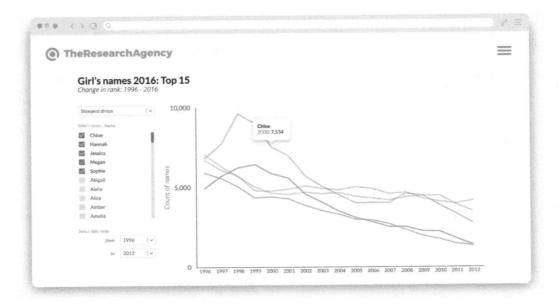

Figure 10.7 Picking names with checkboxes

What can we search for? Can we search for multiple terms? There are obviously a lot, but just how many names are there? Is this all the names in the country?

Either option is going to have a profound effect on how the audience chooses to explore the data.

This is where the default status of the chart has an important role to play. We can use it not just

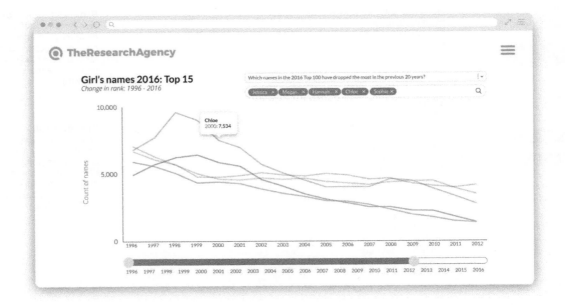

Figure 10.8 Using search to add list items

to tell a story and give a clear indication of the kind of exploration possible but also to give clear hints as to how to explore. With our search field, for example, we can pre-populate it with the names that tell our story, thus showing in detail how the interface element works and prompting the audience to interact with it for themselves.

It's also worth pointing out that we should not be afraid of repeating ourselves, or giving our audience multiple ways to achieve the same effect. There is a tendency, when given all the interface options that interaction gives us, to try to use all of them, all to do something different. But just as using every single visual attribute to mean something different in a chart will quickly get overwhelming and confusing, so will the aircraft cockpit of buttons and selectors. You can never be sure what affordances your audiences may have.

With our 100 baby names, having a search field that updates a list of checkboxes means that our audience has multiple ways to achieve their goal of selecting names: they can search, they can tick, they can scroll and there can be no mistake about what they are doing.

It often seems that people are worried about appearing condescending or servile in helping their audience as much as possible: 'my users are so knowledgeable that they'll just be put off by something so simple.' But no one is going to mind if you're genuinely being helpful. In fact, they're more likely to engage and return if you are.

Feedback

But while a proportion of our affordance with interface elements is to do with the appearance, what we recognise and how it accords with other interfaces we have encountered before, a large amount is to do with function. How an element reacts to how we use it tells us a lot about that element. The scroll bar scrolling when we pull on it, the checkbox checking when we click on it – all of these moments of visual feedback play into our affordance, telling us

we have correctly understood the interface and that our actions are meaningful.

But this has a further, psychological, effect. First of all, that confirmation of affordance is reassuring: we have acted appropriately, we are knowledgeable people. But it is also engaging. The interface prompted, the user acted, the interface responded: we are now having a conversation – the user is now involved.

This is why this visual feedback is so important. Even if the control the user has interacted with isn't supposed to do anything (although why would you be showing them something that doesn't work?), you need to reassure them that that's appropriate. Even if we're just popping up a dialog box to say 'Nothing was supposed to happen', we have to do something to inform the user. The system still needs to reassure them that their actions have import, that they are engaging with the interface correctly.

And not just the interface. The data, too.

Of course poking things in the interface is going to change things in our chart – that's what it's for – but the visual feedback to the poking does more than just show us different data.

Just as the feedback in the interface itself tells us about how it works, so the feedback within the chart tells us about the system we are interacting with. We press this thing, and this other thing pops out. We begin to understand how the machine works, how the different parts of the dataset relate to and interact with each other.

This is, after all, how we learn. We try something, watch the results, update our mental models and try again. It is this loop of experience and feedback that turns an analytical challenge into an instinctive action, from System 2 to System 1. This is why affordance matters so much; we want our audience to be learning from their interaction with the data, not from trying to figure out what all the different widgets in the interface do.

And this is also engaging with that data. The visual feedback involves us in a conversation and then makes that conversation fruitful. We are engaged and learning new things: our connection with and interest in the data is deepened with every interaction.

So our visual feedback has to be meaningful and informative, and this is where the storytelling properties of animation really come into their own. Rather than just switching a line on, we select an option and a line animates in, the label updating dynamically as it switches up and down. The movement is interesting and catches our eye, but also informs us of the consequences of our actions, as well as telling us about the data we've just uncovered. Do this well and the emotional as well as intellectual power is extraordinary.

Responsiveness

There are many great things about smartphones, but mobile interactive data visualisation is not one of them.

For mobile we tend to rely on our basic, simple choices: bar charts and line charts. Even these have to be kept simple and we need to rely on interaction to help us piece out the detail through revelation as the user scrolls, taps and filters.

Responsive design thus narrows our chart choices back down – we need either to be willing to use only simple charts in our story across all platforms or to pare our chart down to its bare minimum elements – only what we need to communicate in the moment and nothing more. Important things need to get bigger and less important things need to shrink or disappear entirely. Fortunately, as we have seen, interactivity means things can disappear but still be there, emerging through clickthroughs and reveals.

However, the same rules also apply to our interface: less space means less complexity – everything is bigger and simpler. This means we really have to abide by our hierarchy of importance, emphasising the key elements. It also means we have to be unambiguous with our signalling, leaning into the

affordance to make sure our audience can immediately see the interface and understand how to use it.

Remember that while we may have to sacrifice detail on an individual chart, the nature of interactivity is that we can have an infinite number of charts, if we wish, building up the complexity of information over time and through interaction.

One of the great achievements of Apple interface design in the original iPhone was realising that scrolling can be a pleasurable experience in itself. That physical push and pull to move content around the screen was a stroke of genius. What it means is that the mobile internet is a feed that scrolls. We can just keep piling chart after chart onto the screen and no one will mind (until it slows down their processor) because that's just how the medium works. And simple chart after simple chart can build subtlety, complexity and depth.

But we also have to remember that it's not just design and experience that need to be responsive, it's also use. Our audience may well want different things from mobile than they do from the desktop experience.

This usually isn't true of data journalism or similar communications, of course. Generally we want to say the same things to the same people no matter where they are; but particularly when it comes to data exploration or corporate data communication, delivery often needs to be different on mobile. Where our audience might expect the desktop visualisation to be more fully featured, they're less likely to expect that on their phones. Their need from mobile, as they sweatily double-check the figures on their way into the meeting, is likely to be very different than their considered fiddling-around back at their desks.

Very often we find ourselves back in the old-fashioned world of separate mobile and desktop development simply because the functionality needs to be separate too. And sometimes you get really lucky and everyone finally admits they don't need a mobile version at all. Bliss is it in that dawn to be alive, but to be a designer? Very heaven.

Integration

With interactive data visualisation, the journey from overview down into detail stops being metaphorical and becomes an actual process. Ben Shneiderman sums it up in his 'visual information-seeking mantra' as 'Overview first, zoom and filter, then details-on-demand'. It is that middle stage that distinguishes interactive data visualisation: zoom and filter – that the reader is able to actively choose parts of the data to concentrate on and then manipulate them, to select and emphasise them, to tell their own story.

As we've seen, it is this active process that allows us to tell our own stories while still allowing audiences to find theirs. To strip back a complex chart to tell one simple thing, all the time knowing that the reader can add all the detail they want back in, once we've got them interested in and informed about the data.

But even while we can hone a chart down to clear details and dramatise it with animation, this can often still be too complicated. Perhaps we need to walk the audience through that complexity a bit more thoroughly, using animation to bring in elements and explain them as we do so (this approach is often put into practice by typing the animation to the window scroll in the browser, so while the audience scrolls down, the chart updates, giving them more granular control over the animation).

Perhaps we in fact have multiple different kinds of interactive chart embedded in a page, focusing on different aspects of the data, or as a dashboard, monitoring different metrics. Perhaps that dashboard has multiple levels, clicking through from summaries to more complex charts.

What all of these experiences need is a way to integrate the different visualisations. A good deal of this is already done, of course: using consistent visual languages, establishing legible information hierarchies, clearly signalling key elements, all these things will mean that our visuals hang together coherently.

But we also need navigation. The reader needs to know where they are in the content and how to get back or move forward. Whether this is navigation that simply helps understand the structure of a single page (jumping back and forth between headlines), or helps them navigate an entire website (with a site menu of sections and breadcrumbs of individual stages), it is vital that it is obviously separate from the charts themselves.

Of course, our navigation design, like all interface, is helped by affordance. The readers will expect the page navigation at the top of the page, maybe in a corner. Forward and back buttons will be at the bottom. As with the design of the interface elements for our visualisations, innovation is the enemy of functionality. Reinventing the contour lines is a poor way to help the mountaineer scale the peak. Our audience need to be able to understand and trust the map we are giving them if they are going to be willing to go exploring.

The journey through the layers of information in a dashboard – from landing page, to information dashboard, to detailed chart to data table (Figure 10.9) – describes perfectly the interactive journey suggested by Ben Shneiderman. We drill down from overview to detail, at each point filtering out unnecessary information to zoom in on what interests us. As we build we need to be thinking how we can avoid overloading the reader with information while still providing them with the tools to discover more detail (Figure 10.10).

Linking charts together also means making sure the reader can navigate easily, being rigorous and consistent with our interface elements and hierarchy so that they can concentrate on the charts and not on relearning how to read with every screen.

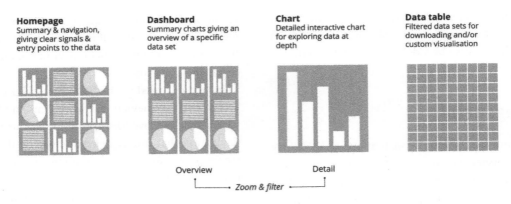

Figure 10.9 Dashboards often mean moving through different layers of information

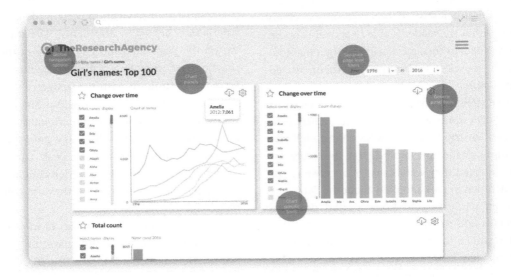

Figure 10.10 Dashboards need a lot of structure to make sure they're legible

Interactivity is hard

Making interactive infographics means not just thinking about the truthfulness, clarity and persuasion of our charts but also our interface, animation and site structure. It is a difficult, complex business. So why do it?

Because we can take more complex data and tell more complex stories with it to more complex audiences.

But that's not a sufficient answer. The real questions are: Why do we want to visualise all this complexity?

Why do we need to cover all these insights? Why do we want all these people to interact with the data?

It is the answer to particularly this last question that is going to help us figure out exactly how we're going to make our visualisation interactive. What is it that we want our audience to go looking for in this data? How will they need to zoom and filter this data to find those things?

Knowing these answers is the key to knowing what chart we are going to choose, what interface functionality we are going to need, and what navigation the audience will need to guide them on their journey from the overview into the detail.

As ever with design, we need to think about how function determines form: until we have properly determined what our interactive does, we can't make any meaningful decisions about what it looks like.

Once we have, then it becomes easy, because we're going to use the audience's affordances to help them explore, which means making only the most obvious, clear and instinctive choices. Once we know what we're making, the making part is easy.

But it's in what happens next that the magic lies. Data visualisation is already a sleight of hand, tricking the brain into seeing meaning it doesn't expect, but this is where it becomes a charm, where the data enchants our audience.

Our audience talks to our data and our data *talks back*. They converse. The audience explores and the data unfolds before them, they ask questions and the data surprises them. Together they develop, together they engage, they build a relationship, *they tell stories*. Together.

This could be the beginning of a beautiful friendship.

 ## Try it yourself!

Now learn HTML, CSS and JavaScript.

Seriously though, as Adam has already outlined, there are an increasing number of tools that will allow you to make interactive data visualisation without needing to get involved in any coding at all. Even if you do intend to build something yourself from scratch, these tools can be really handy in the prototyping of functionality and UX.

Take a wireframe – you did make one at the end of Chapter 9, didn't you? – and try building it using free online tools. Flourish is an amazing resource for making and publishing interactive charts (remember that anything you publish is public by default), as is Datawrapper, and Google Sites is an easy-to-use builder for simple websites.

The handy thing about all these tools is that they largely take care of interface and functionality

questions for you, so you can concentrate on the visual and interactive storytelling:

- Make sure each chart you make says something even without interaction.
- Think about how the chart language you choose will frame exploration.
- Make sure your audience is not overwhelmed with information.
- Remember: it's alright for the reader to break the chart if they want to, but it shouldn't *start* broken.

And once you've made something, test it! Send it to colleagues, annoy your family, I mean, you might as well show it off now, right?

You can find resources to help with all these exercises online at: https://www.addtwodigital.com/book.

Eleven
Refine

Adam Frost

Refining your work is the most valuable and least enjoyable part of the data visualisation process. Although it should happen throughout the **Design** and **Make** stages, we have put refinement at the end of our process, because the majority of checking and testing inevitably takes place towards the end of a project. I should also point out that we are using a broad term here – 'refine' – rather than 'user testing' or 'quality assurance', because we want to cover all the different kinds of oversight and assessment that feature in a data visualisation project, rather than just the kinds that suit larger interactive projects with defined quality assurance (QA) teams.

The first thing to stress about the **Refine** stage is how vulnerable it is. In an ideal world, the Refine stage should be the longest part of any project. You should be testing, gathering feedback, fixing and updating your work and then retesting, over and over again. In reality, the Refine stage is often seen as an afterthought. Other professions are rarely this lax. Every newspaper article will have been scrupulously checked by a sub-editor – and sometimes a lawyer too. If you make a flatscreen TV, you have to check that it won't explode when the viewer turns the volume up. Imagine giving patients a drug that hadn't gone through clinical trials. But a lot of data visualisation projects do precisely this: they get published and the only person who has ever seen them before is the designer and their boss.

Sometimes this doesn't matter, of course. It's an infographic about a new flavour of dog food. It wastes the company's money, and the audience's time (if anyone looks at it), but it's hardly the end of the world. However, we have to assume that most data visualisation projects occur because an organisation has important information to impart, they have a target audience in mind, and they want their audience to understand, enjoy and share the work. They are not auteurs 'just making it for themselves'. So publishing something without checking that it works risks undermining the whole point of the exercise.

Why does the **Refine** stage get rushed or skipped? Here are a few of the most common reasons:

- **Scope creep.** Because a large part of the Refine stage happens at the end of any project, it is most likely to get squeezed as the design and make stages overrun. At the same time, a lot of refining work is invisible to the naked eye (e.g. double-checking data, testing on less common browsers), so it can be hard to persuade clients to extend timelines or budgets unless they are already aware of the difference that proper testing can make.
- **It's painful.** Everyone hates feedback, unless it's, 'That was perfect. Don't change a thing!' This is particularly true of creative types – designers, copywriters, illustrators, animators – who often put a lot of themselves into their work, and find it hard not to take criticism personally. They also tend to dislike revisiting work which they had thought was 'done', and which they have now lost all creative enthusiasm for, especially if another exciting project has come along. So, in my experience, telling the team that a client is not going to bother testing it on any target users rarely encounters any resistance.
- **It's unpredictable.** If you go through the Refine stage properly, your work can end up looking very different at the end of it. Where an organisation has a clear idea of what they want to say with a data visualisation project, this can cause tension, as the audience might not be interested in what the organisation wants to say, or might want answers to a different set of questions. If someone senior has signed off a particular graphic or interactive, then clients are usually unwilling to incorporate user feedback, or even carry out any user testing, because nobody wants to tell senior stakeholders their ideas won't work and, in any case, who paid for this project anyway?

Unless the people who make it are visionary geniuses, with a sixth sense for what their audience needs, an untested data visualisation project will usually die a quick, painless death in a barely visited corner of the internet (especially if it's a pdf). Although, having said that, it might be unlucky enough to be noticed by a site like viz.wtf, in which case it will live on forever as an object lesson in why showing it to other people first matters.

So this is the most important point to make about the Refine stage: nobody likes it, but it doesn't care. It will happen anyway. If you don't do it, your audience will do it for you, and they will find all the mistakes and misjudgements that your editors and testers would have discovered.

A model of refinement

How you organise the **Refine** stage depends on the size, type and importance of your project. I've outlined two project types below – one small and simple, and one large and complex – and tried to illustrate how we follow a similar testing and feedback structure for each, but how different aspects flex up and down in duration and importance based on the nature of the project. Other organisations will approach this differently, or use different terms, and these phases all overlap and cross over to some degree. But I suspect most successful data visualisation projects embed testing and refinement throughout the whole life cycle of the project as we have suggested here (Table 11.1).

Let us start by looking at how we apply this to a smaller project. I've also tried to reflect what happens in reality as well as what should happen in an ideal world. For this small project, I've used the example of an infographic series produced for a client website, designed to appeal to the widest possible audience (Table 11.2).

Next I will outline the steps we would go through for an interactive infographic (Table 11.3). Here I'm imagining it's for a charitable organisation which wants to explain a complex scientific concept to a general audience, particularly those in educational fields. It would combine different media and need to be equally accessible on mobile and desktop.

What I've provided here is a very general overview. There are many good books and articles written on almost every aspect of the testing and refinement process – from how to write a technical specification to how to run a test in a UX lab. There are also countless books and articles on how to make your digital products as usable as possible, which can minimise the chance of major issues occurring in the first place – Steve Krug's classic *Don't Make Me Think!* (2013) is perhaps the best starting point, although Don Norman's *Emotional Design* (2015) is also invaluable. If you are going to be heavily involved in the testing of a product, then it's a good idea to familiarise yourself with all the expert advice that is out there.

However, because many of you won't actually be involved in testing, I've tried to gather just a few useful precepts that have served us well over the years. They won't be applicable to every project, but they might help to save you time, and should stop you publishing something that you'll regret later (the internet never forgets).

Focus groups can make you lose focus

I'm referring here to the focus groups that take place before a product is designed. This is where you ask users what product they think they want or what information they think will be most useful. The first problem is obvious: people don't always know what they want or, if they do, they don't always tell you. The second problem is that users aren't designers, and can't picture a solution that doesn't already exist.

The sad fact is that focus groups are often just an insurance policy. One particularly candid client admitted that *all* of the market research he commissioned was simply a way of deflecting blame when products failed. 'It covers my ass. I can say that the customers told us it was what they wanted.'

Table 11.1 How we test

Phase	Description	Main tools
Research	This is where the original idea for the project is tested, or where a user need is identified.	• Surveys • Focus groups • Stakeholder meetings • Analytics dashboards • Competitor analysis • Briefing document
Requirements	A clear definition of what the product should do, who it is for, and how success should be verified. Without this, testing criteria can't be established.	• Requirements document • Content specification • Technical specification • Brand guidelines • Accessibility guidelines
Internal testing	Ensuring that the product works as specified. For large digital builds, this is often broken down into unit testing, integration testing and system testing.	• Testing plan • Issue tracking software (e.g. Jira) • Device emulators • Project management software • Team communication software (e.g. Slack)
User testing	Checking that users are happy with the product and that it meets business goals. If it doesn't, back to the requirements stage.	• Focus groups • Stakeholder meetings • UX lab testing (e.g. eye tracking, video interviews)
Post-launch	Testing doesn't stop when the project is launched. Users will find issues and they need to be logged and reviewed.	• Customer relationship management software • Customer helpdesk • Focus groups • Bug tracking software

We have made interactive graphics that have started with focus-group sessions, and interactive graphics that have not, and I can't say there has been much difference in the quality or success of the final product. What *does* make a difference is testing when there is something to test. Left to our own devices, we always drop the focus groups and divert the budget into user testing. Research less, test more.

In fact, I'd go further than this. Clients who rely on research and focus groups often mistake this knowledge for expertise and apply the findings in an excessively literal way. I remember one infographic series we created for a scientific journal where a senior stakeholder complained that the section headings were in capital letters. The feedback was: 'Our research suggests that people find it harder to read words in capital letters. Change the headings to sentence case.' It is true that there is research, often inspired by Miles Tinker's *Legibility of Print* (1963), that suggests that humans don't like reading long paragraphs in capital letters. But a six- or seven-word heading? I'm sure the editors of tabloid newspapers, with their millions of readers, would be surprised to hear that their LOUD, ALL-CAPS HEADLINES can't be easily understood. Likewise, AMBULANCE drivers and POLICE officers in POLICE cars. Are people taking longer to get out of burning buildings because the EXIT signs are upper case?

Table 11.2 Refining a small-scale project

Testing a series of infographics		
Phase	**Description**	**Main tools**
Research	Client decides that a particular subject is topical or there is a particular anniversary (e.g. 100 years of air travel). Or perhaps there is new information to publicise about a particular product that they make. They have evidence showing that their target users prefer information in a visual form.	• surveys, competitor analysis and analytics tools confirm that an infographic would deliver the information effectively. • stakeholder meeting where the project is given the green light. • briefing document where the project scope and intentions are laid out and sent to internal designers or external agencies.
Requirements	Client and designers agree on the message that needs to be delivered in the infographic. They also outline the preferred format, whether there need to be separate mobile/desktop versions, a print or PowerPoint version, any social media crops, etc. Success measures (e.g. '5,000 social shares!') are defined.	• should be a requirements doc, but it is usually just a series of emails. • project plan is created so that the client is aware of when their feedback will be needed for each specific asset. • brand guidelines are circulated so that designers and writers can check their work against them.
Internal testing	Each element is tested internally before it is sent to the client. The content wireframe is proofread and the numbers are checked. The same happens with the final infographic designs, plus we check that branding and accessibility guidelines have been adhered to.	• in small projects, edits are usually suggested in slack or emails. Sometimes the graphic is annotated directly (e.g. sticky notes on a pdf). • internal progress meetings allow all team members to raise issues or questions face-to-face.
User testing	The client reviews every stage of the project cycle – any data we have collected, the content wireframe, the designs. Any feedback is incorporated and internally tested before the amended graphic is re-sent to the client. The final graphic is circulated to a test user group (usually organised by the client). This feedback is also incorporated.	• regular progress meetings with the client (one long weekly meeting, shorter daily calls). • project plan to reinforce when feedback required. • emails from client with feedback in bullet points.
Post-launch	The audience may find further content errors: typos, wrong numbers, charts that don't reflect the data and so on.	• analytics dashboards. • emails to helpdesk. • any combination of the tools above may be needed to fix the problem, depending on how bad the mistake is.

The fact is, we capitalise letters for all kinds of reasons, and one of them is to indicate importance or information hierarchy. In our graphics, we sometimes mix upper-case headings and lower-case sub-headings for this reason. Yes, reading a sentence in caps might take the reader a nanosecond longer, but the overall experience of reading and understanding the graphic is accelerated.

Table 11.3 Refining an interactive infographic

Phase	Description	Main tools
Research	The project is usually part of a wider campaign or programme. The interactive graphic is seen as the outreach element. There is often existing client research that we draw on. We supplement this with additional research. In many cases, the client also runs focus groups to test the target audience's level of interest in and prior knowledge of the subject.	• existing research material • focus groups determine the tone and content of the graphic • stakeholder meeting where the project is defined and objectives are set • briefing document where the project scope and intentions are laid out
Requirements	Client and designers agree on both the content and technical requirements. If the client is hosting (which is usually the case), we are given information about any content management systems used or other technical constraints. Browser/device support information is provided.	• requirements document • content specification outlines all copy and interface elements • technical specification. Increasingly this is not a single document – mostly because developers refuse to read it – but a series of features broken down into self-contained cards or stories (more on this below) • project plan • brand and style guidelines
Internal testing	Testing is more formal than with a static graphic, because of the complexity of the project. We recommend agile methodology, which means that testing happens constantly and often. Short daily stand-ups with the whole team (10 minutes maximum) allow for the rapid airing and resolving of issues. QA professionals attend every meeting, even when there is nothing to test. If you're unfamiliar with agile, Wesley Clark's book *Agile Methodology* is a good starting point.	• a test plan outlining exactly what needs to be tested, the tools used to do it (automated v. manual), the schedule and who will do it • a platform like Jira to track and manage bugs (more on this below) • a project management process (e.g. Kanban or Scrum) • device emulators: the type and number will depend on the requirements document • daily stand-ups
User testing	The client checks the content and designs at every stage. A market research agency usually carries out more structured user testing, with our input. This can involve functional elements (Can users find things? Do they understand how the interactive elements work?) where target users are filmed and their interactions are tracked, but also qualitative research – interviews where we ask users what they understood, whether they enjoyed the experience, and what could be improved.	• client emails • a UX lab where users can be studied; there is usually a facilitator in the room and unseen observers stand behind a one-way mirror • video files of user interactions and responses from the UX lab • client/designer meetings to prioritise the UX findings and decide which to act on • a platform like Jira to track and manage client and UX feedback • a progress management process like Kanban or Scrum to manage the overall project

Phase	Description	Main tools
Post-launch	Short version: never launch on a Friday afternoon. Longer version: there will always be unexpected surprises. The boss has spotted something and it needs to be fixed right now! The urgency of the request is not always proportionate to the seriousness of the bug.	<ul><li>a platform like Jira to track and manage new bugs</li><li>emails/meetings to prioritise any bugs or errors</li><li>a wishlist of features for a 'phase 2' (which might never materialise)</li><li>analytics dashboards</li><li>customer relationship management systems</li></ul>

But don't take our word for it, or anyone else's word for it. As we said above, less research, more testing. In the case of the scientific journal, the right answer would have been to create two versions of the graphic – one with the headings in upper case, and one in sentence case – and show these versions to members of the target audience. We would have a test group and a control group, and ask each group if they liked and understood the graphic. In the event, there wasn't time – and besides – the stakeholder had dug his heels in, and it's important to pick your battles. But in other instances, this is how we have resolved these kinds of issues: test. Because there are all kinds of rules out there: people like these colours, people can't read this chart. But those researchers weren't testing your graphic. After all, it's not as if there was one test movie screening in 1901, and every film since has used the same research. Every act of communication is unique.

OK, back to focus groups. Yes, they are of limited use. They are expensive too. But where they have been useful, and helped to improve the final product, they have tended to possess these characteristics:

- The target audience is clearly defined and the focus group is made up exclusively of that audience.
- The client has expertise in running focus groups, or has commissioned an agency that does.
- The focus groups have been small, or have included one-to-one interviews. (Large groups tend to be hijacked by dominant personalities.)

- The focus-group findings are well edited, presented and visualised, so they are easy to refer back to later.
- Full transcripts or videos of the interviews have been made available to us and the client.
- The questions asked give a sense of the audience's prior level of knowledge of the chosen subject.
- We have produced stimulus materials for the group to feed back on. These could be designs that we produced for the original proposal, or pre-existing material on the same subject.
- The client understands the limits of focus groups and doesn't allow the findings to constrain innovation.
- The client combines the focus-group findings with tools that help deduce what people do (e.g. web analytics) as well as what they say they do.

Use the right tools

If your interactive graphic is complex, then you should have a dedicated QA professional on the team, and involve them from the outset of the project. I'm always surprised that anyone would choose to be a QA engineer – like football referees, they seem to be subject to abuse from all sides, particularly if they do their job well. The best testers that I have worked with have a unique combination of sharp eyes, a thick skin and a superb memory. But thank God they *do* exist.

Otherwise you have a game of football without a referee: anarchy.

QA engineers will choose their own favourite tools, but one commonly used example is Jira, which is also great for tracking progress generally. It fits seamlessly with agile processes, encouraging you to break the project down into short, self-contained units and to release something testable every week or fortnight. You don't have to be a QA professional to use it – so if you are having to test an interactive yourself, it's worth trying out Jira beforehand (or an alternative that does the same thing).

Essentially, for anything more substantial than an infographic, relying on emails to report bugs and errors doesn't work. You need a system that lets you record individual issues, describe them in detail (including the browser/device you were using), give them a priority, and assign them to someone. The same system then allows a developer to pick that bug up, fix it, and assign it to a tester for retesting. If it's fixed, great; if not, it gets reassigned

to a developer. It also means that if the problem is about content (missing copy, spelling mistakes, etc.), it can be assigned to an editor. If the problem is about design (we're missing an icon, we don't have a button design for rollovers, etc.), then it can be assigned to a designer. Everyone checks Jira every morning, and sees what their tasks are. A 10-minute daily meeting with the whole team (called a 'stand-up') irons out anything that doesn't make sense. Weekly progress meetings review what's been done the week before and assign tasks that can be realistically completed in the week ahead. A producer or project manager usually oversees the whole process.

You don't need to do it this way, of course, but you do need a system that allows everyone to see any project issues at a glance and understand any dependencies.

I've put one example of an issue-tracking home screen in Figure 11.1, to give you a sense of how it shows you an overview of the whole project. It also

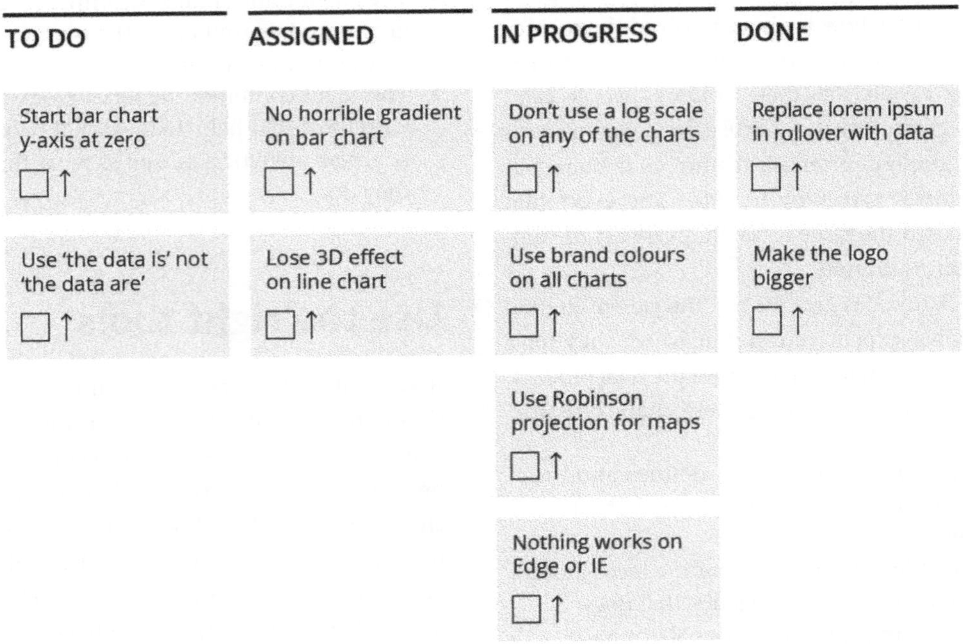

TO DO

Start bar chart
y-axis at zero
☐ ↑

Use 'the data is' not
'the data are'
☐ ↑

ASSIGNED

No horrible gradient
on bar chart
☐ ↑

Lose 3D effect
on line chart
☐ ↑

IN PROGRESS

Don't use a log scale
on any of the charts
☐ ↑

Use brand colours
on all charts
☐ ↑

Use Robinson
projection for maps
☐ ↑

Nothing works on
Edge or IE
☐ ↑

DONE

Replace lorem ipsum
in rollover with data
☐ ↑

Make the logo
bigger
☐ ↑

Figure 11.1 Issue tracking

allows you to zoom and filter out (e.g. see only the tasks assigned to you) or to get detail on demand about specific issues. A tool with good information design helps you to make good information design.

As well as a tool to track bugs, you will also need tools to test them. Most QA professionals have boxes full of old devices that they can test interactives on, and they will also use emulators which let them use their own machines to replicate the hardware and software of other systems. The ideal is always to use actual devices wherever possible and emulators as a back-up. In fact, in some cases, an emulator will be of no use at all. In 2017, we had to build an interactive quiz for an exhibition stand at Cannes that was going to be used on a very specific (and very large) touchscreen TV. We hired that exact model of touchscreen TV, wheeled it into the office, and installed it behind the QA team for the duration of the project. Every couple of hours, we would watch developers stand up and walk over to the screen, tap on it and (usually) swear loudly. It didn't need to work on anything else, so there was no need to test it on anything else.

QA teams will also have tools to test accessibility – Wave seems to be the most commonly used, although axe is also highly regarded. It can also be worth partnering with a specialist accessibility testing company: Nomensa in the UK are excellent, for example.

It's become a cliché, but making sites fully accessible really does benefit all users, not just those with disabilities. You can find handy checklists on the W3C site, but these tend to be the issues that are most commonly overlooked in data visualisation projects:

- **Text description**. All images should have alt tags containing a clear and meaningful description. If your image is a chart, we suggest including a description of the key story (perhaps two sentences) and then, if it is not too huge, a data table.
- **Keyboard controls**. All content needs to be accessible via keyboard controls only. If your chart contains extra data on mouseover, this should also be accessible via the keyboard.

- **Resizing text**. Text can be easily resized without breaking the page. In data visualisation projects, we find that users often zoom in or increase the font size to read details.
- **Contrast**. Text has sufficient colour contrast. This means a ratio of 4.5:1 or greater with the background. This can frustrate some designers, who prefer more subtle colour palettes. But if a significant proportion of your users can't read it, then the beauty of the text colour hardly compensates for its uselessness.
- **Subtitles**. Videos have captions and/or audio descriptions. This is good practice anyway. One Ofcom study from the UK found that of the 7.5 million British TV viewers using subtitles, only 1.5 million had a hearing impairment. Up to 85% of Facebook videos are watched with the sound turned off (Davies, 2019).

Every single test is useful

As well as testing what you make internally – to make sure it functions properly, you will also be showing what you make to external users. This is likely to happen at various points. For example:

- **When you have some test designs**. This often involves printing the designs out and gauging users' reactions, asking if they understand what to click on, checking they understand the information.
- **When you have a first prototype**. By this, I mean a few working screens or charts that users can actually click on and interact with. This often happens in a UX lab and involves close analysis of test users, observing how they respond to the graphic. You will often follow this up with more qualitative questions about what the user understood, how they would improve it and so on. I should add, if you don't have a UX lab, it doesn't matter – as long as you have a quiet room, the right technical set-up and a competent facilitator.
- **When you have a final product**. Sometimes this happens in a UX lab, but often it is a question

of circulating it to as many people as possible, sharing a URL, and getting people to submit their feedback digitally or via email. Breadth is just as important as depth at this point.

Your client is the elephant in the room, of course. They are often the most important test user and can merrily trample on all the other test users, squashing your work to a bloody pulp in the process.

It is easy to get paranoid about testing: to fret about methodology and whether the users are representative and whether the observer-expectancy effect will introduce bias (it will) and whether you're testing it on enough people and whether you're testing the right things.[1] But I promise, the fact that you are even testing your graphic on *anyone* puts you ahead of most of the data visualisation projects being made in the world today. Moreover, a flawless test doesn't exist. So relax, and do your best. Partner with a UX or market research firm if you need to, and if you can afford to. But if you can't, remember that whenever you share your work with someone, you will learn something. Even an informal, unscientific test – showing it to one of your friends – will surprise you. What you thought was of critical importance will turn out to be trivial, whereas something you thought was trivial (e.g. where you put the Submit button) will turn out to be a show-stopper.

The best way of getting useful feedback, even in a less formal test, is to consider the following:

- Give yourself plenty of time to work out the tasks you want to set your users and the questions you want to ask.
- Try everything out yourself several times – there is nothing worse than a test session being held up by a random bug on the landing page.

- Write up the results carefully. Nobody will read the full transcripts, but a summary document or presentation of findings is invaluable, and you will find yourself referring back to it constantly.

And most importantly:

- Only test your work on members of your target audience.

This is the one that our clients keep ignoring, and it genuinely baffles us. We were involved in making an educational website for a science communication charity. It contained games and quizzes introducing children to concepts of evolution and natural selection. It was aimed at primary and secondary school children aged 7–14 and their teachers. One example piece of feedback (with the names changed) was: 'We've tested it on some of the people in the office here. Louise doesn't think we should use cartoons. And Tony doesn't like the fact it's set in a forest.' Maybe they were right. But the point is, unless Louise and Tony are 7 years old, or teachers, their opinions on a website for schoolchildren are not just irrelevant, they are actively counter-productive. Nobody has the same taste at 7 as they do at 9, let alone at 49. It's an issue that recurs particularly often when we make websites for young people – perhaps because testing products on children is more complex, more time-consuming and more expensive. So why not just show it to Tony? Better than nothing, right? No, it's worse. Listening to Tony means you end up with a site for Tony. Next time: why not ask Tony to show it to his kids? Offer them a small,

---

[1]The observer-expectancy effect is a kind of cognitive bias which occurs when the people who run a test or experiment unintentionally influence the participants of an experiment, because a certain outcome is desired. It means that any results that contradict the desired outcome are ignored.

affordable incentive: a voucher for a book shop, or a game store. The feedback you get from them will be more useful than Tony's – and it will be searingly honest too: 'The name is lame' (it was, we changed it) and 'Can the help character be a dog instead?' (yes!).

Another point to consider relates to the accessibility guidelines that we mentioned above. Remember that members of your target audience will include those with disabilities. It is easy to forget this, particularly if (as in the case above) it is a site for children, and your mental image of a 'typical user' may not automatically be someone living with a disability. But one in 20 children in the UK are disabled, as are one in six adults of working age, and almost half of those over 65 (https://www.gov.uk/government/publications/disability-facts-and-figures/disability-facts-and-figures). It is essential to include a similar – and arguably higher – proportion in any user test group.

Of course, once you have shown your interactive graphic to your target audience, the real work begins. You will have a long list of findings. You won't be able to act on everything on this list, not least because some of the users will contradict each other. You need to have a system that prioritises the most important issues and suggests an appropriate fix. We'll move on to this next.

The answer is often deleting

Testers are a bit like Marxists: they are excellent at telling you what the problems are with the current system, but not so good at proposing workable solutions.

Although each issue is unique, what I would say as a general rule is that the problem is usually caused by too much, rather than too little – too much copy, too much design, too many choices – and in consequence the answer is usually deleting rather than adding more.

Let's give you one example from the bad old days. When Tobias and I first started making websites in the late 1990s, we would invariably get feedback that the purpose of the site wasn't self-evident and/or it wasn't obvious how to move around. The solution to both issues, we now know, is to work on the design. If this were a shop, after all, you would be thinking about the shop windows and the floor plan and the signage, so for a website you ought to be doing the same, thinking about how visuals and layout and interface elements can make the users' arrival at and journey through the site as frictionless as possible. But back in the 1990s, clients tended to request a different solution. Adding words. Lots more words. 'Welcome to the home page of our

Figure 11.2 Yahoo and Google landing pages

website! We are LessonPlansUK, the UK's largest provider of lesson plans for secondary school teachers. Click on the Lesson Plans button to see all of our lesson plans. Click on Help to get help. Or click on Contact Us to contact us.'

The misconception persists today: the idea that if users are confused, it is because we haven't *explained* it properly. This may be true, but it doesn't mean your explanations should be text. Or more buttons. Or more anything. The classic example is search engines before and after Google. Readers of a certain age will remember the revelatory appearance of first arriving on the Google home page (Figure 11.2). Before then, search engines were a wall of links and ads and buttons. Google's was clear (and it would get even clearer) and it was obvious what it was *for*.

It's the same with information design. Clarity should be your guiding precept at all times. If your target audience does not understand a chart, including a text box next to the chart with the title: 'How to read this chart' is not going to help you. This approach always reminds us of those 'there, I fixed it' blogs where people replace a section of leaking pipe with a Pringles tube or mend a punctured tyre with foam filler. Just stop. Your chart is too complicated and you need to delete things. Of course, you might be able to add the complexity back in again by walking people into the story gradually (check out the *New York Times*'s 'Sizing Up the Blue Wave' or the *Washington Post*'s 'Great Housing Divide'). But generally speaking, if you find yourself having to add *more* to fix a problem, it's a warning sign.

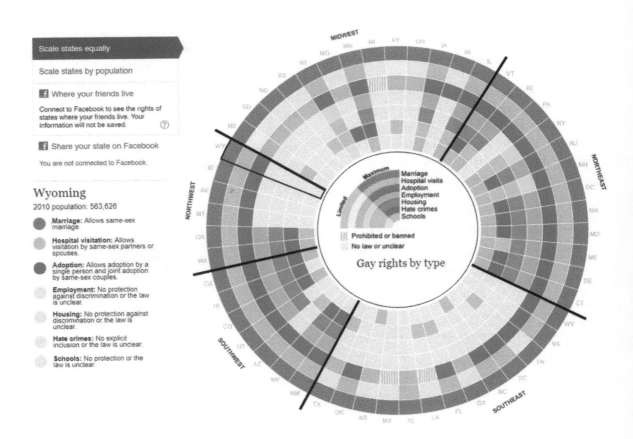

Figure 11.3 Gay rights in the US, state by state

I should say, I'm not referring to adding things you should have included: if your chart needs a legend, you should have added it. I'm referring to when a chart or graphic has failed to be understood or appreciated at a basic level. In these situations, the fix is often to delete not just part of the chart, but the whole chart, and look again at a new solution.

But hang on. Doesn't that mean nothing new or original ever gets made? If you throw things away every time an audience doesn't understand them instantly? Not at all. We're saying it's important to be obvious. To make it clear to the audience what you're telling them and how they can interact with what you've presented. But being obvious doesn't stop you from being original. It sometimes stops you being *subtle* and it definitely stops you being confusing. But I would argue that originality and obviousness are the dream team – an initial 'Huh?' followed by an 'Oh! I get it!' followed shortly after by the silence of intense absorption. (I like to imagine the invention of fire or the wheel being greeted in this way. It's certainly what happened when everyone got iPods in the mid-2000s.)

One example would be Figure 11.3, an interactive chart from the *Guardian*: 'Gay Rights in the US, State by State' (https://www.theguardian.com/world/interactive/2012/may/08/gay-rights-united-states). If you haven't seen it before, I encourage you to take a look now.

When this first appeared in 2012, it was truly original. Feilding Cage and his team had essentially taken an interactive heatmapped spreadsheet and bent it round into a circle. As you roll over the chart, you see which laws restrict freedoms for gay people in individual states. The key is dynamic and gives you information tailored to the state you have chosen.

So where is the 'How to read this chart' paragraph? Nowhere, of course. The originality was inviting, encouraging people to explore. As soon as they did explore, the chart gave them

clear, obvious feedback. The state bar was outlined, the key was updated. 'Oh! I get it!' They learnt by doing.

It looks simple, but achieving this balance of originality and clarity involved a lot of trial and error – check out Feilding Cage's *Guardian* article for more detail on how his team approached their task (Cage, 2012). But, for me, what's apparent is how much they took away, how much they removed and streamlined as they worked.

- **Let's start with the data.** They analysed the thousands and thousands of laws that apply to gay people in the USA and reduced them to seven distinct topics: marriage, hospital visitation, adoption, employment, housing, hate crimes and schools. An easy number of topics to remember, you don't have to keep glancing at the key, it makes the chart a manageable size, and as a bonus, they can use a rainbow palette which suits the theme.
- **The colour density.** Just four bands to represent each state's level of tolerance – grey, hashed grey, a pale colour and the full colour. Think of the number of legal gradations that the designers have included in the 'limited' category, but this act of consolidation speeds up understanding.
- **The chart.** They have 50 states to show and of course they can't delete or hide any of these. But those top-level overview titles help by reducing the 50 states to five areas: Northeast, Southeast, Southwest, Northwest, Midwest. This means we are negotiating a list of five, and then a list of (at most) 13 – the 13 states in the Southeast. In addition, our state's position on the chart approximately correlates to its geographical location, so we can also find it that way. Best of all, in the initial view of the chart, the designers have removed an important dimension of the data: the state's population. Every state – large or small – gets an equal amount of space here. This risks equating California (40 million people) and Wyoming (580,000). It suggests that the decisions that California

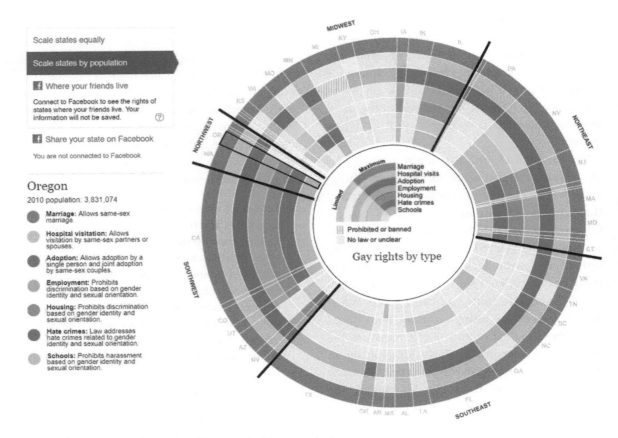

Figure 11.4 Gay rights interactive, scaled by population

takes about how to treat its gay population have the same impact as the decisions taken in Wyoming, which isn't the case. But adding that dimension would make the chart harder to read and, worse, make it look like a chart about population, rather than gay rights. If you don't believe me, click on 'Scale chart by population' on the top left. Because the designers *do* let you add the population variable back in, but you have to choose to do it, and you can only do this after you have taken in the initial, clearer chart. In the 'population' version, California becomes a huge wedge, and Wyoming literally disappears – which shows that accuracy often creates as many problems as it solves (see Figure 11.4).

I'm writing this about an interactive that's almost a decade old, but it is still brilliant. Its brilliance deserves to last for decades more. It works so well because Feilding Cage and his team reviewed and refined their work, gradually removing anything redundant or confusing. Where they couldn't delete (e.g. the 50 states), they added signage (the five top-level areas) and knocked back the state labels, making them two letters in the palest of greys. These are decisions that you can't arrive at without thought, without help, without showing it to others and asking: 'Can you read this? Do you understand this? Have we taken away too much?'

The reward is obvious: your work is discussed, liked and shared thousands of times. Paradoxically, all of the deletion tends to *increase* the number of stories that your users find.

For me, for example, this became not just a story about the persecution of gay people, but also a story about the nature of federalism. I knew that the USA had a federal system but I didn't understand what it meant, I didn't understand the extent of it, and I didn't appreciate how much power individual states had over their citizens' private lives. I've spent most of my life in the UK and, if you're gay, the same laws apply whether you live in Wandsworth or Wales. This is not the case in the USA. If you're gay and you live in Illinois, you are treated like an equal citizen, but if you move to the neighbouring state of Michigan, you can't visit your spouse if they're in hospital, and you can be fired or evicted because you're gay, schools can teach that gay people are evil, and gay adoption is against the law. It's like the USA is 50 different countries – definitely not the united states – and it was this interactive that made me see that clearly for the first time.

This is why we obsess about the value of testing and refinement, and always start by assuming that the problem is *we have left too much in*.

How to be good

The problem with any system is that it relies on human beings sticking to it, and of course they don't. Many of the best practice examples I mention in this book – and plenty of our own work too – will break one or more of the precepts I have just laid out: you will find bugs or spelling mistakes, you will find breaches of accessibility guidelines, a chart will look terrible on a mobile phone or it won't work on Internet Explorer 9. Plus making an interactive project futureproof is impossible: if you don't break it, a Chrome update will.

But I hope I've managed to persuade you that you probably aren't testing and refining enough, and that taking this stage seriously can make a dramatic difference to the quality of your work and its impact on your users. It won't make your work perfect, but it will make it a lot better.

I'd like to end with some final advice on how to make the **Refine** stage run smoothly, both from the client side and from the designer or developer side. Because the best-laid testing plans can often go astray because of what Graham Greene called the human factor.

How to be a good client

1 **Write a detailed brief**. There's no point complaining that the final website isn't developed in PHP if you never specified that it should be. Likewise, if a key performance indicator is 'It has to work on Barry's Blackberry', then let the developers know that from the start.

Remember that in data visualisation, form follows function. The brief must clearly establish the purpose and aim before we can worry about what it might look like. But be specific about what it should look like too – especially with any brand guidelines – and if you have a reference for the kind of thing you're after, include it. See Chapter 9 for some examples of what a good brief should contain.

2 **Involve senior stakeholders from the start.** This is the one that clients should be forced to sign with their own blood. It doesn't matter how busy they are: if person X is the ultimate owner of the project, then they need to be involved in every key decision right from the start. If you only involve person X at the end, then prepare yourself for a world of pain (i.e. changing everything and starting again).

3 **Designers aren't therapists**. Sorry, but if George and Susie don't like each other, then it's not our job to fix it. George might want blue font, and Susie might want red font, for reasons that go back to childhood, but that isn't feedback. You have to figure out the right

answer internally and then let us know whether the font should be red or blue. Or just leave it black – like we originally designed it (that's our 'opinion on this' by the way – our original design). Someone on the client side needs to take all the contradictory feedback, come down on one side, and give the designer or developer a single set of clear instructions (see point 4).

4 **Be clear, but not directive.** Vague feedback is the bane of every designer's life; 'Can it pop more?', 'Not all of the colours work', 'I think some of the text needs rethinking.' Being specific about a problem is the only way it can be solved, for example: 'The title needs to be bolder' or 'The red on that chart is too dark.' However, at the same time, being prescriptive about a solution is often unhelpful too. For example: 'The red on that chart is too dark. Make it this red here' (attaches out-of-focus photo of a random pair of trousers). You have hired designers and developers for their expertise, after all, so let them work out a possible answer first.

5 **Be nice.** At some point in the early 2010s, a lot of our clients seemed to get dispatched to the same assertiveness training course and began sending emails with strange bullet-pointed feedback: 'Please change the word "cabbage" on the home page to the word "artichoke" by 5pm today.' No acknowledgement of the fact that they had used up all their rounds of feedback many weeks ago, or that they had changed the word from 'artichoke' to 'cabbage' and back again five times already. So if you're a client asking for a favour, consider using a less strident tone. It's kindness, not weakness, to say: 'I'm really sorry, I know I've already asked you to change this word five times already, but …' If the budget has run out, be honest about that too: 'I know I should pay you for this, but my budget has

been frozen till June, so …' Designers and developers don't like working for free (see point 6), but they're more likely to do it for nice people.

6 **Pay people.** Most designers and developers will have worked for free at some point in their careers. Particularly if you live in a capitalist society, where the entire system is expressly designed to pay you the lowest possible wage for the highest possible amount of labour (I'm trusting this isn't news to anyone), it is an inevitability that some clients will try to maximise their own profits by reducing their staff costs to less than zero. Designers and developers each have to make their own judgement call about whether and when to work for free. My own view is that you should only say yes if the platform offers a spectacularly huge audience (fancy a column in the *New York Times*?), if you have an empty portfolio and you need some example projects fast, or if it is for a charitable cause that means a lot to you. However, many designers and developers believe that you should *never* work for free, that it only encourages clients to expect it, and that the clients asking you to give your time for nothing are usually on large salaries themselves. 'I'll work for free if you do' is a legitimate answer to a client demanding a freebie.
Clients, you can help. Start with the uncontroversial premise that people should always be paid for their labour. If you are running an internship, provide your interns with a living wage. If you are asking designers or developers to create a test project for an interview, pay them. Why wouldn't you? It doesn't have to be much – just enough to acknowledge that their time is valuable. If you genuinely can't pay – for whatever reason – then never tell designers that a project will be 'good exposure' or 'good experience'. Neither of these things is a unit of currency and they cannot be exchanged for basic daily necessities. If there is no

money for a specific project, set out clearly why this is the case, and let the designer or developer decide for themselves whether they are willing to forfeit their fee.[2]

7   **Remember that you aren't the audience.** Last, but not least, if you are a client commissioning any kind of data visualisation project, remember that you aren't the end user. You are making it for someone else; you are usually doing it to convey a specific message to a wider audience. This might be an internal or external audience, but they will almost always know less about the subject than you, care less about the subject than you, and be less motivated to interact with the subject-matter unless you can persuade them that it is personally relevant to their lives. So put yourself in your audience's shoes continually, and reinforce your assumptions with testing and refining as we have outlined in this chapter.

How to be a good data viz designer

1   **Question the brief.** A brief is a client's best guess at what they want. If you think that parts are missing or misguided, it's a good idea to politely raise this at the start. After all, the client doesn't always have the language or the expertise to fully articulate what they want. It is up to you to engage with the brief and try to understand what it means. Remember that this doesn't mean inventing a different brief that you'd rather work on – your job is to produce work for the client that connects with the client's audience. If the client digs their heels in and insists on an unworkable brief, then we often create a couple of designs, one that sticks to the brief exactly, and one that diverges from it – to show what we think might work better. This is often rejected, but it sets a good precedent for the rest of the project. You are proactive and happy to share your experience – which leads on to point 2.

2   **Share your expertise.** The most common complaint I've heard, echoing around every organisation in which I've worked, is: 'The client is an idiot.' Sometimes the client is the boss – in which case the boss is an idiot. Sometimes the clients are customers, in which case the customers are idiots. Well, thank God they are. Data visualisation, like many industries, only works because there is an asymmetry of information. The client knows less than you, that's why they're paying you for what you do. If you were trying to do what *they* do for a living, you'd be the idiot.
In my experience, the best data viz designers do not have this antagonistic relationship with their clients. If the client doesn't understand something, the designer explains it. If the client sends peculiar feedback, the designer questions it. The fact that the client knows less is an important precondition of the relationship, and what's more, is a gap that can be closed if you continue to share what you know, enabling even more effective collaboration in the future.
And always remember that the point of data visualisation is to help people understand complex information – if the client doesn't understand what you have made, you have probably not done a great job. After all, it is *their* information. You might need to consider their feedback more carefully.

---

[2]Also remember that if you can't pay them, you don't own the work: they do. Unless of course you force them to sign a contract giving you the rights over the work they created for nothing, in which case you are an awful person and I'd direct you to the works of Ayn Rand where you will find your amoral worldview comprehensively validated.

3   **Calm down.** Of course you'd have to have the patience of a saint to abide by the guidance outlined in point 2 all the time. Being told to 'zhoosh up a design', 'push the brand guidelines' (why? where?) or 'give the chart more of a wow factor' is enough to turn even the most mild-mannered designer into the Hulk. Never reply to this kind of feedback immediately. You'll end up writing three emails and never sending them, which will just waste five hours of your life, and besides, you might accidentally send one and regret it. If possible, sleep on it. Tomorrow, you'll realise it's all bound up with point 2 – information asymmetry – and you'll find yourself composing a more thoughtful response. This is also often the moment to play detective. What the client says the work is 'not very exciting', what do they actually *mean*? Is it just a matter of the colours? Is the chart not emphasising its point enough? Or is there a problem in the content, meaning we have to go right back to the wireframe? (This last one is almost always the answer.)

4   **Be on time.** Almost every data visualisation project has a string of dependencies. Task X can't start until task Y is done. Because data visualisation design is a creative endeavour, with multiple right answers, it is possible to spend an almost infinite amount of time experimenting with new visual approaches. But remember, if you are late, someone else gets less time to do their job, or the whole project gets delayed. Make it clear how long you will need to produce work to an acceptable standard and then stick to it.

5   **Be flexible.** At the start of any project, it's a good idea to set how many rounds of feedback are acceptable. Of course, if you are working full-time in a company, this probably won't apply – you'll just have to keep going till the stakeholders are happy. But if you are a contractor or freelancer, you will want to be clear about how many times you can change things without having to charge more. Some designers say three rounds of feedback, others say four, others say as many rounds as you like within a given time period.

For most projects, the client will exceed their rounds of feedback. There are no rules about how you treat these breaches – so much depends on your relationship with the individual client. As a general rule, though, we would say it's good to be flexible. If you have allowed for three rounds of feedback, let the client have four, but warn them that round five will incur extra cost. (You might then allow round five for free if it's only small text changes, but don't tell anyone.)

6   **You're allowed to be paid.** We find it hard to advise designers and developers how much they should be paid. It's usually best to ask around and find out what the going rates are for people of your abilities and experience. What is easier for us to say is that you absolutely *should* be paid. A lot of freelancers are sheepish about invoicing or chasing invoices or adding interest and statutory fixed costs to late payments. But you shouldn't be. If a client doesn't pay you within the contracted period of time, then they have broken the law, and you are perfectly entitled to send firm, reminder emails and add interest to any invoice. If an organisation repeatedly pays you late, consider whether it is worth continuing to work for them. Just remember that your client will rarely be the person organising your payment, and they will often be just as annoyed as you that the finance department has screwed up (again).

Twelve
Resources

Here are a few of our favourite things: the tools we use most often, the books we reread most frequently, the bloggers we admire and the podcasts we devour. We've limited it to a top five for each, otherwise this section would be longer than the rest of the book put together.

Our choices here are subject to change, because new tools and books appear all the time, so for an up-to-date list, check out https://bit.ly/data-viz-best-practice.

It's also worth saying that a lot of these recommendations have been influenced by student feedback, so many thanks to all of our students who have also nominated their favourite things. Note that we are UK-based, and most of our students have been from the UK/USA or English-speaking countries, so the resources listed here are almost all in the English language. Mea culpa. Scusa. 对不起.

Overall top 5

If we were going to pick just five *things* we use most often, it would be:

1 **R/ggplot** for analysis and hypothesis testing
2 **Illustrator** for graphic design
3 **Flourish** for off-the-shelf charts
4 **D3** for custom charts
5 **PowerPoint** because we're all stuck with it and always will be.

We should also mention **pen and paper**, which is where every project starts, every time.

Data visualisation tools (free)

1 **Flourish** Choose from dozens of useful templates and make and publish your own interactive chart in minutes with this free, easy-to-use online toolkit. However, note that the free version does make your data public.

2 **Raw** Upload your data, choose a chart type, drag and drop your variables and *voilà*! A beautiful chart to download as a png or svg. It works in a single page and does not store your data.
3 **Datawrapper** An intuitive interface and beautifully designed charts make this online tool stand out from the crowd. Astonishing range of free map templates too.
4 **Canva** Probably the best place to start if you want to make a quick infographic for free, although Infogram and Venngage are also handy.
5 **D3** This JavaScript charting library is not for the faint-hearted, but the rewards are mighty. It helps if you have Scott Murray's *Interactive Data Visualization for the Web* (2017) as a guide.

Data visualisation tools (paid)

1 **Adobe Illustrator** All of us use it every day. A state-of-the-art vector editing tool, with simple charting tools built in and lots of online community support. Inkscape is a free vector editor, Affinity Designer is cheaper.
2 **After Effects** Also part of the Adobe suite, this is our favourite tool for creating motion graphics and other visual effects.
3 **PowerPoint** An inescapable encumbrance of office life, it now includes libraries of stock images, icons and illustrations. The charting tools are limited, but can do more than you think.
4 **Unity** A game development engine, but also a useful platform for immersive interaction design and 3D visualisation.
5 **Shorthand** A platform for building 'scrollytelling' digital articles, useful for making interactive infographics and long-read data stories. There is a free version too, but it's pretty limited.

Design tools (free)

1 **Coolors** A site that allows you to explore colour palettes made by others and also build your

own, generating random palettes and letting you adjust and adapt them.

2 **ColorBrewer** Online resource for palette optimised for maps (and also visualisations), filterable by accessibility options.

3 **Chroma js colour picker** Online tool for building visualisation palettes, able to extend brand colours into wider palettes suitable for charting.

4 **Grid Calculator** Online tool for generating column grids, useful for setting page layouts, particularly in PowerPoint.

5 **Figma.** An in-browser vector editing tool, useful for tweaking SVG charts made in other tools, but also a fully-fledged design, wireframing and prototyping tool.

Design assets (free)

1 **The Noun Project** Online resource for iconography – designers contribute icons that you can search and download. Most are Creative Commons licences, so check the stipulations.

2 **Unsplash** Stock photo library. Photographers contribute images, and they are usually high-quality and professional. All free to use.

3 **Google Fonts** Font library, all available to download and use for free. Also useful for suggesting font pairings and compatibility.

4 **Humaaans** A large library of illustrations of people. You can download the whole set to work with, or carry out a limited amount of customisation in the browser.

5 **Pexels** Community-sourced stock image and video library. The quality varies, but it is a rare source of free-to-use video clips.

Analysis tools

1 **R/ggplot** Some prefer Python, but R is our first choice for analysis. There is a package for almost every chart you could conceivably want, but ggplot is the best place to start.

2 **Excel** Sometimes you don't need to go beyond Excel. Particularly now it doesn't crash as much as it used to. See Jorge Camões book, *Data at Work* (2016), for how Excel can also be used to make beautiful charts (no, really).

3 **Google Sheets** Not as fully featured as Excel, but this can be a good thing. Its simple interface and ease of use make it a great starting point for arithmophobes. Also great if you are collaborating with others.

4 **OpenRefine** Free data cleaning tool with clear and intuitive functionality. It also has a range of useful online tutorials.

5 **Tableau** When you have Big Data, you'll need one of the Big Beasts – Power BI, QlikView, Spotfire, Tableau. Tableau has the edge for us because its visualisations are slicker. It's expensive though, so try the free version (Tableau Public) first.

People

Historical

1 **William Playfair** – *statistician, engineer, blackmailer and spy*: Instrumental in inventing – or sometimes popularising – all the basic charts: line, bar, bubble and pie. He used them to explain eighteenth-century trade and economics. *Start with: his seminal charts.*

2 **Florence Nightingale** – *nurse and health campaigner*: The Nightingale rose is not just a chart that changed medical history, but also an object lesson in the rhetorical possibilities of data visualisation. *Start with: Diagram of the Causes of Mortality in the Army in the East.*

3 **Charles Booth** – *social researcher*: Booth's heatmaps of nineteenth-century urban poverty were instrumental in the development of social housing and the welfare state. *Start with: his poverty maps of London.*

4   **Otto and Marie Neurath and Gerd Arntz** – *economists and designers*: Otto Neurath thought that visuals were a key instrument in explaining the complexities of the modern world to the general public. The visual language he created (isotypes) remains a foundational element of modern data visualisation. *Start with: the Gerd Arntz web archive.*

5   **Harry Beck** – *designer*: Designer of the London Tube map. His great insight was allowing the functionality of the map to dictate its form. *Start with: the Tube map, of course.*

Data viz thinkers (present day)

1   **Edward Tufte** – *designer and theorist*: The father of visualisation for analysis. Some of his charts (e.g. the slopechart, sparklines, small multiples) are also superb for data communication. An outstanding curator of historical examples too. *Start with: The Visual Display of Quantitative Information* (2001).

2   **Nathan Yau** – *statistician and designer*: A popular and influential data visualiser and communicator, his Flowing Data website is a brilliant resource and his books are invaluable too. *Start with: Data Points* (2013).

3   **Alberto Cairo** – *information designer*, data journalist and academic, Cairo writes interesting, accessible books about data visualisation in real-world contexts. Also uses social media brilliantly. *Start with: The Functional Art* (2013).

4   **Lisa Charlotte Rost** – *theorist, journalist, designer*: Rost's blog posts for Datawrapper are lucid, wise, helpful, and right about everything. An absolute must-read. *Start with: any of her blog posts.*

5   **Moritz Stefaner** – *self-proclaimed truth and beauty operator*: Stefaner's conceptual, often playful, work is underpinned by a deep commitment to comprehensibility and accessibility. His podcasts (see below) contain invaluable guidance and advice for fellow practitioners. *Start with: his website.*

Data viz best practice (present day)

1   **David McCandless** – *journalist and designer*: The man who created an industry. His first book, *Information is Beautiful* (2012), proved that a book of charts could be interesting, witty – and also a best-seller. *Start with: Information is Beautiful.*

2   **Valentina D'Efilippo** – *Information designer, creative director and teacher*: D'Efilippo is notable for her large, detailed and intricate works of visualisation. Always an inspiration. *Start with: her website.*

3   **Mona Chalabi** – *data journalist*: Increasingly visible in the media, Chalabi's hand-drawn visualisations are provocative, playful and completely unique. Isotypes for the twenty-first century. *Start with: her hand drawn charts on Instagram.*

4   **Stefanie Posavec and Giorgia Lupi** – *designers*: Both influential designers in their own right, their 'Dear Data' project put their own individual experiences at the centre of their charting – with spectacular results. *Start with: Dear Data.*

5   **Adolfo Arranz** – *visual journalist*: Where data viz meets figurative art, Adolfo Arranz's work for the *South China Morning Post* is simply breathtaking. Also inspirational in a similar vein: Jane Pong, Alberto Lucas Lopez, Juan Velasco and Fernando Baptista. Important precursors: Nigel Holmes, John Grimwade, Peter Grundy. *Start with: Arranz's work for the South China Morning Post.*

Wider influences

1   **Scott McCloud** – *comic book artist*: Alongside Will Eisner's work, McCloud's two comics about comics are entertaining and profoundly important explorations of visual storytelling: *Start with: Making Comics* (2006).

2   **Daniel Kahneman** – *behavioural economist*: The work of Kahneman and Tversky changed

psychology for ever and their exploration of cognitive biases is vital to understanding how human beings read (and misread) the world. *Start with: Thinking, Fast and Slow* (Kahneman, 2011).

3 **Don Norman** Hard to imagine what interface design would look like today without Don Norman's wise and humane interventions. His work on the importance of emotions in design also remains invaluable. *Start with: The Design of Everyday Things* (1988).

4 **George Lakoff and Mark Johnson** Their work on how humans convert reality into metaphor is particularly applicable to data visualisation, where we continually use visual metaphors to accelerate understanding. Their book will change the way you see the world. *Start with: Metaphors We Live By* (1980).

5 **Will Storr** – *writer* There are lots of theories of story construction, from Aristotle to Robert McKee, but Storr's examination of how stories work offers a brilliant introduction to the field. *Start with: The Science of Storytelling* (2019).

Other resources

1 **Data Stories** A podcast hosted by Moritz Stefaner and Enrico Bertini featuring discussions of the practice and excellent interviews with prominent data viz figures.

2 **99% Invisible** A podcast exploring the human stories behind design and architecture and its often-unexpected cultural effects.

3 **The Data Visualization Society** Ever-expanding, the society now hosts conferences and publishes on Medium, as well as being a vibrant community.

4 **The Nib** A journal of documentary comics and visual journalism. Its statistics section, featuring a mixture of comics and visualisation, is inspirational.

5 **The Pudding** Ground-breaking digital data journalism site, full of excellent data-driven stories and engaging interactives.

Data journalism teams

1 **New York Times** Brilliant journalism combined with ground-breaking visual storytelling. The *Washington Post* team is also excellent.

2 **South China Morning Post**. A lot of news teams have given up on illustrations and 'traditional' information graphics. Thank God the SCMP haven't. Beautiful graphics on fascinating subjects.

3 **Economist** World-class charts on a range of subjects (not just economic). Great on social media too.

4 **Financial Times** Perhaps the best data journalism team in the UK at present, the FT excels not just at static graphics, but at interactive and animated data visualisation too.

5 **Guardian** Great visual journalism and, unlike *The Economist* and the *Financial Times*, none of it is behind a paywall (at least, not at the moment).

Free data sources

1 **Our World in Data** Max Roser's team provides a brilliant data service – for free. Some of the most interesting data in the world, superbly organised and visualised.

2 **World Bank** An invaluable catalogue of vital, interesting data. Their time series often stretch back to the mid-twentieth century, offering a valuable long-term perspective on key trends. Their data is often drawn from other high-quality sources such as the FAO, ILO, WHO and others.

3 **Kaggle** A data-sharing community, among other things. People upload their favourite datasets, and subjects range from stock prices to *Star Trek*.

4 **Google Dataset Search** Launched in 2018, this offers a quick and easy way to locate free, online data.

5 **Google Trends** Needs no introduction. Worth reading Seth Stephens-Davidowitz's *Everybody Lies* (2017) before you use it, though.

Part II

Finding the Right Chart For Your Story

Finding the right chart for your story

This section consists of a series of story types and the kinds of charts and maps that work best for telling each story. All of the visuals have been tried and tested in client projects. Our hope is that, if you're ever stuck for ideas, you can flick through these pages and find inspiration. All of the charts use genuine data – the sources are at the bottom of each page.

What you will notice is that there are always several right answers for every story. It depends on what you want to say and who your audience is. For some audiences, you will want simple bar or line charts; for others, something more novel or perhaps no chart at all. In Chapter 2, we discussed the best choices for each audience type.

You will notice that there are many chart types that aren't included in these pages, for example, no Marimekko charts, no radial bar charts, no 3D scatter charts. Just because a chart exists, it doesn't mean that it's a useful communication tool. We are not showing you every chart you can use, just the charts that we believe you should.

Another caveat: there is a definite bias towards static charts here. Because this is a book, we have inevitably told stories and used charts that work well in print. If you were making an interactive, you might go more ambitious (think Gapminder) or even less (lots of bar charts, like a corporate dashboard). You would also be more likely to use maps, which come into their own when interactivity is added. We have discussed the kinds of choices you make in interactive storytelling in Chapters 9 and 10.

We have grouped the charts into their primary story type – change over time, comparison, composition and so on. Often charts tell more than one story. For example, a change-over-time chart often compares multiple variables too, or indicates the composition of a marketplace. However, the audience always notices one story first (if you've designed it right). There is always an organising metaphor. So our change-over-time stories are for when you want your audience to notice what's rising or falling (or staying the same) before anything else.

Some of the time, you will be linking several chart types together. For example:

- you might start with a **comparison** chart: 'Here is the GDP of the G7 countries right now. '

- then perhaps a **composition** chart: 'Here is the total GDP of the G7 compared to the rest of the world (e.g. in 2019, they had 39% of the world's GDP). '

- finally **change over time**: 'Here is how the G7's share of global GDP has increased since 1945. '

We have put a few of these multi-step stories at the end of this section. Notice that, in each case, we keep each part of the story as a separate chart, and rarely recommend merging disparate story types into one composite visual. This is about communicating to people who know less about the subject than you, and this means small pieces of self-contained and coherent information, progressively disclosed (see Chapter 4 for more on story structure).

We've put the svgs of all these charts here: www.addtwodigital.com/book/downloads. Feel free to use, adapt and modify them, under Creative Commons 4.0. This means you have to credit us, but that's all. The main tools we used were ggplot, Flourish, Raw and Illustrator. We'd highly recommend all four.

Change over time

1. One data series, two years

Number of measles cases in Europe (2014–2018)

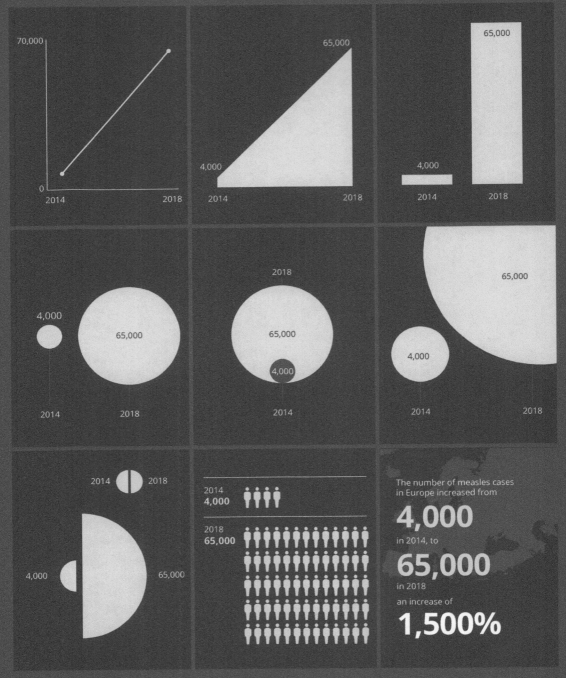

The number of measles cases in Europe increased from

4,000

in 2014, to

65,000

in 2018

an increase of

1,500%

Sources: Royal Stastistical Society / WHO

Change over time

2. One data series, several years

British people who believe there is nothing wrong with sex before marriage (%)

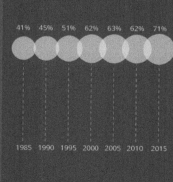

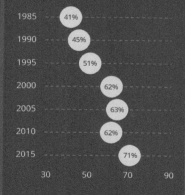

71% of British people believe there is nothing wrong with sex before marriage, up from **41%** in 1985

Source: NatCen BSA Survey

Change over time

3. One data series, with annotation

The population of Ireland

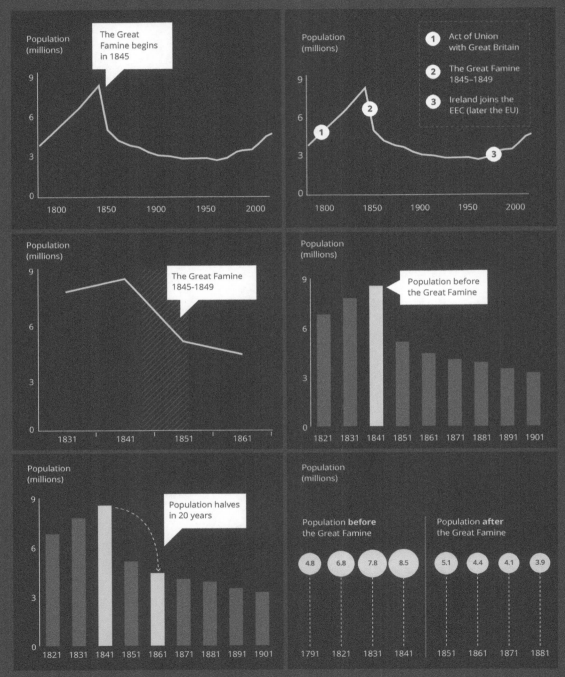

Source: Library Ireland; Annales de Demographie Historique, 1979

Change over time

4. Several data series, two years

Percentage of adult males who are smokers (2000 vs 2016)

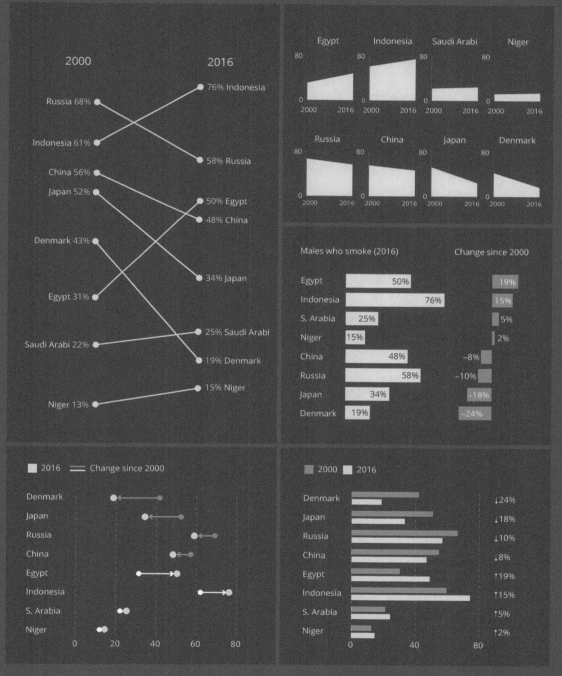

Change over time

5. Several data series, several years

Percentage of British people in each group that own their own home* (1987–2017)

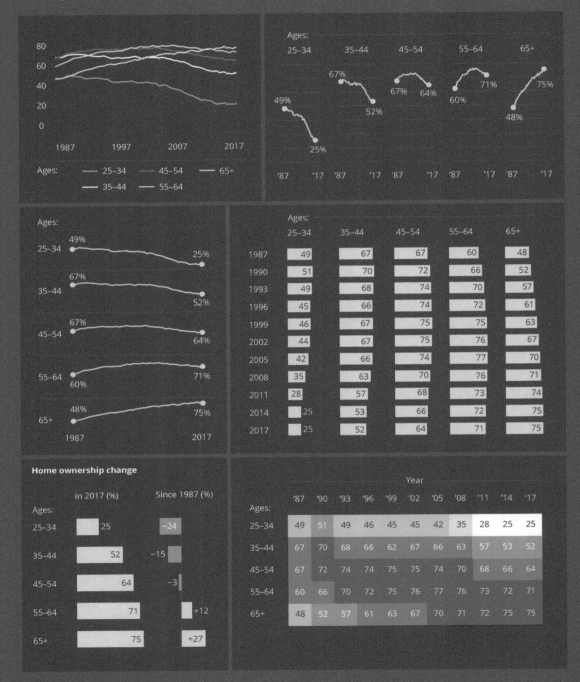

	Ages:				
Year	25–34	35–44	45–54	55–64	65+
1987	49	67	67	60	48
1990	51	70	72	66	52
1993	49	68	74	70	57
1996	45	66	74	72	61
1999	46	67	75	75	63
2002	44	67	75	76	67
2005	42	66	74	77	70
2008	35	63	70	76	71
2011	28	57	68	73	74
2014	25	53	66	72	75
2017	25	52	64	71	75

Home ownership change

Ages:	in 2017 (%)	Since 1987 (%)
25–34	25	−24
35–44	52	−15
45–54	64	−3
55–64	71	+12
65+	75	+27

	Year										
Ages:	'87	'90	'93	'96	'99	'02	'05	'08	'11	'14	'17
25–34	49	51	49	46	45	45	42	35	28	25	25
35–44	67	70	68	66	62	66	66	63	57	53	52
45–54	67	72	74	74	75	75	74	70	68	66	64
55–64	60	66	70	72	75	76	77	76	73	72	71
65+	48	52	57	61	63	67	70	71	72	75	75

Source: Resolution Foundation
*Including mortgage holders

Change over time

6. Several data series against an average

Total fertility rates (births per woman), 1960–2017

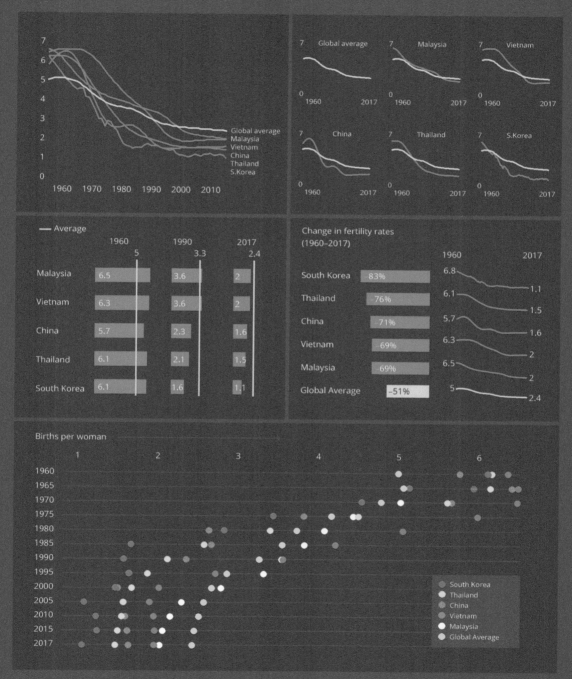

Source: World Bank

Change over time

7. Ranking

Murder rate per 100,000 people in G10 countries, 2010–2015

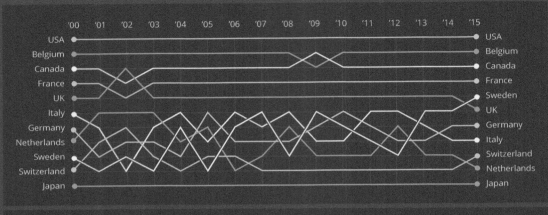

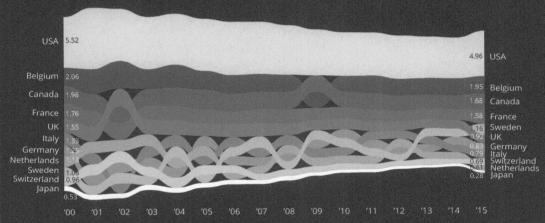

	Murder rate (per 100,000)	Rank change since 2000
1 USA	4.96	=
2 Belgium	1.95	=
3 Canada	1.68	=
4 France	1.58	=
5 Sweden	1.15	+4
6 UK	0.99	-1
7 Germany	0.83	=
8 Italy	0.79	-2
9 Switzerland	0.69	+1
10 Netherlands	0.61	-2
11 Japan	0.28	=

	'00	'01	'02	'03	'04	'05	'06	'07	'08	'09	'10	'11	'12	'13	'14	'15
USA	1	1	1	1	1	1	1	1	1	1	1	1	1	1	1	1
Belgium	2	2	2	2	2	2	2	2	2	3	2	2	2	2	2	2
Canada	3	3	4	3	3	3	3	3	3	2	3	3	3	3	3	3
France	4	4	5	4	4	4	4	4	4	4	4	4	4	4	4	4
Sweden	9	10	9	10	7	10	7	6	9	6	7	8	9	6	6	5
UK	5	5	3	5	5	5	5	5	5	5	5	5	5	5	5	6
Germany	7	9	8	9	8	6	8	8	7	8	6	7	8	8	7	7
Italy	6	7	10	7	6	8	6	7	6	8	8	6	6	7	8	8
Switzerland	10	8	7	8	10	9	9	10	10	10	10	10	10	10	10	9
Netherlands	8	6	6	6	8	7	10	9	7	9	9	9	7	9	9	10
Japan	11	11	11	11	11	11	11	11	11	11	11	11	11	11	11	11

Source: World Bank

Change over time

8. Margin of error

Percentage who feel safe walking alone after dark (England and Wales)

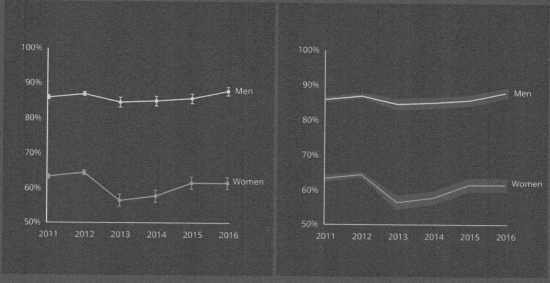

Source: Crime Survey for England and Wales, 95% confidence interval shown.

9. Projections

World population (1900 to 2100)

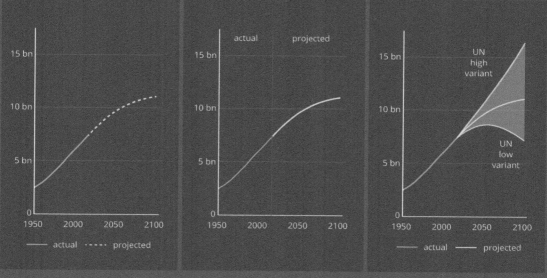

Source: United Nations

Change over time
10. Off-the-charts

The price of bread in Berlin, Germany (1918–23)

continues for 35,000 more pages

Date	Loaf of bread (Marks)
Dec 1918	0.5
Dec 1921	4
Jan 1923	250
Mar 1923	463
June 1923	1,465
July 1923	3,465
Aug 1923	69,000
Sept 1923	1,512,000
Oct 1923	1,743,000,000
Nov 1923	201,000,000,000

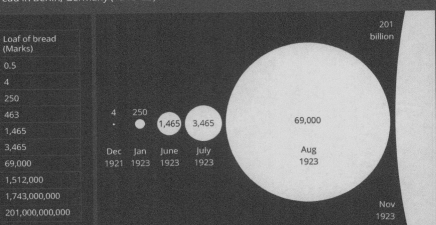

4	250	1,465	3,465	69,000	201 billion	
Dec 1921	Jan 1923	June 1923	July 1923	Aug 1923	Nov 1923	

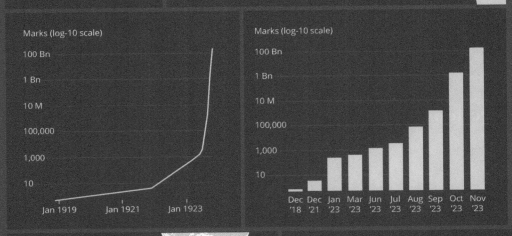

Marks (log-10 scale)

100 Bn
1 Bn
10 M
100,000
1,000
10

Jan 1919 — Jan 1921 — Jan 1923

Marks (log-10 scale)

100 Bn
1 Bn
10 M
100,000
1,000
10

Dec '18 | Dec '21 | Jan '23 | Mar '23 | Jun '23 | Jul '23 | Aug '23 | Sep '23 | Oct '23 | Nov '23

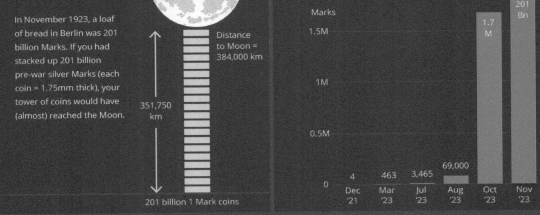

In November 1923, a loaf of bread in Berlin was 201 billion Marks. If you had stacked up 201 billion pre-war silver Marks (each coin = 1.75mm thick), your tower of coins would have (almost) reached the Moon.

Distance to Moon = 384,000 km

351,750 km

201 billion 1 Mark coins

Marks

1.5M
1M
0.5M
0

	4	463	3,465	69,000	1.7 M	201 Bn
	Dec '21	Mar '23	Jul '23	Aug '23	Oct '23	Nov '23

Source: Encyclopaedia Britannica

Change over time
11. Too much data

Social acceptance of LGBT people (Global Acceptance Index) – 2004–08 and 2009–13

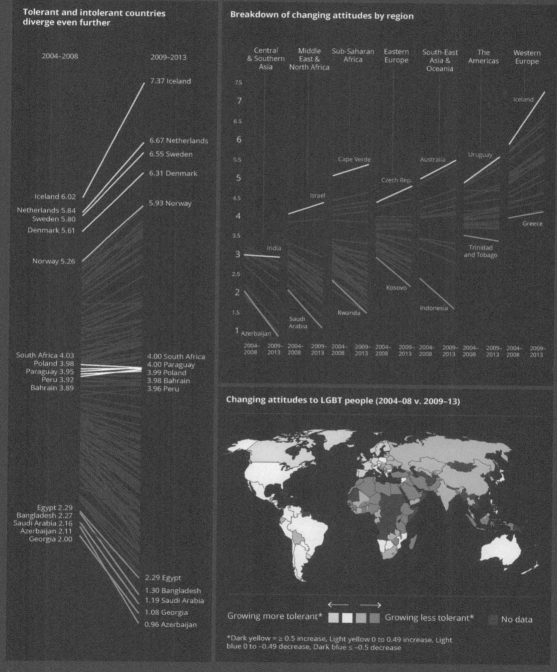

Tolerant and intolerant countries diverge even further

2004–2008 / 2009–2013

7.37 Iceland

6.67 Netherlands
6.55 Sweden
6.31 Denmark

Iceland 6.02

Netherlands 5.84
Sweden 5.80
Denmark 5.61

5.93 Norway

Norway 5.26

South Africa 4.03   4.00 South Africa
Poland 3.98   4.00 Paraguay
Paraguay 3.95   3.99 Poland
Peru 3.92   3.98 Bahrain
Bahrain 3.89   3.96 Peru

Egypt 2.29
Bangladesh 2.27
Saudi Arabia 2.16
Azerbaijan 2.11
Georgia 2.00

2.29 Egypt
1.30 Bangladesh
1.19 Saudi Arabia
1.08 Georgia
0.96 Azerbaijan

Breakdown of changing attitudes by region

Central & Southern Asia / Middle East & North Africa / Sub-Saharan Africa / Eastern Europe / South-East Asia & Oceania / The Americas / Western Europe

Iceland

Cape Verde
Australia
Uruguay

Czech Rep.

Israel
Greece

India
Trinidad and Tobago

Kosovo

Saudi Arabia / Rwanda / Indonesia

Azerbaijan

Changing attitudes to LGBT people (2004–08 v. 2009–13)

Growing more tolerant*   Growing less tolerant*   No data

*Dark yellow = ≥ 0.5 increase, Light yellow 0 to 0.49 increase, Light blue 0 to –0.49 decrease, Dark blue ≤ –0.5 decrease

Sources: Williams Institute, Global Acceptance Index

295

Global searches for football by month (indexed, 2008–18)

Dec 48
Nov 66
Jan 39
Feb 31
Oct 69
Mar 28
Apr 39
Sep 81
May 29
Aug 53
Jul 33
Jun 35

Jan
Dec   Feb
Nov   Mar
Oct   Apr
Sep   May
Aug   Jun
Jul

Population of Shenzhen, China

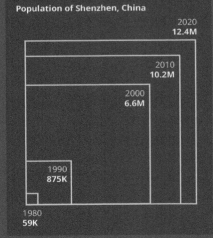

2020 **12.4M**
2010 **10.2M**
2000 **6.6M**
1990 **875K**
1980 **59K**

Animal heart rates (beats per minute)

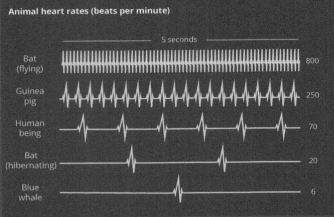

5 seconds

Bat (flying)	800
Guinea pig	250
Human being	70
Bat (hibernating)	20
Blue whale	6

Change in animal sizes (50,000 BC vs today)

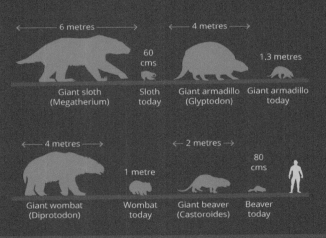

6 metres
60 cms
Giant sloth (Megatherium) — Sloth today

4 metres
1.3 metres
Giant armadillo (Glyptodon) — Giant armadillo today

4 metres
1 metre
Giant wombat (Diprotodon) — Wombat today

2 metres
80 cms
Giant beaver (Castoroides) — Beaver today

Earth's prehistory

Slimeball   Billiard ball   Snowball   Glitterball

4.6 bn years ago
Earth is covered in slime, with no life on it

4.5 bn years ago
The Moon is formed after a Mars-sized rock hits Earth

750M years ago
Temperatures plunge and Earth is covered in snow

335M years ago
A single supercontinent (Pangaea) and a huge glittering ocean

Average life expectancy in Russia and the Soviet Union (1880–1960)

years
15 ——— 70

1892:
Drought
and famine.
Life expectancy
falls to 21

1917-22:
Revolution
and Civil War

1933:
Stalinist
collectivisation

1943:
During WWII,
life expectancy
falls to 16

1880 · 1900 · 1920 · 1940 · 1960

Top 15 names in England & Wales (1944, 1974, 2004)

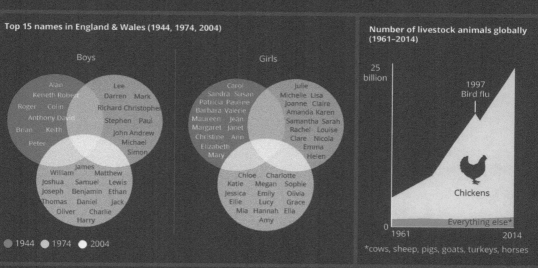

Boys

Alan
Keneth Robert
Roger   Colin
Anthony David
Brian   Keith
Peter

Lee
Darren Mark
Richard Christopher
Stephen Paul
John Andrew
Michael
Simon

William James Matthew
Joshua Samuel Lewis
Joseph Benjamin Ethan
Thomas Daniel Jack
Oliver Charlie
Harry

Girls

Carol
Sandra Susan
Patricia Pauline
Barbara Valerie
Maureen Jean
Margaret Janet
Christine Ann
Elizabeth
Mary

Julie
Michelle Lisa
Joanne Claire
Amanda Karen
Samantha Sarah
Rachel Louise
Clare Nicola
Emma
Helen

Chloe Charlotte
Katie Megan Sophie
Jessica Emily Olivia
Ellie Lucy Grace
Mia Hannah Ella
Amy

● 1944 ● 1974 ● 2004

Number of livestock animals globally (1961–2014)

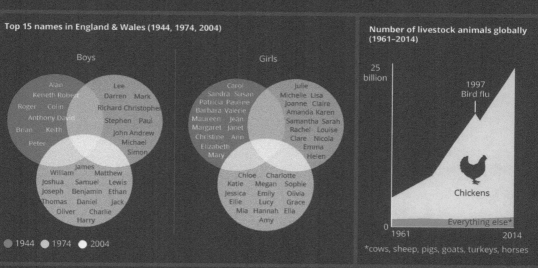

25
billion

1997
Bird flu

Chickens

Everything else*

0
1961 · 2014

*cows, sheep, pigs, goats, turkeys, horses

Change in height in males (1850–1980)

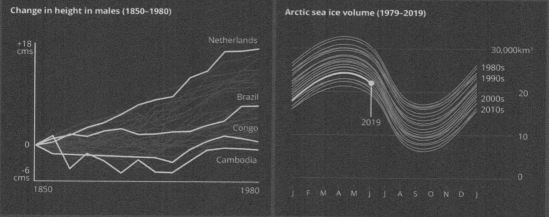

+18
cms

Netherlands

Brazil

Congo

0

Cambodia

-6
cms

1850 · 1980

Arctic sea ice volume (1979–2019)

30,000km³

1980s
1990s

2000s
2010s

2019

20

10

0

J F M A M J J A S O N D J

Sources: Google Trends (football data), Natural History Museum (animal size, animal heart rates), Gapminder
(Russia life expectancy), Our World in Data (livestock and height data), Guardian/ Polar Science Centre (sea ice),
ONS (baby names)

Comparison

1. Five items or fewer

Largest animals that have ever lived (average weight in tonnes)

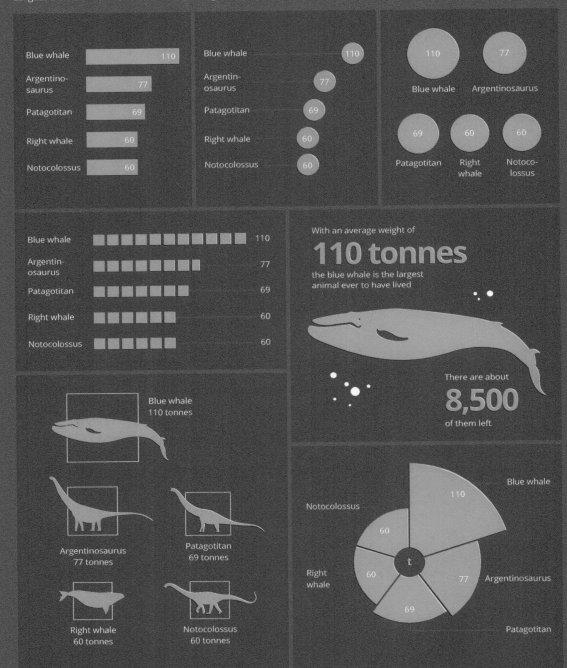

Blue whale	110
Argentino-saurus	77
Patagotitan	69
Right whale	60
Notocolossus	60

Blue whale 110
Argentinosaurus 77
Patagotitan 69
Right whale 60
Notocolossus 60

Blue whale 110
Argentin-osaurus 77
Patagotitan 69
Right whale 60
Notocolossus 60

With an average weight of

110 tonnes

the blue whale is the largest animal ever to have lived

There are about

8,500

of them left

Blue whale
110 tonnes

Argentinosaurus
77 tonnes

Patagotitan
69 tonnes

Right whale
60 tonnes

Notocolossus
60 tonnes

Blue whale 110
Argentinosaurus 77
Patagotitan 69
Notocolossus 60
Right whale 60

Source: Natural History Museum, UK. This is correct as of Jan 2019. Larger dinosaurs are being found all the time, but none so far have come close to the size of the blue whale.

Comparison

2. Five items or fewer, percentage

Water content (%)

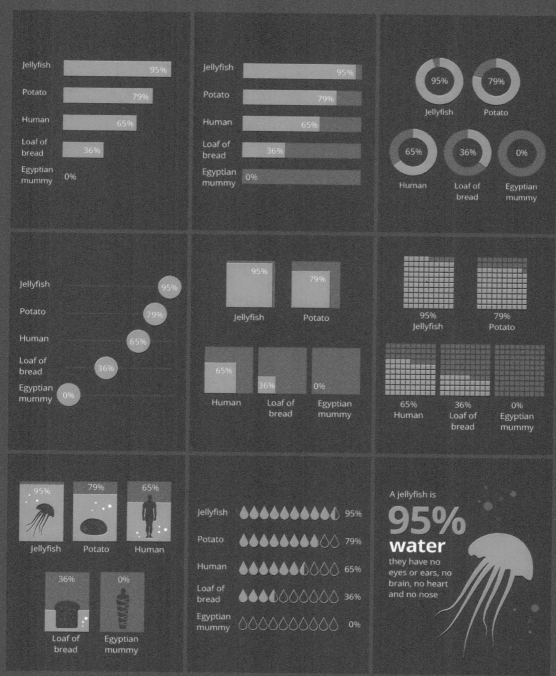

Jellyfish	95%
Potato	79%
Human	65%
Loaf of bread	36%
Egyptian mummy	0%

Jellyfish Potato

Human Loaf of bread Egyptian mummy

Jellyfish 95%
Potato 79%
Human 65%
Loaf of bread 36%
Egyptian mummy 0%

95% Jellyfish 79% Potato

65% Human 36% Loaf of bread 0% Egyptian mummy

Jellyfish Potato Human

Loaf of bread Egyptian mummy

Jellyfish		95%
Potato		79%
Human		65%
Loaf of bread		36%
Egyptian mummy		0%

A jellyfish is

95%
water

they have no
eyes or ears, no
brain, no heart
and no nose

Comparison

3. 10-20 datapoints

Number of baby boys for every 100 baby girls, 2017 (highest ratio)

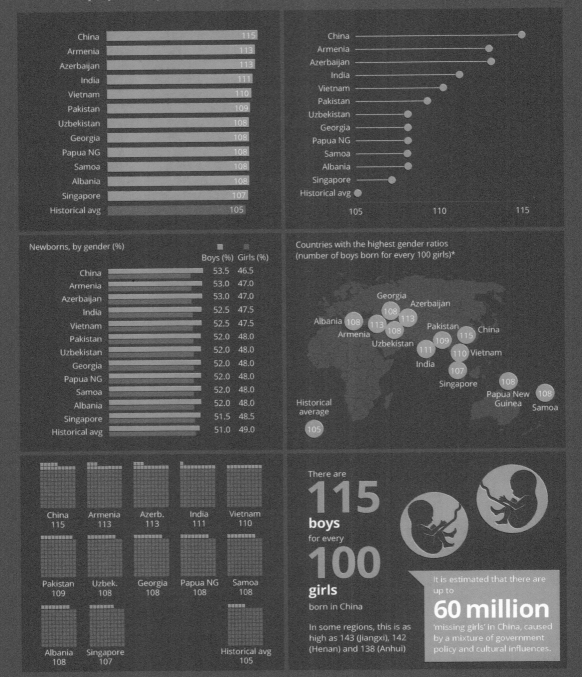

	Boys (%)	Girls (%)
China	53.5	46.5
Armenia	53.0	47.0
Azerbaijan	53.0	47.0
India	52.5	47.5
Vietnam	52.5	47.5
Pakistan	52.0	48.0
Uzbekistan	52.0	48.0
Georgia	52.0	48.0
Papua NG	52.0	48.0
Samoa	52.0	48.0
Albania	52.0	48.0
Singapore	51.5	48.5
Historical avg	51.0	49.0

Newborns, by gender (%)

Countries with the highest gender ratios
(number of boys born for every 100 girls)*

There are

115
boys
for every
100
girls

born in China

In some regions, this is as high as 143 (Jiangxi), 142 (Henan) and 138 (Anhui)

It is estimated that there are up to

60 million

'missing girls' in China, caused by a mixture of government policy and cultural influences.

China 115 · Armenia 113 · Azerb. 113 · India 111 · Vietnam 110
Pakistan 109 · Uzbek. 108 · Georgia 108 · Papua NG 108 · Samoa 108
Albania 108 · Singapore 107 · Historical avg 105

Source: World Bank

Comparison

4. 10–20 datapoints, %

Percentage who believe that parts of neighbouring countries 'really belong to us' (among NATO members, 2020)

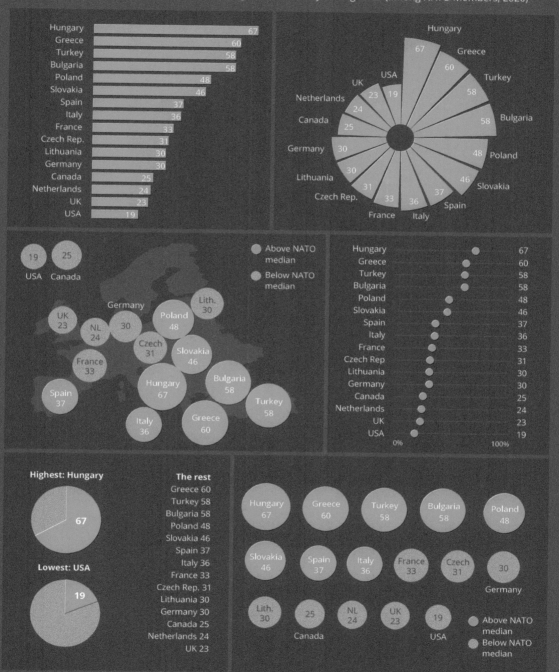

Source: Pew Research Center, February 2020, 'NATO Seen Favorably Across Member States'

Comparison

5. Many categories, two variables

Graduate population (%) in selected European countries and their capital cities

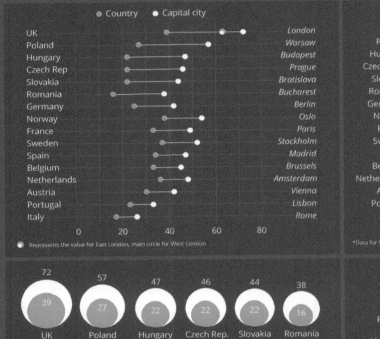

● Country   ● Capital city

UK	London
Poland	Warsaw
Hungary	Budapest
Czech Rep	Prague
Slovakia	Bratislava
Romania	Bucharest
Germany	Berlin
Norway	Oslo
France	Paris
Sweden	Stockholm
Spain	Madrid
Belgium	Brussels
Netherlands	Amsterdam
Austria	Vienna
Portugal	Lisbon
Italy	Rome

○ Represents the value for East London, main circle for West London

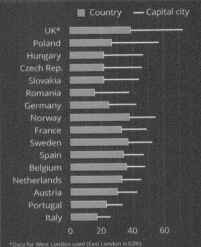

■ Country   — Capital city

UK*, Poland, Hungary, Czech Rep., Slovakia, Romania, Germany, Norway, France, Sweden, Spain, Belgium, Netherlands, Austria, Portugal, Italy

*Data for West London used (East London is 63%)

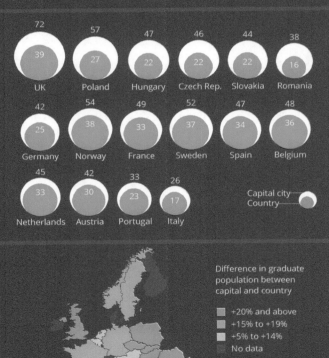

	Country	Capital
UK	72	39
Poland	57	27
Hungary	47	22
Czech Rep.	46	22
Slovakia	44	22
Romania	38	16
Germany	42	25
Norway	54	38
France	49	33
Sweden	52	37
Spain	47	34
Belgium	48	36
Netherlands	45	33
Austria	42	30
Portugal	33	23
Italy	26	17

Capital city — / Country —

Difference in graduate population between capital and country

■ +20% and above
■ +15% to +19%
■ +5% to +14%
■ No data

	Country	Capital	Difference
UK*	39	72	+33
Poland	27	57	+30
Hungary	22	47	+25
Czech Rep.	22	46	+24
Slovakia	22	44	+22
Romania	16	38	+22
Germany	25	42	+17
Norway	38	54	+16
France	33	49	+16
Sweden	37	52	+15
Spain	34	47	+13
Belgium	36	48	+12
N'lands	33	45	+12
Austria	30	42	+12
Portugal	23	33	+10
Italy	17	26	+9

*Data for W. London used for UK

Source: Eurostat

Comparison

6. Many categories, many variables

Selected food exports for USA, China, France, Germany and the Netherlands, 2018

Percentage of global export market

	Potatoes	Onions	Cucumbers	Tomatoes	Mushrooms	Peppers	Carrots	Cheese	Eggs
USA	5	7	2	3	2	4	9	5	5
China	6	14	2	2	10	1	14	<1	4
France	15	2	1	4	2	1	3	11	1
Germany	9	1	1	<1	2	<1	3	14	7
Netherlands	18	19	21	20	15	20	16	13	23

● Top exporter among the five countries

Percentage of global export market

	Potatoes	Onions	Cucumbers	Tomatoes	Mushrooms	Peppers	Carrots	Cheese	Eggs
USA	5	7	2	3	2	4	9	5	5
China	6	14	2	2	10	1	14	<1	4
France	15	2	1	4	2	1	3	11	1
Germany	9	1	1	<1	2	<1	3	14	7
Netherlands	18	19	21	20	15	20	16	13	23

Percentage of global export market

	Potatoes	Onions	Cucumbers	Tomatoes	Mushr'ms	Peppers	Carrots	Cheese	Eggs
USA									
China									
France									
Germany								14	
Netherlands	18	19	21	20	15	20	16		23

■ Top exporter among the five countries

Sources: CIA World Factbook, Tridge, worldstopexports.com

Comparison

7. Many countries, many variables

Social attitudes in selected European countries (2018)

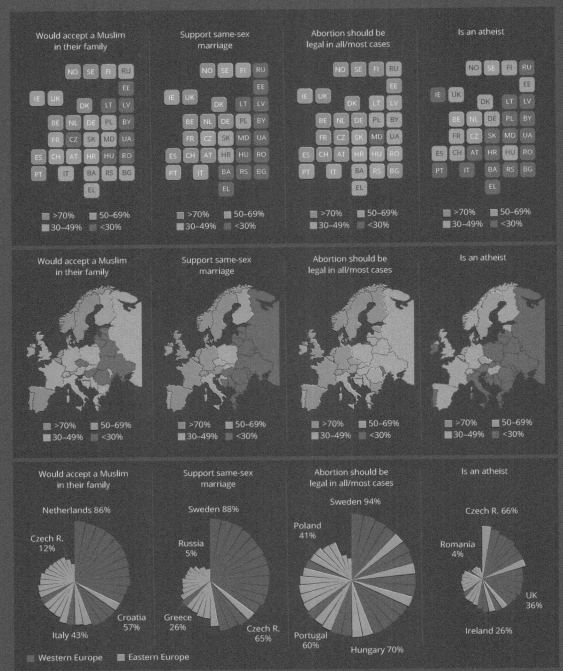

Would accept a Muslim in their family

>70% 50–69%
30–49% <30%

Support same-sex marriage

>70% 50–69%
30–49% <30%

Abortion should be legal in all/most cases

>70% 50–69%
30–49% <30%

Is an atheist

>70% 50–69%
30–49% <30%

Would accept a Muslim in their family

>70% 50–69%
30–49% <30%

Support same-sex marriage

>70% 50–69%
30–49% <30%

Abortion should be legal in all/most cases

>70% 50–69%
30–49% <30%

Is an atheist

>70% 50–69%
30–49% <30%

Would accept a Muslim in their family

Netherlands 86%

Czech R. 12%

Italy 43%

Croatia 57%

Support same-sex marriage

Sweden 88%

Russia 5%

Greece 26%

Czech R. 65%

Abortion should be legal in all/most cases

Sweden 94%

Poland 41%

Portugal 60%

Hungary 70%

Is an atheist

Czech R. 66%

Romania 4%

UK 36%

Ireland 26%

■ Western Europe ■ Eastern Europe

304

Would accept a Muslim in their family (%)

Nor. 82, Swe. 80, Fin. 66, Russia 34, Est., Irel. 60, UK 53, Den. 81, Lith., Lat., Bela., NL, Belg. 77, 86, Germ. 55, Pol., Ukr., Spain, Port. 74, 66, Swit., Aust., Cz. 57, Slvk., Hn., Ml., Bul., 70, Fra., Italy 43, Cro., Bos. 31, Rm. 43, 32, Gre., Serb.

Support same-sex marriage (%)

Irel. 66, UK 77, Nor. 72, Swe. 88, Fin. 64, Russia, Est. 23, Lat., NL 82, Den. 86, 86, Lith. 32, Pol., Bela., Ukr., Belg., Spain 77, Germ. 73, Swit., 65, Slvk., Ml., Port. 59, Fra., 72, Cz. 31, Hn., Rm., Bul., Italy 59, Aust., Cro. 26, Bos., Serb., Gre.

Abortion should be legal in all/most cases (%)

Irel. 66, UK 81, Nor. 81, Swe. 94, Fin. 87, Est., Russia 36, Den. 92, Pol. 41, Lith. 55, Lat. 42, Bela., Belg. 84, NL 84, Germ. 76, Ukr., Ml., Rm., Spain 72, 81, Swit., Slvk. 84, Hun., 58, 80, Fra. 60, Aust., Cz. 60, Serb., Port., Italy 65, Cro. 47, Bos. 45, Gre., Bul.

Is an atheist (%)

Irel. 26, UK 36, Nor. 47, Swe. 60, Fin. 37, Est. 45, Den. 46, Pol., Lith., Lat., Russia, NL, Germ., Slvk., Bela., Belg. 54, 53, 36, 66, Bos., Ukr., Spain 37, Swit. 29, Cz., Cro., Ml., Rm., Port. 31, Fra., Aust., Ser., Hn., Bulg., Italy, Gre.

■ Western Europe   ■ Eastern Europe

Would accept a Muslim in their family

Netherlands, Norway, Denmark, Sweden, Belgium, Spain, Portugal, Finland, France, Ireland, Switzerland, Croatia, Germany, Austria, UK, Slovakia, Italy, Serbia, Bosnia, Russia, Poland, Bulgaria, Greece, Moldova, Romania, Estonia, Ukraine, Hungary, Latvia, Georgia, Lithuania, Belarus, Czech R., Armenia
40   80

Support same-sex marriage

Sweden, Netherlands, Denmark, Belgium, Spain, UK, Switzerland, Germany, France, Norway, Austria, Ireland, Czech R., Finland, Portugal, Italy, Slovakia, Poland, Croatia, Hungary, Greece, Romania, Estonia, Bulgaria, Latvia, Belarus, Bosnia, Serbia, Lithuania, Ukraine, Russia, Moldova, Georgia, Armenia
40   80

Abortion should be legal in all/most cases

Sweden, Denmark, Finland, Netherlands, Belgium, Czech R., UK, France, Norway, Estonia, Bulgaria, Germany, Switzerland, Austria, Spain, Slovakia, Hungary, Ireland, Italy, Serbia, Portugal, Croatia, Romania, Armenia, Latvia, Lithuania, Bosnia, Greece, Belarus, Poland, Russia, Ukraine, Moldova, Georgia
40   80

Is an atheist

Czech R., Sweden, Belgium, Netherlands, Norway, Denmark, Estonia, Finland, France, UK, Germany, Switzerland, Spain, Hungary, Austria, Slovakia, Ireland, Italy, Bulgaria, Latvia, Russia, Portugal, Lithuania, Serbia, Croatia, Belarus, Ukraine, Poland, Greece, Romania, Armenia, Bosnia, Moldova, Georgia
40   80

■ Western Europe   ■ Eastern Europe

Source: Pew Research Center. Some countries omitted in maps 1, 2 and 4.

Comparison

8. Margin of error

Deaths from conflict in selected countries (2011–15)

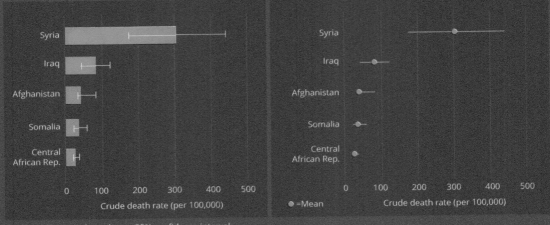

Syria
Iraq
Afghanistan
Somalia
Central African Rep.

0   100   200   300   400   500

Crude death rate (per 100,000)

● =Mean

Source: WHO, error bars show a 95% confidence interval

9. Off-the-charts

Size of stars (in solar radii)

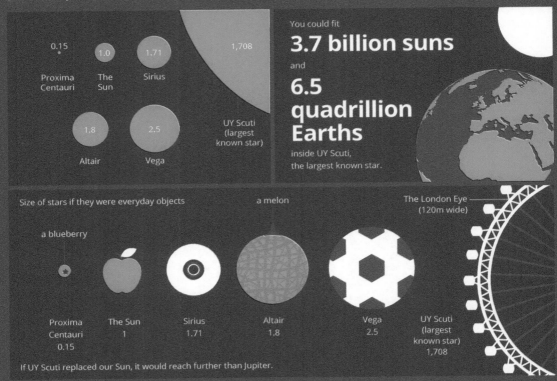

0.15
Proxima Centauri

1.0
The Sun

1.71
Sirius

1.8
Altair

2.5
Vega

1,708
UY Scuti (largest known star)

You could fit

3.7 billion suns

and

6.5 quadrillion Earths

inside UY Scuti, the largest known star.

Size of stars if they were everyday objects

a melon

a blueberry

The London Eye (120m wide)

Proxima Centauri 0.15

The Sun 1

Sirius 1.71

Altair 1.8

Vega 2.5

UY Scuti (largest known star) 1,708

If UY Scuti replaced our Sun, it would reach further than Jupiter.

Source: NASA

Comparison

10. Too many datapoints

Main language spoken (other than English and Welsh): England and Wales Census, 2011*

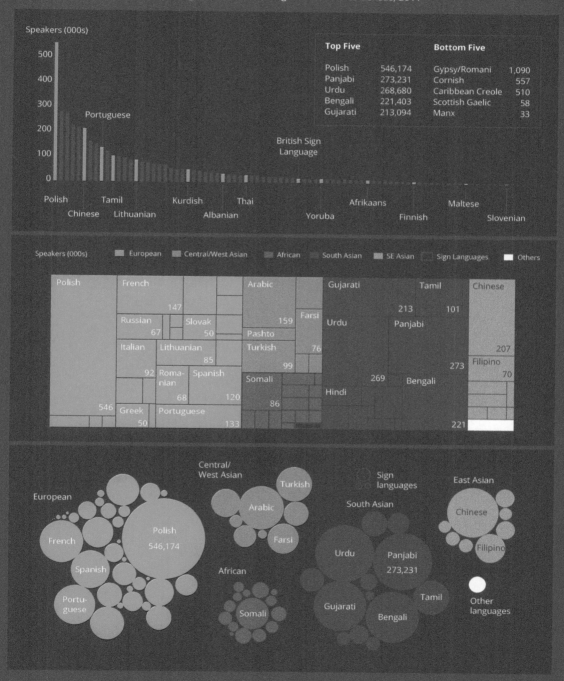

Speakers (000s)

	Top Five		Bottom Five	
	Polish	546,174	Gypsy/Romani	1,090
	Panjabi	273,231	Cornish	557
	Urdu	268,680	Caribbean Creole	510
	Bengali	221,403	Scottish Gaelic	58
	Gujarati	213,094	Manx	33

*49.8 million residents state that their main language is English. Of the 562,000 Welsh speakers, it is unknown how many of these use Welsh as their main language. Source: ONS/UK Census 2011

307

Comparison
11. Miscellaneous

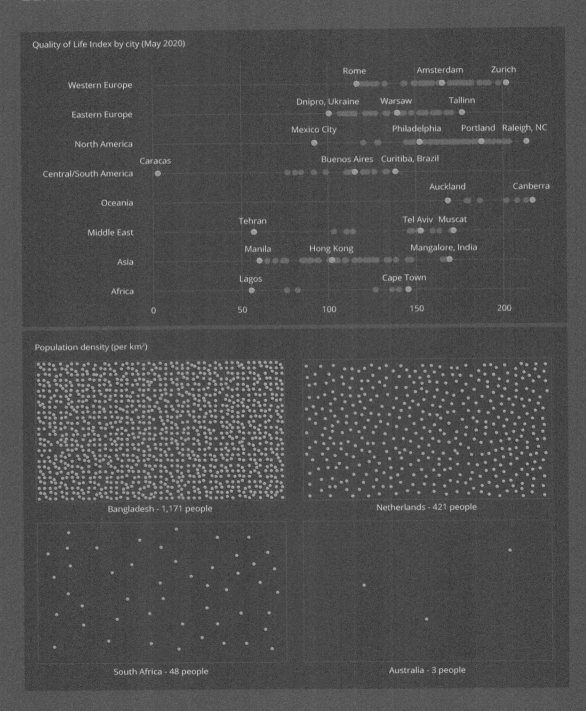

Quality of Life Index by city (May 2020)

Western Europe	Rome, Amsterdam, Zurich
Eastern Europe	Dnipro, Ukraine, Warsaw, Tallinn
North America	Mexico City, Philadelphia, Portland, Raleigh, NC
Central/South America	Caracas, Buenos Aires, Curitiba, Brazil
Oceania	Auckland, Canberra
Middle East	Tehran, Tel Aviv, Muscat
Asia	Manila, Hong Kong, Mangalore, India
Africa	Lagos, Cape Town

Population density (per km²)

Bangladesh - 1,171 people

Netherlands - 421 people

South Africa - 48 people

Australia - 3 people

What percentage of the population do you think are Muslim?

Average estimate in each country

Reality

Country	Average estimate	Reality
Canada	22	3
France	28	9
Germany	21	4
NL	20	5
Spain	19	4
Sweden	23	8
Italy	19	5
Australia	17	3
US	14	1
UK	17	4
Poland	5	<1
Japan	4	<1

If US states were countries (by GDP), 2019

Poland
Azerbaijan
Uruguay
Ireland
Ethiopia
Uganda
Thailand
Bulgaria
Vietnam
Sri Lanka
Bolivia
Serbia
South Africa
Iran
Canada
Myanmar
Hungary
Algeria
Israel
Morocco
Qatar
The Netherlands
Malaysia
Turkey
Saudi Arabia
Pakistan
Switzerland
Venezuela
Austria
India
Kazakhstan
Denmark
Oman
Belgium
Singapore
Slovakia
New Zealand
Kuwait
Hong Kong
Greece
Sweden
Romania
Ecuador
Peru
Taiwan
Kenya
Brazil
Finland
Lebanon
Mexico

GDP/GSP > $3 trillion $1–$2.9 trillion $500Bn–$999Bn $250Bn–$499Bn   <$250Bn

Student debt in selected countries

Percentage of students with debt

Country	Percentage
England	94
Australia	78
New Zealand	72
Canada	60
Japan	37

Average amount of debt (in GDP)

£40,452
£8,528
£19,535
£14,342
£23,008

Sources: City Quality of Life by city from Numbeo (crowd-sourced) (taken 15th May 2020), population density from UN Statistics Division, US states GDP from BEA. estimate of Muslim population from Ipsos MORI 'Perils of Perception' (2018) student debt from OECD and UCU.

Composition

1. Percentage, small dataset, one point in time

Percentage of overweight and obese adults in the USA (2016)

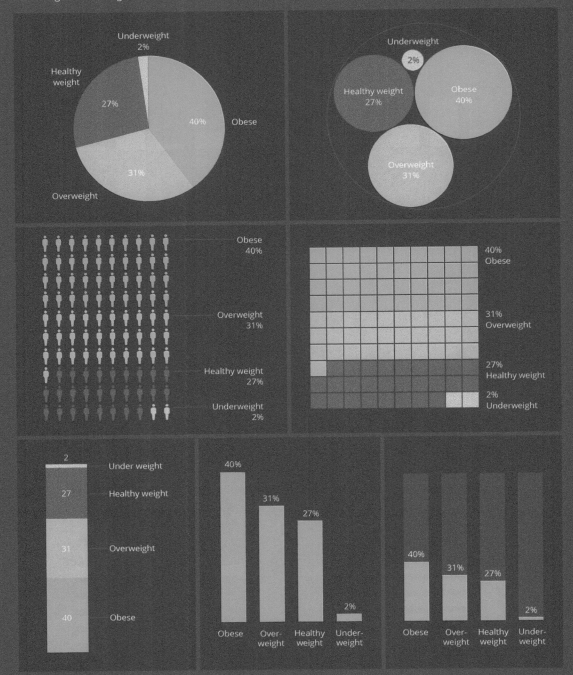

Source: CDC, https://www.cdc.gov/nchs/fastats/obesity-overweight.htm

Composition

2. Percentage, comparing against others

Percentage of daily energy intake by food group (selected countries, 2013)

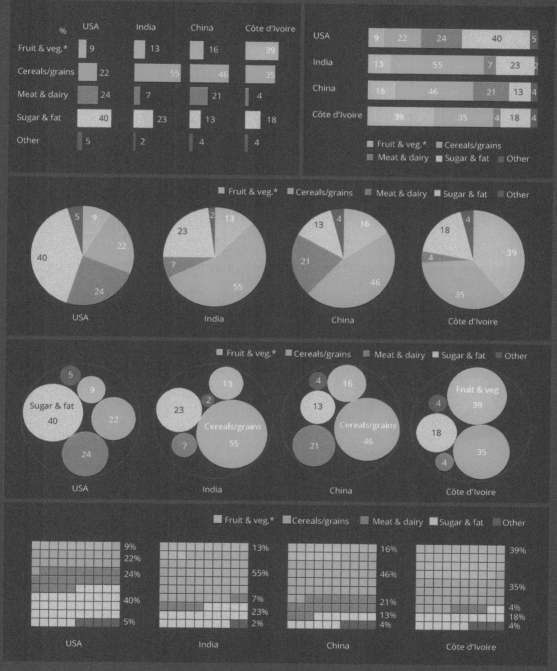

Source: UN FAO via Our World in Data

* Includes starchy roots

Composition

3. Nested categories

Nationality of people living in Qatar, 2019 (thousands, estimated)

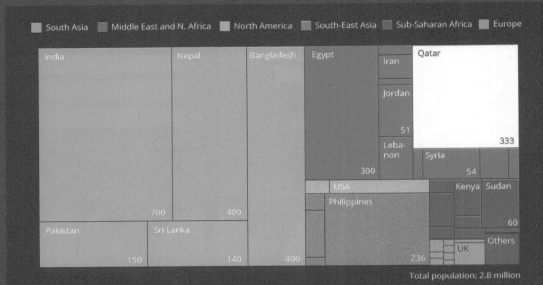

Total population: 2.8 million

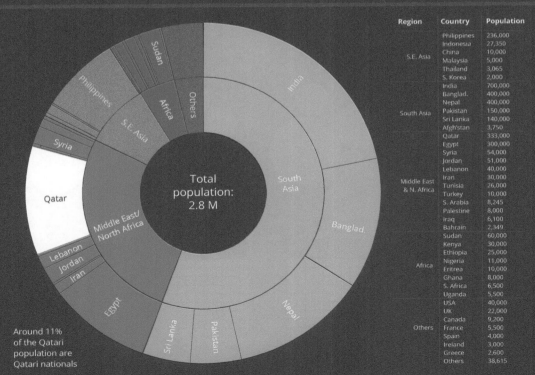

Total population: 2.8 M

Around 11% of the Qatari population are Qatari nationals

Region	Country	Population
S.E. Asia	Philippines	236,000
	Indonesia	27,350
	China	10,000
	Malaysia	5,000
	Thailand	3,065
	S. Korea	2,000
South Asia	India	700,000
	Banglad.	400,000
	Nepal	400,000
	Pakistan	150,000
	Sri Lanka	140,000
	Afgh'stan	3,750
Middle East & N. Africa	Qatar	333,000
	Egypt	300,000
	Syria	54,000
	Jordan	51,000
	Lebanon	40,000
	Iran	30,000
	Tunisia	26,000
	Turkey	10,000
	S. Arabia	8,245
	Palestine	8,000
	Iraq	6,100
	Bahrain	2,349
Africa	Sudan	60,000
	Kenya	30,000
	Ethiopia	25,000
	Nigeria	11,000
	Eritrea	10,000
	Ghana	8,000
	S. Africa	6,500
	Uganda	5,500
Others	USA	40,000
	UK	22,000
	Canada	9,200
	France	5,500
	Spain	4,000
	Ireland	3,000
	Greece	2,600
	Others	38,615

Source: Priya DSouza Communications

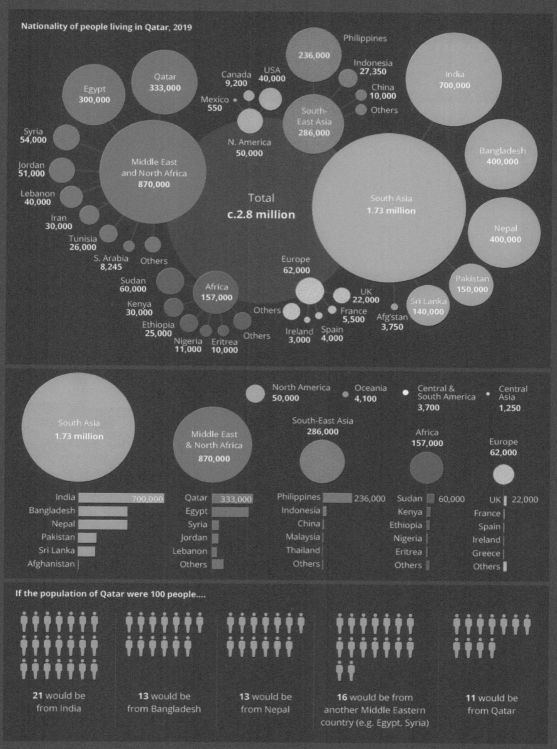

Nationality of people living in Qatar, 2019

Philippines 236,000
Indonesia 27,350
China 10,000
Others
India 700,000

Canada 9,200
USA 40,000
Mexico 550

Egypt 300,000
Qatar 333,000

South-East Asia 286,000

N. America 50,000

Bangladesh 400,000

Syria 54,000
Jordan 51,000
Lebanon 40,000
Iran 30,000
Tunisia 26,000
S. Arabia 8,245

Middle East and North Africa 870,000

Total c.2.8 million

South Asia 1.73 million

Nepal 400,000

Others

Africa 157,000

Europe 62,000

Sudan 60,000
Kenya 30,000
Ethiopia 25,000
Nigeria 11,000
Eritrea 10,000

Others

UK 22,000
France 5,500
Afg'stan 3,750

Pakistan 150,000

Sri Lanka 140,000

Others
Ireland 3,000
Spain 4,000

South Asia 1.73 million

Middle East & North Africa 870,000

South-East Asia 286,000

North America 50,000
Oceania 4,100
Central & South America 3,700
Central Asia 1,250

Africa 157,000

Europe 62,000

	South Asia		Middle East & N. Africa		South-East Asia		Africa		Europe	
India	700,000	Qatar	333,000	Philippines	236,000	Sudan	60,000	UK	22,000
Bangladesh		Egypt		Indonesia		Kenya		France	
Nepal		Syria		China		Ethiopia		Spain	
Pakistan		Jordan		Malaysia		Nigeria		Ireland	
Sri Lanka		Lebanon		Thailand		Eritrea		Greece	
Afghanistan		Others		Others		Others		Others	

If the population of Qatar were 100 people....

21 would be from India

13 would be from Bangladesh

13 would be from Nepal

16 would be from another Middle Eastern country (e.g. Egypt, Syria)

11 would be from Qatar

Source: Priya DSouza Communications

313

Composition
4. Too many datapoints

Composition of the human body (mass, kg, based on a 70kg adult human)

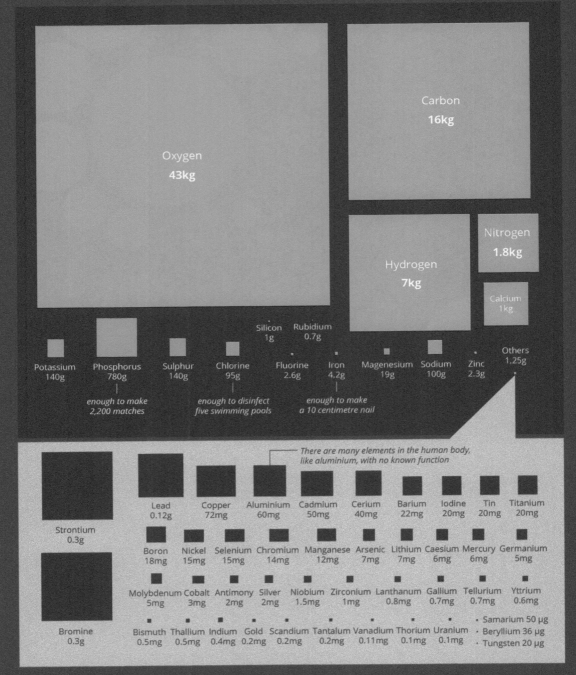

Oxygen
43kg

Carbon
16kg

Hydrogen
7kg

Nitrogen
1.8kg

Calcium
1kg

Silicon 1g

Rubidium 0.7g

Others
1.25g

Potassium 140g
Phosphorus 780g
Sulphur 140g
Chlorine 95g
Fluorine 2.6g
Iron 4.2g
Magenesium 19g
Sodium 100g
Zinc 2.3g

enough to make 2,200 matches

enough to disinfect five swimming pools

enough to make a 10 centimetre nail

There are many elements in the human body, like aluminium, with no known function

Strontium 0.3g

Lead 0.12g
Copper 72mg
Aluminium 60mg
Cadmium 50mg
Cerium 40mg
Barium 22mg
Iodine 20mg
Tin 20mg
Titanium 20mg

Boron 18mg
Nickel 15mg
Selenium 15mg
Chromium 14mg
Manganese 12mg
Arsenic 7mg
Lithium 7mg
Caesium 6mg
Mercury 6mg
Germanium 5mg

Molybdenum 5mg
Cobalt 3mg
Antimony 2mg
Silver 2mg
Niobium 1.5mg
Zirconium 1mg
Lanthanum 0.8mg
Gallium 0.7mg
Tellurium 0.7mg
Yttrium 0.6mg

Bromine 0.3g

Bismuth 0.5mg
Thallium 0.5mg
Indium 0.4mg
Gold 0.2mg
Scandium 0.2mg
Tantalum 0.2mg
Vanadium 0.11mg
Thorium 0.1mg
Uranium 0.1mg

- Samarium 50 µg
- Beryllium 36 µg
- Tungsten 20 µg

Source: Emsley, John, The Elements, 3rd edn, Clarendon Press, Oxford, 1998 via ThoughtCo.com

Composition
5. Miscellaneous

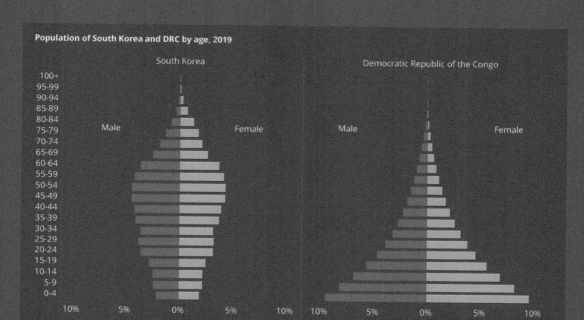

Population of South Korea and DRC by age, 2019

South Korea

Democratic Republic of the Congo

100+
95-99
90-94
85-89
80-84
75-79
70-74
65-69
60-64
55-59
50-54
45-49
40-44
35-39
30-34
25-29
20-24
15-19
10-14
5-9
0-4

Male — Female

10% 5% 0% 5% 10%

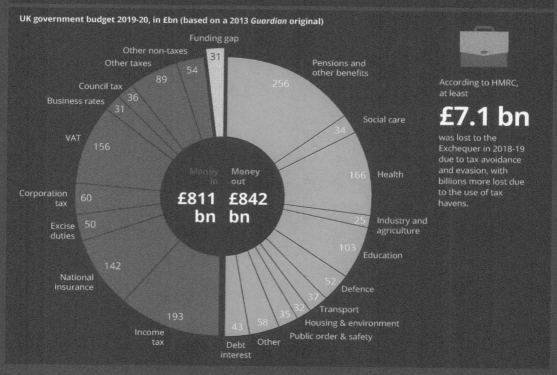

UK government budget 2019-20, in £bn (based on a 2013 *Guardian* original)

Funding gap 31

Other non-taxes 54
Other taxes 89
Council tax 36
Business rates 31

VAT 156

Corporation tax 60

Excise duties 50

National insurance 142

Income tax 193

Debt interest 43
Other 58
Public order & safety 35
Housing & environment 32
Transport 37
Defence 52
Education 103
Industry and agriculture 25
Health 166
Social care 34
Pensions and other benefits 256

Money in £811 bn   **Money out £842 bn**

According to HMRC, at least

£7.1 bn

was lost to the Exchequer in 2018-19 due to tax avoidance and evasion, with billions more lost due to the use of tax havens.

Sources: Population pyramid data from PopulationPyramid.net, UK Budget data from gov.uk, original design concept by the *Guardian*.

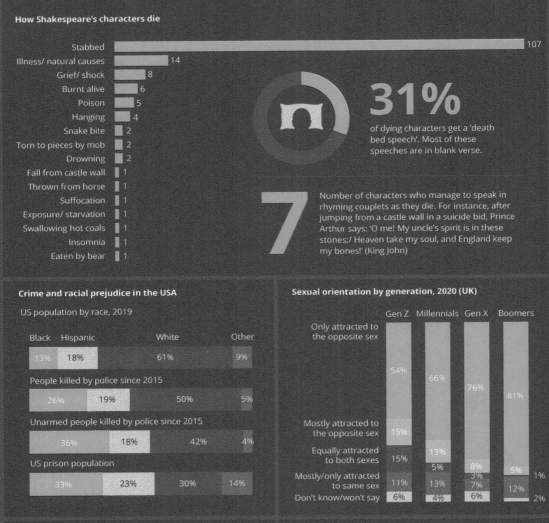

How Shakespeare's characters die

Stabbed	107
Illness/ natural causes	14
Grief/ shock	8
Burnt alive	6
Poison	5
Hanging	4
Snake bite	2
Torn to pieces by mob	2
Drowning	2
Fall from castle wall	1
Thrown from horse	1
Suffocation	1
Exposure/ starvation	1
Swallowing hot coals	1
Insomnia	1
Eaten by bear	1

31% of dying characters get a 'death bed speech'. Most of these speeches are in blank verse.

7 Number of characters who manage to speak in rhyming couplets as they die. For instance, after jumping from a castle wall in a suicide bid, Prince Arthur says: 'O me! My uncle's spirit is in these stones;/ Heaven take my soul, and England keep my bones!' (King John)

Crime and racial prejudice in the USA

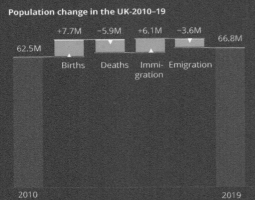

US population by race, 2019

Black	Hispanic	White	Other
13%	18%	61%	9%

People killed by police since 2015

| 26% | 19% | 50% | 5% |

Unarmed people killed by police since 2015

| 36% | 18% | 42% | 4% |

US prison population

| 33% | 23% | 30% | 14% |

Sexual orientation by generation, 2020 (UK)

	Gen Z	Millennials	Gen X	Boomers
Only attracted to the opposite sex	54%	66%	76%	81%
Mostly attracted to the opposite sex	15%			
Equally attracted to both sexes	15%	13%	8%	5%
		5%	3%	1%
Mostly/only attracted to same sex	11%	13%	7%	12%
Don't know/won't say	6%	4%	6%	2%

Population change in the UK-2010–19

62.5M
+7.7M Births
−5.9M Deaths
+6.1M Immi-gration
−3.6M Emigration
66.8M

2010   2019

Percentage of people who have paid a bribe this year to access public services (2017)

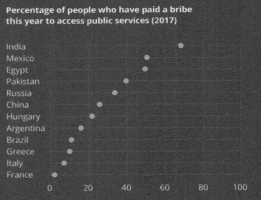

India
Mexico
Egypt
Pakistan
Russia
China
Hungary
Argentina
Brazil
Greece
Italy
France

0   20   40   60   80   100

Sources: Shakespeare data from Adam Frost, US ethnicity and crime data from *Washington Post* and Pew Research, sexual orientation data from Ipsos MORI UK, population change data from ONS UK, bribery data from Transparency International via Our World in Data

Distribution

1. A single distribution

Film noir movies (1940–2020)

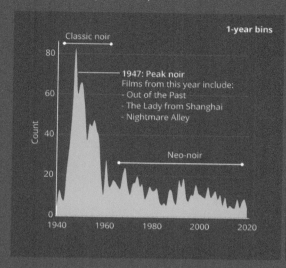

1-year bins

Classic noir

1947: Peak noir
Films from this year include:
- Out of the Past
- The Lady from Shanghai
- Nightmare Alley

Neo-noir

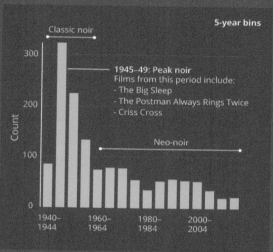

5-year bins

Classic noir

1945–49: Peak noir
Films from this period include:
- The Big Sleep
- The Postman Always Rings Twice
- Criss Cross

Neo-noir

2. Comparing two distributions

Age of leading men and leading women in 200 key romantic movies (1905–2015)

Female
Male

Men are on average seven years older than women in romantic movies.

Age of male actors

Bill Murray in Lost in Translation

Age of female actors

Scarlett Johansson in Lost in Translation

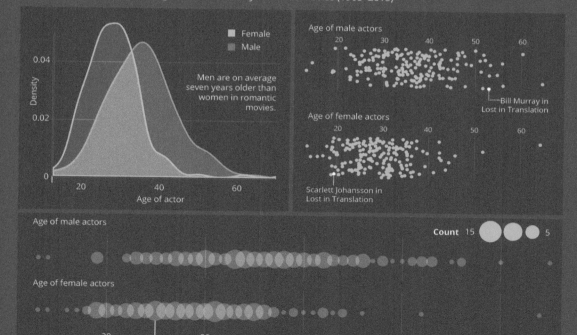

Age of male actors

Count 15 ⬤⬤⬤ 5

Age of female actors

A total of 14 female actors in our 200 romantic films were 25 years old, including Audrey Hepburn in Sabrina (opposite the 55-year-old Humphrey Bogart) and Kim Novak in Vertigo (opposite the 50-year-old James Stewart).

Source: Adam Frost while researching British Film Institute graphics.
Data here: https://bit.ly/noir-films-all and here: https://bit.ly/love-films-all

Distribution

3. Comparing many distributions

Duration of hit songs (2000–17)

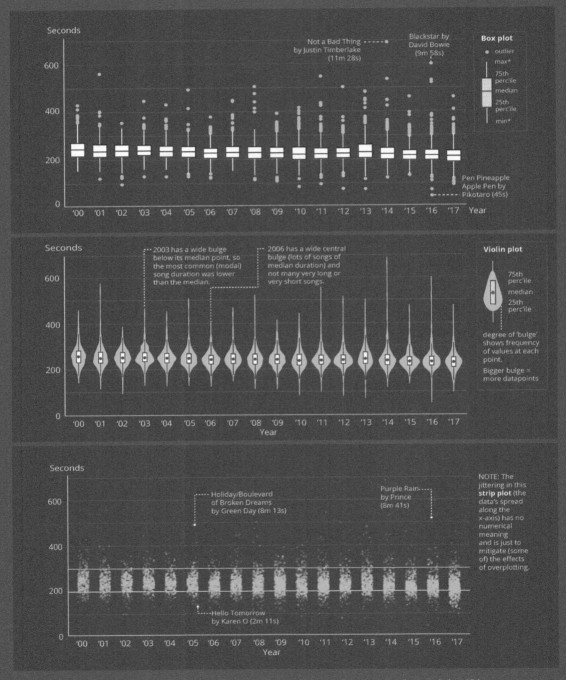

*Not quite the min and max in this case. For example, min = smallest value within 1.5 x interquartile range below 25th percentile. This variant of a box plot is often used so that outliers don't skew the 'whiskers' at either end of the plot.

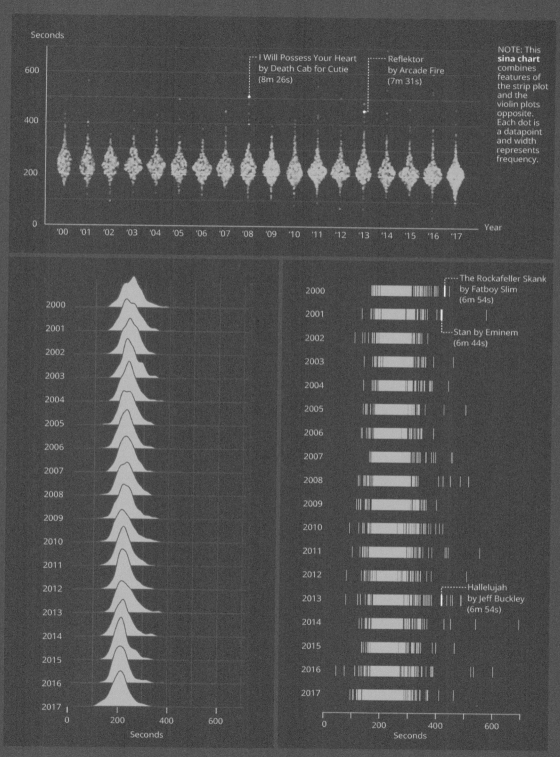

Seconds

600

400

200

0

I Will Possess Your Heart
by Death Cab for Cutie
(8m 26s)

Reflektor
by Arcade Fire
(7m 31s)

NOTE: This
sina chart
combines
features of
the strip plot
and the
violin plots
opposite.
Each dot is
a datapoint
and width
represents
frequency.

'00 '01 '02 '03 '04 '05 '06 '07 '08 '09 '10 '11 '12 '13 '14 '15 '16 '17   Year

2000
2001
2002
2003
2004
2005
2006
2007
2008
2009
2010
2011
2012
2013
2014
2015
2016
2017

0   200   400   600
Seconds

2000
2001
2002
2003
2004
2005
2006
2007
2008
2009
2010
2011
2012
2013
2014
2015
2016
2017

The Rockafeller Skank
by Fatboy Slim
(6m 54s)

Stan by Eminem
(6m 44s)

Hallelujah
by Jeff Buckley
(6m 54s)

0   200   400   600
Seconds

Source: Michael Tauberg, https://medium.com/@michaeltauberg/music-and-our-attention-spans-are-getting-shorter-8be37b5c2d67

Correlation

1. Comparing countries or categories

Age at first marrriage and number of babies per woman in selected African countries (2005)

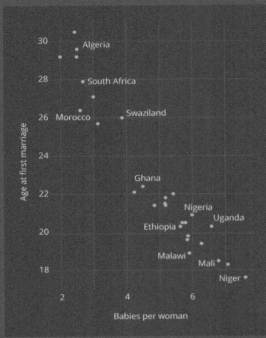

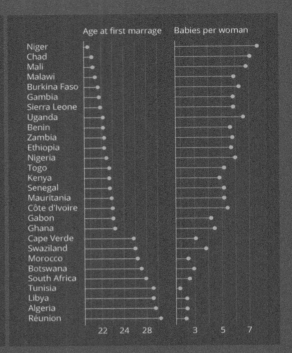

Sources: World Bank, Gapminder Foundation

2. Change over time

Percentage of 25–34-year-olds who own a home v. number of buy-to-let mortgages (UK, 2000–17)

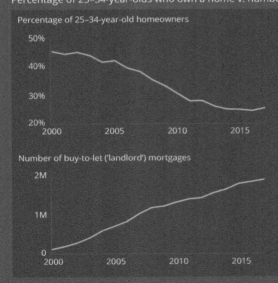

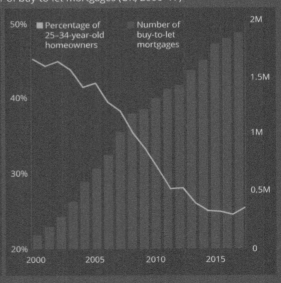

Source: Resolution Foundation, Game of Homes report

Correlation

1. Comparing countries or categories

Age at first marrriage and number of babies per woman in selected African countries (2005)

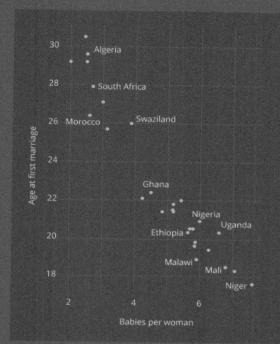

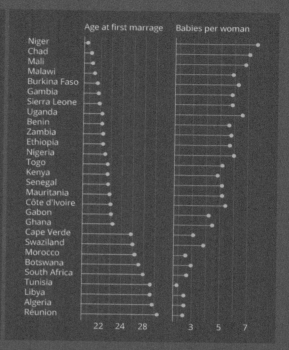

Sources: World Bank, Gapminder Foundation

2. Change over time

Percentage of 25–34-year-olds who own a home v. number of buy-to-let mortgages (UK, 2000–17)

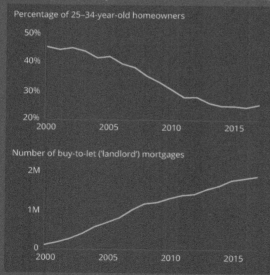

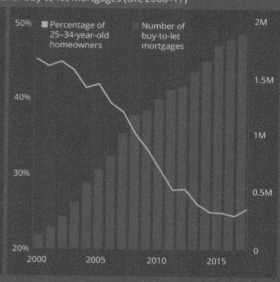

Source: Resolution Foundation, Game of Homes report

Geospatial

1. 10 datapoints or fewer

Number of power cuts reported by businesses in a typical month (most recent year)*

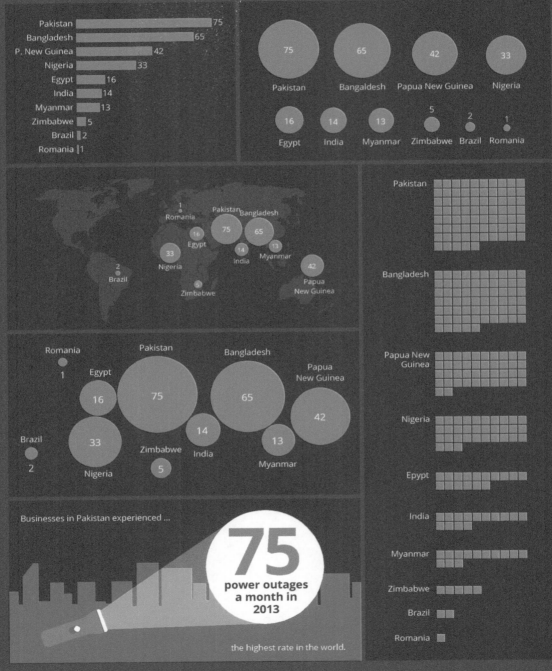

Pakistan	75
Bangladesh	65
P. New Guinea	42
Nigeria	33
Egypt	16
India	14
Myanmar	13
Zimbabwe	5
Brazil	2
Romania	1

Businesses in Pakistan experienced ...

75 power outages a month in 2013

the highest rate in the world.

Source: Our World in Data. The most recent year varies from 2009 for Brazil to 2016 for Zimbabwe.

2. One country or area, all regions

GDP per capita (in euros), UK and Ireland, by NUTS-3 region, 2014

Legend (map):
- < €5,000
- €5,000–€10,000
- €10,000–€15,000
- €15,000–€20,000
- €20,000–€30,000
- > €30,000

Headquarters of Apple, Boston Scientific, and other multinationals

Legend (hex map):
- < €5,000
- €5,000–€10,000
- €10,000–€15,000
- €15,000–€20,000
- €20,000–€30,000
- > €30,000

Top 3 richest regions
(GDP per capita)
1. City of London — €113,000
2. Dublin — €89,000
3. Westminster — €78,000

Bottom 3 regions
185. Shetland Islands — €1,200
186. Orkney Islands — €810
187. Western Isles — €750

Scotland

Northern Ireland

Ireland

Wales

England

Note: Hex maps like this work better when they are interactive

Legend (treemap):
- Scotland
- Wales
- England
- London
- N. Ireland
- Ireland

Edinburgh, 28   Aberdeen, 27

Tyneside

Leeds 31

Manchester

Birmingham

Cambs.   Suffolk

Herts. 45

Berks.

Bath 25

53

West Surrey

Tower Hamlets 41   City of London 113

Westminster 89

Richmond

Belfast

Dublin

Kerry & Cork 35   78

Numbers show GDP in €'000s

Geospatial
3. Global data, single point in time

Air passengers carried (in millions), by country (2018)*

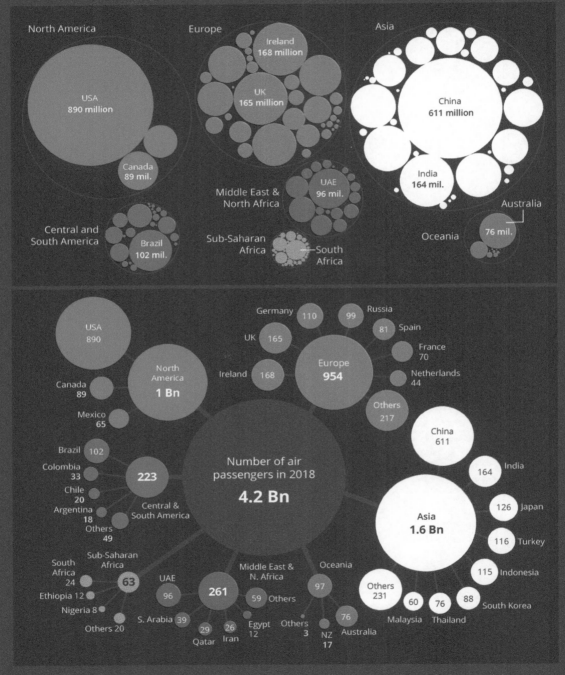

**Data missing for some countries, some countries use data from earlier than 2018. Dataset here: https://bit.ly/air_travel_data
Sources: World Bank - International Civil Aviation Organization, Civil Aviation Statistics of the World and ICAO staff estimates

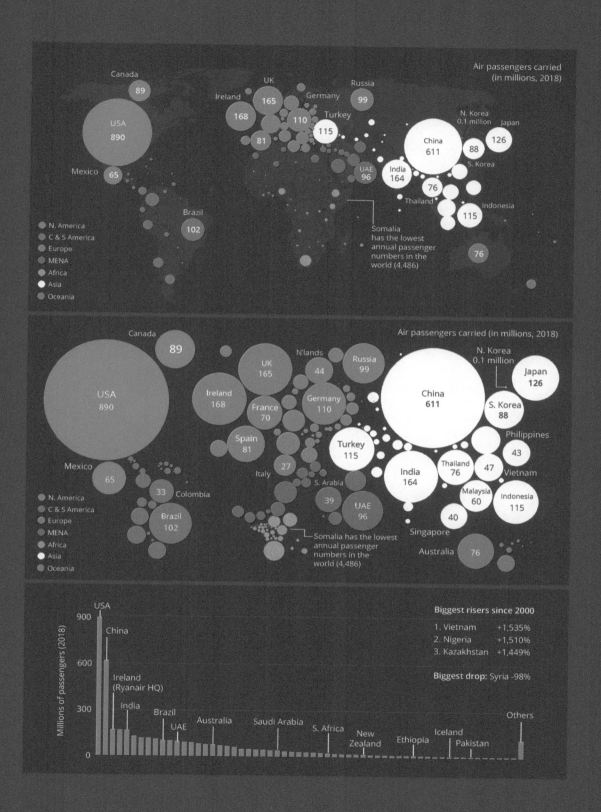

Air passengers carried
(in millions, 2018)

Canada 89

USA 890

Mexico 65

Ireland 168

UK 165

Germany 110

81

Russia 99

Turkey 115

UAE 96

India 164

N. Korea 0.1 million

China 611

88

S. Korea

Japan 126

Thailand 76

Indonesia 115

Brazil 102

Somalia
has the lowest
annual passenger
numbers in the
world (4,486)

76

- N. America
- C & S America
- Europe
- MENA
- Africa
- Asia
- Oceania

Air passengers carried (in millions, 2018)

Canada 89

USA 890

N'lands 44

UK 165

Russia 99

N. Korea
0.1 million

Japan 126

Ireland 168

France 70

Germany 110

China 611

S. Korea 88

Mexico 65

Spain 81

Italy 27

Turkey 115

India 164

Thailand 76

47

Philippines 43

Vietnam

Colombia 33

S. Arabia

39

UAE 96

Malaysia 60

Indonesia 115

Brazil 102

Somalia has the lowest
annual passenger
numbers in the
world (4,486)

40

Singapore

Australia 76

- N. America
- C & S America
- Europe
- MENA
- Africa
- Asia
- Oceania

USA

China

Ireland
(Ryanair HQ)

India

Brazil

UAE

Australia

Saudi Arabia

S. Africa

New
Zealand

Ethiopia

Iceland

Pakistan

Others

900

600

300

0

Millions of passengers (2018)

Biggest risers since 2000

1. Vietnam   +1,535%
2. Nigeria   +1,510%
3. Kazakhstan +1,449%

Biggest drop: Syria -98%

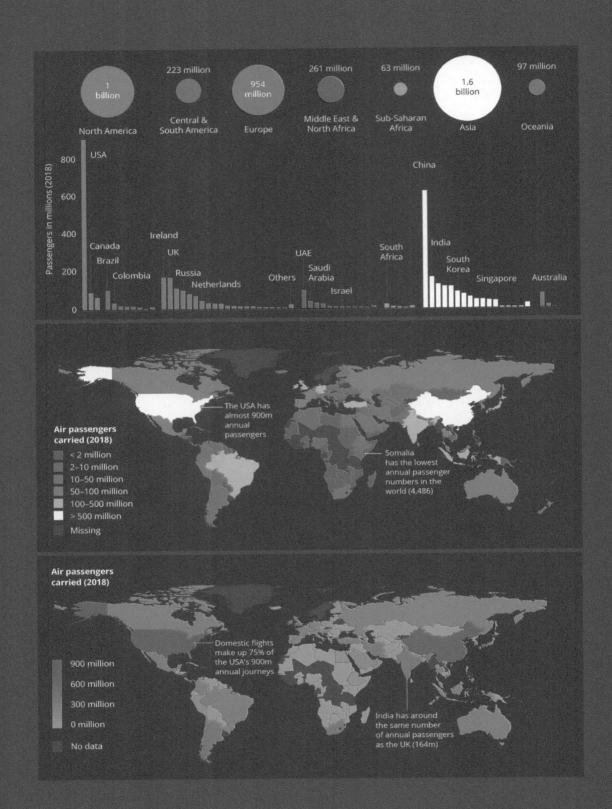

1 billion — North America

223 million — Central & South America

954 million — Europe

261 million — Middle East & North Africa

63 million — Sub-Saharan Africa

1.6 billion — Asia

97 million — Oceania

Passengers in millions (2018)

USA

China

Ireland

Canada

UK

Brazil

India

Colombia

Russia

South Korea

Netherlands

UAE

Saudi Arabia

South Africa

Others

Israel

Singapore

Australia

Air passengers carried (2018)

< 2 million
2–10 million
10–50 million
50–100 million
100–500 million
> 500 million
Missing

The USA has almost 900m annual passengers

Somalia has the lowest annual passenger numbers in the world (4,486)

Air passengers carried (2018)

900 million
600 million
300 million
0 million
No data

Domestic flights make up 75% of the USA's 900m annual journeys

India has around the same number of annual passengers as the UK (164m)

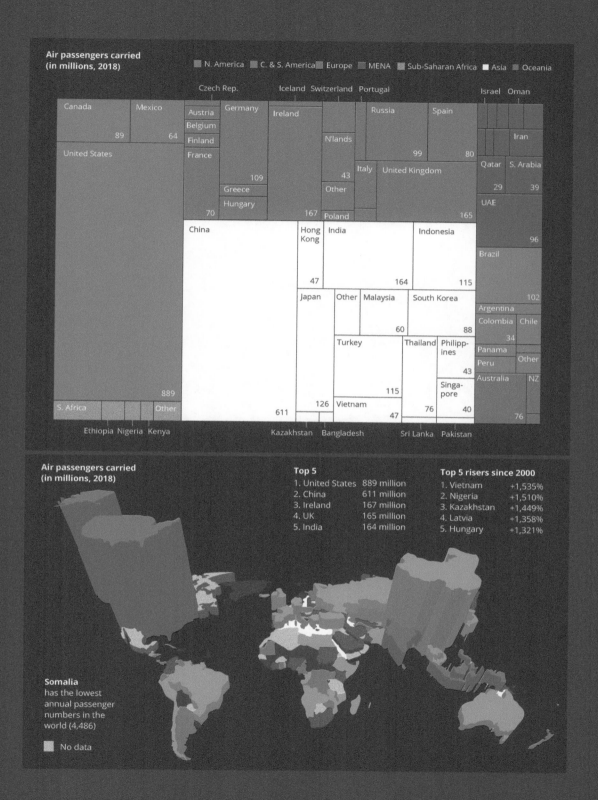

Air passengers carried (in millions, 2018)

Legend: N. America · C. & S. America · Europe · MENA · Sub-Saharan Africa · Asia · Oceania

Canada	89
Mexico	64
United States	889
Germany	109
Greece / Hungary	70
Ireland	167
N'lands	43
Russia	99
Spain	80
United Kingdom	165
Iran	96 (UAE)
Qatar	29
S. Arabia	39
Brazil	102
Argentina / Colombia / Chile	34
Australia	76
China	611
Hong Kong	47
India	164
Indonesia	115
Japan	126
Malaysia	60
South Korea	88
Turkey	115
Thailand	76
Philippines	43
Singapore	40
Vietnam	47

Labels: Czech Rep., Iceland, Switzerland, Portugal, Israel, Oman, Austria, Belgium, Finland, France, Italy, Other, Poland, Panama, Peru, Other, NZ, Other, Kazakhstan, Bangladesh, Sri Lanka, Pakistan, S. Africa, Ethiopia, Nigeria, Kenya

Air passengers carried (in millions, 2018)

Top 5
1. United States — 889 million
2. China — 611 million
3. Ireland — 167 million
4. UK — 165 million
5. India — 164 million

Top 5 risers since 2000
1. Vietnam — +1,535%
2. Nigeria — +1,510%
3. Kazakhstan — +1,449%
4. Latvia — +1,358%
5. Hungary — +1,321%

Somalia
has the lowest annual passenger numbers in the world (4,486)

No data

The shrinking of the Aral Sea

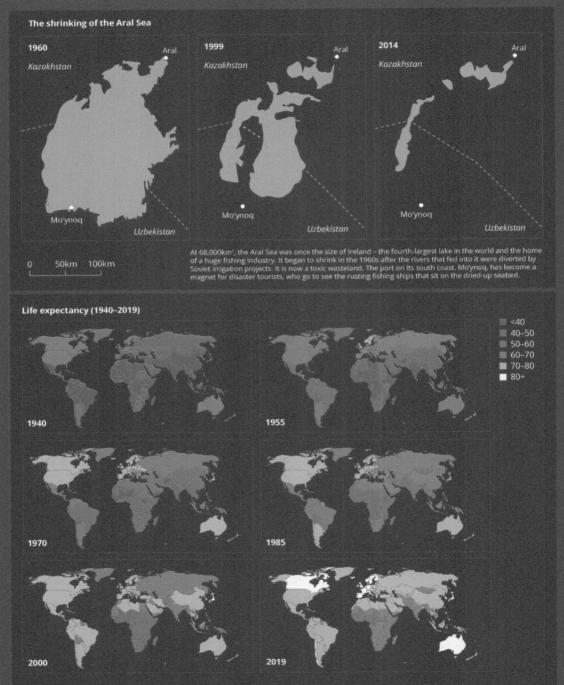

1960

Kazakhstan

Aral

Mo'ynoq

Uzbekistan

1999

Kazakhstan

Aral

Mo'ynoq

Uzbekistan

2014

Kazakhstan

Aral

Mo'ynoq

Uzbekistan

0   50km   100km

At 68,000km², the Aral Sea was once the size of Ireland – the fourth-largest lake in the world and the home of a huge fishing industry. It began to shrink in the 1960s after the rivers that fed into it were diverted by Soviet irrigation projects. It is now a toxic wasteland. The port on its south coast, Mo'ynoq, has become a magnet for disaster tourists, who go to see the rusting fishing ships that sit on the dried-up seabed.

Life expectancy (1940–2019)

- <40
- 40–50
- 50–60
- 60–70
- 70–80
- 80+

1940

1955

1970

1985

2000

2019

In 1940, the lowest life expectancy was **24.5** years of age in Sierra Leone. Today the lowest is **53.3** in the Central African Republic. The highest life expectancy in 1940 was **66.7** in Sweden. The highest today is **84.6** in Japan.

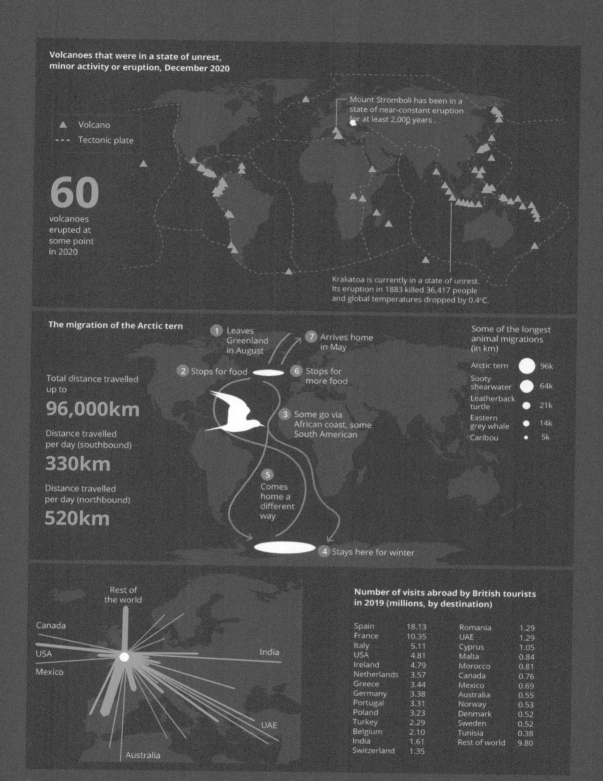

Volcanoes that were in a state of unrest, minor activity or eruption, December 2020

▲ Volcano

- - - Tectonic plate

60 volcanoes erupted at some point in 2020

Mount Stromboli has been in a state of near-constant eruption for at least 2,000 years .

Krakatoa is currently in a state of unrest. Its eruption in 1883 killed 36,417 people and global temperatures dropped by 0.4°C.

The migration of the Arctic tern

1. Leaves Greenland in August
2. Stops for food
3. Some go via African coast, some South American
4. Stays here for winter
5. Comes home a different way
6. Stops for more food
7. Arrives home in May

Total distance travelled up to
96,000km

Distance travelled per day (southbound)
330km

Distance travelled per day (northbound)
520km

Some of the longest animal migrations (in km)

Arctic tern	96k
Sooty shearwater	64k
Leatherback turtle	21k
Eastern grey whale	14k
Caribou	5k

Rest of the world

Canada

USA

Mexico

India

UAE

Australia

Number of visits abroad by British tourists in 2019 (millions, by destination)

Spain	18.13	Romania	1.29
France	10.35	UAE	1.29
Italy	5.11	Cyprus	1.05
USA	4.81	Malta	0.84
Ireland	4.79	Morocco	0.81
Netherlands	3.57	Canada	0.76
Greece	3.44	Mexico	0.69
Germany	3.38	Australia	0.55
Portugal	3.31	Norway	0.53
Poland	3.23	Denmark	0.52
Turkey	2.29	Sweden	0.52
Belgium	2.10	Tunisia	0.38
India	1.61	Rest of world	9.80
Switzerland	1.35		

Sources: Encyclopaedia Britannica (Aral Sea), Our World in Data, UN Population Division (Life expectancy), Volcano Discovery (volcano map)/ BBC Earth, Guardian Environment (Arctic tern), Office for National Statistics (outbound tourism data)

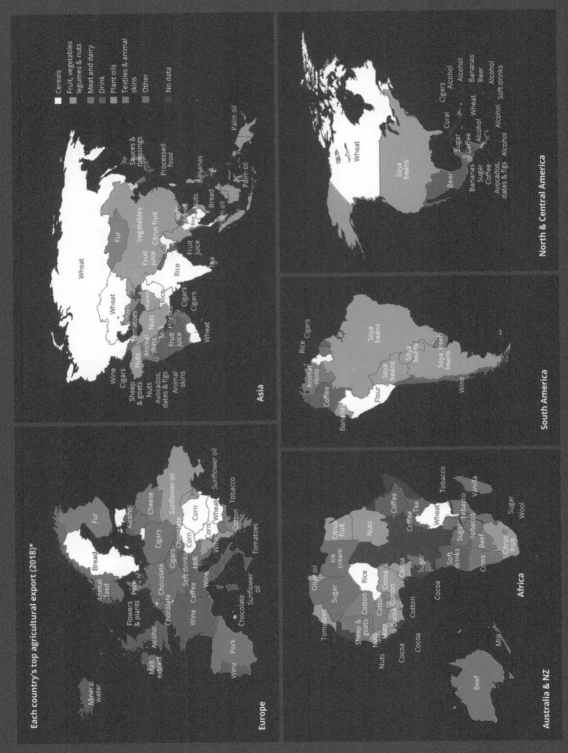

Each country's top agricultural export (2018)*

Legend:
- Cereals
- Fruit, vegetables legumes & nuts
- Meat and dairy
- Drink
- Plant oils
- Textiles & animal skins
- Other
- No data

Asia

Wheat, Wheat, Fur, Vegetables, Citrus fruit, Sauces & dressings, Processed food, Bananas, Bread, Palm oil, Palm oil, Palm oil, Nuts, Fruit juice, Rice, Tea, Fruit juice, Rice, Cotton, Tomatoes, Nuts, Horses, Milk, Animal skins, Fruit juice, Cigars, Cigars, Wheat, Wine, Cigars, Sheep & goats, Nuts, Avocados, dates & figs, Animal skins

North & Central America

Wheat, Soya beans, Beef, Coral, Sugar, Cigars, Coffee, Alcohol, Bananas, Sugar, Coffee, Avocados, dates & figs, Alcohol, Wheat, Alcohol, Alcohol, Alcohol, Bananas, Beer, Alcohol, Soft drinks

South America

Rice, Cigars, Animal skins, Coffee, Bananas, Soya beans, Soya beans, Flour, Soya beans, Soya beans, Beef, Wine

Europe

Mineral water, Bread, Fur, Alcohol, Cheese, Sunflower oil, Sunflower oil, Tobacco, Animal feed, Pork, Cigars, Corn, Wheat, Corn, Cotton, Flowers & plants, Chocolate, Cigars, Chocolate, Milk, Wine, Wine, Tomatoes, Malt extract, Alcohol, Chocolate, Soft drinks, Coffee, Wine, Sunflower oil, Wine, Pork, Chocolate

Africa

Tomatoes, Olive oil, Sugar, Ice cream, Citrus fruit, Nuts, Coffee, Coffee, Tea, Wheat, Tobacco, Tobacco, Vanilla, Sugar, Tobacco, Citrus fruit, Sugar, Wool, Sheep & goats, Nuts, Cotton, Cocoa, Cocoa, Rice, Cocoa, Sugar, Soft drinks, Beef, Cocoa, Nuts, Cotton, Cocoa, Cows, Cotton, Cocoa, Cocoa

Australia & NZ

Beef, Milk

Sources: *data from WTO country profiles, smaller countries omitted

330

Countries sized by population (2020)

⬡ = 1 million people

With around four people per square kilometre, Canada has one of the lowest population densities in the world.

Russia's 145 million people live on over 17 million km² of land. Russia has almost twice as much land as China but around 10% of the population.

4.5 billion people live in Asia. That's 60% of the world's population. 36% of the world live in China or India.

With its population of 268 million, Indonesia has around 10 times as many people as Australia. But Indonesians live in a country less than a quarter of Australia's size.

There are more people living in India (1.35bn) than the whole of Africa (1.22bn).

With its population of 196 million, Nigeria is by far Africa's largest country. DRC, Egypt and Ethiopia are a distant second, all with populations of just over 100 million people.

Inspired by an original design by Simon Scarr

Any countries with a population of fewer than 500,000 people are not shown. Sorry, Iceland.

Other chart types

1. Targets and deviation

Vaccine safety (2018)

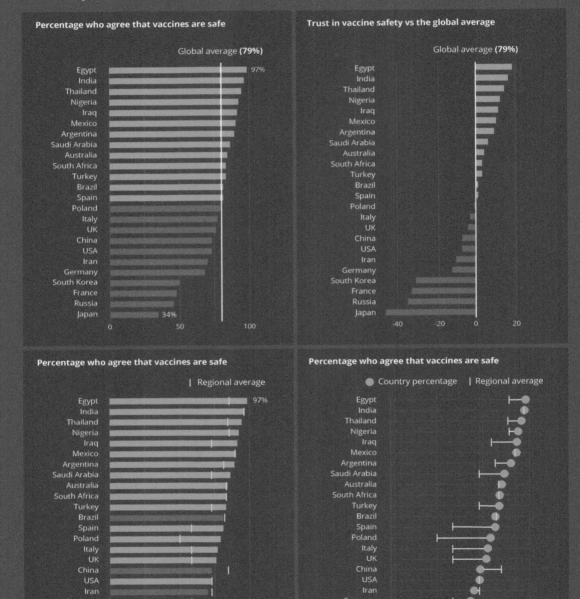

Other chart types
2. Timelines

Selected British Romantic writers – a timeline

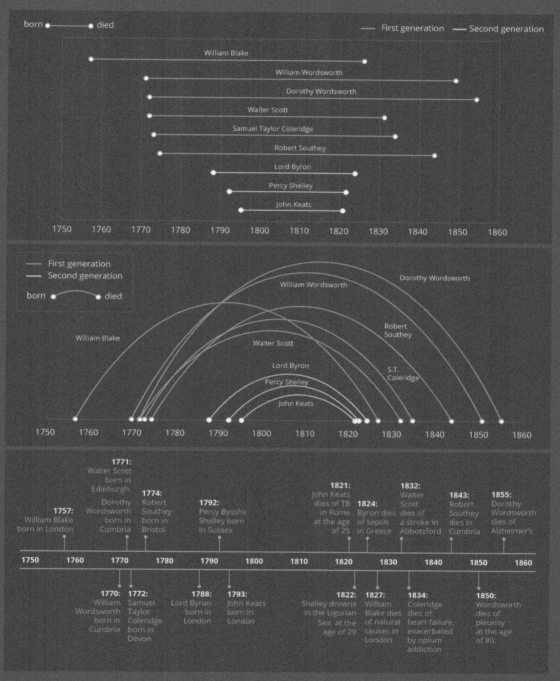

Source: Encyclopaedia Britannica

Other chart types

3. Movement and flow

Value of US goods exports in $bn (by destination, 2000)

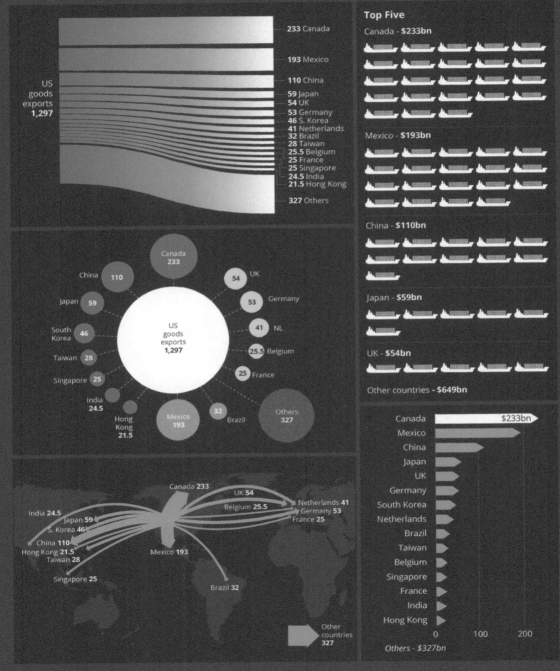

Top Five

Canada - $233bn

Mexico - $193bn

China - $110bn

Japan - $59bn

UK - $54bn

Other countries - $649bn

*Goods only, in billions of dollars, provisional figures. Ship icon by Sascha Elmers / Noun Project. Data Sources: Census.gov, USTR. Sankey flow chart template from Flourish

Other chart types

4. Overlap

The world of Sherlock Holmes

Which Sherlock Holmes story is the best?

According to Conan Doyle*

According to Sherlockians**

The Five Orange Pips

The Speckled Band

The Silver Blaze

The Second Stain

A Scandal in Bohemia

The Man with the Twisted Lip

The Red-Headed League

The Devil's Foot

The Final Problem

The Blue Carbuncle

The Musgrave Ritual

The Priory School

The Dancing Men

The Six Napoleons

The Empty House

The Reigate Squire

The Bruce-Partington Plans

*Ranked by Conan Doyle:
http://www.sherlock-holmes.co.uk/library/doyle.html
**Ranked by fans:
http://www.bestofsherlock.com/story/storyhm.htm

Holmes likes to take on cases that are singular, remarkable and curious

5 cases

10 cases

11 cases

Singular

Remarkable

18 cases

7 cases

5 cases

Curious

4 cases

The 18 cases described as singular, remarkable AND curious are:

Reigate Squire	Sign of the Four
Red-Headed League	Retired Colourman
Speckled Band	Case of Identity
Bruce-Partington Plans	Silver Blaze
Crooked Man	Norwood Builder
Hound of the Baskervilles	Resident Patient
Golden Pince-Nez	Devil's Foot
Greek Interpreter	Three Garridebs
Wisteria Lodge	Creeping Man

*One of these adjectives is used in every single case. Other adjectives that feature widely include: extraordinary, strange, novel, uncommon and peculiar.

The supporting characters are almost as famous, but are scattered throughout the stories

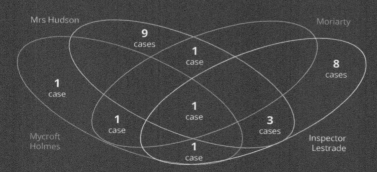

Mrs Hudson

Moriarty

9 cases

1 case

8 cases

1 case

1 case

1 case

Mycroft Holmes

1 case

3 cases

1 case

Inspector Lestrade

The only case featuring all four of these characters is The Empty House. It is also one of the favourites of both Conan Doyle and Sherlockians. In it, Holmes 'comes back to life' after his apparent death at Moriarty's hands at the Reichenbach Falls.

Source: Adam Frost and Jim Kynvin

Chart combinations

1. A change for the better

US attitudes on gender in the workplace

Most Americans no longer care whether their boss is male or female

Would you prefer to work for a male or female boss? (2017)

Female boss

Male boss

55%
Don't mind

This represents a dramatic shift in attitudes since 1975

Would you prefer to work for a male or female boss? (%)

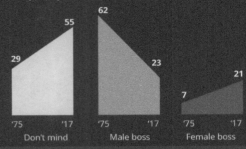

29 → 55	62 → 23	7 → 21
'75 → '17	'75 → '17	'75 → '17
Don't mind	Male boss	Female boss

Younger Americans are least likely to say they would like a male boss

Would you prefer to work for a male or female boss? (2017, %)

	Women under 50	Men under 50
Don't mind	42	67
Male boss	25	17
Female boss	31	16

There could be several reasons why attitudes have changed

 47% of the US labour force is now female, up from 30% in 1950.

 Attitudes to working women have changed, with less than 1 in 5 now believing that women should have 'traditional roles'

 The bad behaviour of male figures in authority has been widely publicised, in part because of the #MeToo movement

---

However let's not get too excited yet...

Percentage earned by women in comparison to men

Parity

100

85%

64%

50

0

1980 2018

The average woman still earns only 85% of what a man earns, and the gap has barely shifted since 2005.

And we might say we want more female bosses, but we don't currently have them.

Female representation

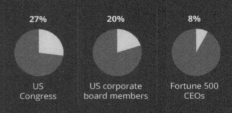

27%	20%	8%
US Congress	US corporate board members	Fortune 500 CEOs

We need policy-makers and businesses to step up and make workplaces safer and more equal environments for women.

Advice for this story type

1. Start with a hero dataset and then bring in supplementary data to root your story in a wider context.
2. Introduce tone and perspective shifts with 'but' and 'however'. Your dataset might contain good news but there are always downsides or ongoing dilemmas, and these nuances make for a richer story.
3. Vary your chart types to signal that you are moving between different aspects of your story.
4. Use colour and textual cues to guide reader towards the most pertinent aspect of each chart.
5. Ensure that your text complements the visuals, and does not simply duplicate what is in the chart.
6. End with a clear conclusion or call to action.

Source: Gallup, World Bank, Pew Research Center

Chart combinations

2. A change for the worse

Levels of home ownership in the UK

Young people in the UK can longer afford to buy their own home.

Percentage in each age range that own a home

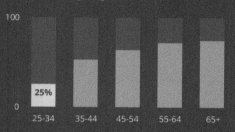

100

25%

0

25-34 35-44 45-54 55-64 65+

Before the 1990s, your age used to make very little difference to your ability to buy a home.

Percentage in each age range that own a home (2017)

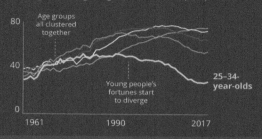

80 Age groups all clustered together

40

Young people's fortunes start to diverge

25–34-year-olds

0

1961   1990   2017

Since the 1980s, a series of policy decisions have made home ownership harder for the young.

 The financial sector was deregulated in the 1980's leading to an era of 'cheap money'.

 There has been a supply shortage: the number of new houses being built has dropped each decade since the 1960s. Most social housing has been sold off and not replaced.

 The advent of 'buy to let' mortgages in the 1990s made it easier for existing homeowners to buy multiple properties and rent them out.

All of this has helped to stoke almost continuous runaway house price inflation.

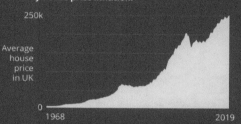

250k

Average house price in UK

0

1968   2019

In 1968, the average house was **3 times** the average salary, by 2019, it was **6.4 times** the average salary.

At the same time, young people are facing unprecedented financial pressures.

94%

of students leave university in debt, owing an average of **£50,800** (up from £16,200 in 2011)

52%

of people on zero- hours contracts are 17-34. Youth unemployment is **12.5%** (it is 4.9% overall).

What needs to change?

Several solutions have been proposed.

 A new government-backed lending model
The current Help to Buy Scheme does not target low-earners. 65% of those who have used the scheme could have afforded a house anyway.

 Disincentivising landlordism
The way rental income is taxed should be reviewed. It is currently too lucrative for people to own multiple properties.

 A review of the planning system
There are too many restrictions on where to build new homes. In Surrey, just outside of London, more land is devoted to golf courses than houses.

Advice for this story type

1. Start with what has changed, and then bring in contextual data to explain why things might have worsened.
2. Try to keep your tone neutral even though you are presenting data which is likely to shock and anger people.
3. Use simple, clear charts. Because this is bad news, you don't want to suggest that you are treating it trivially.
4. Use icons to lift explanatory charts and to separate out your key points.
5. Use a highlight colour and clear copy to guide the reader towards the most relevant part of each visual. Change your visuals when you are looking at a different aspect of the problem.
6. Don't leave people in despair. Finish with an overview of how the situation might be changed or improved.

Source: Resolution Foundation

Chart combinations

3. A neutral or historical change

Declining fertility rates

Global fertility rates have fallen by more than half since 1960.

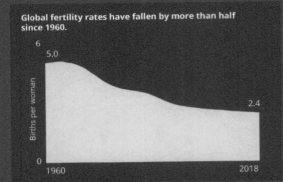

Births per woman

6
5.0

2.4

0

1960   2018

Although the rate of decline varies hugely by country, women are having fewer babies everywhere.

	S. Korea	UAE	Thailand	Colombia
Countries with large drops	8 / 6.1 → 1.0	6.9 → 1.4	6.1 → 1.5	6.7 → 1.8
	Ethiopia	Nigeria	Uganda	Afghanistan
Countries with lower drops	8 / 6.8 → 4.2	6.4 → 5.4	7.0 → 5.0	7.5 → 4.5

1960   2018   1960   2018   1960   2018   1960   2018

Low fertility rates are largely a success story, reflecting the fact that fewer children are dying in infancy.

Child mortality rates per 1,000 live births (1960 v 2019)

Algeria	Brazil	Chile	Egypt	India
146 / 20	127 / 12	131 / 6	212 / 17	161 / 28
Kenya	Pakistan	Turkey	UAE	USA
118 / 32	185 / 56	172 / 9	135 / 6	26 / 6

1960
2019

It is also linked to the transformation of women's lives in many countries.

	Algeria	Kenya	S.Korea	Greece
Female school completion rate (lower secondary, %)	95 / 5	79 / 9	100 / 34	94 / 49
	India	Thailand	Afghanistan	Turkey
Female contraceptive prevalence (%)	54 / 14	78 / 15	23 / 2	73 / 32

Female labour force participation rates have also rocketed since 1980, e.g. from 7% to 24% in Pakistan, from 30% to 52% in Brazil.

2018
1971

But low fertility causes problems too. Population pyramids become inverted, unbalancing societies.

Population profile in 2020

	Canada	Germany	Japan
60+	24%	29%	34%
45-59			
30-44			
15-29			
<15	16%	14%	12%

By 2100, 183 out of the world's 195 countries will have declining populations because of low fertility.

What does this mean for the future?

Most experts believe that declining fertility will require a total reorganisation of society. Predictions include:

 Much later retirement age because of the reduced size of the adult workforce

 Changes in the tax system to reflect increasing healthcare costs for older populations

 Dramatic changes in migration policy as countries compete for skilled migrants

 Government programmes to increase fertility rates, and improved employment rights for parents

---

Advice for this story type

1. With a neutral dataset, your storytelling has to work harder. Start simple, with a single stat or chart, as it's not a dataset people are likely to have thought much about before.
2. As you move through your story, isolate only the most interesting datapoints - delete ruthlessly.
3. By bringing in secondary datasets, you can add drama and show that your apparently neutral dataset has both positive and negative connotations.
4. Be bold with your designs. Avoid too many bars/lines; consider more unusual charts (here, nested bubbles).
5. Draw everything together at the end of your story. And if possible, look ahead to what the future might hold.

Sources: World Bank, Our World in Data, BBC News, The Lancet, Population Pyramid.net. Icons from DesignBite, Sergey Krivoy & Ahargun Ahduy via Noun Project

Chart combinations
4. Comparison - an outlier or exception
The case of Uruguay

Uruguay hit the headlines in Autumn 2020 for having one of the world's most effective Covid responses.

Confirmed daily cases per million, South America

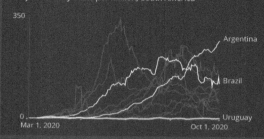

However, this didn't surprise anyone in South America. This tiny country had long been an outlier in the region.

GDP per capita (current US$), South America

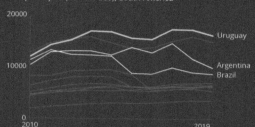

Not only are Uruguayans relatively wealthy, but they share their wealth more equally.

Top 5 performing countries, South America

Inequality level (GINI index, 2017)	Poverty headcount (% of population)	Public health spending (% of GDP)
Uruguay 39.7	Uruguay 7.9	Uruguay 6.1
Argentina	Chile	Colombia
Peru	Ecuador	Bolivia
Bolivia	Peru	Ecuador
Chile	Argentina	Paraguay
0 50	0 30	0 8

On social and political issues, Uruguay is also exceptional.

 Best performer in region on women's rights (0.28 score in Gender Inequality Index). Abortion legal since 2012.

 Highest levels of LGBT tolerance in the Americas (5.56 GAI Score, Williams Institute). Gay marriage legal since 2013.

 Liberal drug and alcohol laws. Marijuana legal since 2017 and can be bought in shops.

 Highest political transparency score in region (70 out of 100). Lower levels of perceived corruption than most European countries.

The country is also an ecological pioneer

98%

of its energy comes from renewable sources

16.1 USA
China 7.2
4.7 Argentina
Uruguay 2

It emits just 2 metric tons of CO_2 per person per year

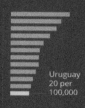

Uruguay 20 per 100,000

It has the lowest number of deaths from air pollution in the region

All of this meant that Uruguay was in a better position when the Covid crisis struck.

 65% of people trust their institutions, the highest level in the region. This meant public health recommendations were followed by most people.

 In a 2009 survey, almost 30% of Uruguayans said 'most people can be trusted'. Only 17% of Argentinians, 9% of Brazilians and 4% of Colombians said the same.

Would other countries benefit from copying Uruguay's social model?

Advice for this story type

1. When you telling a story about an outlier, always keep the competitive context in view, so the audience is continually reminded of how far your outlier deviates from 'normal' or average performance
2. If your chosen example excels in just one area, explain why this area is important. If it excels in many (as in this example), group the different elements into categories.
3. If you can, explain why and how your outlier managed to attain its exceptional position.
4. Use a single highlight colour for your outlier in each chart or illustration.
5. End by telling your audience why this information is important. Should we be imitating this exceptional entity?

Sources: Johns Hopkins University, World Bank, Transparency International, Williams Institute, Our World in Data. Renewable icon by Made x Made

Chart combinations
5. Comparison - a mixed picture
The impact of Covid on UK business

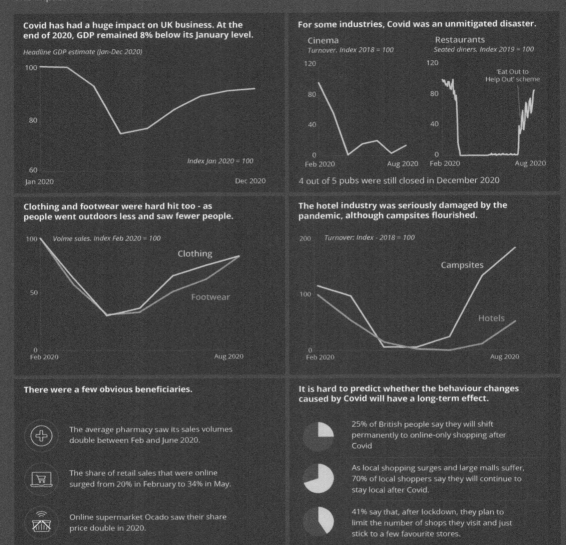

Covid has had a huge impact on UK business. At the end of 2020, GDP remained 8% below its January level.

Headline GDP estimate (Jan-Dec 2020)

Index Jan 2020 = 100

Jan 2020 — Dec 2020

For some industries, Covid was an unmitigated disaster.

Cinema
Turnover. Index 2018 = 100

Restaurants
Seated diners. Index 2019 = 100

'Eat Out to Help Out' scheme

Feb 2020 — Aug 2020

4 out of 5 pubs were still closed in December 2020

Clothing and footwear were hard hit too - as people went outdoors less and saw fewer people.

Volme sales. Index Feb 2020 = 100

Clothing

Footwear

Feb 2020 — Aug 2020

The hotel industry was seriously damaged by the pandemic, although campsites flourished.

Turnover: Index - 2018 = 100

Campsites

Hotels

Feb 2020 — Aug 2020

There were a few obvious beneficiaries.

The average pharmacy saw its sales volumes double between Feb and June 2020.

The share of retail sales that were online surged from 20% in February to 34% in May.

Online supermarket Ocado saw their share price double in 2020.

It is hard to predict whether the behaviour changes caused by Covid will have a long-term effect.

25% of British people say they will shift permanently to online-only shopping after Covid

As local shopping surges and large malls suffer, 70% of local shoppers say they will continue to stay local after Covid.

41% say that, after lockdown, they plan to limit the number of shops they visit and just stick to a few favourite stores.

Advice for this story type
1. A mixed picture can be confusing unless you structure your story effectively. Clearly demarcate the story's positive and negative elements before starting. Avoid using examples that don't show a clear trend or outcome.
2. Decide what you want your story arc to be: will you start with the negative examples or the positive? Bad news is more attention-grabbing, so it's often sensible to start with this by default.
3. Use text and chart changes to make it clear that you are shifting angle or perspective.
4. In mixed picture stories, your ending is likely to be inconclusive. Explain some of the uncertainties and invite your audience to speculate about possible implications.

Source: ONS, Cinema UK, Top Table, Yougov. Icons from Blangcon, Vectorstall via the Noun Project

Chart combinations

Sex and gender in the UK

The *Observer*'s **Sex Survey revealed striking differences between British men and women's sexual behaviour.**

Men
promiscuous
untruthful
discontent

Women
monogamous
trusting
more content

Men claim to have had more sexual partners.

Men
12

Women
7

Men are more likely to be both jealous *and* unfaithful.

Cheated on their partner

Men 22%
Women 12%

Suspect their partner of cheating

Men 14%
Women 12%

They are more likely to pay for sexual services.

Use online pornography

Men 76%
Women 36%

Have used a prostitute

Men 22%
Women <1%

And to be drawn to risky or reckless behaviour.

Used the internet to get casual sex

Men 20%
Women 7%

Had sex with someone and not known their name

Men 29%
Women 10%

Had unsafe sex

Men 30%
Women 22%

But despite all their (apparent) sexual adventures...

Men are less likely than women to be happy with their sex lives

60% Men
66% Women

And they are getting unhappier all the time

73% 2008
60% 2014

Advice for this story type

1. When you are comparing two categories, keep your slides as simple and uncluttered as possible, so that the relationship between the categories is the obvious focus of every slide.
2. Use consistent colours for your two categories. Use charts (like bars or bubbles) that clearly demarcate the categories as distinct and separate.
3. Be clearly aware of the differences and similarities between your two categories, and use this to structure your story. 'They are similar in many ways, but...' or 'They are different in many ways, but...'
4. Draw the story to an obvious close. Is one category winning or losing out? Why? What might happen next?

Source: Observer Sex Survey 2014

References

AA Motoring (2019) 'Why does my speedo read higher than road side speed monitors?', AA Website, 25 November, https://www.aa.co.nz/cars/motoring-blog/why-does-my-speedo-read-higher-than-road-side-speed-monitors/

Alexander, M. et al. (2018) *The Excel Bible* (Wiley).

An, D. (2017) 'Find out how you stack up to new industry benchmarks for mobile page speed', February, https://www.thinkwithgoogle.com/intl/en-ca/marketing-strategies/app-and-mobile/mobile-page-speed-new-industry-benchmarks/

Arranz, A. et al. (2018) 'The history of the Forbidden City: A Visual Explainer', *South China Morning Post*, May-December, https://multimedia.scmp.com/infographics/culture/article/3016607/history-of-the-forbidden-city/index.html

Arranz, A et al. (2019) 'How Bruce Lee and street fighting in Hong Kong helped create MMA', 21 May, https://multimedia.scmp.com/infographics/sport/article/3010883/bruce-lee-and-mixed-martial-arts/index.html

Ashkenas, J. and Parlapiano, A. (2014) 'How the recession reshaped the economy, in 255 charts' *New York Times*, 6 June, https://www.nytimes.com/interactive/2014/06/05/upshot/how-the-recession-reshaped-the-economy-in-255-charts.html

Badger, E., Miller, C. C. et al. (2018) 'The punishing reach of racism', *New York Times*, 19 March.

Barber, M. (1977) 'John le Carré: An interrogation', *New York Times*, 25 September, https://archive.nytimes.com/www.nytimes.com/books/99/03/21/specials/lecarre-interrogation.html

Berlin, B. and Kay, P. (1969) *Basic Color Terms: Their Universality and Evolution* (University of California Press).

Bertin, J. (1967) *Semiology of Graphics* (ESRI Press, 2010).

Booker, C. (2005) *The Seven Basic Plots: Why We Tell Stories* (Continuum).

Borgenheimer, L., Blickle, P. et al. (2014) 'A nation divided', *Die Zeit*, 19 November, https://www.zeit.de/feature/german-unification-a-nation-divided

Borges, J. L. (2004) *A Universal History of Iniquity* (Penguin).

Brandreth, G. (ed.) (2013) *The Oxford Dictionary of Humorous Quotations* (Oxford University Press).

Buchanan, K. (2015) 'It took 40 years, But Harrison Ford is now a *Star Wars* fan', *Vulture*, 11 July, https://www.vulture.com/2015/07/after-38-years-harrison-ford-is-a-star-wars-fan.html

Cage, F. (2012) 'How we visualised gay rights in America', theguardian.com, 10 May, https://www.theguardian.com/news/datablog/2012/may/10/data-visualisation-us-gay-rights

Cairo, A. (2013) *The Functional Art* (New Riders).

Cairo, A. (2016) *The Truthful Art*, Kindle edition (New Riders).

Camoes, J. (2016) *Data at Work* (New Riders).

Clark, W. (2019) *Agile Methodology: A Beginner's Guide to Agile Method and Principles* (independently published).

Cleveland, W. (1985) *Elements of Graphing Data* (Wadsworth).

Cleveland, W. and McGill, R. (1984) 'Graphical perception: Theory, experimentation, and application to the development of graphical methods', *Journal of the American Statistical Association*, 79(387), 531–54.

Darley, J. M. and Gross, P. H. (1983) 'A hypothesis-confirming bias in labeling effects', *Journal of Personality and Social Psychology*, 44(1), 20–33, https://doi.org/10.1037/0022-3514.44.1.20

Davenport, C., Haner, J., Buchanan, L. and Watkins, D. (2015) 'Greenland is melting away', *New York Times*, 27 October, https://www.nytimes.com/interactive/2015/10/27/world/greenland-is-melting-away.html

Davies, H. J. (2019) 'Lights, camera, caption', theguardian.com, 21 July, https://www.theguardian.com/tv-and-radio/2019/jul/21/subtitles-tv-hearing-no-context-twitter-captions

D'Efilippo, V. and Ball, J. (2013) *The Infographic History of the World* (Collins).

Drake, N., Jacobs, B.T. et al. (2019) 'Atlas of Moons', National Geographic, 9 July, https://www.nationalgeographic.com/science/graphics/the-atlas-of-moons

Edgers, G. (2016) 'The inside story of when Run-DMC met Aerosmith and changed music forever', *Washington Post*, 18 May, https://www.washingtonpost.com/graphics/lifestyle/walk-this-way/

Few, S. (2007) 'Save the pies for dessert', Perceptual Edge, https://www.perceptualedge.com/articles/visual_business_intelligence/save_the_pies_for_dessert.pdf

Few, S. (2011) 'Visual business intelligence', Perceptual Edge, https://www.perceptualedge.com/blog/?p=103

Few, S. (2012) *Show Me the Numbers* (Analytics Press).

Harford, T. (2020) *How to Make the World Add Up* (Bridge Street Press).

Hastorf, A. H. and Cantril, H. (1954) 'They saw a game; a case study', *Journal of Abnormal and Social Psychology*, 49(1), 129–134. https://doi.org/10.1037/h0057880

Healy, K. (2019) *Data Visualisation: A Practical Introduction* (Princeton University Press).

Henley, J., Topham, T. et al. (2013) 'Firestorm', *Guardian*, 23 May, https://www.theguardian.com/world/interactive/2013/may/26/firestorm-bushfire-dunalley-holmes-family.

Himmelman, J. (2013) 'A game of shark and minnow', *New York Times*, 27 October, , https://www.nytimes.com/newsgraphics/2013/10/27/south-china-sea/index.html

Kahneman, D. (2011) *Thinking, Fast and Slow* (Penguin).

Kirk, A. (2019) *Data Visualisation* (Sage).

Klein, M. C. (2014) 'How Americans die', Bloomberg, 17 April, https://www.bloomberg.com/graphics/dataview/how-americans-die/

Knaflic, C. N. (2015a) *Storytelling with Data* (Wiley).

Knaflic, C. N. (2015b) 'Storytelling with Data at Google Talks', https://www.youtube.com/watch?v=8EMW7io4rSI

Kopf, D. (2018) 'A brief history of the scatter plot', Quartz, 31 March, https://qz.com/1235712/the-origins-of-the-scatter-plot-data-visualizations-greatest-invention

Krug, S. (2013) *Don't Make Me Think*, 3rd edn (New Riders).

Lambrechts, M. (2016) 'How Belgium is heating up', http://www.maartenlambrechts.be/vis/warm2015/

Leo, S. (2019) 'Mistakes, we've drawn a few', Medium, 27 March, https://medium.economist.com/mistakes-weve-drawn-a-few-8cdd8a42d368

Links, J. G. (1966) *Venice for Pleasure* (Pallas Athene).

Livingston, G. (2011) 'In a down economy, fewer births', Pew Research Center, 12 October, https://www.pewsocialtrends.org/2011/10/12/in-a-down-economy-fewer-births/

Marcus, A. (ed.) (2018) *Design, User Experience, and Usability, Part I* (Springer).

McCandless, D. (2012) *Information is Beautiful* (Harper Collins).

McCandless, D. (2017) 'Hans Rosling – the world's greatest data-storyteller', informationisbeautiful.net, https://informationisbeautiful.net/2017/hans-rosling-the-worlds-greatest-data-storyteller/

McCloud, S. (2001) *Understanding Comics* (HarperCollins).

McCloud, S. (2006) *Making Comics* (HarperCollins).

Meirelles, I. (2013) *Design for Information* (Rockport).

Mellnik, T., Cameron, D. et al, (2016) 'America's great housing divide: Are you a winner or loser?', 28 April, https://www.washingtonpost.com/graphics/business/wonk/housing/overview/

Morelli, A. (2013) 'The Water We Eat', https://thewaterweeat.com/

Morris, E. (2012) 'Hear, All Ye People; Hearken, O Earth', *New York Times,* 8 August, https://opinionator.blogs.nytimes.com/2012/08/08/hear-all-ye-people-hearken-o-earth/

Munzner, T. (2014) *Visualization Analysis and Design* (AK Peters).

Murray, E. and Kriebel, A. (2018) *Makeover Monday* (Wiley).

Murray, S. (2017) *Interactive Data Visualization for the Web*, 2nd edn (O'Reilly).

Norman, D. (1988) *The Design of Everyday Things* (Basic Books).

Norman, D. (2005) *Emotional Design* (Basic Books).

Norton, M., Mochon, D. and Ariely, D. (2011) 'The IKEA effect: When labor leads to love', *Journal of Consumer Psychology*, 22(3), 453–60, https://www.hbs.edu/ris/Publication%20Files/11-091.pdf

O'Brien, O. and Cheshire, J. (2016) 'Interactive mapping for ltarge, open demographic data sets using familiar geographical features', *Journal of Maps*, 12(4), 676–83.

Orwell, G. (2013) *Nineteen Eighty-Four* (Penguin).

Ovenden, M. (2013) *London Underground by Design* (Penguin).

Playfair, W. (2005) *The Commercial and Political Atlas and Statistical Breviary*, ed. H. Wainer and I. Spence (Cambridge University Press).

Puleston, J. and Sazuki, S. (2014) *The Quest To Design The Perfect Icon* (ESOMAR).

Rogers, S. (2013a) *Facts are Sacred* (Faber).

Rogers, S. (2013b) 'A conversation with Stephen Few', simonrogers.net, https://simonrogers.net/2013/03/15/a-conversation-with-stephen-few-about-data-visualisation-kind-of/

Romano, A., Sotis, C., Dominioni, G. and Guidi, S. (2020a) 'The public do not understand logarithmic graphs used to portray COVID-19', London School of Economics blog, 19 May, https://blogs.lse.ac.uk/covid19/2020/05/19/the-public-doesnt-understand-logarithmic-graphs-often-used-to-portray-covid-19/

Romano, A., Sotis, C., Dominioni, G. and Guidi, S. (2020b), 'The scale of COVID-19 graphs affects understanding, attitudes, and policy preferences', *Health Economics*, 29(11), 1482–94, https://www.autoblog.com/2010/12/14/gas-gauge/

Rozenblit, L. and Keil, F. (2002) 'The misunderstood limits of folk science: An illusion of explanatory depth', *Cognitive Science*, 26(5), 521–62, https://www.ncbi.nlm.nih.gov/pmc/articles/PMC3062901/

Shariatmadari, D. (2015) 'Daniel Kahneman: "What would I eliminate if I had a magic wand? Overconfidence"', *Guardian*, 18 July, https://www.theguardian.com/books/2015/jul/18/daniel-kahneman-books-interview

Shea, T. (2016) 'How does your gas gauge really work?', https://www.autoblog.com/2010/12/14/gas-gauge/

Shneiderman, B. (1996) 'The eyes have it: A task by data type taxonomy for information visualization', in *Proceedings: IEEE Symposium on Visual Languages* (IEEE Computer Society Press), pp. 336–43.

Silver, N. (2015) *The Signal and the Noise* (Penguin).

Svenson, O. (1981) 'Are we all less risky and more skillful than our fellow drivers?', *Acta Psychologica*, 47(2), 143–8, https://www.sciencedirect.com/science/article/abs/pii/0001691881900056

Tarran, B. (2015) 'An interview with David McCandless', *Significance* Magazine online, 12 January, https://www.significancemagazine.com/culture/75-knowledge-in-focus-an-interview-with-david-mccandless

Thomas, F. and Johnston, O. (1981) *Disney Animation: The Illusion of Life* (Abbeville Press).

Tinker, M. (1963) *Legibility of Print* (Iowa State University Press).

Tufte, D. (2001) *The Visual Display of Quantitative Information* (Graphics Press).

Tufte, D. (2006) *Beautiful Evidence* (Graphics Press).

Watkins, D. et al. (2018) 'Sizing Up the 2018 Blue Wave', *New York Times*, 7 Nov, https://www.nytimes.com/interactive/2018/11/07/us/politics/how-democrats-took-the-house.html

Wexler, S. et al. (2017) *The Big Book of Dashboards* (Wiley).

Wilkinson, L. (1999) *The Grammar of Graphics* (Springer).

Wong, D. (2010) *The Wall Street Journal's Guide to Information Graphics* (Norton).

Worth, J. (n.d.) 'If the moon were only 1 pixel', https://joshworth.com/dev/pixelspace/pixelspace_solarsystem.html

Wu, J., Watkins, D. et al. (2020) 'Who gets to breathe clean air in Delhi?', *New York Times*, 17 December, https://www.nytimes.com/interactive/2020/12/17/world/asia/india-pollution-inequality.html

Yau, N. (2013) *Data Points* (Wiley).

Zacks, J. and Tversky, B. (1999) 'Bars and lines: A study of graphic communication', *Memory & Cognition*, 27(6), 1073–9.

Index